MAX POWER

Check Point Firewall

Performance Optimization

Second Edition

Second Edition

ISBN-13: 978-1981481224

ISBN-10: 1981481222

Copyright © 2018 by Shadow Peak Inc. All rights reserved.

Cover Images provided by iStock

TABLE OF CONTENTS

LIST OF FIGURES

LIST OF TABLES

FOREWORD

What a long, strange trip it's been, and it's come full circle.

Back in 1996, I started working for a company that was a Check Point reseller. While it wasn't originally why I started working there, I soon found myself supporting customers running Check Point FireWall-1 and, through many trials and tribulations, became an expert on the product.

Back in those early days, there was no SecureKnowledge. The only public forum that existed was the old FireWall-1 Mailing List. Realizing other people were struggling with the product, I started a website that contained the knowledge I collected. A few of you might remember the old PhoneBoy FireWall-1 FAQ or even the FireWall-1 Gurus Mailing List. Some of you may have a copy of the book *Essential Check Point FireWall-1*. I'm the guy behind those resources.

Back when I was on the front lines supporting FireWall-1, performance was rarely a consideration. The software ran on large Unix workstations or the odd Windows NT machine. Internet connections were measured in kilobytes, not megabits or even gigabits. Policies were a simple allow/block of traffic by ports and IP addresses.

While firewalls are only one of the many security controls organizations should deploy in order to protect their critical assets, they still play a key role in the overall strategy. We still expect them to block traffic that isn't explicitly allowed, but what is explicitly allowed cannot be defined in terms of just ports and IP addresses. This definition requires deeper inspection of traffic, both for the things we want to allow (specific applications), and the things we don't want to allow (malicious content or exfiltration of sensitive data).

This deeper inspection of traffic comes at a cost. In some cases, organizations are bearing this cost, but many organizations have chosen to forego the deeper inspection, prioritizing fast connectivity over security. Given that the number of reported breaches keeps increasing year after year with rapidly escalating remediation costs, prioritizing fast connectivity over security is a deeply flawed long-term strategy.

This book will ensure you are getting the best out of your investment in Check Point Security Gateways, and it starts with a lot of stuff that has nothing to do with the firewall: basic networking. I can't tell you how many times I helped people troubleshoot "firewall" problems only to find the problem was somewhere else. Tim gives you the practical knowledge you need to verify network traffic is flowing to the firewall smoothly.

Once network packets get to the firewall, there are plenty of things you need to do to ensure they are processed optimally. Back in the early days, there was no CoreXL or SecureXL to worry about. There wasn't even ClusterXL in the earliest days, but Tim takes you through it all, step by step, giving you a strong foundation on which to ensure your gateways will operate at peak performance. You'll also be able to troubleshoot potential performance issues, regardless of where they might be in the configuration.

I've known Tim for many years on CPUG (Check Point User Group at https://cpug.org) where he has helped thousands of Check Point administrators with practical advice on how to solve their performance-related issues. He's also contributing significantly to CheckMates, Check Point's recently launched user community initiative! If you look closely at https://community.checkpoint.com, you'll see a familiar face posting there fairly regularly: me. I would probably post there even if I wasn't in charge of the CheckMates community, but it certainly doesn't hurt that I am. As I said at the beginning, my long, strange trip has officially come full circle.

Like Tim's previous edition of *Max Power*, if you maintain Check Point Security Gateways, you need this book. The advice provided herein is sound, field-tested, and updated for Check Point's latest Security Gateway release (at time of printing): R80.10!

Dameon D. Welch-Abernathy

a.k.a. "PhoneBoy"

PREFACE

Knowledge is the only instrument of production that is not subject to diminishing returns.

   - J.M. Clark

Why was this book created?

As someone who both teaches Check Point firewall classes for a Check Point Authorized Training Center (ATC) and performs firewall consulting engagements, I noticed that just about every customer firewall I encountered was not tuned properly for optimum performance. In fact an amusing irony was this: The larger and more expensive the firewall, the more likely it was not tuned properly and network performance was suffering. While there were extensive reference documents available at Check Point's SecureKnowledge site concerning firewall performance optimization, there didn't seem to be a ready step-by-step guide available to maximize firewall performance.

The majority of properly sized Check Point firewalls perform very well when deployed in a customer network. However there are wildly differing network designs and priorities in every customer's network, and conditions can arise that hamper the performance of the firewall such as:

- You have recently enabled several new features on your firewall that were not anticipated when the firewall was originally sized and purchased
- Your organization is experiencing rapid growth and your network security requirements are rapidly outstripping your security budget

- Your firewall will be replaced when next year's capital budget becomes available, but you need to "buy some time" performance-wise for an older firewall until the replacement arrives

- A major redesign or cleanup of the networks surrounding the firewall has shifted far more traffic load onto the firewall than originally planned

- You have inherited an existing firewall already in production (of which you have very limited knowledge), and perceived firewall performance has suddenly decreased but there is no obvious reason why

Over time, I found myself following the same sequence of discovery, analysis and remediation for the same common performance problems I saw over and over. My experiences have been expanded upon and documented in the book you are now reading. I've held nothing back; every tip, technique and tidbit of knowledge I've discovered over the years concerning Check Point firewall performance optimization is in this book.

Second Edition Notes

When the first edition of *Max Power* was published in early 2015, the latest version of Check Point code available was R77.20, and code releases as far back as R75.20 were still officially supported. R77.30, with great new features such as the Dynamic Dispatcher, wasn't available yet and R80 seemed like a distant dream.

However at long last R80.10 is available, and is chock full of new features that mitigate many of the performance limitations explored in the first edition. At the time of this second edition's publication, R77.30 is the oldest supported release and will be covered side-by-side with R80.10. Even if you are still using R77.30 gateway exclusively and have no immediate plans to upgrade your gateways to R80.10+, I have carefully constructed the recommendations in this book to "future-proof" them as much as possible, such that the extensive performance benefits of R80.10 can be realized immediately when you do eventually upgrade.

How to use this book

This book is not intended as an introduction to Check Point firewalls; the basics of Check Point initial setup, policies, and configuration is not covered here. It is assumed the reader of this book has at least 6 months experience managing Check Point firewalls in a production environment. If you are looking for a good Check Point introduction, the 3-day Check Point Certified Security Administrator (CCSA) class offered by your preferred Check Point Authorized Training Center (ATC) does a very good job. *Shameless Plug Alert*: I teach all of the classroom-led and online Check Point classes for my company Shadow Peak Inc. which is a Check Point ATC. If you work for a Check Point Partner, you may be able to use CO-OP marketing funds to attend official Check Point classes hosted by an ATC free of charge!

The ordering of the chapters is very deliberate; they take a bottom-up approach to optimizing performance and I strongly recommend going through the chapters in order as you begin your endeavors. As the lower OSI layers of the firewall and surrounding network are optimized, your changes may actually push even more errors and issues into upper layers where they can be addressed in later chapters. I feel it is critical to provide not just the "What" and the "How", but the *Why*. I can't predict every possible outcome you might encounter when running the discovery commands, and providing the background for why the output is important will help you make the right decision should you encounter an unusual situation that is "off the rails" and not covered by this book.

If you are new to R80+ management, CheckMates (community.checkpoint.com) has an excellent series of free training videos called "R80.x Training Videos" that would be well worth your time to peruse prior to migrating to R80+ management. At press time these videos were available at this location:

https://community.checkpoint.com/docs/DOC-2158-r80-training-videos

The commands provided should be safe to run during production unless otherwise noted, however it is your responsibility to keep track of what was modified so you can quickly change things back if problems arise.

Conventions

This book assumes you are using the Gaia operating system on your firewall. While many of the counters and other information we wish to examine can be obtained through the clish command shell, in general we will examine these parameters using expert mode commands via the bash shell.

As far as firewall hardware, the expert mode commands in this book will apply on Check Point appliance series 2200-23000 inclusive. The optimization steps in this book **do not** apply to the following:

- *Azure/AWS Deployments*
- *Crossbeam*
- *Embedded Gaia 600-1400 Series*
- *IPS-1 Appliances*
- *LTE/GX*
- *Nokia IP Appliances Running IPSO*
- *Sofaware/Edge Appliances (including Series 80)*
- *41000-64000 Models*

The optimization techniques described in this book also do not apply to the VSX product; however Michael Endrizzi of Midpoint Technology (https://dreezman.wordpress.com/) has some outstanding VSX-specific CoreXL/SecureXL optimization tips on his "VSX & CoreXL Training" page here: https://dreezman.wordpress.com/2015/01/24/corexl-training-youll-love-the-price/

SecureKnowledge (SK) articles are referenced throughout the book that can be consulted for more information. In every case the SK number (i.e. sk13214) will be provided as well as the title of the SK. These SK articles can most definitely be removed, revamped or combined together by Check Point as their support site evolves. If you search for a specific SK number and it no longer exists, try searching for the provided title of the SK article. That will hopefully lead you to where the needed content has ended up. If perusing the electronic copy of this book, SK hyperlinks are "hot" and clickable; but keep in mind that not all SK articles are public. If you receive an error message when trying to access a hyperlinked SK, log into Check Point's site with your User Center credentials and try again. SK articles are constantly being updated. If while running discovery commands you see something that doesn't match what is shown in this book, a visit to the SK articles quoted in the chapter might be in order to see if something has changed in later releases.

And Now for a Word

Even if you happen to obtain a PDF copy of this book other than by purchasing it legitimately via maxpowerfirewalls.com, I still hope this book helps you and your organization get the most out of your Check Point firewalls. Yes you read that right! I didn't write this book to get rich. Legitimate electronic copies of this book are distributed in only one format: PDF. It has no annoying Digital Rights Management (DRM); you can read this book on all your devices past, present, and future with no restrictions.

This book is not free; if it has helped you (and particularly if it has saved your behind and/or made you look like a rock star to your customers, colleagues, and/or management) I hope you would see the value in picking up a legit electronic or hardcopy edition of this book for yourself and/or your organization via maxpowerfirewalls.com. Thanks!

Addendums

Three addendums were released for the first edition of *Max Power* and posted free of charge at maxpowerfirewalls.com. I intend to continue this practice for this second edition of this book, so be sure to check the above URL occasionally for updates. I will make announcements at CPUG (cpug.org) and CheckMates (community.checkpoint.com) upon release of any addendums for this book.

About the Author

Timothy C. Hall

CISSP, CCSM, CCSI, CCNA Security

Mr. Hall has been performing computer security work for over 20 years and has been providing security consulting services for organizations along the Colorado Front Range full-time since 1999. He has worked with Check Point firewall for over twenty years. Mr. Hall holds a B.S. in Computer Science from Colorado State University and has been teaching Check Point firewall classes continuously since 2003.

As one of the top ten active participants on the Check Point User Group website forum (CPUG.org) with over 2,000 posts, and a perennial Top 3 contributor at CheckMates (community.checkpoint.com), Mr. Hall frequently lends his expertise to solving problems posted by Check Point users all over the world. Mr. Hall is also credited as a contributor to numerous editions of the official Check Point training courseware over the years including version R80.10.

ACKNOWLEDGEMENTS

Special Thanks to **Robbie Elliott**, Security Engineering (SE) Director for Check Point in the Western USA. Robbie is a long time Check Pointer who, before joining Check Point in 2006, was an end user and a consulting engineer, and since joining Check Point has been an SE, a SE Manager, and is now the SE Director. I have known and worked with Robbie on projects large and small for more than a decade. Thanks for the collaboration and idea sharing, and for always being a good soundboard for content.

I'd also like to thank **Eric Anderson** of Netanium Inc. for proofreading and sanity-checking the contents of this book, and continuing to operate an extremely valuable resource to the Check Point user community: the Check Point User Group (CPUG) forum located at https://www.cpug.org/.

CHAPTER 1
INTRODUCTION & CONCEPTS

The enemy of a good plan is the dream of a perfect plan.

- Carl von Clausewitz

Introduction

Performance tuning is not an exact science. In fact the process is frequently referred to as the "Art and Science" of performance tuning. In each chapter the background of what is about to be examined will be visited first. I promise to only provide the amount of background you need for the task at hand and not venture into obscure or esoteric areas. This background information is critical should you encounter a situation not covered by this book. By having the necessary foundation and background you should hopefully be able to make an informed decision about how to handle your findings.

In many chapters, the next section "Discovery and Analysis" will always start with a quick series of commands we will run from an expert mode prompt on your firewall. Unless otherwise noted these commands should be safe to run during production. Ideally you should run most of them during the times when your firewall is at its busiest and from the active cluster member in a High Availability (HA) setup; we discuss how to determine your firewall's busiest periods later in this chapter.

In general it is recommended to implement only the changes for a particular chapter and then re-assess how your system is behaving before moving onto the next chapter (or OSI Layer) of your configuration for tuning. As you adjust the lower layers of your firewall, the now proper functioning of those lower layers may actually exacerbate any performance problems being experienced in higher layers. The methodology in this book seeks to avoid pushing problems back into a lower layer underneath where you are working. Should this unfortunate situation occur, tuning changes made at higher layers will seem to have no meaningful effect on performance due to the actual problem being somewhere lower. For the same reason I don't recommend trying to skip ahead; if a network-level issue is hampering performance you can tune CoreXL and SecureXL until you turn blue in the face and nothing will seem to help. To say this situation can be frustrating is a gross understatement. Follow the procedures and chapters in order, these techniques have served me well.

Background: Check Point History & Architecture

Check Point began shipping firewall products in 1993, and until five years later in 1998 the end user of Check Point firewalls was required to provide both the hardware and operating system on which to run the Check Point software. This led to Check Point's solution being dubbed a "software-based" firewall as compared to firewalls offered by Cisco and Juniper which are sold all-in-one as hardware, OS, and firewall software in a single integrated bundle.

While Nokia and Check Point themselves began shipping turnkey hardware solutions in 1998 and 2007 respectively, at its heart Check Point is still a software-based firewall in many respects. Check Point sells a wide variety of firewall appliances from very small

SOHO appliances all the way up to chassis-based systems capable of passing hundreds of Gbps of data. The use of so-called "open hardware" such as a Dell or HP server for the firewall is also supported, but the vast majority of new Check Point firewall installations today consist of firewall appliances manufactured by Check Point. There is still a clear delineation between the operating system of the firewall (Gaia – based on RedHat Enterprise Linux 5) and the actual Check Point firewall inspection code (CPshared, INSPECT driver, SecureXL driver). This delineation is much less clear on solutions such as Cisco and Juniper which hide most of the internals of the OS from the end user. Fortunately Check Point does not hide the internals from firewall administrators, and the full power of many Linux utilities and tools are available for our use which comes in quite handy. As such many of the techniques detailed in this book will be useful on most generic Linux systems as well.

Your Best Friend: GA Jumbo Hotfix Accumulators

When attempting to troubleshoot firewall performance problems I cannot stress enough how important it is make sure you are using the latest Generally Available (GA) Jumbo Hotfix Accumulator. There have been literally hundreds of different performance problems fixed by the various Jumbo Hotfix Accumulators. Few things are more frustrating than isolating a difficult firewall performance issue after hours (or even days or weeks) of hard work, only to discover that the performance problem has already been found and fixed by Check Point.

It is well worth the risk to preemptively install the latest GA Jumbo Hotfix Accumulator take *as long as it has been continuously available for at least 2 weeks.* While I have had very good luck installing the GA takes, I have seen occasions where certain Jumbo Hotfix Accumulators labeled "GA" were abruptly yanked back and replaced by a new take number. You can probably take a wild guess why that occurred, so as long as they have been continuously available for 2 weeks I'd say the GA versions are pretty safe to install. Jumbo HFAs can be easily installed via the Check Point Upgrade Service Engine (CPUSE) from clish, or the Gaia web interface as shown here:

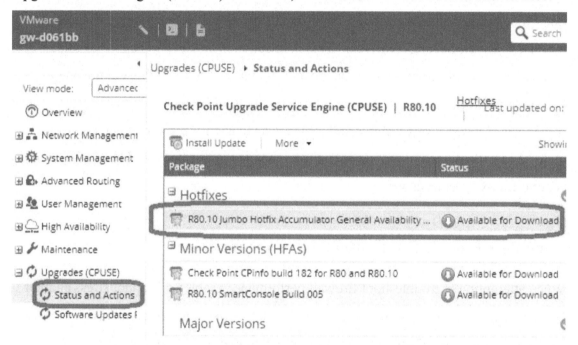

Figure 1-1: Utilizing CPUSE to Install Jumbo HFAs

There are also "ongoing" takes as well, and my luck has not been as good with those. Generally I wouldn't recommend installing an "ongoing" Jumbo Hotfix Accumulator take, unless it contains a very specific fix to solve a critical problem you are currently experiencing. Ongoing takes should *not* be installed preemptively. For more information about Jumbo Hotfix Accumulators see: sk98028: **Jumbo Hotfix Accumulator FAQ**.

Finally it can sometimes be helpful to make sure you are running the latest copy of the R80.10 SmartConsole as there have been numerous fixes and enhancements lately that are detailed here: sk119612: R80.10 SmartConsole Releases.

Methodology

We will employ a bottom-up approach and ensure the lower OSI layers of the firewall are delivering packets cleanly and efficiently before attempting any tuning operations on higher layers.

Latency vs. Loss

During the tuning process there is one key element that must always be determined: is the unacceptable performance being caused by excessive (or highly variable) latency of packet delivery, or is it flat-out packet loss? Packet loss tends to be the most destructive from a performance perspective but do not underestimate the impact of inconsistent packet delivery latency (called jitter) on network performance. Traditionally jitter most impacts real-time streaming applications such as voice and video, but excessive jitter can confuse TCP's congestion control mechanism and degrade network performance for non-streaming protocols such as HTTP and FTP as well. As an example, the Common Internet File System (CIFS) protocol used in Microsoft Windows environments is particularly vulnerable to dismal performance caused by high packet latency; more on this effect in Chapter 8.

A great trick to help you determine whether a particular network path is experiencing latency or loss is to send extra-large test packets with the `ping` command, which have a knack for irritating any underlying network problems thus making them more pronounced and easier to identify:

Gaia/Linux: `ping -s 1400 129.82.102.32`

Windows: `ping -l 1400 129.82.102.32`

Better yet, most Linux-based versions of the `ping` command also support a flood option (`-f`) which instead of sending one echo request per second, will send a flood of them as fast as it can and note how much loss and/or latency is encountered.

Test Environment Setup

Generally speaking your testing workstation should be as close to the firewall as possible to minimize the effects of your internal network as shown here:

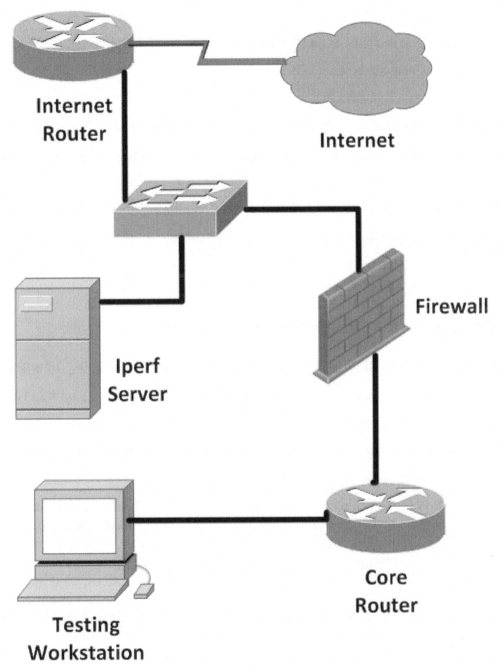

Figure 1-2: Testing Workstation Setup

Ideally your testing workstation is only one router hop away from the inside interface of the firewall where the bulk of internal traffic is arriving. While Internet speed test sites are available and can be used (Comcast's speed test [http://speedtest.xfinity.com/] is my current favorite – I've seen that tool easily shove 900Mbps downstream and over 800Mbps upstream), you may want to consider setting up your own testing server on the network attached to the firewall's external interface as shown in the prior figure. There is an excellent free tool called **iPerf** (https://iperf.fr) that can be used on the testing workstation and testing server to generate network load through the firewall. Internet speed tests are subject to the variability of the Internet and may not provide consistent results like your own **iPerf** setup will.

A Millisecond in the Life of a Frame

Prior to tuning our firewall for network performance, a basic understanding of how packets are received, processed, and transmitted by Gaia (which is based on Red Hat Enterprise Linux) is necessary. This has been simplified to just the amount of detail we need to know for our tuning efforts and will be referred to numerous times as we determine why one of these stages failed and a packet was lost:

> **Stage 1**: A frame begins arriving on the wire; the NIC checks the destination MAC address on the incoming frame. If the destination MAC address matches the NIC's, or the destination MAC is a broadcast/multicast, or the NIC is set to promiscuous mode by a packet capture utility like **tcpdump**, the NIC controller copies the frame into a physical area of built-in RAM on the NIC card itself.

> **Stage 2**: The NIC controller signals the NIC's device driver running in the kernel of the operating system to retrieve the frame from the NIC's RAM with a hardware interrupt (hi).

Stage 3: The NIC kernel driver begins processing the hardware interrupt, retrieves the frame from the NIC's hardware buffer, and does various sanity checks on the frame. If the frame checks out, it places the frame into a reserved area in the host's RAM memory called a "receive socket buffer".

Stage 4: The NIC driver populates an RX ring buffer slot with a descriptor referencing the location of the newly received frame in memory. Hardware interrupt processing is complete.

Stage 5: The NIC driver schedules a soft interrupt (si/SoftIRQ) with the CPU to retrieve frames via the RX ring buffer at its convenience.

Stage 6: At a later time the CPU begins SoftIRQ processing and looks in the ring buffer. If a descriptor is present, the CPU retrieves the frame from the associated receive socket buffer, clears the descriptor referencing the frame in the ring buffer, and sends the frame to all "registered receivers" which will either be the SecureXL acceleration driver (if SecureXL is enabled) or the Check Point INSPECT driver (if SecureXL is disabled). If a `tcpdump` capture is currently running, libpcap will also be a "registered receiver" in that case and receive a copy of the frame as well.

Stage 7: If SecureXL is active, the packet reaches SecureXL Acceleration Layer first. Existing connections subject to throughput acceleration may be forwarded immediately to the outbound SecureXL layer after performing optimized inspection operations. (SecureXL is covered in Chapters 9 and 11)

Stage 8: If SecureXL can't handle the packet exclusively in its Accelerated Path, the packet is sent to Check Point INSPECT driver (F2F) for processing in the Firewall Path or the Medium Path. (The different paths are covered in Chapter 9)

Stage 9: The Check Point INSPECT driver processes the packet (Does the rulebase allow it? Should the packet be NATed?). (i->I) If allowed by policy the packet continues and destination NAT is applied.

Stage 10: Packet is forwarded to the Gaia IP driver for routing; the egress interface is determined by an IP routing table lookup.

Stage 11: The Gaia IP driver sends the packet to the Check Point INSPECT driver for final processing (o->O)

Stage 12: Packet reaches outbound SecureXL acceleration driver.

Stage 13: Packet is copied to a "send socket buffer" bound for the egress interface determined by the IP routing lookup.

Stage 14: The Linux packet scheduler adds a descriptor to the TX ring buffer pointing to the location of a send socket buffer containing packet in memory.

Stage 15: The NIC driver takes the packet, adds Ethernet framing, and sends it to the NIC's RAM buffer via hardware interrupt.

Stage 16: The NIC transmits the frame on the wire via the egress interface.

More often than not, many Check Point firewall performance issues are caused by problems during the receive operation (Stages 1-9) and almost never during the transmit operation (Stages 10-16). Buffering misses, corrupted packets, or NIC card overruns are examples of issues encountered during the receive operation leading to packet loss, which can be devastating to firewall performance.

Discovery

As stated earlier, hopefully you have a short path between your testing workstation to your speed testing server through the firewall. You will need to discover both the switching and routing path from your testing workstation, through your internal network, through the firewall, and to the Internet testing server. The logical path can be discerned with the **traceroute/tracert** command which will show all Layer 3 routers in the path. Another useful command built into Windows is **pathping**; this is an enhanced

version of **traceroute** that will blast each hop it discovers with lots of traffic to see if
that particular hop is the culprit for excessive packet delay or loss:

```
C:\>pathping -n 4.2.2.2

Tracing route to 4.2.2.2 over a maximum of 30 hops

 0    10.30.11.222
 1    10.30.11.254
 2    ███████.238.226
 3    ███████.224.41
 4    205.214.65.5
 5       *        4.53.14.89
 6       *        4.69.145.139
 7    4.2.2.2

Computing statistics for 175 seconds...
               Source to Here   This Node/Link
Hop   RTT    Lost/Sent = Pct   Lost/Sent = Pct   Address
 0                                                10.30.11.222
                                0/ 100 =   0%     |
 1    0ms    0/ 100 =   0%      0/ 100 =   0%     10.30.11.254
                                0/ 100 =   0%     |
 2    0ms    0/ 100 =   0%      0/ 100 =   0%     ███████.238.226
                                0/ 100 =   0%     |
 3    0ms    0/ 100 =   0%      0/ 100 =   0%     ███████.224.41
                                0/ 100 =   0%     |
 4    0ms    0/ 100 =   0%      0/ 100 =   0%     205.214.65.5
                                0/ 100 =   0%     |
 5    28ms   0/ 100 =   0%      0/ 100 =   0%     4.53.14.89
                                0/ 100 =   0%     |
 6    ---    100/ 100 =100%     100/ 100 =100%    4.69.145.139
                                0/ 100 =   0%     |
 7    15ms   0/ 100 =   0%      0/ 100 =   0%     4.2.2.2

Trace complete.
```

Figure 1-3: Windows *pathping* Command Example

If the firewall shows as stars (* * *) in the **traceroute/pathping** output, it would
be helpful to permit service "Any" from your testing workstation IP address to the
firewall object itself in the security policy. This rule will need to be one of the first rules
in your rulebase and placed prior to the firewall stealth rule. Using the **netstat -rn**
command (which works on both Gaia and Windows) can also help determine the routing
path.

Determining the Layer 2 switching path is a little more difficult and may involve tracing cables. If you are using Cisco switches in your network, from the firewall you can sniff and decode Cisco Discovery Protocol (CDP) frames from the switch attached to the firewall with this command:

```
tcpdump -vn -s 1500 -i (interface) 'ether[20:2] == 0x2000'
```

```
# tcpdump -vn -s 1500 -i Mgmt 'ether[20:2] == 0x2000'
03:57:11.920646 CDPv2, ttl: 180s, checksum: 692 (unverified), leng
  Device-ID (0x01), length: 7 bytes: 'Switch0'
  Version String (0x05), length: 189 bytes:
    Cisco IOS Software, C3550 Software (C3550-IPSERVICESK9-M),
        Version 12.2(44)SE6, RELEASE SOFTWARE (fc1)
    Copyright (c) 1986-2009 by Cisco Systems, Inc.
    Compiled Mon 09-Mar-09 20:28 by gereddy
  Platform (0x06), length: 17 bytes: 'Cisco WS-C3550-48'
  Address (0x02), length: 13 bytes: IPv4 (1) 10.30.11.200
  Port-ID (0x03), length: 16 bytes: 'FastEthernet0/10'
  Capability (0x04), length: 4 bytes: (0x00000029): Router,
        L2 Switch, IGMP snooping
  Protocol-Hello option (0x08), length: 32 bytes:
  VTP Management Domain (0x09), length: 14 bytes: 'shadowpeak.com'
  Native VLAN ID (0x0a), length: 2 bytes: 11
  Duplex (0x0b), length: 1 byte: full
  AVVID trust bitmap (0x12), length: 1 byte: 0x00
  AVVID untrusted ports CoS (0x13), length: 1 byte: 0x00
  Management Addresses (0x16), length: 13 bytes:
        IPv4 (1) 10.30.11.200
```

Figure 1-4: *tcpdump* Decode of CDP Traffic

From your testing workstation, you can do something similar in Wireshark. Start a capture on your network interface and use the following filter:

```
eth.dst == 01:00:0c:cc:cc:cc
```

Filter: eth.dst == 01:00:0c:cc:cc:cc   ▼ Expression

No.	Time	Source	Destination	Protocol
12	0.16851700	Cisco_68:59:8a	CDP/VTP/DTP/PAgP/UD	CDP

⊞ Frame 12: 388 bytes on wire (3104 bits), 388 bytes captured
⊞ IEEE 802.3 Ethernet
⊞ Logical-Link Control
⊟ Cisco Discovery Protocol
    Version: 2
    TTL: 180 seconds
  ⊞ Checksum: 0x66c4 [correct]
  ⊞ Device ID: Switch0
  ⊞ Software Version
  ⊞ Platform: Cisco WS-C3550-48
  ⊞ Addresses
  ⊞ Port ID: FastEthernet0/10
  ⊞ Capabilities
  ⊞ Protocol Hello: Cluster Management
  ⊞ VTP Management Domain: shadowpeak.com
  ⊞ Native VLAN: 11
  ⊞ Duplex: Full
  ⊞ Trust Bitmap: 0x00
  ⊞ Untrusted port CoS: 0x00
  ⊞ Management Addresses

Figure 1-5: Wireshark Decode of CDP Traffic

The CDP traffic should tell you enough about the locally attached switch to identify it. Keep in mind that there may be many other switches in the path between your testing workstation and the firewall depending upon the architecture of your network; *you need to discover them all.* If they are Cisco switches and you can obtain command-line access to them, running the Cisco IOS command **show cdp neighbors** is helpful for identifying adjacent switches. Make a quick diagram of all the devices in your testing path for future reference as you will need it later. It doesn't need to be elaborate or pretty.

Network Device Health Check

Now that you have discovered all the intervening devices in your network test path (which can include routers, switches, other vendor's firewalls as well as in-line appliances such as IPS & Web filters) it is time to assess their health. The procedure to do this will vary depending on the vendor involved, but more often than not the intervening devices will be some kind of Cisco box or something that is running a variant of the Linux OS. Specific commands for these two common devices will be included; if you don't have administrative access to these devices you may need to ask someone on your network team to run them for you. When assessing the health of a network device, there are five basic things you should look at:

- **CPU Load** (Cisco: `show proc cpu`; Linux: `top`)

- **Free Memory** or lack thereof (Cisco: `show proc mem`; Linux: `free -m`)

- **Network Interface Errors** such as CRC/framing errors and interface crashes or resets. Don't forget to check both the ingress interface for network traffic (which is the one that will show up in a `traceroute`) and the egress interface. (Cisco: `show interface` and look at "input error", "output error", and "carrier transitions" counters; Linux: `netstat -ni` and look for RX-ERR and RX-OVR; `ifconfig (interface)` and check "carrier" value)

- **Network Buffer Processing Errors** - Don't forget to check both the ingress interface for network traffic (which is the one that will show up in a `traceroute`) and the egress interface. (Cisco: `show buffers` and look for misses; Linux: `netstat -ni` and look for RX-DRP)

- **Device Uptime** in case the device is unstable or crashing constantly (Cisco: `show version`; Linux: `uptime`)

Any devices with nonzero error counters (especially if they are actively incrementing), experiencing a CPU pegged at a perpetually high utilization value, unusually low on free memory, or with a suspiciously short uptime should be investigated and hopefully corrected before you begin your tuning efforts on the firewall. You may have just found your main network performance problem and for once the firewall was not completely to blame! Amazing!

Monitoring Blade Present?

Do you have the Monitoring Blade (CPSB-MNTR) as part of your Security Management Server (SMS) license? The easiest way to tell is by starting the SmartView Monitor GUI application. From R77.30 management this is easily accomplished by starting the SmartView Monitor tool from the SmartConsole link located at the top of every R77.30 GUI tool.

For R80+ management, this is a little more involved. Select the "Tunnel & User Monitoring" link from the R80+ SmartConsole as shown here:

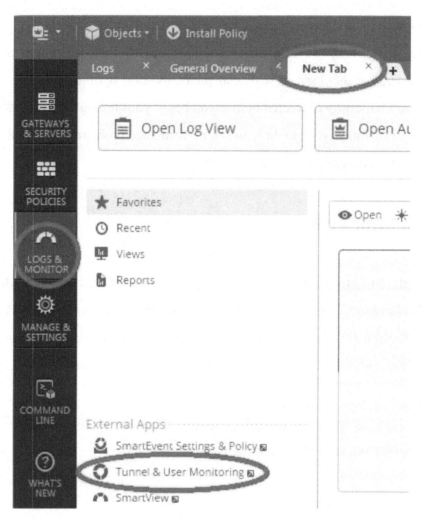

Figure 1-6: Invoking SmartView Monitor from the R80+ SmartConsole

Now look at the categories displayed by the SmartView Monitor:

Monitoring Blade   **No Monitoring Blade**

Figure 1-7: Monitoring Blade Additional Reports

The R80+ SmartConsole can directly provide the same Traffic/System Counters functionality as the SmartView Monitor, by right-clicking a firewall object on the "Gateways and Servers" tab and selecting "Monitor". A command-line alternative for any missing functions of the SmartView Monitor will be provided where needed, but it is far more convenient to access this data graphically in the SmartView Monitor. Another option is to contact your Check Point reseller and request a 30-day evaluation license that will enable the enhanced SmartView Monitor reports. Once the evaluation license is properly attached the full reporting capabilities of the SmartView Monitor will be available to you. If you have some leftover year-end money in your budget my first recommendation is *always* to purchase the Monitoring Blade if you don't already have it, as its graphing capabilities make performance troubleshooting much easier.

Determining the Busiest Times of Day

Generally speaking, we will want to analyze performance and run various commands during the busiest periods on the firewall, and on the active cluster member if High Availability is employed. While performance issues can be investigated after-the-fact with tools such as **sar** and **cpview** as detailed in Chapter 14, the available level of granularity will be much lower if using these tools in historical mode.

If you have the Monitoring Blade, determining the busiest time of day will be a snap; on the left-hand side of the SmartView Monitor select the System Counters...Firewall History report. Select the gateway you wish to inspect and once the report appears, select "Last Week" for the timeframe. Note the busiest times of day for the firewall. In many organizations it tends to be in the morning and immediately after lunch break. Another very busy period can be when nightly backup traffic traverses the firewall.

If you do not have the Monitoring Blade, run the **sar -u** command on the firewall:

```
[Expert@firewall:0]# sar -u
Linux 2.6.18-92cpx86_64 (gw-35dd56)

00:00:01  CPU  %user  %nice  %system  %iowait  %steal  %idle
00:10:01  all  0.44   0.00    0.40     0.06     0.00   99.10
00:20:01  all  0.48   0.00    0.42     0.07     0.00   99.04
00:30:01  all  0.43   0.00    0.41     0.06     0.00   99.10
00:40:01  all  0.43   0.00    0.41     0.05     0.00   99.11
00:50:01  all  0.47   0.00    0.41     0.06     0.00   99.06
01:00:01  all  0.43   0.00    0.40     0.06     0.00   99.11
01:10:01  all  0.43   0.00    0.40     0.05     0.00   99.12
01:20:01  all  0.48   0.00    0.41     0.07     0.00   99.04
01:30:01  all  0.43   0.00    0.40     0.06     0.00   99.10
01:40:01  all  0.43   0.00    0.40     0.06     0.00   99.11
01:50:01  all  0.47   0.00    0.40     0.07     0.00   99.06
02:00:01  all  0.43   0.00    0.40     0.06     0.00   99.11
02:10:01  all  0.43   0.00    0.40     0.06     0.00   99.11
02:20:01  all  0.48   0.00    0.41     0.07     0.00   99.04
02:30:01  all  0.44   0.00    0.40     0.07     0.00   99.09
02:40:01  all  0.44   0.00    0.40     0.06     0.00   99.10
02:50:01  all  0.47   0.00    0.41     0.06     0.00   99.06
03:00:01  all  0.43   0.00    0.40     0.06     0.00   99.11
03:10:02  all  0.43   0.00    0.40     0.05     0.00   99.11
03:20:01  all  0.51   0.00    0.42     0.06     0.00   99.01
03:30:01  all  0.48   0.00    0.42     0.06     0.00   99.03
03:40:01  all  0.44   0.00    0.40     0.05     0.00   99.10
03:50:01  all  0.48   0.00    0.42     0.07     0.00   99.03
04:00:01  all  0.44   0.00    0.40     0.06     0.00   99.09
04:10:01  all  0.44   0.00    0.41     0.05     0.00   99.10
Average:  all  0.45   0.00    0.41     0.06     0.00   99.08
[Expert@firewall:0]#
```

Figure 1-8: *sar* Command Example

The **sar** command will report the CPU utilization for the current day every 10 minutes; look at the idle percentage and note the lowest value so far today. Take the current day number, subtract 1 (i.e. if the date is April 08 then subtract 1 to get 07) and run the command **sar -u -f /var/log/sa/sa07** (don't forget the leading zero if the day number is a single digit). Repeat this procedure for the last 7 days. Hopefully you should start to see a pattern of the busiest times of day. Note them for future reference.

An alternative way to help determine the busiest time of day is invoking **cpview** in historical mode with **cpview -t**, going to the "CPU" screen, then using the "-" and "+" keys to move forwards and backwards in time as shown below. The historical mode of **cpview** will be covered further in Chapter 14.

```
|-----------------------------------------------------------|
| CPVIEW.CPU                                 01Nov2017  8:40:01 |
|-----------------------------------------------------------|
| [01Nov2017  8:40:01] HISTORY. Use [-],[+] to change timesta |
|-----------------------------------------------------------|
| Overview SysInfo Network CPU Software-blades Advanced      |
|-----------------------------------------------------------|
| Overview Top-Protocols Top-Connections                    |
|-----------------------------------------------------------|
| CPU:                                                      |
|                                                           |
|    CPU    User System  Idle      I/O wait    Interrupts   |
|     0      0%    0%    100%          0%          1,025     |
|     1      0%    0%    100%          0%          1,025     |
|     2      0%    0%     99%          0%          1,025     |
|     3      0%    0%     99%          0%          1,025     |
|     4      0%    0%     99%          0%          1,025     |
|     5      0%    0%     99%          0%          1,025     |
|     6      0%    0%     99%          0%          1,026     |
|     7      0%    0%     99%          0%          1,026     |
|                                                           |
|                                                           |
|-----------------------------------------------------------|
```

Figure 1-9: Using *cpview* to Determine Firewall's Busiest Period

Introduction & Concepts: Key Points

- Installing the latest Generally Available (GA) Jumbo Hotfix Accumulator on your firewall and Security Management Server is strongly recommended.

- Keep in mind that poor network performance is commonly caused by excessive (or highly variable) packet latency and/or packet loss.

- Fully document the network path you will use for performance testing.

- Inspect every hop in the network testing path for excessive CPU load, lack of free memory, network interface errors, network buffer processing errors, and unexplained crashes/reboots.

- The Monitoring Blade is highly recommended for streamlined firewall performance troubleshooting.

- The SmartView Monitor and the `sar -u` command can be employed to determine the busiest times of day on the firewall.

CHAPTER 2
LAYERS 1&2 PERFORMANCE
OPTIMIZATION

There is a construct in computer programming called the 'infinite loop' which enables a computer to do what no other physical machine can do - to operate in perpetuity without tiring. In the same way it doesn't know exhaustion, it doesn't know when it's wrong and it can keep doing the wrong thing over and over without tiring.

- John Maeda

Background

In this chapter we will examine elements associated with the physical (OSI Layer 1) and Data Link (OSI Layer 2) parts of your network (including the firewall). But wait a minute you say, isn't this book supposed to be about firewall performance optimization? Well of course it is, but if the underlying physical network is losing or mangling frames the performance of the firewall will most certainly suffer. You may be 100% positive that your network is running cleanly. But is it really? Perhaps you inherited the firewall and associated networks from a former employee that is long gone. Perhaps another team of employees manages the network themselves, and you're only allowed to touch the firewall. Perhaps major changes have been made to the network architecture and no one has checked up on how the various components of your network are performing since the change.

We will perform as much discovery from the firewall and testing workstation as possible, but depending on the complexity of your network you will almost certainly need command-line access to the manageable switches and routers in your network to ensure they are running cleanly. Or alternatively, if another person or team manages your network infrastructure, you may need them to run the listed commands for you and provide the output.

Discovery

Log in to your firewall in expert mode.

Question: What interfaces exist on your firewall?

Answer: Run `ifconfig -a` (Ensure the PROMISC flag does not appear on any interfaces unless you are actively running a `tcpdump`)

Question: What kind of NIC hardware are you using on all interfaces?

Note: The option after the ls command is a numeric 1

```
ls -1 /sys/class/net | grep -v ^lo | xargs -i ethtool -i {} | grep driver
```

```
ls -1 /sys/class/net | grep -v ^lo | xargs -i ethtool -i {} | grep driver
driver: e1000
driver: e1000
driver: e1000
driver: e1000
driver: e1000
driver: e1000
driver: e1000
driver: e1000
driver: e1000
driver: e1000
driver: e1000
driver: e1000
driver: e1000
driver: e1000
driver: e1000
```

Figure 2-1: Using *ethtool* to Check NIC Driver Type

Question: What link speeds are your NICs using?

```
ls -1 /sys/class/net | xargs -i -t ethtool {} | grep -i speed
```

Note: The option after the ls command is a numeric 1

```
ls -1 /sys/class/net | xargs -i ethtool {} | grep -i speed
        Speed: 1000Mb/s
        Speed: 1000Mb/s
        Speed: 1000Mb/s
        Speed: 1000Mb/s
        Speed: 1000Mb/s
        Speed: 1000Mb/s
        Speed: 1000Mb/s
        Speed: 1000Mb/s
        Speed: 1000Mb/s
        Speed: 1000Mb/s
        Speed: 1000Mb/s
        Speed: 1000Mb/s
        Speed: 1000Mb/s
        Speed: 1000Mb/s
```

Figure 2-2: Displaying Speed of all Network Interfaces

Question: Are my interfaces stable and have there been any carrier transitions?

Answer: Run **ifconfig -a | more**. For each interface there is a counter called "carrier" which should be zero:

```
[Expert@firewall:0]# ifconfig -a
eth0  Link encap:Ethernet  HWaddr 00:0C:29:D0:BC:DA
      inet addr:172.31.128.99  Bcast:172.31.128.255  Mask:255.25
      UP BROADCAST RUNNING MULTICAST  MTU:1500  Metric:1
      RX packets:799844 errors:1 dropped:0 overruns:0 frame:0
      TX packets:919880 errors:0 dropped:0 overruns:0 carrier:0
      collisions:0 txqueuelen:1000
      RX bytes:1070993267 (1021.3 MiB)  TX bytes:81534121 (77.7
      Interrupt:75 Base address:0x2000
```

Figure 2-3: Using *ifconfig* to Detect Carrier Transitions

Question: Any interfaces with a nonzero RX-OVR or RX-ERR value?

Answer: Run **netstat -ni** on the firewall from expert mode and examine the RX-OVR and RX-ERR counter for all interfaces.

Preferred NIC Hardware: Intel

Hopefully the **ethtool** command revealed that your firewall is using all Intel NICs (driver name will be e1000, e1000e, igb, ixgbe, or w83627) on your firewall, which are by far the most common ones in use on recent Check Point appliance hardware. As long as your firewall is running the latest Generally Available (GA) Jumbo Hotfix Accumulator, your NICs will always be using the latest supported NIC drivers available. Older NIC drivers can sometimes cause performance and/or stability issues with the firewall, although these type of issues are rare as long as the firewall is running at least version R77.30. The Check Point Technical Assistance Center (TAC) can provide the latest NIC driver version (in hotfix form) for your firewall's version if you'd prefer not to install the latest Jumbo Hotfix Accumulator.

But what if you're seeing some driver names that were not mentioned above? Consult the following table:

Table 1: Vendor Summary of NIC Driver Names Shown by *ethtool*

Driver Name	NIC Vendor	Notes
e1000, e1000e, igb, ixgbe, w83627	Intel	Recommended with latest GA Jumbo Hotfix loaded
mlx5_core, mlx_compat	Mellanox	Relatively new 40Gbit fiber card for 15000/23000 appliance series only
bge, tg3	Broadcom	Not recommended for use with production traffic
be2net	Emulex	Not recommended for use with production traffic
sk98lin	SysKonnect/Marvell	Obsolete

If some or all of your NICs are manufactured by Broadcom, Emulex or SysKonnect/Marvell, I've got a bit of bad news for you. I've encountered performance problems every single time I've dealt with these NICs; they are never included on newer Check Point firewall appliances for this reason. On numerous occasions involving open hardware firewalls, I've moved network connections away from these NICs (which are usually built-in to the motherboard of an open server) to Intel-branded NICs added in an expansion slot, and seen *at least* a doubling of performance with no additional tuning whatsoever. While the principles in this book will still apply, I'm afraid you will be facing an uphill battle performance-wise if NIC brands other than Intel or Mellanox are in use on your firewall. I've even seen situations where these other NICs degrade performance when they aren't even in use (i.e. not configured and nothing even plugged into them), and it was necessary to disable them in the server's BIOS due to some kind of bus contention to get decent performance from the other Intel NICs!

If your open hardware firewall does not possess enough free NIC ports for your environment, and you are forced to utilize a non-Intel/Mellanox NIC, use it only for firewall cluster sync or possibly firewall management; never use them to pass actual production traffic as the performance will almost certainly be dismal. A call to the Check Point TAC to obtain the latest Broadcom or Emulex drivers for your release of code is also a very good idea if you are forced to use them. To make matters even worse, Broadcom and Emulex NICs cannot take advantage of the Multi-Queue feature (covered in Chapter 12) and I've also heard anecdotal reports of various issues between Broadcom/Emulex NICs and SecureXL. Stick with Intel NICs if at all possible!

The RX "Dark Triad"

On your firewall run command **netstat -ni**:

```
[Expert@firewall:0]# netstat -ni
Kernel Interface table
Iface  RX-OK RX-ERR RX-DRP RX-OVR    TX-OK TX-ERR TX-DRP TX-OVR
eth0   799796      1      0      0   917594      0      0      0
eth1   521824      2      4      0  1342053      0      0      0
eth2   467258      0      0      0   459184      0      0      0
eth3   467032      0      0      0  5944661      0      0      0
lo     285998      0      0      0   285998      0      0      0
[Expert@firewall:0]#
```

Figure 2-4: *netstat -ni* Command Example

Notice the three fields RX-ERR, RX-DRP, and RX-OVR listed for each interface. I affectionately refer to these three counters as the "*Dark Triad* of lousy network performance". If any of these counters are nonzero the Linux OS is not cleanly delivering packets to Check Point's firewall code for processing. These counters are not part of Check Point's software but are embedded in the Red Hat Linux OS upon which Gaia is based. "Dark Triad" is an academic term I appropriated from the Psychology field that describes conniving and psychopathic behavior. I associate the three RX counters with these traits:

- **RX-OVR** – (Overrun) Narcissism, Pride, & Egotism: *I can handle our monstrous network load at full line speed, oh wait no I can't arghhhhh drop drop drop*

- **RX-ERR** – (Error) Psychopathy: *I'm a corrupt frame tainting all of network society*

- **RX-DRP** – (Drop) Machiavellianism and overwhelming self-interest, no morality: *I don't care if your stupid frames get dropped or not, I have more important things to do* – Covered in Chapter 7

We must ensure clean delivery of packets to Check Point's firewall code prior to attempting any tuning of Check Point software elements such as CoreXL and SecureXL.

Network Interface Stability and Error Counters

The "carrier" counter shown by `ifconfig -a` indicates the number of times the interface has physically lost link integrity from the attached switch port since the firewall was booted. Typically this counter would only be incremented if the switch was rebooted, the network cable was unplugged, or the network cable is loose. If the counter is nonzero check the fit of the cable on both ends of the connection. Also check the uptime of the switch (`show version` for Cisco switches) to see if the switch has crashed or been rebooted. Rectify any issues found to ensure a solid network connection before proceeding.

Mitigating Overruns: Interface Bonding vs. Flow Control

The RX-OVR counter for all interfaces displayed by `netstat -ni` should be zero. Nonzero values indicate a NIC hardware overrun is occurring during Stage 1 of the "A Millisecond in the Life of a Frame" discussion in Chapter 1. An overrun means that frames arrived from the network faster than the NIC card could buffer them in its local RAM. You would think that because a NIC can operate at a line speed of 1Gbps that it can actually keep up with the RAM buffering requirements when operating at full utilization. Sadly this is not true, especially when most incoming frames are the minimum size. I have personally seen Intel Gigabit NICs start to accumulate overruns when sustained interface throughput goes north of 950Mbps at a 1Gbps link speed. Needless to say this is not a good thing, and causes frame loss which must then be recovered by higher-layer protocols such as TCP which will of course degrade performance.

There are two possible corrective actions for this situation: bonded interfaces or NIC flow control.

Use of a bonded interface (or using an interface capable of higher speed such as 10Gbps) is the recommended course of action if RX-OVR situations are being encountered on a regular basis. The single interface experiencing overruns is paired (bonded) with another physical interface. The two bonded physical interfaces now appear as one logical aggregate Ethernet interface in the Gaia web interface, CLI, and the

SmartConsole/SmartDashboard. The bonded physical interfaces share the same IP address, but now there are two separate pieces of NIC hardware processing the same stream of frames; a bonded setup should hopefully result in zero overrun conditions. Consult the Check Point documentation for information on setting up a bonded interface; it can be done quite easily from the Gaia web interface as shown here:

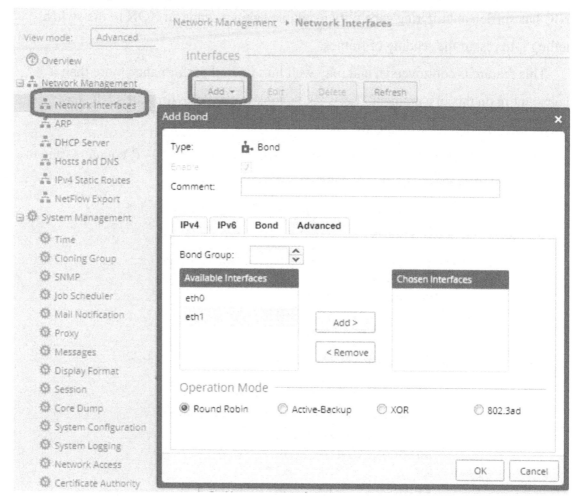

Figure 2-5: Creating a Bonded Interface

Alternatively, Gigabit Ethernet and higher provides a flow control capability between a NIC and the switch; generally speaking this feature is on by default in the firewall's NIC but off by default on most switches. Essentially when the NIC is starting to run low on RAM buffering, it sends a special control frame called a "pause frame" to the switch basically saying "I can't keep up, stop sending me traffic for a bit (XOFF)". Once the NIC has sufficient buffering capability available again it sends an XON to the switch telling it to restart the sending of frames.

This feature is controversial and may well hurt overall performance more than it helps; more on this in a moment. Let's take a look to see if the firewall's NIC has attempted flow control with the switch.

Follow-up Question: Has the interface showing nonzero RX-OVR counters tried to implement flow control with the switch?

```
ethtool -S (interface) | grep -i flow_control
ethtool -a (interface)

  # ethtool -S Lan1 | grep -i "flow_control"
      rx_flow_control_xon: 0
      rx_flow_control_xoff: 0
      tx_flow_control_xon: 0
      tx_flow_control_xoff: 0
```

Figure 2-6: Using *ethtool -S* to Check Flow Control Counters

```
      [Expert@fw:0]# ethtool -a eth0
      Pause parameters for eth0:
      Autonegotiate:   on
      RX:              off
      TX:              on
```

Figure 2-7: Using *ethtool -a* to Check Interface Flow Control Settings

If the `tx` flow control parameters are nonzero, the firewall's NIC has tried to signal the switch that it is about to be overrun and to "please slow down". However by default flow control is off on most switches, so the `rx` values will almost certainly be zero unless the switch has flow control enabled as well. It is actually possible for the RX-OVR counter in the `netstat -ni` output to be zero, but the `tx_flow_control_xon` and `tx_flow_control_xoff` counters are nonzero. How can this be? Essentially the NIC signaled the switch that it was almost out of RAM buffering capacity (thus causing the nonzero `tx_flow_control` counters) but it did not actually run out and drop any frames. For now just keep an eye on the RX-OVR counter for this interface; a bonded configuration may be needed at some point.

Why is bonding so strongly preferred over using flow control? Gigabit Ethernet flow control is essentially trying to perform congestion management for the network to prevent NIC overruns. However the vast majority of traffic in most networks is TCP-oriented, which has its own congestion control mechanisms. Because there are now two different congestion control mechanisms being implemented when NIC flow control is switched on, they can interact in unexpected ways that can actually hurt performance by making a sending TCP system slow down much more than it should. One example of this phenomenon is known as "Head of Line Blocking". (Google "Beware Ethernet Flow Control" for a great article describing this effect) So the bottom line is this: I can only recommend enabling flow control in lieu of interface bonding for two scenarios if you are accumulating RX-OVR events on an interface:

- The vast majority of traffic in your network is non-TCP (UDP, ICMP, etc) and does not have its own congestion control mechanisms
- You don't have another free physical interface available to implement bonding

Even if you have one or both of these conditions present, definitely retest the performance of your network carefully after enabling flow control. There is an even chance flow control will hurt firewall network performance more than it helps.

Other Network Interface Errors

If the RX-ERR counter displayed by **netstat -ni** is nonzero, frames are being received by the NIC that are corrupt in some way and being discarded. To see more detail about why, run:

```
ethtool -S (interface) | grep -i errors

  # ethtool -S Lan1 | grep -i errors
        rx errors:  0
        tx errors:  0
        rx_length_errors:  0
        rx_over_errors:  0
        rx_crc_errors:  0
        rx_frame_errors:  0
        rx_missed_errors:  0
        tx_aborted_errors:  0
        tx_carrier_errors:  0
        tx_fifo_errors:  0
        tx_heartbeat_errors:  0
        tx_window_errors:  0
        rx_long_length_errors:  0
        rx_short_length_errors:  0
        rx_align_errors:  0
        rx_csum_offload_errors:  0
```

Figure 2-8: Using *ethtool* to View NIC Error Counters

The specific fields we are interested in are:

> `rx_errors`: (number of frames with an error; sum of all values listed below)
> `rx_length_errors`
> `rx_crc_errors`
> `rx_frame_errors`
> `rx_align_errors`

Any nonzero values here could well indicate a bad cable or the presence of electromagnetic interference near the network cable, especially if the cable run is in excess of 50 meters. Try using a new cable that is Cat5e or Cat6 rated for short runs; if the condition persists with a Cat5e cable you may want to try a Cat6 cable which is somewhat more resistant to interference than Cat5e over longer cable runs. Also if the "carrier" counter for that interface is nonzero, it is possible that the RX-ERR counter got incremented when link integrity was lost during the reception of a frame, thus causing a single mangled frame to increment the RX-ERR counter.

What about RX-DRP?

You may be wondering why we didn't cover RX-DRP, the final member of the RX "Dark Triad" in this chapter. Generally this counter is not directly related to the health of the attached network and will be covered in Chapter 7.

Firewall Hardware Health Check

Hardware problems can severely impact firewall performance in ways you aren't expecting. Run this command on the firewall: `cpstat -f sensors os`. (This command will definitely work on all Check Point Appliances; it should work with open hardware firewalls as well if you are using R77.20 or later) You'll see output like this:

```
[Expert@firewall:0]# cpstat -f sensors os

Temperture Sensors
----------------------------------------------------
|Name         |Value|Unit       |Type          |Status|
----------------------------------------------------
|CPU 2 Temp 87    |degrees C|Temperature|      1
|M/B  Temp |29     |degrees C|Temperature|      0|
|CPU 1 Temp|42     |degrees C|Temperature|      0|
----------------------------------------------------


Fan Speed Sensors
-------------------------------------
|Name         |Value|Unit|Type|Status|
-------------------------------------
|Case Fan 2|1985 |RPM |Fan |      0|
|Case Fan 3|2033 |RPM |Fan |      0|
|CPU  2 Fan |0    |RPM |Fan |      1
|CPU 1 Fan |6026 |RPM |Fan |      0|
|Case Fan 1|2008 |RPM |Fan |      0|
-------------------------------------
```

Figure 2-9: Checking Temperatures and Fan Speeds with *cpstat*

See the problem? CPU #2's fan has failed, and as a result it is running extremely hot. The CPU is almost certainly being throttled to a lower clock speed so it doesn't literally burst into flames. To check for a downclocking situation occurring run this command:

```
dmidecode -t processor | grep -i "speed"

# dmidecode -t processor | grep -i "speed"
        Max Speed: 2400 MHz
        Current Speed: 2400 MHz
        Max Speed: 2400 MHz
        Current Speed: 2400 MHz
[Expert@firewall:0]#
```

Figure 2-10: Checking for CPU Downclocking Due to Thermal Overload

This command will show the current and maximum speed of all CPU cores. (You can use the Gaia clish command **show asset all** to view CPU speed as well). All processors should be running at maximum speed at all times. This may seem like a bizarre corner case, but I have seen it numerous times in the field. Obviously an RMA for the firewall is in order, but do not attempt to open the case of your Check Point appliance to reseat the CPU fan cable as doing so may void the firewall's warranty.

One other situation to be on the lookout for is the various voltage levels and their state which is also part of the **cpstat** command output:

```
Voltage Sensors
------------------------------------
|Name   |Value|Unit |Type    |Status|
------------------------------------
|VBat   |2.99 |Volts|Voltage|     0|
|VSB    |3.23 |Volts|Voltage|     0|
|+5V    |4.97 |Volts|Voltage|     0|
|VCore2|0.96 |Volts|Voltage|     0|
|AVCC   |3.23 |Volts|Voltage|     0|
|+3.3   |3.23 |Volts|Voltage|     0|
|+1.5V |1.62 |Volts|Voltage|     0|
|VCore1|0.90 |Volts|Voltage|     0|
------------------------------------
```

Figure 2-11: Checking Power Supply and Motherboard Voltages

If low or high voltages are reported with a nonzero status, it could indicate that various motherboard components (such as capacitors) are in the process of failing and eventually will impact the reliability of the firewall. Another interesting command to run is **cpstat -f power_supply os** to check the status of the firewall's power supplies. If any abnormalities are observed on a Check Point appliance, a call to the Check Point TAC is probably not a bad idea as the firewall appliance may need to be replaced.

If using an open hardware firewall and "Out of normal bound" errors are encountered when trying to run the preceding commands, consult the following: sk94629: How to enable temperature and fan sensors for SecurePlatform / GAiA OS on Open Servers.

Firewall Open Hardware – BIOS Tuning

If utilizing so-called "open hardware" for your firewall it is important to make several BIOS configuration adjustments to ensure optimal performance. These are general recommendations; specific BIOS setting names will vary slightly between hardware vendors, so you may need to do a little research and exploration to find the relevant settings to adjust.

If using open hardware for the firewall that has multiple power supplies, a power supply problem can actually cause system CPUs to be placed in a disabled state which is absolutely disastrous from a performance perspective. See the following SK for an explanation of this rare but nasty corner case: sk103348: Output of 'cat /proc/cpuinfo' command and of 'top' command show only one **CPU core** on multi-processor Open Server.

In general any BIOS setting that permits the CPU frequency to vary from its base processor speed (either faster or slower) should be disabled. While the Gaia operating system itself performs just fine with varying CPU frequencies, portions of the Check Point firewall code such as the Secure Network Distributor (SND), Dynamic Dispatcher, and ClusterXL assume that all cores are equal at all times in regards to clock speed and processing power.

If firewall CPU clock speeds vary in the slightest these features will perform in a suboptimal fashion; CPU clock speed adjustments can take many forms but here is a sampling of those that should be ***disabled*** on open hardware firewalls:

- Intel Turbo Boost/Turbo Mode
- Intel SpeedStep
- Energy Saving: P-States, C-States, & HPC Optimizations
- SMT/Hyperthreading (only supported on Check Point firewall appliances)
- IO Non Posted Prefetching
- X2APIC Support
- Dynamic Power Capping Function
- Intel Virtualization Technology **

Other relevant BIOS settings to check:

- Boot Mode: Legacy BIOS (i.e. non-UEFI)
- CPU and Memory Speed: Maximum Performance
- Memory Channel Mode: Independent
- Thermal/Fan Mode: Maximum Performance
- AES-NI Support: Enabled

** Use of Intel Virtualization Technology CPU extensions to accelerate local emulation of suspicious executables by the Threat Emulation feature is not supported on open firewall hardware, but is supported on certain Check Point appliances as discussed here: sk92374: Intel Virtualization Technology (VT) support compliance on Check Point appliances.

Spanning Tree Protocol Sanity Check

Next we will discuss the spanning tree protocol implemented by switches. What's that you say? I thought this book was about firewall performance optimization, why the heck are we talking about the spanning tree protocol used by switches? Spanning tree issues on switches can cause intermittent network slowdowns and downright outages, but invariably the firewall gets blamed for it. I've been involved in numerous consulting engagements to troubleshoot "intermittent performance issues on the firewall" only to discover a severe spanning tree issue that needs to be rectified. Let's dive right in:

> The **Spanning Tree Protocol (STP)** is a network protocol that ensures a loop-free topology for any bridged Ethernet local area network. The basic function of STP is to prevent bridge loops and the broadcast radiation that results from them. Spanning tree also allows a network design to include spare (redundant) links to provide automatic backup paths if an active link fails, without the danger of bridge loops, or the need for manual enabling/disabling of these backup links.

Wikipedia does a great job of summarizing the Spanning Tree Protocol (STP) in a nutshell. While the firewall itself does not directly participate in the STP, the performance impact of a STP issue will affect the firewall as much as the rest of the network. All switches in a network send special control frames called Bridge Protocol Data Units (BPDUs) out all switch ports, for the purpose of electing a root bridge and disabling (partitioning) any switch ports necessary to ensure a loop-free architecture. The firewall itself never sends BPDUs or otherwise participates in the spanning tree algorithm. Switch ports that have been disabled by STP will glow an amber color on a Cisco switch as opposed to the usual green. There are many extensions of the STP such as Rapid STP, Per-VLAN STP, and Multiple STP; for simplicity's sake we will only focus on the STP as originally defined in the IEEE 802.1D standard.

When a switch port first comes up, by default spanning tree will enter a "listening and learning" phase on the port. The switch will listen to traffic coming inbound to the port but not forward any frames. The switch is "listening" to the source MAC addresses received on the interface, trying to determine if that the same source MAC address has been "seen" on a different switch port. If the same unicast MAC address appears on more than one switch port interface, it could indicate the presence of a bridging loop in the network which can slow or outright crash the entire network. In this case the port will never leave the "listening and learning" phase and be left in a partitioned/disabled state, unable to forward any traffic.

This listening and learning phase will typically last for 12-15 seconds during which the port will glow amber on the front of a Cisco switch. Once the timer has expired without any conflicting MAC addresses detected, the switch port will turn green and enter forwarding state.

This listening and learning phase can be shortened to essentially zero by setting the switch port to "portfast" mode. When enabled, portfast allows the switch port to skip the learning and listening phase and immediately go active. However care must be taken to ensure that no other switches are attached to a switch port with portfast enabled, as it can cause immediate spanning tree issues and potentially impact the performance of the network. BPDU Guard (discussed later) can be enabled in the switch to prevent this problem from occurring.

What can go wrong with STP? The most common scenarios I've run into when troubleshooting a "firewall performance issue" that turns out to be STP-related are:

- Rogue root bridges
- A constantly shifting root bridge due to a persistent network flap (especially on trunk ports)

- STP has been disabled completely (this is NOT the same as setting portfast on a port, it is *far* worse)

- Different variants of STP (i.e. PVSTP, RSTP, MST) are in use on the same network, and are not interoperating properly with each other

Question: What is the current state of the STP? Who is the root bridge?

On the firewall run the following:

```
tcpdump -vvv -ni (interface) stp
```

```
[Expert@firewall:0]# tcpdump -vvv -ni Mgmt stp
04:21:17.046566 802.1d config 800b.00:0c:31:68:59:
       root 800b.00:0c:31:68:59:80
       pathcost 0 age 0 max 20 hello 2 fdelay 15
```
Figure 2-12: Using *tcpdump* to View STP Traffic

Every few seconds you should see a BPDU sent by the local switch if STP is enabled. One of the pieces of information displayed will be the MAC address of the root bridge. Make a note of this MAC address for future reference.

Question: How long has the current root bridge been the root?

Answer: The only way to obtain this information is to run a **show spanning-tree detail** command on a Cisco switch itself; unless an unusual event has occurred (power outage, switch replacement) the time displayed here should be a fairly long time ago:

```
Switch0>show spanning-tree detail

 VLAN0011 is executing the ieee compatible Spanning Tree protocol
   Bridge Identifier has priority 32768, sysid 11,
         address 000c.3168.5980
   Configured hello time 2, max age 20, forward delay 15
   We are the root of the spanning tree
   Topology change flag not set, detected flag not set
   Number of topology changes 102 last change occurred 1d18h ago
         from FastEthernet0/18
   Times:   hold 1, topology change 35, notification 2
            hello 2, max age 20, forward delay 15
   Timers: hello 0, topology change 0, notification 0, aging 300
```

Figure 2-13: Displaying Cisco Spanning Tree Detail

If not it could indicate a rogue root bridge being introduced into the network, or that some kind of network flap is present. Features on Cisco switches that can prevent these two events from impacting your network are Root Guard and BPDU Guard. Root Guard designates one or more key switches in your network that are eligible to be the root; other switches may participate in spanning tree by sending BPDUs, but if they attempt to elect themselves the root bridge they are immediately disconnected from the network. On the other hand, BPDU Guard will automatically disable any switch port receiving a BPDU that has been set to portfast; recall in our portfast discussion earlier that portfast should never be enabled on a switch port attached to another switch. Root Guard and BPDU Guard are very important features that should be enabled in any network consisting of 3 or more switches to ensure the stability of the network. The Cisco command **show spanning-tree summary** will indicate if Root Guard and/or BPDU Guard are active.

If the STP is completely disabled on the switch (you don't see any BPDUs at all while running **tcpdump** on the firewall) there is a possibility that bridging loops can form between two or more switches. When a bridging loop forms, traffic cycles endlessly between two or more switches, thus consuming valuable switch CPU resources and network bandwidth. There is no Time-To-Live (TTL) mechanism implemented for Layer 2 frames by a switch; a Layer 3 router uses TTL values to detect and discard looping packet traffic after too many hops. As more and more traffic is pulled into the bridging loop, network performance is significantly reduced. Eventually the amount of traffic being passed by the two or more switches involved becomes too great and crashes at least one of them, finally breaking the loop and causing a full-blown network outage. The switch(es) recover, and everything is fine until of course it all happens again.

Needless to say, disabling the STP on your organization's switches is not a good idea. Set the necessary switch ports for portfast mode if you want them to come up and start forwarding as soon as a network cable is plugged in; disabling the STP completely is *not* the right way to accomplish this.

Question: Is portfast enabled on the switch ports attached to the firewall?

Answer: There is no way to assess this solely from the firewall, unless you physically unplug the cable and plug it back in to see what happens (obviously this will cause an outage on that interface). If the switch port LED goes green immediately when it is plugged in portfast is enabled; it if remains amber-colored for about 15 seconds then goes green portfast is not enabled. On the switch the **spanning-tree portfast** or **set spantree portfast** commands are used to enable portfast on a switch port. To check if a certain switch port is set to portfast on a Cisco, run the Cisco IOS command **show run interface (interfacename)**, if **spanning-tree portfast** appears in the output as shown the port is indeed set to portfast:

```
Switch0#show run interface FastEthernet 0/1
Building configuration...

Current configuration : 136 bytes
!
interface FastEthernet0/1
 switchport access vlan 11
 switchport mode access
 spanning-tree portfast
end
```

Figure 2-14: Checking Portfast Setting on Cisco

Generally speaking, portfast should be set on all switch ports the firewall is attached to, especially if the firewall is in a High Availability (HA) cluster. Failure to set portfast on switch ports attached to a firewall cluster may cause a 12-15 second network outage every time a failover occurs from one cluster member to another. These so-called "slow" failovers are explored further in Chapter 6.

Increasingly Rare but Still Deadly: Duplex Mismatches

Do you have any interfaces running at Fast Ethernet (100Mbps) speed?

```
ethtool (interface)
```

```
[Expert@firewall:0]# ethtool Lan1
Settings for Lan1:
        Supported ports: [ TP ]
        Supported link modes:    10baseT/Half 10bas
                                 100baseT/Half 100b
                                 1000baseT/Full
        Supports auto-negotiation: Yes
        Advertised link modes:   10baseT/Half 10bas
                                 100baseT/Half 100b
                                 1000baseT/Full
        Advertised auto-negotiation: Yes
        Speed: 100Mb/s
        Duplex: Half
        Port: Twisted Pair
        PHYAD: 1
        Transceiver: internal
        Auto-negotiation: on
        Supports Wake-on: pumbag
        Wake-on: g
        Current message level: 0x00000001 (1)
        Link detected: yes
[Expert@firewall:0]#
```

Figure 2-15: Using *ethtool* to Check NIC Speed

Network interface speed and duplex can be easily changed from the firewall's Gaia web interface or clish if necessary:

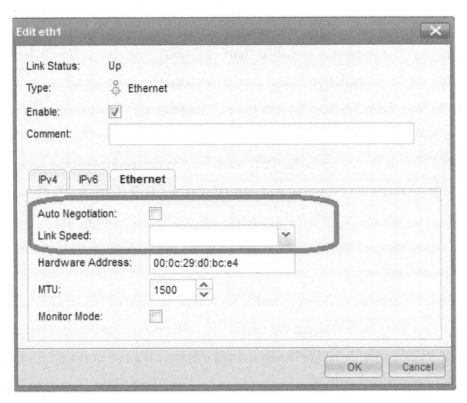

Figure 2-16: Gaia Web Interface NIC Speed Setting

Hopefully all NICs on your firewall are running at gigabit speed (1000Mbps) or better. If any interfaces are running at Fast Ethernet (100Mbps) speed, watch out for duplex mismatches which will cause overall throughput of those interfaces to plunge as their load ramps up due to rapidly increasing frame loss. Network performance in both directions is impacted, but traffic sent from the full-duplex side to the half-duplex side is more severely degraded, due to more frequent frame loss that is not immediately caught at Layer 2.

As an example, suppose box *F* and box *H* are connected via a crossover cable. *F* is hardcoded for 100Mbps full-duplex and H is hardcoded for 100Mbps half-duplex. If *F* is in the process of sending a frame and *H* starts to transmit a frame at the same time when a duplex mismatch is present, a so-called "half-collision" will occur. *H* will detect the collision, log the frame as deferred, and then try to send the same frame again after a negligible backoff delay (usually far less than 1 millisecond). However since *F* is set for full-duplex with collision detection disabled, *F* has no idea that the frame it just sent was mangled and lost. It is now up to the TCP stack on *F* to determine that the packet contained within that frame was lost and to send it again; unfortunately this process takes several orders of magnitude longer than simply having the NIC retransmit it, and the amount of delay imposed to successfully get an intact packet from *F* to *H* in this case will definitely be noticeable.

As the overall amount of network traffic increases, the rate of half-collisions (and therefore packet loss) increases and the useful network throughput plunges rapidly. Box *H* will log CRC, framing & late collision interface errors; if a late collision occurs *H* will not attempt to send the frame again so there can be some frame loss from *H* to *F* as well. *F* will not log late collisions but will tend to log runts & framing errors as *H* abruptly ceases transmission in the middle of a frame when it senses a collision is occurring.

So hopefully the above example has clarified the need to ensure there is not a duplex mismatch present. The next question is, are your 100Mbps interfaces capable of running at gigabit speed? On all modern Check Point hardware all ports are at least 100/1000 capable. Check the capabilities of your switch, it may have been upgraded to support gigabit speed but the firewall's NIC is still hardcoded at 100Mbps. Get that fixed! If both the firewall and the switch are gigabit-capable and set to auto, but they don't seem to link up at 1000Mbps, check your network cable. A regular Category 5 (Cat5) cable cannot link at gigabit speed and will try to fall back to 100Mbps (or not work at all). A Cat5e or better yet Cat6 cable is required for gigabit speeds. One significant bonus of

Gigabit Ethernet is that a duplex mismatch is extremely unlikely to occur, because proper duplex negotiation was finally made mandatory in the Gigabit Ethernet specification.

Layers 1&2 Performance Optimization: Key Points

- Using firewall NICs manufactured by Intel or Mellanox only is strongly recommended.

- RX-ERR and RX-OVR counters should be zero on all firewall interfaces.

- Check that the firewall's network interfaces (and those on surrounding network devices such as switches) are stable by ensuring the "carrier" counter is zero.

- If NIC interfaces are being overrun (nonzero RX-OVR counter) consider interface bonding.

- Implementing Ethernet flow control is generally not recommended but may be helpful in some scenarios where protocols lacking their own congestion control mechanisms comprise the majority of network traffic.

- Ensure that all firewall interfaces are running at their maximum supported line speed (ideally 1Gbps or higher).

- Check the hardware sensor reports for your firewall to determine if cooling fans have failed or voltages are out of spec; on open hardware ensure the BIOS settings are tuned appropriately.

- Spanning Tree Protocol issues on network switches can kill network performance, but the firewall will almost certainly be blamed for it.

- The most common STP issues are: turning off the algorithm completely, a constantly shifting root bridge, or a flapping link somewhere in the network.

- Portfast mode should be enabled on all switch ports attached to the firewall, especially if it is part of a firewall cluster.

- Watch out for duplex mismatches at Fast Ethernet (100Mbps) speeds.

CHAPTER 3
LAYER 3 PERFORMANCE OPTIMIZATION

People think computers will keep them from making mistakes. They're wrong. With computers you make mistakes faster.

- Adam Osborne

Background

Now that we have ensured that the OSI Layer 1&2 components of our network are reliably delivering packets, we move up the OSI stack to Layer 3 (Network Layer).

Discovery & Analysis

Question: Is the firewall statically routed or using dynamic routing to populate its routing table?

Answer: We want to ensure that the firewall's routing table is stable and not constantly unconverged due to a flapping route somewhere in our network. This is not a concern on a statically routed firewall. To determine if your Gaia firewall is statically routed, from clish run the **show route summary** command which will provide a count of the routes in the firewall routing table and how they were learned.

If the only nonzero counters shown are **connected**, **kernel**, and **static** on Gaia, then your firewall is statically routed. (On SecurePlatform run: **netstat -rn**. Do any routes have a flag of **R**, **D**, or **M**? If so your firewall is dynamically routed. If not your firewall is statically routed).

If the firewall is dynamically routed, check the age of dynamic routes with the **show route** command from clish on Gaia, or the **cligated** command on SecurePlatform. The age of all dynamic routes should be a fairly large number that corresponds with the last time a network outage or downtime event occurred. If the counters are constantly resetting, there is probably a flap present in the network that should be rectified.

Special Case: The Dual Default Gateway Problem

Is the firewall connected to your core internal router on a dedicated VLAN/segment with no other systems present? In other words, is your firewall connected to your core internal router with a transit network used solely to forward traffic between the firewall and core router like this:

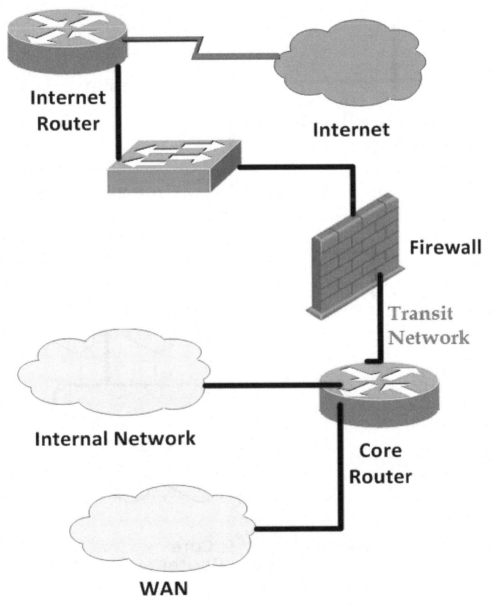

Figure 3-1: A Private Firewall-Core Router Transit Network

Or do you have something like this:

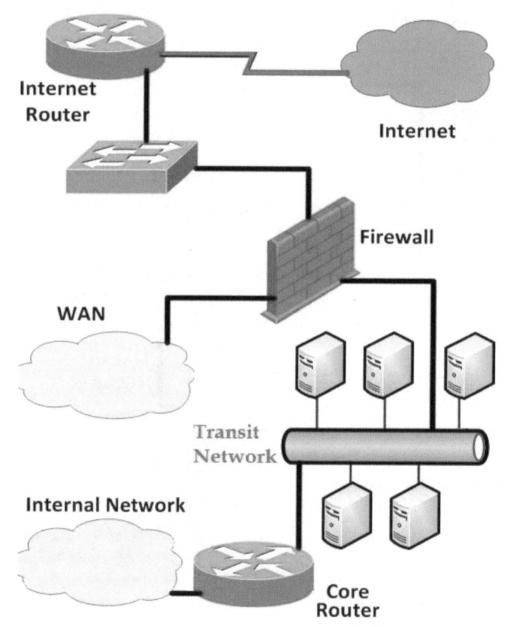

Figure 3-2: Non-private Transit Network between Firewall and Core Router

I may have some bad news for you; this latter network architecture is infamous for causing network performance issues. Ideally the VLAN between the firewall's internal interface and your internal core router is simply used to transit traffic between the two entities. When there are other systems present on that transit VLAN, those systems have two possible gateways for routing and are in a kind of a "no man's land" in regard to routing. So what should those systems' default gateway be? In most scenarios I've seen the default gateway is set to be the internal core router and things seem to work. However this setup will cause one of the following to occur:

- Traffic initiated from these systems to the Internet and/or firewall DMZs will flow asymmetrically to and from the firewall
- The core router will issue ICMP Redirect packets to dynamically update the routing tables of the no-man's-land systems, encouraging them to send Internet/DMZ traffic directly to the firewall and avoid asymmetry

Let's explore these two scenarios. The former is a minor issue while the latter can be a major issue from a network performance perspective.

Asymmetric Path Issue

In the first scenario let's suppose one of the no-man's-land systems (a user workstation) between the firewall and the internal core router needs to send traffic to a system located on the internal network. The destination IP is determined to be nonlocal, so the workstation sends the packet to its default route (the internal core router) in the forward direction (Stage 1). The packet is sent to the destination inside the network by the core router, and on the return path the core router sends the reply directly to the workstation (Stage 2). Everything was symmetric and handled properly; no problems here:

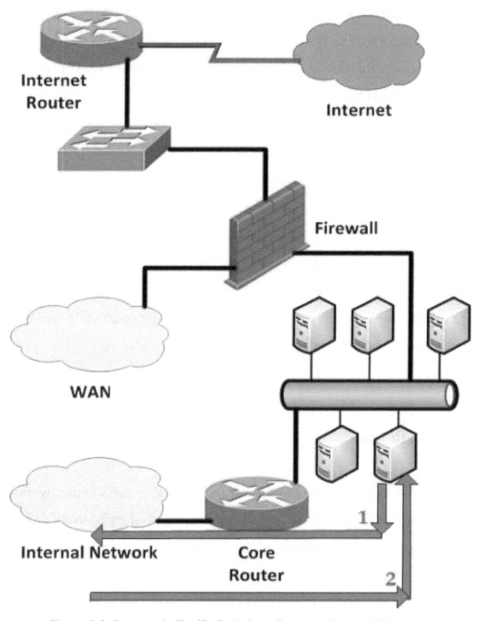

Figure 3-3: Symmetric Traffic Path from Server to Internal Network

Now let's suppose a system in no man's land initiates a connection to the Internet:

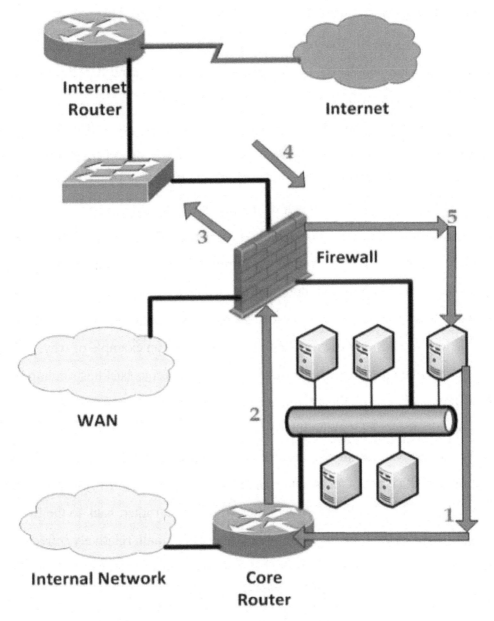

Figure 3-4: Asymmetric Traffic Path to the Internet for Server

Once again the destination IP is determined to be nonlocal, so the workstation sends the packet to its default gateway: the internal core router (Stage 1). Notice that the packet went towards the internal network and not towards the Internet, at least initially. Upon receipt let's assume the core router is not configured to send ICMP redirects. In this case the core router will "hairpin" or "u-turn" the packet right back out the same interface it was received back towards the firewall (Stage 2). Let's assume the firewall accepts the packet and forwards it to the Internet (Stage 3). The reply returns to the firewall on its external interface (Stage 4). *The firewall then sends it directly to the no-man's-land system* (Stage 5). Notice how the forward path and the return path were not completely identical, which is by definition asymmetric. From the firewall's enforcement perspective the connection *was* symmetric, since the traffic crossed the same firewall internal interface on both the forward and return path.

Normally this situation will not cause a dramatic performance issue, but in general it is desirable to avoid asymmetric routing in a network. As an example of why, let's suppose the internal core router is overloaded due to numerous backups running between several different VLANs on the internal networks. A user on the no-man's-land workstation initiates an FTP to the Internet and GETs a large file. The main flow of traffic (and largest packets) in this case is in the return direction from the Internet to the workstation, and the core router is not involved with routing this heavy traffic. There is a stream of ACKs being sent by the system through the core router, back to the firewall and to the Internet in the forward direction, but these are small, relatively infrequent packets that are not dramatically impacted. In this case the user sees very good file transfer performance and is not directly affected by the heavy load on the core router.

However *in the same FTP connection session* the user attempts a file PUT operation. Now the heaviest flow of traffic is in the forward direction from the user's workstation to the Internet, which must flow through the overloaded core router and back through the firewall. The user now sees ridiculously bad file transfer performance due to the overloaded core router losing and/or inordinately delaying the heavy flow of traffic. This is a textbook example of why it is desirable to avoid asymmetric routing in the network; it can cause strange, inconsistent performance issues such as these.

ICMP Redirect Issue

The second possibility in our Dual Default Gateway discussion is far less obvious, and will almost certainly cause intermittent performance issues and even brief outages in some extreme cases. Let's step through it.

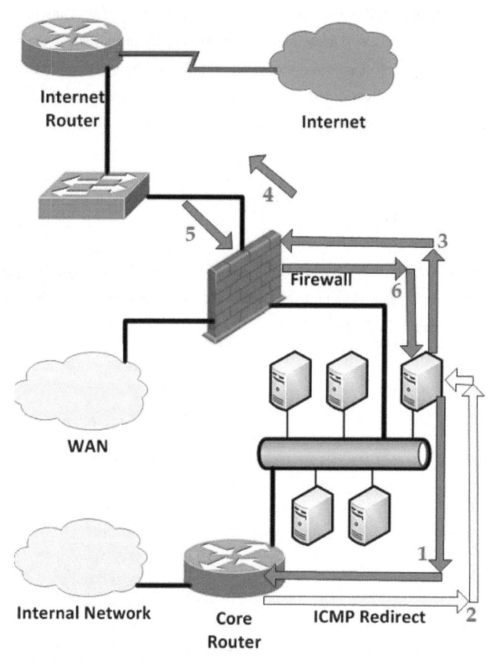

Figure 3-5: ICMP Redirect from Core Router to Force Symmetric Path for Server

The workstation in question initiates a connection to a system on the Internet. Let's suppose the destination IP address is 129.82.102.32. Once again the destination IP is determined to be nonlocal, so the system sends the packet to its default gateway which is the core router (Stage 1). Notice that the packet went towards the internal network and not towards the Internet, at least initially. Upon receipt let's assume the core router is configured to send ICMP Redirects. Upon consulting its routing table, the core router notices that the workstation sent the packet to the "wrong" default gateway. If the core router is configured to issue ICMP redirects, it forwards the packet to the firewall AND sends a special ICMP message called a redirect (ICMP Type 5) to the workstation basically saying "hey you went the wrong way, instead of using me as the gateway for this destination host address, send it to the firewall instead" (Stage 2). Upon receipt of this special ICMP packet, the workstation dynamically adds a temporary static, host-based route to its routing table for address 129.82.102.32 with its next hop being the firewall's internal interface address. All future packets to 129.82.102.32 are now sent directly to the firewall (Stage 3), thus assuring network path symmetry. FTP performance to this Internet destination from the workstation will now be completely unaffected by the performance state of the internal core router.

This sounds great, but danger lurks. There are many things that can go wrong here and all of them will impact the network performance of the user's workstation. First off, how do we know if this situation is present in our network? On the user workstation, initiate some traffic to a few Internet sites, then run a **netstat -s** command and under the ICMP section look for a counter called **Redirects**. If it is nonzero and increments every time a unique Internet site is visited, the situation discussed is present *and you should not rely on this mechanism for a properly functioning network.*

However this situation may be present in your network but everything seems to be working just fine! You are lucky, but eventually you *will* have this hurt you at some point; it is not a question of *if* but *when*. Why? Here is a sampling of a few things that can go wrong:

- The router is rate-limited on the number of ICMPs it is allowed to send. If it cannot send ICMPs fast enough to keep up with demand, asymmetry will return at seemingly random intervals and potentially degraded performance with it.

- ICMP messages are not sent reliably. There is no direct mechanism to detect if they were lost and resend them.

- If a workstation is communicating with a large number of destination IP addresses on the Internet, the workstation's routing table can fill up with hundreds or thousands of routing table entries, thus degrading route lookup performance on the host.

It is risky from a performance perspective to have a Dual Default Gateway scenario as has been described here, and it may be impacting your network's performance right now without you even being aware of it. Unless you want to start hard-coding static routes on all workstations located in no man's land, you'll need to create an isolated VLAN solely for transit between the internal core router and the firewall as follows:

1. In an outage window, move the VLAN implemented between the core router and firewall and its IP addressing scheme to somewhere inside the network. No changing of IP addressing or default gateways will be required on the no-man's-land workstations being moved.

2. Next create a new private VLAN. Plug the firewall internal interface into this VLAN and give it a new IP addressing scheme (anything from the private

RFC1918 ranges is fine, as long as it does not conflict with your internal networks or any business partners you are connected to). Allocate a new IP address for the internal router on this new network as well and plug it in. Don't forget to update the firewall object's topology with this change in the SmartDashboard/SmartConsole, and reinstall policy.

3. Change the default route on the core router to point to the firewall's new internal address.

4. On the firewall, change the next hop for all internally facing routes (routes for which the next hop is the internal core router) to the core router's new IP address on the private VLAN.

Core Router Supernet Loops

This issue is caused by adding supernetted routes to the firewall's routing table for the entire RFC1918 private address space, pointing to the internal core router. The core router then typically has a default route pointing back to the firewall. So suppose the firewall has all RFC1918 address space routed to the core internal router, and of course a default route leading to the Internet.

Firewall Routes:

- 10.0.0.0/8 -> core router
- 172.16.0.0/12 -> core router
- 192.168.0.0/16 -> core router
- default -> Internet perimeter router

On the internal core router, there are 10 RFC1918 private networks actually in use with directly attached or static routes referencing them, and a default gateway.

Core Router Routes:

- 192.168.0.0/21 -> some internal nexthop

- 192.168.9.0/24 - direct

- 192.168.10.0/24 - direct

- default -> firewall

Now suppose a packet arrives at the core router from an internal VLAN bound for a destination of 192.168.66.11. The core router doesn't have a route for that network, so the packet matches the default route and is sent to the firewall. Assuming the firewall security policy allows it, the firewall is likely to Hide NAT the packet's source IP address, and then based on IP routing sends it back out the same interface back to the core router, who then flips the packet right back to the firewall. If Hide NAT was performed earlier, the firewall will kill the packet at that point because it is arriving with a source IP address that the firewall assigned in the NAT operation, which should not happen.

However if there was no Hide NAT rule matching the traffic (or it matched an anti-NAT rule), the packet will loop between the firewall and core router until the Time-To-Live (TTL - default value 255) field in the IP header is finally decremented to zero, at which point the packet will be discarded. Now imagine for a moment an aggressive, self-propagating worm rampaging inside your network. The worm is sending hundreds or thousands of probe packets per second to randomized nonexistent RFC1918 addresses that don't exist in your internal network, and each one of these individual packets is getting looped 255 times between the core router and the firewall. This looping effect repeatedly crashed entire networks when the Code Red and Nimda worms got loose inside various networks during the 1990's, and it took *weeks* for some organizations to fully recover and have a functional network again.

There are two solutions to this problem:

1) On the firewall, only route the specific RFC1918 networks you are actually using to your internal core router. In our example the only RFC1918 related routes on the firewall should be for 192.168.0.0/21, 192.168.9.0/24, and 192.168.10.0/24.

2) If you *must* supernet all the RFC1918 routes from your firewall to core router, then add the following Null0 routes on your core router:

- 192.168.0.0/16 -> Null0
- 172.16.0.0/12 -> Null0
- 10.0.0.0/8 -> Null0

WARNING: If you are using any RFC1918 address space on your firewall DMZ networks (or accessing these RFC1918 networks through site-to-site VPNs), make sure to add specific static routes to those networks on your core router (with the firewall as the next hop) before adding the Null0 routes above!

ICMP: Canary in the Coal Mine

ICMP isn't just all about `ping` and `traceroute`; the various type and code values of ICMP datagrams can sometimes indicate that performance-impacting conditions are occurring within the network. Running a `netstat -s` on the firewall shows counters for how many different types of ICMP messages have been received by the Gaia OS on the firewall. Particular ones that can impact performance and be helpful to investigate further are:

- Fragmentation required but DF set (Type 1, Code 4)
- Precedence cutoff in effect (Type 1, Code 15)
- Source Quench (Type 4, Code 0) – very rare
- Redirect (Type 5)
- Time Exceeded (Type 11)

If nonzero values are noted for any of these in the **netstat -s** output, it is entirely possible they came from the Internet and you have no control over their generation. However if you are seeing these types of ICMP datagrams arriving on any of the firewall's internal interfaces via **tcpdump**, it is definitely worth your time to investigate further. To display all ICMP traffic on an internal interface that is not associated with ping testing traffic, use this command:

```
tcpdump -eni (interface name) icmp and not icmp[0]=0 and not icmp[0]=8
```

ARP Neighbor Table Overflows

One interesting side effect of not having a private transit network between the internal interface of the firewall and your internal core router, is that the firewall will have to maintain far more IP address to MAC address mappings in its ARP cache than it otherwise would. This is especially true if there are hundreds or thousands of workstations/servers located on VLANs directly attached to the firewall's various interfaces. Such a large network will of course have far more broadcast traffic flooded to all stations on the network including the firewall, resulting in reduced overall network throughput.

However one situation that can occur in this case will severely damage the firewall's performance (almost to the point of looking like rolling outages in some cases): an overflow of the firewall's ARP cache. By default, the R77.30/R80.10 Gaia OS has a default value of 4096 ARP cache slots available for use. The default under older firewall code versions was much lower (in R75.40 Gaia the default limit was 1024). *These ARP cache slots are shared by all interfaces (both untagged and tagged) of the firewall.* If the ARP cache table fills up (let's say the limit in our example is 1024), the firewall will not be able to cache an IP address to MAC address mapping for the 1025th workstation. Successful communication between that workstation and the firewall will be impossible until an ARP cache slot becomes available. Once the mapping is finally formed and cached in the firewall's ARP table, communication with that workstation will now succeed, but some other workstation's MAC to IP address mapping will now be "odd man out". The process continues with firewall connectivity issues that seem to roll through the entire network randomly, severely impacting performance.

Another problematic situation that can exhaust the available ARP cache space on the firewall no matter how high you crank it is the following: adding the firewall's default route with a local *network interface* defined as the next hop, instead of using an actual gateway IP address as a next hop. Most of the time trying to do this will not work at all, but if proxy ARP is enabled on your upstream Internet router, it will cheerfully answer ARP requests for every single IP address on the Internet and reply with its own MAC address. Internet connectivity will be fine until the firewall's ARP cache is exhausted at which point the "rolling outage" behavior will begin and performance will be absolutely

terrible. To check for this condition on your firewall run **netstat -rn | grep**
^0.0.0.0. If the gateway address (second column) is listed as **0.0.0.0**, you will most
definitely need to fix that during a maintenance window. Remove the network interface
next hop and add the correct next hop gateway IP address corresponding to your
upstream Internet router.

Do you have this ARP cache overflow occurring on your firewall? Run **dmesg |**
grep -i "table overflow" on the firewall. If no output is returned you are
probably OK; however if you see numerous "neighbour table overflow" messages, an
ARP cache overflow is occurring on the firewall and you are probably seeing the "rolling
outage" symptoms described to some degree.

However as an extra sanity check, during the firewall's busiest period execute
arp -an | wc -l on the firewall to obtain a count of the active number of ARP cache
slots in use:

```
[Expert@firewall:0]# arp -an | wc -l
3212
[Expert@firewall:0]#
```

Figure 3-6: Obtaining Count of IP-MAC Address Mappings with the *arp* Command

Now go to the Gaia Web interface for the firewall and select Network
Management...ARP. The field "Maximum Entries" under ARP Table Settings will
display the maximum number of ARP table slots available:

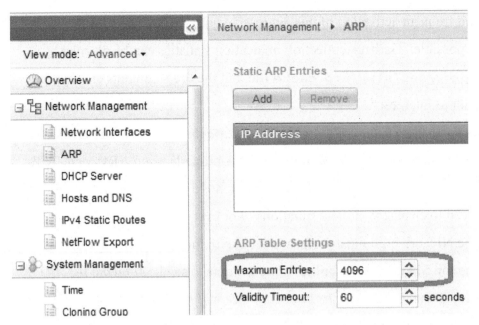

Figure 3-7: Gaia Web Interface ARP Maximum Entries Setting

Compare the value shown with the `arp -an | wc -l` command you ran earlier that gave the current count in the ARP table. If the number reported by the `arp` command is more than 50% of the "Maximum Entries" value, I'd recommend doubling this Maximum Entries value to ensure sufficient headroom for potential future growth of the ARP cache. The basis for this recommendation: by default when the number of total ARP entries becomes more than ½ of the Maximum Entries value (2048 by default which is 4096/2) Gaia has crossed a threshold known as "gc2" in the ARP driver. Aggressive garbage collection is then automatically undertaken by Gaia, in an attempt to reduce the number of entries in the ARP cache back below the gc2 threshold. This garbage collection expends significant CPU time on the firewall by sending large numbers of ARP requests into the network, in an attempt to determine which ARP entries it can expire early from the cache prior to their normal expiration. In general it is desirable to avoid frequent activation of this aggressive garbage collection of the ARP cache whenever possible. Garbage collection invocation statistics can be gleaned by inspecting the `/proc/net/stat/arp_cache` file, but the file's contents are cryptic and pretty difficult to interpret.

Please resist the urge to arbitrarily crank the ARP Maximum Entries to the highest allowed value of 16384 unless absolutely necessary. A properly sized ARP cache will help ensure the most efficient operation of the firewall; 4096 is a reasonable default value and you won't need to change it in most situations. For every frame that is to be transmitted by the NIC driver, it must perform a lookup in the ARP cache to determine the proper destination MAC address for the frame it wants to send. *Allowing the ARP cache to needlessly grow well beyond its necessary size will incur a slight performance penalty for **every single frame sent by the firewall,*** because the ARP cache lookups performed by the NIC driver will take longer than they otherwise would.

Layer 3 Performance Optimization: Key Points

- If participating in a dynamic routing protocol such as OSPF, ensure the firewall's routing table remains properly converged, and there is not a persistent routing flap somewhere in the network.

- Use a dedicated transit VLAN between the firewall and internal core router; other workstations or servers should not be placed on the transit VLAN.

- Asymmetric paths in a network can cause intermittent, one-way performance issues.

- Do not rely on the ICMP redirect mechanism for proper routing.

- Core Router Supernet Loops can occur when routes for the entire RFC1918 address space are implemented on the firewall, with the internal core router as the next hop.

- If numerous ICMP packets not associated with ping testing traffic are arriving on the internal and/or DMZ interfaces of the firewall, it may indicate performance problems elsewhere within your network.

- ARP neighbor table overflows can cause intermittent firewall connectivity problems, especially if a dedicated transit VLAN is not used between the firewall and internal core router.

CHAPTER 4
BASIC GAIA OPTIMIZATION

What makes a great standalone piece of hardware is not the same thing as what makes a great networking device. One can work as an essentially closed system. The other is absolutely dependent on its openness.

-Douglas Rushkoff

Background

In this chapter we will profile the CPU utilization of the firewall in preparation for CoreXL/SecureXL tuning, and perform various Gaia optimizations that are independent of whether CoreXL & SecureXL are enabled or not. An important concept is that a minimum amount of processing overhead is incurred on a per-packet level, rather than per-byte of actual data sent. A system that is processing a large number of small packets with only a few bytes in the payload of each packet, works almost as hard as a system processing the same number of packets containing the typical MTU limit of 1500 bytes of data in each packet. Clearly the overall data throughput in these two scenarios will be radically different even if the CPU load looks the same. Jumbo frames are supported by almost all Check Point firewalls and tend to be commonly deployed with the 41000-64000 series of appliances, are also sometimes deployed with the 13000-23000 series appliances, but much less often with lower models due to the wholesale network architecture changes typically required to avoid fragmentation.

Discovery and Analysis

The Discovery and Analysis procedures in this chapter should ideally be conducted during your firewall's busiest period as determined in Chapter 1.

A Great Shortcut: healthcheck.sh

While I still feel it is important for Check Point administrators to be familiar with all the underlying commands needed to assess firewall performance, Check Point has made a great tool available called **healthcheck.sh**: sk121447: How to perform an automated health check of a Gaia based system. When executed, this script examines the Gaia system (regardless of whether it is a firewall or Security Management Server) and highlights any areas that could be detrimental to performance, a sampling of which is shown here:

```
[Expert@fw:0]# ./healthcheck.sh
+-----------------------------------------------------------------
| Physical System Checks
+--------------------+------------------------------------+---------
| Category           | Title                              | Result
+====================+====================================+=========
| System             | Uptime                             | INFO
|                    | OS Version                         | OK
+--------------------+------------------------------------+---------
| NTP                | NTP Daemon                         | WARNING
|                    | NTP Logs                           | WARNING
+--------------------+------------------------------------+---------
| Disk Space         | Free Disk Space                    | OK
+--------------------+------------------------------------+---------
| Memory             | Physical Memory                    | WARNING
|                    | Swap Memory                        | OK
|                    | Hash Kernel Memory (hmem)          | OK
|                    | System Kernel Memory (smem)        | OK
|                    | Kernel Memory (kmem)               | OK
+--------------------+------------------------------------+---------
| CPU                | CPU idle%                          | OK
|                    | CPU user%                          | OK
|                    | CPU system%                        | OK
|                    | CPU wait%                          | OK
|                    | CPU interrupt%                     | OK
+--------------------+------------------------------------+---------
| Interface Stats    | RX Errors                          | OK
|                    | RX Drops                           | OK
|                    | TX Errors                          | OK
|                    | TX Drops                           | OK
```

Figure 4-1: Script *healthcheck.sh* Summarized Results

```
# System Checks:
###########################
Uptime Check Info:
The system has been rebooted within the last week.
Please review "/var/log/messages" files (if they have not rolled ove


# NTP Checks:
###########################
NTP Daemon: Unable to talk to the NTP daemon.
NTP Logs: NTP entries not found in "/var/log/messages".

NTP Information:
Please use sk92602 and sk83820 for asssitance with verifying NTP is


# Memory Checks:
###########################

# Core File Checks:
###########################
Usermode Cores:
-rw-r--r-- 1 admin root  15M Dec  1 17:09 scanengine_k.8300.core.gz
-rw-r--r-- 1 admin root 7.5M Aug 24 20:34 sim_ex.25491.core.gz

Core files detected on this system.
Please upload the following to Check Point for analysis:
 -Current cpinfo from this system
 -Usermode core files from /var/log/dump/usermode/
```

Figure 4-2: Script *healthcheck.sh* Detailed Results

Software Blades Performance Impact

Question: What software features/blades are enabled on the firewall and what is their general performance impact?

Answer: The easiest way to determine this is to open the firewall object for editing in the SmartConsole, and at the bottom of the General Properties screen on the Network Security tab, you will see a series of checkboxes. A check next to a feature indicates that it is enabled. Alternatively to obtain this information via the CLI, on R75.47 or later firewalls you can run the **enabled_blades** command. If using R80+ management, running a License Report will show a handy summary of which blades are enabled on all managed gateways in a single PDF report. The License Report is accessed here:

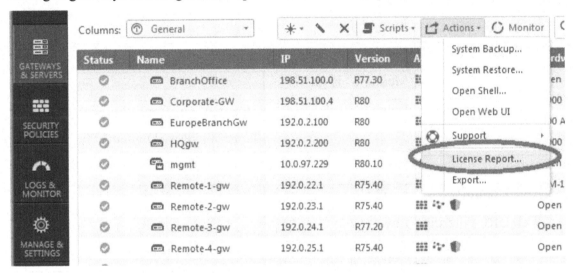

Figure 4-3: R80+ SmartConsole License Report

Following is a list of the available blades on the Security Gateway, and based on my experience the relative performance impact incurred by enabling each blade. For now it is sufficient for you to simply note which blades are enabled on your firewall; in later chapters we will examine how to tune and optimize the performance of these various blades.

Table 2: Relative Performance Impact of Various Firewall Features

Feature	Performance Impact	Notes
Firewall	Low	Always enabled
IPSec VPN	Low->Medium	Dependent on amount of encrypted/decrypted traffic
Mobile Access	Low->Medium	Dependent on amount of encrypted/decrypted traffic
IPS	Low->High	Highly Variable
Anti-Bot	Medium**	
Anti-Virus	Medium->High**	
Identity Awareness	Low	Heavy use of firewall processes in a large Windows Domain***
Monitoring	Low	Separate kernel driver loaded
App. Control	Low**	
Web URL Filtering	Low**	
Content Awareness	Medium**	Heavy use of firewall processes***
DLP	Very High**	Heavy use of firewall processes***
Threat Emulation	Medium**	Heavy use of firewall processes***
Threat Extraction	Medium**	Heavy use of firewall processes***
QoS	High	Separate kernel driver loaded

** Potentially Very High Performance Impact if HTTPS Inspection is enabled for this blade via the HTTPS Inspection Policy.

*** Trips to process space on the firewall to handle traffic (the "Fourth Path") are covered extensively in Chapter 10.

The "top" & "free" Gaia/Linux Commands

Question: What is the current CPU load on the firewall?

Answer: From expert mode run the command **top**. Immediately your entire screen will be populated with a list of the busiest processes on the system. The line we want to focus on is here:

```
top - 04:44:04 up 1 day, 19:35,  2 users,  load average: 0.16, 0.10,
Tasks: 212 total,  1 running, 211 sleeping,  0 stopped,  0 zombie
Cpu(s):  0.2%us,  0.4%sy,  0.0%ni, 99.3%id,  0.0%wa,  0.0%hi,  0.0%si
Mem:   8028904k total,  2767484k used,  5261420k free,   272012k buff
Swap: 18900432k total,       0k used, 18900432k free,  1004712k cache
```

PID	USER	PR	NI	VIRT	RES	SHR	S	%CPU	%MEM	TIME+	COMMAND
9776	admin	21	0	69000	8244	3960	S	1	0.1	27:00.64	DAService
6031	admin	15	0	367m	50m	24m	S	1	0.6	12:01.78	fw_full
1	admin	18	0	1976	724	624	S	0	0.0	0:01.36	init
2	admin	RT	-5	0	0	0	S	0	0.0	0:00.08	migration/0
3	admin	15	0	0	0	0	S	0	0.0	0:00.00	ksoftirqd/0
4	admin	RT	-5	0	0	0	S	0	0.0	0:00.00	watchdog/0
5	admin	RT	-5	0	0	0	S	0	0.0	0:01.22	migration/1
6	admin	15	0	0	0	0	S	0	0.0	0:00.07	ksoftirqd/1
7	admin	RT	-5	0	0	0	S	0	0.0	0:00.00	watchdog/1
8	admin	RT	-5	0	0	0	S	0	0.0	0:00.07	migration/2
9	admin	15	0	0	0	0	S	0	0.0	0:00.00	ksoftirqd/2
10	admin	RT	-5	0	0	0	S	0	0.0	0:00.00	watchdog/2
11	admin	RT	-5	0	0	0	S	0	0.0	0:00.01	migration/3
12	admin	15	0	0	0	0	S	0	0.0	0:00.00	ksoftirqd/3
13	admin	RT	-5	0	0	0	S	0	0.0	0:00.00	watchdog/3
14	admin	RT	-5	0	0	0	S	0	0.0	0:00.01	migration/4
15	admin	15	0	0	0	0	S	0	0.0	0:00.00	ksoftirqd/4
16	admin	RT	-5	0	0	0	S	0	0.0	0:00.00	watchdog/4

Figure 4-4: *top* Command Showing Aggregate CPU Load

On the **Cpu(s)** line is a real-time summary of your firewalls processing load, averaged across all cores. On most production firewalls, the majority of CPU time is expended in system/kernel space (sy) and processing soft interrupts (si). Let's examine each field in detail.

Top Output: "us" – Process Space

CPU cycles being used to service processes. You may see a large number of fw_worker processes using quite a bit of CPU. This is normal on systems with CoreXL enabled (we will cover CoreXL in detail during a later chapter). The **fw_worker** process represents a firewall kernel instance on a multi-core Check Point firewall that utilizes CoreXL. If an excessive amount of CPU time (>40%) is being expended by processes other than an **fw_worker**, the situation may warrant further examination. Ignore any processes shown enclosed in brackets [] as these are kernel/system threads. Further down on the **top** display you will be able to see the top processes that are currently consuming CPU. Look at the **%CPU** column. Is there one process using large amounts of CPU? It could be a runaway process or one that is crashing and restarting constantly. Run the command **cpwd_admin list**:

```
[Expert@firewall:0]# cpwd_admin_list
```

APP	PID	STAT	#START	START_TIME		MON	COMMAND
HISTORYD	5695	E	1	[08:05:30]	15/3/2015	N	cpview_his
CPD	5698	E	1	[08:05:30]	15/3/2015	Y	cpd
MPDAEMON	5822	E	1	[08:05:31]	15/3/2015	N	mpdaemon ,
CPHAMCSET	6015	E	1	[08:05:35]	15/3/2015	N	cphamcset
CI_CLEANUP	6027	E	1	[08:05:40]	15/3/2015	N	avi_del_tn
CIHS	6031	E	1	[08:05:40]	15/3/2015	N	ci_http_se
FWD	6045	E	1	[08:05:41]	15/3/2015	N	fwd
FWM	6050	E	1	[08:05:41]	15/3/2015	N	fwm
STPR	6053	E	1	[08:05:41]	15/3/2015	N	status_prc
CPSM	6438	E	1	[08:05:44]	15/3/2015	N	cpstat_mor
CPVIEWD	6921	E	1	[08:05:59]	15/3/2015	N	cpviewd
SVR	7770	E	1	[08:06:02]	15/3/2015	N	SVRServer
CPSEAD	7852	E	1	[08:06:02]	15/3/2015	N	cpsead
CPWMD	7924	E	1	[08:06:04]	15/3/2015	N	cpwmd -D -
CPHTTPD	7927	E	1	[08:06:04]	15/3/2015	N	cp_http_se
DASERVICE	7952	E	1	[08:06:04]	15/3/2015	N	DAService_

Figure 4-5: Using *cpwd_admin list* to Find Restarting Firewall Processes

This command shows the last time a key firewall process was restarted. The
START_TIME values for all processes monitored by the Check Point Watchdog Daemon
(**cpwd**) should be very close to each other, and roughly correspond to when the system
was first booted. Use the **uptime** command to confirm. If the **START_TIME** of one of
the processes isn't close to the others, take a look in the directory
/var/log/dump/usermode on the firewall as there may be core dumps present for any
processes that have crashed. These core dumps can be submitted to the Check Point
TAC for a root cause determination. Also the **cpview** tool can be used to track a
running count of monitored processes restarted by **cpwd**:

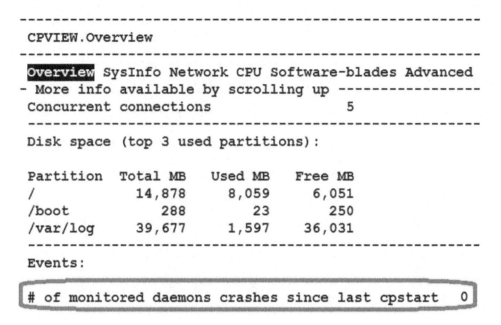

```
------------------------------------------------------
  CPVIEW.Overview
------------------------------------------------------
 Overview SysInfo Network CPU Software-blades Advanced
- More info available by scrolling up ----------------
 Concurrent connections                    5
------------------------------------------------------
 Disk space (top 3 used partitions):

 Partition   Total MB   Used MB    Free MB
 /            14,878     8,059      6,051
 /boot          288         23        250
 /var/log    39,677      1,597     36,031
------------------------------------------------------
 Events:

 # of monitored daemons crashes since last cpstart   0
```

Figure 4-6: Viewing Monitored Daemon Crashes from *cpview*

For certain processes there is a log file available which may prove helpful if the process is logging any errors just before terminating abnormally:

- fwd: $FWDIR/log/fwd.elg
- fwm: $FWDIR/log/fwm.elg
- cpm: $FWDIR/log/cpm.elg
- vpnd: $FWDIR/log/vpnd.elg
- cpd: $CPDIR/log/cpd.elg

For example to look at the latest entries in the **fwd** process log, type **tail** $FWDIR/log/fwd.elg. Further debugging of runaway or misbehaving processes can be accomplished with these commands:

- **fw debug fwd on|off** (Debugs go to **$FWDIR/log/fwd.elg**)

- **fw debug fwm on|off** (Debugs go to **$FWDIR/log/fwm.elg**)

- **$FWDIR/scripts/cpm_debug.sh -t <TOPIC> -s <SEVERITY>**

- **vpn debug on|off** (Debugs go to **$FWDIR/log/vpnd.elg**)

- **cpd_admin debug on|off** (Debugs go to **$CPDIR/log/cpd.elg**)

If you enable debug on a process, make sure to turn it off when done! To identify the function of these or any other daemon process names that may be encountered, consult sk97638: Check Point Processes and Daemons.

But suppose you see a strange-looking process hogging CPU in the **top** output:

PID	USER	PR	NI	VIRT	RES	SHR	S	%CPU	%MEM	TIME+	COMMAND
15215	admin	25	0	660m	180m	144m	R	94	0.0	20198:16	/bin/cat

Figure 4-7: A Process Consuming Excessive CPU

Huh? Why is the **cat** command eating so much CPU and what process launched this beast? The built-in Gaia tool **pstree** can help give us the answer:

```
[Expert@gw:0]# pstree
init-+-acpid
     |-cpwd-+-CvpnUMD
     |      |-fw_full-+-cp_file_convert---20*[{cp_file_convert}]
     |      |         |-scrubd--configure_scrub---configure_scrub-+-cat
     |      |         |                                           |-fold
     |      |         |                                           `-tr
     |
```

Figure 4-8: Using *pstree* to Help Identify a CPU-Hogging Process

As it turns out this process is related to the **scrubd** process which sk97638 lists as part of the Threat Extraction blade feature. Using **pstree** can help us determine the origin of a runaway process when the name of the process itself (or its arguments) is not enough to determine its purpose and whether we should do something about it.

Another command that can provide some insight for a mystery process consuming excessive CPU is **lsof** (LiSt Open Files). Once the process ID has been determined (15215 in our example) run **lsof -p 15215**. The output will show all files currently being accessed by the process, along with all open network connections and TCP/UDP ports the process is currently listening on (if any).

A final option that is guaranteed to satisfy even the most voracious seeker of information about a pesky process, is to install the **strace** binary (similar to the **truss** command on Solaris) and dynamically attach it to the problematic process with the **-p** option. This allows real-time monitoring of all system calls made by the process in an attempt to determine what it is trying to accomplish. **strace** is not included by default with Gaia (and its use is not officially supported) but you can install the precompiled CentOS version of **strace** available here:

http://vault.centos.org/3.8/os/i386/RedHat/RPMS/strace-4.5.14-0.EL3.1.i386.rpm

Top Output: "sy" &"si" – System Space

CPU cycles being used to service kernel drivers and modules shown in top output. It is normal to see the vast majority of CPU cycles expended in these two areas with **top**, since the Check Point INSPECT and SecureXL kernel drivers perform most of the security inspection functions on the firewall. Firewall Path and Medium Path processing typically shows up as CPU usage in **sy** space; Accelerated Path and SoftIRQ processing typically shows up as CPU usage in **si** space (the various processing paths are covered in Chapter 9). Unlike processes running in process space, visibility into what service or function is consuming excessive CPU in system space is limited. However some insight can be gained by running **cpview** and selecting CPU...Top Connections to see the top individual connections by CPU consumption. This usage data can be summarized for all Firewall Worker cores or even viewed for individual cores if needed.

Top Output: "wa" – Waiting for I/O Operation

This value should be between 0 and 5% at most. This field specifies the amount of time a CPU is blocked (unable to do anything else) while waiting for an I/O operation of some kind to complete. The most common culprit is waiting for the hard drive of the firewall to respond to a request. This may occur a fair amount right after the firewall is booted up, as the needed executable code is paged in from the hard disk and cached in RAM. This number will also spike for a few moments during a policy load which is completely normal. However this **wa** activity should eventually die down to practically zero on a properly configured firewall. If more than 5% of CPU is consistently being wasted in a waiting state, your firewall almost certainly does not have enough RAM or is experiencing problems with some kind of hardware peripheral.

Gaia Memory Management

Run the command **free -m**. Some sample output is provided:

```
[Expert@firewall:0]# free -m
             total     used     free   shared  buffers   cached
Mem:          7840     3760     4079        0      276     1126
-/+ buffers/cache:     2357     5483
Swap:        18457        0    18457
[Expert@firewall:0]#
```

Figure 4-9: Viewing Gaia Memory Statistics with *free -m*

Let's discuss this in detail; the first number on the second line (7840 in our sample output) is the total amount of RAM installed in the firewall, or at least how much that is recognized by the operating system. The second number (3760) is the total amount of RAM consumed for execution of code and buffering/caching of hard drive operations. **shared** is always zero. **buffers** indicates RAM that is allocated for buffering of disk I/O operations. **cached** is the amount of RAM allocated to store directory listings and file attributes for fast filesystem access. The RAM allocated to both buffering and caching is not being used for actual execution of code, and could be freed and reallocated at any moment if more RAM was needed for code execution.

This brings us to the third line: 2357 is the amount of RAM allocated on the system for code execution; it does not include the RAM allocated for buffering and caching. 5483 is the amount of currently free RAM available to be allocated for execution. Notice that if you subtract the amount of RAM allocated for buffering and caching (276+1126=1402) from the total amount of RAM reported used on the second line of output (3760), you get approximately the value 2357, which is the used amount reported on the third line of output. Therefore in our example, 2357 represents the true amount of RAM consumed by the firewall for execution of code. The value reported by your firewall on the second line (4079 in our example) may look extremely low in some cases, leading you to conclude that the firewall is running low on RAM. Nothing could be further from the truth. The `free` value reported on the third line (5483 in our example) reports the true amount of RAM readily available for code execution when not taking buffering and caching into account.

Ideally, the fourth line of the free command output is reporting zero for swap used as shown the previous screenshot. If this value is nonzero, this indicates that the firewall is (or was) low on free RAM memory at one point and had to page at least a portion of the system memory allocated for processes out to disk. *The larger this swap used number the bigger the performance hit*. This use of virtual memory due to a lack of RAM can be highly destructive to firewall performance and should be avoided if at all possible.

Question: My system is low on free memory as reported on the third line of the `free -m` output and/or "Swap used" is being shown as nonzero. What is consuming so much memory on the firewall?

Answer: Run the `top` command and then hit M (upper-case M). This will change the default sorting which would normally show the processes using the most CPU first; now the processes using the most memory will be shown first. Once again disregard the `fw_worker` processes which we will discuss in a later chapter. Do you see any other processes using an extremely large amount of memory in the `RES` column? It is possible that process is a runaway or otherwise leaking memory. Depending on the identity of the offending process you may be able to kill it (and let it automatically restart) without causing a service outage. Contact the Check Point TAC for assistance in making this determination.

Question: My `free -m` output is reporting the total amount of RAM as approximately 4096, but I know for a fact the system has at least 6GB of RAM. What's wrong?

Answer: The Gaia operating is running in 32-bit mode. If a firewall was initially configured with less than 6GB of RAM then had its memory upgraded later, Gaia may still be running in 32-bit mode. As long as a minimum of 6GB RAM is present in the system, you can set Gaia for 64-bit operation to take advantage of that additional memory capacity. Check the edition (32-bit or 64-bit) by running the clish command `show version os edition`. To change from 32-bit to 64-bit operation run the command `set edition 64-bit` from clish, execute a `save config` command, and then reboot the system.

Gaia Memory Zone Reclaim

NUMA (Non-Uniform Memory Access) allows multiple cores to access the system's RAM simultaneously in the Gaia operating system. It does this by dividing the system's RAM into several zones and allocating each core its own dedicated zone of memory. When a particular zone runs low on memory and cannot satisfy a memory allocation request, a "reclaim" routine can be launched in an attempt to free up memory inside that same zone that is not currently being used, or is not expected to be used soon. Unfortunately this reclaim process is quite intensive, and can cause seemingly random slowdowns when memory-intensive processes are attempting to execute on the firewall.

Run the following command: `cat /proc/sys/vm/zone_reclaim_mode`. The returned result should be "0" for optimum Gaia memory management, and is normally set to zero by default. If you receive a "no such file or directory" error message, it means that either the system's processing hardware is not capable of NUMA, or that the Gaia OS is running in 32-bit mode in which case NUMA cannot be used. When `zone_reclaim_mode` is set to zero and a zone does not have enough free memory to satisfy an allocation request, the needed memory is simply allocated from another zone that does have enough free memory instead of embarking on the intensive zone reclaim procedure.

If `zone_reclaim_mode` is somehow set to a non-zero value on your firewall, see the following SK for instructions about how to permanently set it to zero: sk109772: R77.30 NGTP, NGTX and HTTPS Inspection performance and memory consumption optimization.

Firewall Disk Space Check

Question: Is my firewall running out of disk space?

Answer: Run the command `df -h`. If any partitions show more than 90% utilization, cleanup of files will need to be attempted. Determine which partition is near-full (/, /opt, /var/log, etc) and run this command:

```
find /var/log -mount -type f -size +1000000 -ls
```

Look at the largest files and delete them if possible; old cpinfos or debug captures frequently consume large amounts of disk space and can be removed. If no files show up in the find output, remove one zero from the **+1000000** part of the command and run it again. If you can't seem to find any large user-generated files to delete, try the cleanup script provided by Check Point here: sk91060: Removing old Check Point packages and files after an upgrade on Security Gateway / Security Management Server. If you still cannot free enough disk space on Gaia, consider using the `lvm_manager` script to reallocate the partition sizes as detailed here: sk95566: Managing partition sizes via LVM manager on Gaia OS. Note that on releases R80 and later, the `lvm_manager` tool can only be successfully used when the system has been booted into Maintenance Mode first.

Check Point Specific Commands

Question: Is the firewall running out of resources such as memory when processing traffic?

Answer: Run the command `fw ctl pstat` on the firewall. Focus on the `System Capacity Summary`, `System Kernel Memory (smem)`, and `Kernel Memory (kmem)` sections:

```
[Expert@firewall:0]# fw ctl pstat

System Capacity Summary:
  Memory used: 11% (181 MB out of 1587 MB) - below watermark
  Concurrent Connections: 0% (43 out of 24900) - below watermark
  Aggressive Aging is not active

Hash kernel memory (hmem) statistics:
  Total memory allocated: 163577856 bytes in 39936 (4096 bytes) ]
  Total memory bytes  used: 19019912    unused: 144557944 (88.37%
  Total memory blocks used:     6544   unused:    33392 (83%)    ]
  Allocations: 20380914 alloc, 0 failed alloc, 20203364 free

System kernel memory (smem) statistics:
  Total memory  bytes  used: 247632308    peak: 271764448
  Total memory bytes wasted: 16011980
    Blocking  memory  bytes    used:  5100120    peak:  5765280
    Non-Blocking memory bytes used: 242532188    peak: 265999168
  Allocations: 28039 alloc, 0 failed alloc 24316 free, 0 failed
  vmalloc bytes  used:        0 expensive: yes

Kernel memory (kmem) statistics:
  Total memory  bytes  used: 102898324    peak: 138183348
  Allocations: 20398669 alloc, 0 failed alloc
             20219537 free, 0 failed free
  External Allocations: 0 for packets, 43491586 for SXL
```

Figure 4-10: Viewing Check Point-specific Kernel Memory Statistics

If **smem** or **kmem** are reporting any failed allocations, system memory is running low which will definitely impact performance. Allocation failures under **Hash Memory (hmem)** are not as serious; essentially the firewall wanted to allocate some RAM to optimize searches in the state tables via hashing but could not due to a shortage of RAM. Firewall state table lookups will still succeed; they will just not be quite as optimized.

Question: During the firewall's busiest periods we see intermittent connection failures. What is the state table limit for number of concurrent connections? Has my firewall bumped into the limit?

Answer: By default for a new Gaia firewall installation there is no configured hard limit on the number of concurrent connections. On the Capacity Optimization screen of the firewall object in SmartConsole, the default setting for a new Gaia installation is "Automatically" as shown here:

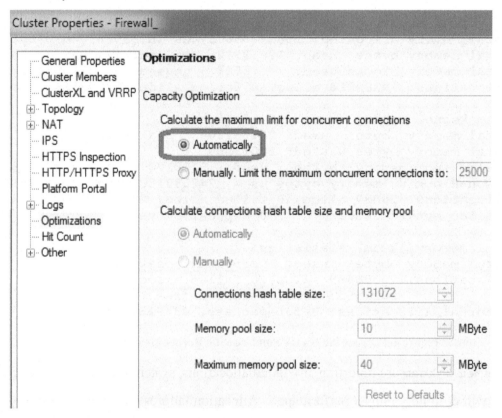

Figure 4-11: Capacity Optimization Screen – "Automatic" Setting

Generally the only limiting factor with the "Automatically" setting enabled is the amount of physical memory available on the firewall to track the connections. Examine your firewall's setting on this screen. If it is not set to "Automatically" and your firewall is using the Gaia OS, you should set it to "Automatically" immediately and install policy. If the firewall was upgraded from SecurePlatform or IPSO (where automatic connection table size is not supported) any hard-coded connection-table limits will be retained in Gaia after the upgrade.

If there is still a hard limit set on your firewall object (let's suppose it is the SecurePlatform/IPSO default of 25,000), you can check if the firewall has run up against the limit by executing the command **fw tab -t connections -s** on the firewall. If the value for **PEAK** is 25,000, at some point since being booted the firewall ran out of space in the state table to track new connections. In that case, any new connections attempted in excess of 25,000 were dropped regardless of what rule the security policy matched, since there was no way for the firewall to keep track of the connection. This situation will result in dismal firewall performance when it occurs, as some connections will succeed (when there are a few connection table slots free) and some connections will fail (when the limit is reached). *If using Gaia always make sure this is set to "Automatically"!* For more information about the other options on this screen consult: sk39555: Capacity Optimization and Connections Table.

Question: My connection table has a very large number of connections it is tracking, far beyond what it should be and it is impacting firewall performance. How can I see what source IP addresses are consuming the most connection table slots?

Answer: Run this command on the firewall:

```
fw tab -u -t connections |awk '{ print $2 }'|sort -n |uniq -c|sort -nr|head -10
```

This handy command will provide an output something like this:

```
12322 0a1e0b53
212 0a1e0b50
```

.
.

The first number in the output will be the number of connection table slots consumed, and the second value will be the source IP address of the offender in hexadecimal. The top offenders will be listed first. In our example the top offender is **0a1e0b53** (0a=10, 1e=30, 0b=11, 53=83) or 10.30.11.83. This IP address is consuming about 12,322 slots in the connections table, which is quite excessive for a single IP address unless it is some kind of proxy server or terminal server. If that IP address is not some kind of server, the classic scenarios that cause this behavior are:

- The host is infected with some kind of self-propagating virus or worm that is sending thousands of short-lived connection requests

- The host is running a port scan or performing some kind of network discovery that involves sending a very high number of connection requests (as in the case of an auditor, penetration tester, or the CEO's extremely bored but very bright child)

Remediations to deal with this annoying situation (other than not-so-politely telling the perpetrator to knock it off) are covered in the Chapter 7 section "CoreXL Firewall Worker Load Distribution" and Chapter 13. Another useful tool that can provide further visibility into precisely who is hogging slots in the connections table is the "Check Point Top Talkers" script by Craig Dods:

http://expert-mode.blogspot.com/2013/05/checkpoint-top-talkers-script-display.html.

However one limitation of the "Top Talkers" script is that SecureXL must be enabled. If SecureXL is disabled for some reason on your firewall (more on this in Chapter 9) you can still use the alternative **fw tab** command shown at the start of this section.

The "sar" Command and Using top in Batch Mode

Running some kind of continuous system-monitoring script is a time-honored technique employed by system administrators to catch degraded performance "in the act" and have statistics available to review. While there are a truly bewildering quantity of system counters and statistics that can be monitored, from a firewall performance perspective there are two general things we will want to look at first during a period of degraded performance:

- Network Error Counters – Did the firewall suddenly start racking up errors at the network level thus causing packet loss?

- CPU Utilization – Did one or more firewall CPUs get pegged at 100 percent utilization, thus causing network latency to spike dramatically?

But how do we look at these things during a period of degraded performance when we are not sure when it will occur? We can examine a spike in network errors after the fact with the **sar -n EDEV** command like this:

```
[Expert@firewall:0]# sar -n EDEV
Linux 2.6.18-92cp (firewall)      03/23/15

00:00:01  IFACE  rxerr/s  txerr/s  rxdrop/s  txdrop/s  txcarr/s
00:10:01     lo     0.00     0.00      0.00      0.00      0.00
00:10:01   eth0     0.00     0.00      0.00      0.00      0.00
00:10:01   eth1     0.00     0.00      0.00      0.00      0.00
00:10:01   eth2     0.00     0.00      0.00      0.00      0.00
00:10:01   eth3     0.00     0.00      0.00      0.00      0.00
00:20:01     lo     0.00     0.00      0.00      0.00      0.00
00:20:01   eth0     0.00     0.00    780.00      0.00      0.00
00:20:01   eth1     0.00     0.00      8.00      0.00      0.00
00:20:01   eth2     0.00     0.00      0.00      0.00      0.00
00:20:01   eth3     0.00     0.00      0.00      0.00      0.00
```

Figure 4-12: Using *sar -n EDEV* to Determine When Network Errors Occurred

If the **sar** command's 10-minute granularity period for these counters is too imprecise, you could also run the command **netstat -c -ni 5** which will continuously display network statistics every 5 seconds. Unfortunately, there is no direct way to have the **netstat** command print a timestamp every time it writes output without creating a more complex shell script, so you may be stuck babysitting this output waiting for something bad to happen performance-wise.

    sar can also show us historic CPU utilization per core by running **sar -P ALL**:

```
[Expert@firewall:0]# sar -P ALL
Linux 2.6.18-92cp (firewall)      03/23/15

00:00:01 CPU   %user   %system   %iowait   %idle
00:10:01 all    0.28      1.38      0.00    98.32
00:10:01   0    0.11      1.55      0.03    98.31
00:10:01   1    0.43      1.99      0.00    97.55
00:10:01   2    0.03      0.54      0.00    99.42
00:10:01   3    0.51      2.01      0.01    97.41
00:10:01   4    0.01      0.56      0.00    99.42
00:10:01   5    0.60      2.00      0.00    97.40
00:10:01   6    0.03      0.55      0.00    99.41
00:10:01   7    0.49      1.84      0.00    97.67
00:20:01 all    0.20      1.28      0.00    98.51
00:20:01   0    0.03      1.67      0.01    98.29
00:20:01   1    0.38      1.62      0.00    98.00
00:20:01   2    0.02      0.64      0.00    99.33
00:20:01   3    0.33      1.54      0.00    98.13
00:20:01   4    0.01      0.69      0.00    99.30
00:20:01   5    0.46      1.86      0.00    97.68
00:20:01   6    0.02      0.69      0.00    99.28
00:20:01   7    0.32      1.57      0.00    98.10
```

Figure 4-13: Viewing Historic CPU Utilization with *sar -P*

    While the historical data reported by the **sar** command can be useful, it can definitely be overwhelming unless you have a good idea of what you are looking for. A picture is worth a thousand words, so if you find yourself staring down the barrel of hours and hours of poring through **sar** data trying to find a performance problem, consider the **ksar** tool. **ksar** can be used to browse and graph **sar** data like this:

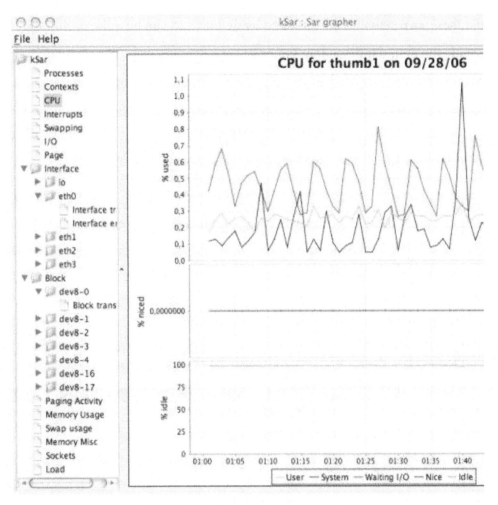

Figure 4-14: Using *ksar* to Graph *sar* Data

While not included with the Gaia operating system, `ksar` can be downloaded for free from https://sourceforge.net/projects/ksar. For more information about `sar` see sk112734: How to collect System Activity Report using the "sar" command. In Chapter 14 we also cover the ability of the SmartView Monitor to provide historical graphing of system resource utilization.

While these **sar** statistics are gathered by default and can be quite useful, they do not quite provide the granular detail that the **cpview** command can. For example in the **sar** output above hardware interrupt processing (**hi**), software interrupt processing (**si**) and system processing (**sy**) are all combined under the **%system** counter. But what if we need to see each of these three elements individually or we see an intermittently spiked **%user** value and want to know which process caused it?

We can monitor CPU usage at regular intervals with the **top** command in batch mode with its output being continuously redirected to a file, however in order to see individual core utilization while running **top** in batch mode a bit of setup is required. First off run the **top** command:

```
top - 04:44:04 up 1 day, 19:35,  2 users,  load average: 0.16, 0.10,
Tasks: 212 total,  1 running, 211 sleeping,  0 stopped,  0 zombie
Cpu(s):  0.2%us,  0.4%sy,  0.0%ni, 99.3%id,  0.0%wa,  0.0%hi,  0.0%si
Mem:  8028904k total,  2767484k used,  5261420k free,  272012k buff
Swap: 18900432k total,       0k used, 18900432k free,  1004712k cach

  PID USER      PR  NI  VIRT  RES  SHR S %CPU %MEM    TIME+  COMMAND
 9776 admin     21   0 69000 8244 3960 S    1  0.1 27:00.64 DAService
 6031 admin     15   0  367m  50m  24m S    1  0.6 12:01.78 fw_full
    1 admin     18   0  1976  724  624 S    0  0.0  0:01.36 init
    2 admin     RT  -5     0    0    0 S    0  0.0  0:00.08 migration/0
    3 admin     15   0     0    0    0 S    0  0.0  0:00.00 ksoftirqd/0
    4 admin     RT  -5     0    0    0 S    0  0.0  0:00.00 watchdog/0
    5 admin     RT  -5     0    0    0 S    0  0.0  0:01.22 migration/1
    6 admin     15   0     0    0    0 S    0  0.0  0:00.07 ksoftirqd/1
    7 admin     RT  -5     0    0    0 S    0  0.0  0:00.00 watchdog/1
    8 admin     RT  -5     0    0    0 S    0  0.0  0:00.07 migration/2
    9 admin     15   0     0    0    0 S    0  0.0  0:00.00 ksoftirqd/2
   10 admin     RT  -5     0    0    0 S    0  0.0  0:00.00 watchdog/2
   11 admin     RT  -5     0    0    0 S    0  0.0  0:00.01 migration/3
   12 admin     15   0     0    0    0 S    0  0.0  0:00.00 ksoftirqd/3
   13 admin     RT  -5     0    0    0 S    0  0.0  0:00.00 watchdog/3
   14 admin     RT  -5     0    0    0 S    0  0.0  0:00.01 migration/4
   15 admin     15   0     0    0    0 S    0  0.0  0:00.00 ksoftirqd/4
   16 admin     RT  -5     0    0    0 S    0  0.0  0:00.00 watchdog/4
```

Figure 4-15: Using *top* to Display Aggregate CPU Utilizations

Now hit the numeric "1" key to display individual CPU usage, and then hit capital "W" to write the current display configuration to the `.toprc` file:

```
top - 10:12:39 up 5 days,  1:12,  2 users,  load average: 0.09, 0.12,
Tasks: 165 total,    2 running, 163 sleeping,    0 stopped,    0 zombie
Cpu0  :   0.0%us,  0.0%sy,  0.0%ni, 99.7%id,  0.0%wa,  0.0%hi,  0.3%si
Cpu1  :   0.0%us,  0.3%sy,  0.0%ni, 96.6%id,  0.0%wa,  0.0%hi,  3.0%si
Cpu2  :   0.0%us,  0.0%sy,  0.0%ni, 96.0%id,  0.0%wa,  0.0%hi,  4.0%si
Cpu3  :   0.3%us,  1.4%sy,  0.0%ni, 95.3%id,  0.0%wa,  0.0%hi,  3.0%si
Cpu4  :   0.0%us,  0.0%sy,  0.0%ni, 97.3%id,  0.0%wa,  0.0%hi,  2.7%si
Cpu5  :   0.3%us,  1.0%sy,  0.0%ni, 94.4%id,  0.0%wa,  0.0%hi,  4.3%si
Cpu6  :   0.0%us,  0.3%sy,  0.0%ni, 96.0%id,  0.0%wa,  0.0%hi,  3.7%si
Cpu7  :   0.7%us,  1.0%sy,  0.0%ni, 94.6%id,  0.0%wa,  0.0%hi,  3.7%si
Mem:    4078260k total,  3931836k used,   146424k free,   297928k buff
Swap:   8385920k total,       92k used,  8385828k free,  1155324k cach
Wrote configuration to '/home/admin/.toprc'
  PID USER       PR  NI  VIRT  RES  SHR S %CPU %MEM    TIME+  COMMAND
 7504 admin      19   0  110m  51m 5176 S    1  1.3 108:56.32 DAServic
   11 admin      RT  -5     0    0    0 S    0  0.0   7:19.17 migratio
 9339 admin      15   0  2172 1124  832 R    0  0.0   0:00.01 top
    1 admin      15   0  2044  724  624 S    0  0.0   0:01.63 init
    2 admin      RT  -5     0    0    0 S    0  0.0   0:23.44 migratio
    3 admin      15   0     0    0    0 S    0  0.0   0:03.64 ksoftirq
    4 admin      RT  -5     0    0    0 S    0  0.0   0:00.05 watchdog
    5 admin      RT  -5     0    0    0 S    0  0.0   5:32.21 migratio
    6 admin      15   0     0    0    0 S    0  0.0   0:02.84 ksoftirq
    7 admin      RT  -5     0    0    0 S    0  0.0   0:00.10 watchdog
```

Figure 4-16: Using *top* to Display Separate CPU Utilizations by Default

Exit **top** and restart it. Notice how all individual CPU core utilization statistics now display by default, which will carry over into our batch mode monitoring. Now suppose you know that a period of intermittent performance problems is likely to happen in the next hour (3600 seconds), and you would like to monitor the CPU utilization and top processes closely during that period. The command would be: **top -b -d 5 -n 720 > outputfile**. This command will save a copy of all CPU statistics every 5 seconds 720 times (for a total of 3600 seconds) and then terminate. It is very important to always use the **-n** option to specify the number of iterations! Otherwise the **top** command will run until you stop it with a CTRL-C, the firewall is rebooted, or it runs out of disk space, whichever comes first.

Another interesting option is using the **cpview -p** command which immediately dumps all data from all possible screens of the **cpview** tool at once; this command can be quickly executed multiple times when problems begin and its extensive output analyzed later. This command can also be run over and over again by a script every few seconds trying to catch an intermittent problem "in the act". The **cpview** tool also has its own "batch" mode as well, but the output is voluminous and looks nothing like the **cpview** screens you are used to seeing. Troubleshooting intermittent or past performance issues is explored more thoroughly in Chapter 14.

Firewall Gateway Thresholds

If you suspect that the firewall's overall CPU usage is getting pegged during the periods of intermittently slow performance (or you see suspicious-looking CPU utilization spikes in the Firewall History report of SmartView Monitor), it is critical to catch the firewall "in the act" so you can run tools like **top** or **cpview** to determine what precisely is happening during the incident. In the SmartView Monitor by right-clicking on a firewall gateway object and selecting "Configure Thresholds", you can enable the automatic sending of a SNMP trap or email when the overall CPU usage exceeds a set threshold (the default is 90%):

Enabled	Threshold	Operator		Value	Action	
☐	CPU usage	more than	▼	90%	alert	▼
☐	Free disk space	less than	▼	15%	alert	▼
☑	Status connection	not	▼	connected	alert	▼
☑	Firewall Policy	equal	▼	not installed	alert	▼
☑	Firewall Policy install time	changed	▼		alert	▼
☑	Firewall Policy name	changed	▼		alert	▼
☑	Synchronization state	equal	▼	not synchronized	alert	▼
☑	QoS Policy	equal	▼	not installed	alert	▼
☑	QoS Policy install time	changed	▼		alert	▼
☑	QoS Policy name	changed	▼		alert	▼

Figure 4-17: SmartView Monitor Threshold Settings

These alerts can be globally configured for all firewalls or for individual ones. This setup can provide the "heads-up" you need to quickly log in to the firewall and begin troubleshooting during a performance-related incident. The IP address for the SNMP trap receiver and email setup parameters for these alerts are configured in the SmartDashboard/SmartConsole under Global Properties...Log and Alert...Alerts. For more information about email alerts see: sk25941: Configuring 'Mail Alerts' using **'internal_sendmail'** command.

Although not directly related to performance, I would highly recommend configuring the "Firewall Policy install time...changed" threshold with an email alert. This feature will send an email any time the firewall policy is reinstalled. Example: A colleague makes some big security policy changes, installs the policy to the firewall, and then (in true Murphy's Law fashion) leaves for lunch and forgets their cell phone. You get a call from the Help Desk 10 minutes later concerning various issues that are now occurring, because of course any network problem is always the firewall's fault. Wouldn't it have been nice to receive an email right before that call, letting you know that something in the firewall policy was recently changed and installed?

Gaia OS Monitoring with cpview

An incredible wealth of monitoring information concerning the firewall's Gaia OS is available through the **cpview** tool. Even more exciting is that the great statistics available from **cpview** can not only be examined in real-time, but past statistics are available as well. By default all Check Point firewalls store 30 days of historical statistics accessible through **cpview**; a daemon process called **historyd** makes this happen. The historical mode of **cpview** can be accessed by passing the **-t** option; once active you can "step forward" or "step back" in increments of 60 seconds on almost all available screens in **cpview**. As you might suspect, the historical mode of **cpview** is absolutely invaluable for performing a post-mortem of performance issues, or troubleshooting intermittent issues after they have occurred. This historical mode of **cpview** is explored thoroughly in Chapter 14.

For now we will concern ourselves with using **cpview** in real-time to monitor the health and utilization of the Gaia operating system; let's jump right in with some screenshots showing what are probably the four most useful Gaia-related screens. These are presented with no commentary and should be pretty self-explanatory.

```
|---------------------------------------------------------
| CPVIEW.Overview
|---------------------------------------------------------
| Overview SysInfo Network CPU Software-blades Advanced
|---------------------------------------------------------
| CPU:
|
| ┌─────────────────────────────────┐
| │ Num of CPUs:       4            │
| │                                 │
| │        CPU        Used          │
| │         2          2%           │
| │         3          2%           │
| │         0        100%           │
| └─────────────────────────────────┘
|  --------------------------------------------------------
| Memory:
|
| ┌─────────────────────────────────────────┐
| │           Total MB   Used MB   Free MB   │
| │ Physical     1,450       556       893   │
| │ FW Kernel    1,160       277       882   │
| │ Swap         2,047       540     1,506   │
| └─────────────────────────────────────────┘
|  --------------------------------------------------------
| Network:
|
| ┌─────────────────────────────────────────┐
| │ Bits/sec                        81,788   │
| │ Packets/sec                         16   │
| │ Connections/sec                      4   │
| │ Concurrent connections              62   │
| └─────────────────────────────────────────┘
|  --------------------------------------------------------
| Disk space (top 3 used partitions):
|
| Partition  Total MB   Used MB   Free MB
| /            10,911     5,439     4,908
| /boot          288         23       250
| /var/log    10,911        882     9,465
```

Figure 4-18: *cpview* Overview Screen

```
|--------------------------------------------------------------.
| CPVIEW.SysInfo
|--------------------------------------------------------------.
| Overview SysInfo Network CPU Software-blades Advanced
|--------------------------------------------------------------.
| Configuration Information:
|
| Platform              Gaia 32Bit
| Configuration         Cluster Security Gateway
| Cluster status        Active
| SecureXL Status       on
| CoreXL Status         on
| CoreXL instances      3
| SMT Status            Unsupported
|
| ---------------------------------------------------------
| General information:
|
| System uptime         3 days, 18:42:24
| Last policy install time   23Oct2017 11:24:26
| Last policy name      Alpha_Standard
| ---------------------------------------------------------
| Version Information:
|
| fw1_wrapper package version    R80.10
|
|                   Branch Name        Build Number
| FW User Mode      R80_10_jumbo_hf    991140020
| FW Kernel         R80_10_jumbo_hf    991140025
'
```

Figure 4-19: *cpview* SysInfo Screen

```
|-----------------------------------------------------------------------
| CPVIEW.Network.Interfaces                            26Oct2017 11:0
|-----------------------------------------------------------------------
| Overview SysInfo Network CPU Software-blades Advanced
|-----------------------------------------------------------------------
| Traffic Interfaces Top-Protocols Top-Connections
|-----------------------------------------------------------------------
| Overview Traffic
|-----------------------------------------------------------------------
| RX Traffic:
|
| Interface      packets        pps       peak      Mbits       Mbps
| lo              264K           1         13        1,318          0
| eth0          3,687K          18        145        3,457          0
| eth1          2,693K           7         60        1,807          0
| eth2         12,433K          37        393        9,998          0
| eth3         12,116K          39        720       24,550          0
| eth4          2,522K           7         10        1,641          0
| eth5          2,505K           7          8        1,623          0
| TOTAL        36,223K         116        N/A       44,397          0
| --------------------------------------------------------------------
| TX Traffic:
|
| Interface      packets        pps       peak      Mbits       Mbps
| lo              264K           1         13        1,318          0
| eth0          3,636K          21         75       11,039          0
| eth1          2,719K           7        119        2,357          0
| eth2         13,181K          36        379       18,130          0
| eth3          3,298K          10        174        2,223          0
| eth4          2,524K           7         10        1,637          0
| eth5          2,507K           7          8        1,623          0
| TOTAL        28,133K          89        N/A       38,330          0
| --------------------------------------------------------------------
| Errors and Drops:
```

Figure 4-20: *cpview* Network.Interfaces Screen

```
|-------------------------------------------------------------
| CPVIEW.CPU.Top-Connections                              2(
|-------------------------------------------------------------
| Overview SysInfo Network CPU Software-blades Advanced
|-------------------------------------------------------------
| Overview Top-Protocols Top-Connections
|-------------------------------------------------------------
| Instances0-2
|-------------------------------------------------------------
| Instances0 Instances1 Instances2
|-------------------------------------------------------------
| CPU Utilization (CPU Connections Statistics should be on. R(
|
| Average connection CPU utilization              0.00%
|
|                            Connections        CPU utilization
| Top connections                      0                 0.00%
| Other connections                   13                 0.00%
| Total connections                   13                 0.00%
|          ---------------------------------------------------
| Top Connections
|
| Connection            Protocol    % out of CPU
```

Figure 4-21: *cpview* CPU.Top-Connections Screen

Basic Gaia Optimization: Key Points

- Enabling some firewall blades can have dramatic impact on firewall performance.

- The **top** command can be used to profile the firewall's CPU usage in both process space and system/kernel space.

- The **free** command can be used to assess whether the firewall has sufficient RAM available or is having to dip into performance-killing virtual memory.

- Ensure Gaia is running in 64-bit mode if the firewall has at least 6GB of memory.

- Clean up old files if disk space is low on the firewall.

- All Gaia firewalls should have their Capacity Optimization set to "Automatic" to avoid running out of connection table entries.

- The **sar** command and using the **top** command in batch mode can provide live monitoring of firewall performance.

- **cpview** is an outstanding tool that can provide live and historical firewall performance statistics.

CHAPTER 5
ACCESS CONTROL POLICY TUNING

If you spend more on coffee than on IT Security, you will be hacked. What's more, you deserve to be hacked.

- Richard Clarke

Background

In this chapter we will discuss optimization strategies for the Access Control policy layers in the R80+ SmartConsole. While the screenshots and overall tone of this chapter will assume you are utilizing R80+ management, the recommendations have been carefully crafted to be applicable to R77.30 management as well, and "future-proofed" for when you do eventually upgrade to R80.10+ firewall code. The recommendations made in this chapter will improve firewall performance regardless of the state and/or configuration of CoreXL/SecureXL on your firewall; tuning these critical acceleration technologies is covered in later chapters. We will eschew the normal command-line discovery phase in this chapter since the policy layers configuration is performed from the SmartDashboard/SmartConsole GUI. As we proceed it is assumed that you are following along in your own policy configurations and making adjustments as we go.

This chapter is not intended as an introduction to how policy layers are handled in R80+ management; it is assumed that you are already working with policy layers or are otherwise familiar with them. The CCSA (Check Point Certified Security Administrator) class offered by your local Check Point Authorized Training Center (ATC) is a good start in this area. If you are completely new to R80+ management and policy layers, CheckMates (community.checkpoint.com) has an excellent series of free training videos called "R80.x Training Videos" that would be well worth your time to peruse prior to going through this chapter. At press time these free videos were available at this location:

https://community.checkpoint.com/docs/DOC-2158-r80-training-videos

For starters let's define precisely what specific sets of rules comprise the Access Control policy layers in R80+ management that will be covered in this chapter:

- **Network Access Layer**: Filtering by IP Addresses & Port Numbers
- **APCL/URLF Layer**: Application Control & URL Filtering
- **Content Awareness** (R80.10+ only): Data Loss Prevention (DLP) "Lite" & File Type Identification
- **NAT Policy**: Network Address Translation rules

While the policy layers below are also part of the Access Control policy, they will not be covered in this book because these features are either infrequently used or do not have a direct impact on overall firewall performance:

- **Quality of Service** (QoS -formerly known as Floodgate-1)
- **Desktop Security**
- **Mobile Access Blade** (MAB)
- **Data Loss Prevention** (DLP)

Due to their heavy impact on how traffic can be (or not be) potentially accelerated by SecureXL, optimization of Threat Prevention policies is covered in Chapter 9. Threat Prevention consists of the IPS, Anti-Bot, Anti-Virus, Threat Emulation and Threat Extraction features.

Optimization of HTTPS Inspection and its policy is covered in Chapter 10.

Policies: R77.30 vs. R80+ Management

The following diagram summarizes the overall changes in policy location between the R77.30 SmartDashboard application and the R80+ SmartConsole. In R80+ management, configuration of some features is still performed in a legacy SmartDashboard application separate from the R80+ SmartConsole application.

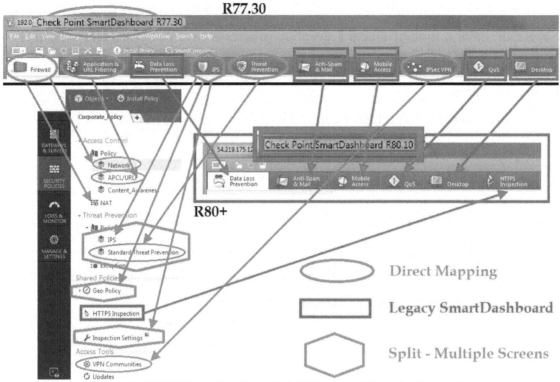

Figure 5-1: R77.30 SmartDashboard & R80+ SmartConsole Comparison

The policy tuning covered in this chapter will all take place in the R80+ SmartConsole. For those still using R77.30 management, the recommendations will still be mostly valid, but they may look a little different in the R77.30 SmartDashboard.

Firewall Topology

Before we proceed any further, it is critical to make sure that your firewall topology is completely and correctly defined on your firewall/cluster object. Failure to ensure that this configuration is correct will cause big problems later and make achieving reasonable firewall performance nearly impossible. Specifically, your firewall's topology configuration will heavily impact policies that utilize the built-in object "Internet" and those that make reference to DMZ networks. An incorrect or incomplete firewall topology configuration will cause huge amounts of traffic to be improperly processed by many different firewall features, thus making even LAN to LAN communication through the firewall unbearably slow.

WARNING: Take extreme care when changing a network interface from External to Internal (or vice-versa) as well as toggling the checkbox "Interface leads to DMZ". Changing this setting or other interface topology values can have a dramatic impact on anti-spoofing and blade enforcement, which can in turn either drop or impede insane amounts of network traffic causing an outage. If the Internal/External/DMZ definitions on your firewall's interfaces need to be corrected, schedule a maintenance window to make the change.

In the SmartDashboard open your firewall/cluster object for editing and select Network Management (called "Topology" in R77.30 management):

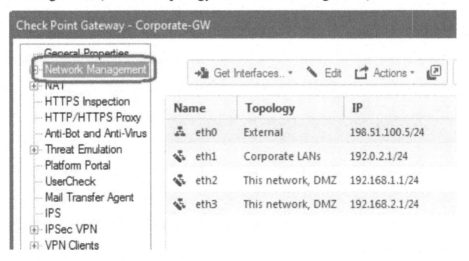

Figure 5-2: Firewall Network Management Topology Screen

You should see a list of your firewall's interfaces. Examine them closely. Does the interface facing the Internet have a "Network Type" of "External"? It should. Generally only the external-facing interface should be defined as "External" and all other interfaces should be defined as "Internal". In some environments it is definitely possible to have more than one interface defined as "External", such as when using more than one Internet Service Provider.

In R80+ management, anything under "Topology" other than External means the interface is defined as Internal. (In the R77.30 SmartDashboard it will explicitly say "Internal" in the Topology column instead). In our example screenshot, one interface is defined as External while the other three are defined as Internal. In the following section we will examine how our interface topology is currently defined, but don't change anything in your configuration just yet!

Now we need to view each of the individual interfaces defined as Internal and go to their Topology screen, first we will examine eth1:

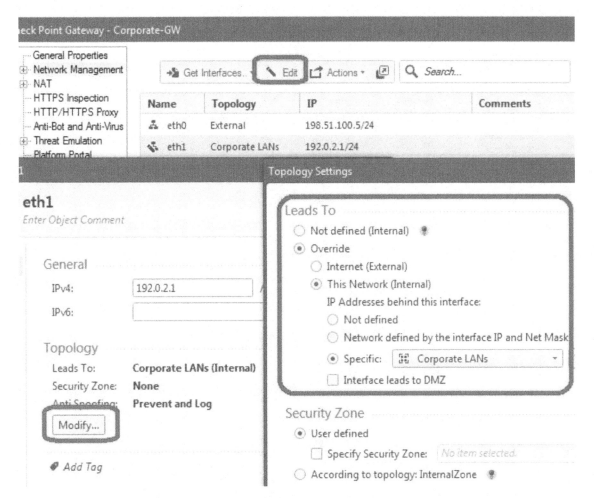

Figure 5-3: Firewall Interface Topology Settings – eth1

This interface is defined as Internal and probably leads to our organization's main internal network. Let's examine eth2 next:

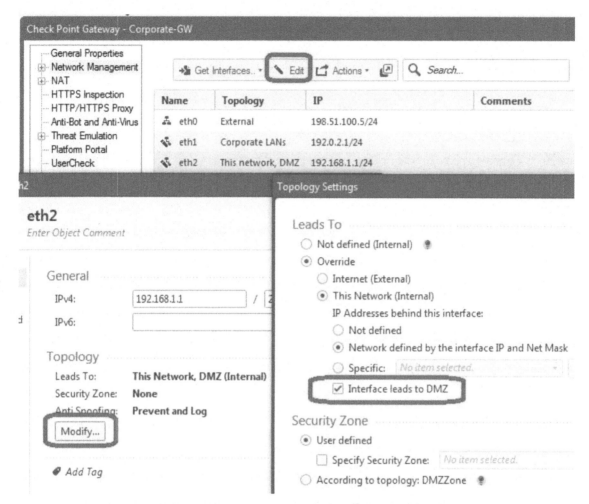

Figure 5-4: Firewall Interface Topology Settings – eth2

eth2 is also defined as Internal but notice that "Interface leads to DMZ" checkbox is set, which would indicate that this interface leads to a DMZ network hosting servers that a sensitive from a security perspective. But what does this checkbox actually do? To summarize, it has an enormous impact on how the dynamic object "Internet" is calculated, and can also directly impact which traffic the DLP blade and the Threat

Prevention blades Anti-Virus & Threat Emulation will inspect. For the complete list of blades this checkbox affects, see sk108057: What does the box "**Interface leads** to DMZ" control in **interface** topology?

There is another big thing to watch out for in the firewall topology definition: missing interfaces. Suppose that for our example firewall, you configured a new interface eth3 in the Gaia web interface. You assigned the new interface an IP address and set up the required routing. In the SmartConsole you then created a new network object for the eth3 network, assigned a NAT, and added a security policy rule letting the new network pass traffic. Everything is working great, BUT you forgot one important thing: adding the eth3 interface to the firewall object's topology. This new network is not explicitly defined as "Internal" (actually it is not defined *at all* in the firewall's topology), so therefore it must be External! *In that case all traffic going to and from the eth3 interface will be considered External.* This will have dire performance ramifications for how the object "Internet" will be calculated and applied in our policies.

WARNING: If you determine that there are missing interfaces in your firewall's topology definition, you might be tempted to click the "Get Interfaces" button on the Network Management screen of the firewall object in the R80.10 SmartConsole. But before you do that, look carefully at the Get Interfaces button. Does it provide two possible choices ("Get Interfaces With Topology" and "Get Interfaces Without Topology") or only one (Get Interfaces With Topology)? If there is only one choice you need to STOP and upgrade your R80.10 SmartConsole software to at least build 005 as specified here: sk118518: How to get the interfaces without changing the current topology in SmartConsole R80 and above. This will give you the "Get Interfaces

*Without Topology" menu choice which is the appropriate one to use in this case to add any missing interfaces. Clicking "Get Interfaces **With** Topology" will attempt to modify the interface topology definition of all existing interfaces as well, which may impact anti-spoofing enforcement, which could cause a huge outage and even disrupt your ability to manage the firewall! Should you find yourself cut off from managing or installing policy to the firewall due to misconfigured anti-spoofing enforcement, run these expert mode commands on the firewall to recover the ability to install policies (the last two lines assume that SecureXL is enabled on the firewall):*

```
fw ctl set int fw_antispoofing_enabled 0
sim feature anti_spoofing off
fwaccel off;fwaccel on
```

The Dynamic Object "Internet"

Proper use of the object "Internet" in your APCL/URLF policy layers is one of the most important weapons in your arsenal for policy optimization, but only if the firewall's topology is completely and correctly defined as covered in the last section. Typically the object "Internet" is applied in the Destination of an APCL/URLF rule like this:

Figure 5-5: Object "Internet" in R80+ Management

In the R77.30 SmartDashboard however, viewing the object "Internet" includes an additional tidbit that describes it quite well:

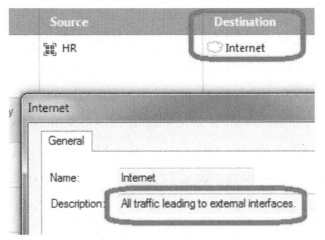

Figure 5-6: Object "Internet" in R77.30 Management

So at long last, we are ready to describe exactly what object "Internet" will match when used in our policies:

- Traffic whose routing destination is via an interface explicitly defined in the firewall's topology as "External"

- Traffic whose routing destination is via an interface with checkbox "Interface leads to DMZ" set

- Traffic whose routing destination is via an interface that does not explicitly appear in the firewall object's topology definition at all. (Yes that means that all individual subinterfaces assigned for 802.1q VLAN tagging must be listed in the firewall's topology and have their topology set correctly)

Later in this chapter the object "Internet" will be used extensively to optimize the application of policy layers.

Security Zones - R80.10

Another interesting option for R80.10+ policies is the use of Security Zone objects. Long a staple on other vendor's firewall products, the use of Security Zone objects in policy layers requires R80.10+ code to be running on the firewall. While Security Zones can be instrumental in constructing a more simplified policy, they do have one glaring limitation as of the R80.10 release: they cannot be used in manual NAT rules.

Use of Security Zones in the source and destination columns of various policy rules vs. using host/network/group objects doesn't seem to make much difference from a firewall performance perspective. Traffic traversing an R80.10+ gateway will always have its source and destination Security Zones calculated, regardless of whether the firewall's various policy layers are using Security Zone objects or not. Assigning a Security Zone object to an interface, then using that Security Zone object in a rule's source/destination in lieu of a big group of networks located behind that interface can be pretty convenient though.

Bottom Line: Use Security Zones if you want for convenience and policy simplification; at this time they appear to be a non-factor in regards to firewall performance.

Geo Policy: Your Secret Weapon

Geo Policy is an incredibly underrated feature for firewall performance improvement that is almost certainly not being utilized to its full potential in your environment. In R77.30 and earlier, Geo Policy (formerly called Geo Protection) was an inseparable part of the Intrusion Prevention System (IPS) blade, and as a result required a valid IPS license/contract to be present on the firewall.

However in a major shift for R80.10, Geo Policy has been extricated from the IPS blade and is now just another part of the main Access Control policy. As a result, changes to the Geo Policy will take effect upon an Access Policy installation; a Threat Prevention policy installation is not necessary. In addition, the IPS blade does not even need to be enabled (or licensed) on an R80.10+ gateway at all to take advantage of Geo Policy.

Customers that have implemented a well-crafted Geo Policy report a firewall CPU utilization drop of *at least* 10%, and sometimes much more depending on the size of their Internet-routable address space. A big part of the "background noise" of the Internet is automated probes and scans from compromised systems seeking other systems to infect.

The larger the block of Internet-routable addressing assigned to an organization, the more of this "background noise" arrives at its firewall. This constant stream of compromise attempts must be inspected and eventually dropped by the firewall; with Internet-routable subnets in excess of a /24 (255+ hosts) this performance-draining effect becomes much more pronounced. Ironically the vast majority of these attempts are of a generic nature and are not particularly aimed at your organization. Wouldn't it be nice to save precious firewall resources for actual concentrated attacks against your organization, and not waste time on all this "trash traffic" from the far corners of the Internet you don't care about? Enter Geo Policy.

Geo Policy allows highly efficient bulk drops of traffic to and from particular countries. If you know for a fact that your organization does not have operations or customers/partners in most countries of the world, why would you want to even inspect traffic to and from those countries? Just drop it all! By blocking large parts of the Internet with which there is no need for your organization to communicate, the amount of processing overhead consumed by the incessant background noise of the Internet can be substantially reduced.

So if you know for sure which countries your organization needs to communicate with, shouldn't you just block all other countries? Which countries are the most well-known for hosting attacks?

A great starting point is blocking the 20 most populous countries of the world if you can. Without getting into the murkiness of geopolitics, if a certain percentage of a country's people are dedicated to cybercrime with all its various forms and motivations, blocking the most populous countries first tends to yield the biggest "bang for the buck" in regards to your Geo Policy. Here are the top 20 countries by population to consider blocking, if a country in this list is a political rival or flat-out enemy of the country in which your organization is based, they are probably a good candidate to block:

China, India, United States, Indonesia, Brazil, Pakistan, Nigeria, Bangladesh, Russia, Japan, Mexico, Philippines, Ethiopia, Vietnam, Egypt, Turkey, Germany, Iran, Congo (Democratic Republic), Thailand

Drops performed by Geo Policy are executed by the firewall very early in its processing, long before any other policy layer is ever consulted and can save truly amazing amounts of CPU overhead.

Configuring Geo Policy

Prior to enabling Geo Policy for the first time, it is strongly recommended to make sure that the latest Geo Policy database update has been downloaded and installed as specified here: sk92823: Geo Protection fails to update.

The first step is determining which Geo Protection profile is assigned to your gateway. In R77.30 management the Geo Protection elements are part of the IPS profile assigned to the gateway, while in R80+ management the Geo Policy profile assignment is part of the Shared Policies:

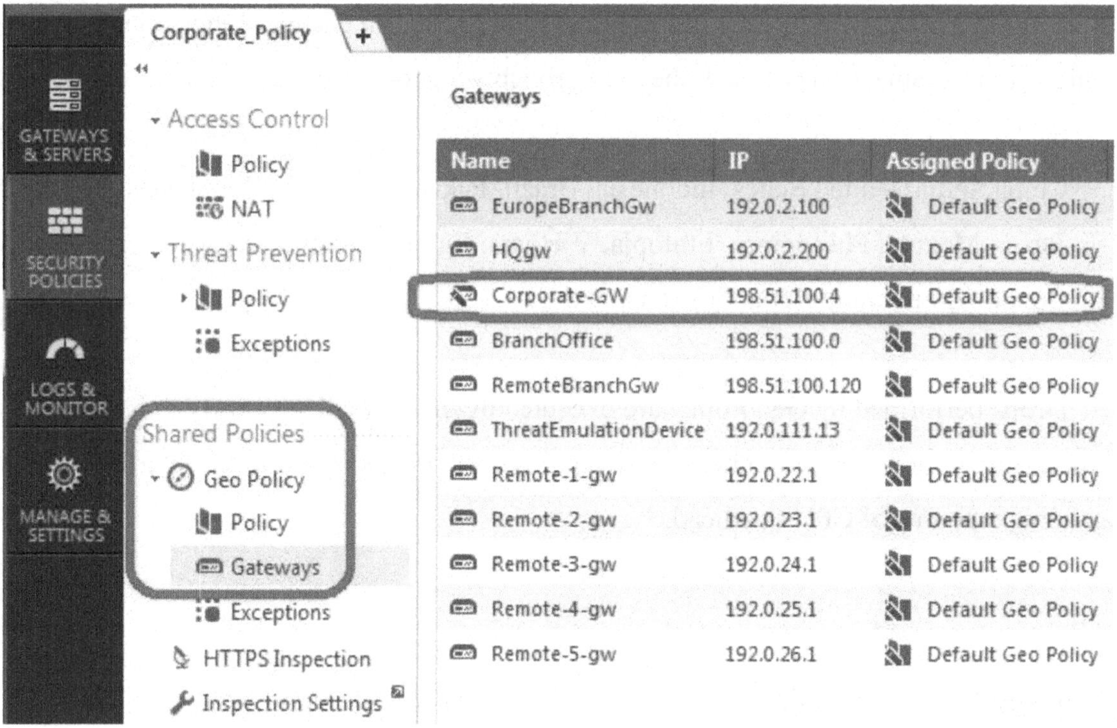

Figure 5-7: Geo Policy Firewall Profile Settings

In this case the name of the Geo Policy currently assigned to our gateway Corporate-GW is called "Default Geo Policy". Next we go to the Policy configuration screen and select the proper Geo Policy (if there is more than one):

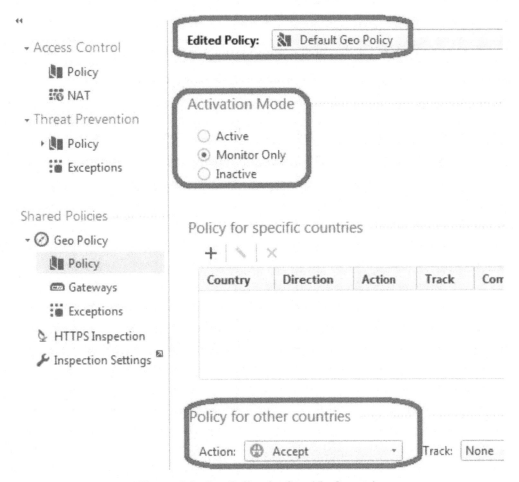

Figure 5-8: Geo Policy for Specific Countries

If setting up the Geo Policy for the first time, setting "Activation Mode" to "Monitor Only" as shown is highly recommended. Once log analysis has confirmed that the new Geo Policy will not disrupt production traffic, the Activation Mode can be set later to "Active". Note also that the "Policy for other countries" is set to "Accept" which indicates we plan to explicitly block traffic with Geo Policy from the countries we don't want, while letting traffic from all other countries continue on for further inspection by the various policy layers (at which point it might end up being dropped anyway). This "blacklist" approach is by far the most common, but a "whitelist" approach can be employed as well with a special hotfix. See the following for more details: sk110683: IPS **Geo Protection** drops the wrong traffic when it is configured as a whitelist.

Next we configure the countries we want to block; in most cases we will want to select "From and To Country" for Direction to both stop attacks originating from that country, and also stop possible malware inside our network from "phoning home" to that country. Also be sure to set Track field to Log for ease of troubleshooting:

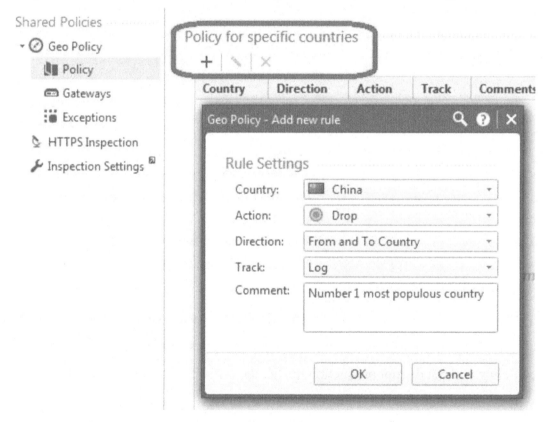

Figure 5-9: Using Geo Policy to Block a Specific Country

Once all countries have been added that you wish to block, simply reinstall the Access Policy to the firewall for it take effect. Note that exceptions can be added for Geo Policy if you have a customer or business partner located in a country that you would otherwise want to block. Once Geo Policy is configured and applied, there should be an immediate drop in Firewall CPU utilization, especially if your organization has a large block of routable addresses on the Internet. Don't forget to examine the Geo Protection logs over a reasonable time period and eventually set it to Active mode!

Policy Layer "Cleanup" Rules & Performance

Prior to R80+ management, when the phrase "Cleanup Rule" was encountered, most Check Point administrators would assume the term referred to the final explicitly created rule in a typical firewall's rulebase. This rule would match any other traffic that did not match a higher rule, drop it, and usually log it as well. Most Check Point administrators are also aware of the invisible so-called "implicit drop" at the end of the firewall's main rule base. Traffic discarded by this final implicit drop rule was also sometimes referred to as traffic that "fell off the end of the rulebase". However this condition would never occur if an explicit cleanup rule was already present at the end of the rule base, as the implicit drop could never be reached. The whole "unless traffic is specifically allowed deny it" concept is a fundamental part of every vendor's firewall including Check Point.

However what was not so obvious in R77.30 management and earlier was the presence of an invisible cleanup rule at the end of other policies such as APCL/URLF and Threat Prevention, and its default action was *Accept*. Unfortunately most firewall administrators were not aware of this fact, and would add an explicit Accept to the end of these policies like this:

Figure 5-10: The Unnecessary Default APCL/URLF Policy "Cleanup Rule"

To make matters worse, the final Accept rule as shown above was included by default in the R77.30 and earlier APCL/URLF policies. Why is this fact important from a firewall performance perspective?

This final explicit Accept rule is not necessary in R77.30 unless you want to log all other applications/URLs that have been allowed and classified by APCL/URLF; using it will keep all your outbound traffic to the Internet and all defined DMZs from being eligible for acceleration via SecureXL. Recall earlier what object "Internet" actually means; traffic whose destination is an interface not explicitly defined as Internal, or is designated as a DMZ. Do you really need to see thousands of extra log entries noting the presence of the TLS protocol on port 443, or that (surprise, surprise) the SSH protocol is constantly appearing on port 22? Of course APCL/URLF rules with Block action should always be matched on an explicit rule and logged.

However if you have any APCL/URLF rules that permit applications/categories for all internal users but do not log them, those rules should be removed, unless they trump a more generalized Block action later in the APCL/URLF rulebase. As mentioned earlier there is no "implicit drop" at the end of an APCL/URLF policy as there is at the end of a main firewall security policy; if no APCL/URLF rule is matched the connection is simply allowed to continue, without application identification or URL categorization being performed. Traffic that "falls off the end" of an APCL/URLF policy in our example policy is potentially eligible for acceleration by SecureXL, while traffic that matches an "Any/Internet/Any Recognized/Allow" rule will *not* be eligible for full acceleration by SecureXL.

Removing that final rule in an R77.30 APCL/URLF policy, combined with using specific Sources/Services in all other R77.30 APCL/URLF rules, can yield astounding performance gains due to large amounts of traffic becoming eligible for processing in the Accelerated Path by SecureXL which is covered in Chapter 9. Bear in mind though that if logging is disabled for Allowed Applications/URLs (or the final "Any Internet Any_Recognized" rule is removed), that some statistical reporting (such as user browsing times for permitted Applications & URL Categories) will not be available in SmartEvent.

Under R80+ management however, the ambiguity surrounding implied cleanup rules has been clarified significantly as you can see in the following two screenshots:

Figure 5-11: A Missing Cleanup Rule Flagged by the R80+ SmartConsole

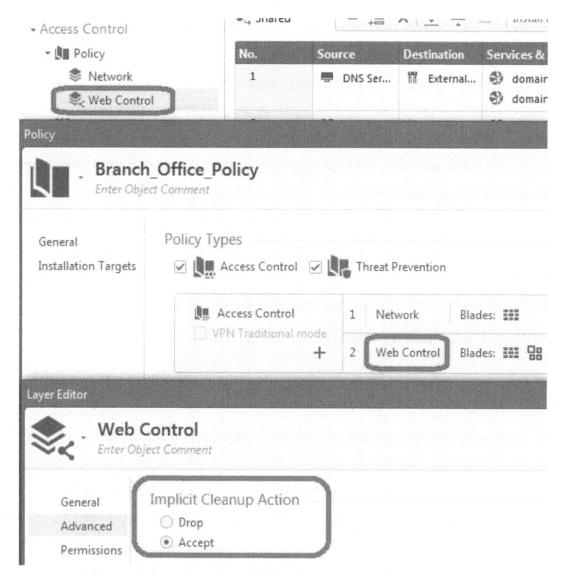

Figure 5-12: Changing the Default Action of the Implicit Cleanup Rule

As you can see in the first screenshot if an explicit cleanup rule is not present in a policy layer, a notification appears stating what the default action will be if traffic "falls off the end" of that policy layer. The second screenshot shows that the action of the Implicit Cleanup Action of a policy layer can now be toggled by the user.

So the bottom line from a performance tuning perspective is this: Resist the urge to add an explicit cleanup rule that accepts traffic at the end of your policy layers, especially those performing APCL/URLF and Threat Prevention. Avoiding an explicit cleanup rule that accepts traffic in these policy layers can potentially make much more traffic eligible for acceleration by SecureXL.

For a Network Policy Access layer that makes its filtering decisions based only on IP addresses and/or port numbers, use of an explicit cleanup rule with a drop action is still appropriate and will have no impact on potential acceleration of traffic.

Gateway Performance: Ordered vs. Inline/Unified Layers

This book is not intended to be an introduction to the pros and cons of using Ordered policy layers (which is what you will initially start with after upgrading an existing R77.30 Security Management Server to R80+ management) vs. the use of Unified/Inline layers (which requires an R80.10+ firewall). From the firewall's perspective, the use of Ordered vs. Unified/Inline layers has very little impact on policy evaluation overhead and general firewall performance, assuming that the recommendations in this chapter are followed.

The main benefit of using the new Unified/Inline layers is increased granularity of administrative control and the ability to see your entire security policy in one consolidated view. While this can definitely optimize the use of an administrator's time when making and tracking policy configuration changes, Ordered Layers vs.

Inline/Unified Layers has little impact on the firewall performance side of things which is the focus of this book.

General Access Control Policy Best Performance Practices

The best practices covered in this section apply to the following Access Control policy layers:

- **Network Access**: Filtering by IP Addresses & Port Numbers
- **APCL/URLF**: Application Control & URL Filtering
- **Content Awareness** (R80.10+ only): Data Loss Prevention (DLP) "Lite" & File Type Identification
- **NAT Policy**: Network Address Translation rules

Optimization of Threat Prevention policy layers is covered in Chapter 9, while HTTPS Inspection policies are covered in Chapter 10.

Column-based Matching & Early Drop

A major improvement from the traditional "top-down, first-fit" method of finding a rulebase match was extended to practically all policy layer types in the R80.10+ firewall code. While Column-based matching did exist in some policy types for firewalls using R77.30, R80.10+ firewalls take full advantage of this new rule-matching technique. Instead of stepping through rules one-by-one trying to find a match (and taking the first match found), Column-based matching excludes all rules that cannot possibly match the candidate traffic based on the values in various rulebase columns, then attempts top-down, first-fit evaluation of the "surviving" rules with an Accept/Allow action that were not previously excluded. Rather than bogging down in the details of how this relatively new Column-based matching works, we will simply use it to shape our policy recommendations. While the biggest "bang for the buck" will be achieved if using R80.10+ firewalls in your environment, some policy evaluation performance gains can be eked out with these recommendations on R77.30 firewalls as well. Once upgraded to R80.10+, the policy evaluation performance gains on the firewall will be fully realized. This new Column-based rulebase matching technique works just fine with both Ordered and Unified/Inline layers.

Detailed documentation concerning Column-based matching was pretty scant at press time; see this CheckMates thread called "Unified Policy Column-based Rule Matching" for the latest information available: https://community.checkpoint.com/message/10388

"Any" is the Enemy

Let's cut to the chase right now: *Avoid using "Any" in the Source, Destination & Service fields in as many policy layer rules as possible, but most especially in the Destination column.* In the prior section we briefly discussed "Column-based rule matching" which essentially excludes certain rules in a policy from consideration prior to commencing the traditional "top-down, first-fit" matching. As policies grow larger and larger, the overhead expended by the firewall to find a match solely using the traditional "top-down, first-fit" method of policy rule matching becomes very high. SecureXL Session Rate Acceleration (covered in Chapter 11) tries to combat this ever-increasing impact, by forming Accept Templates in an attempt to avoid as many rule base lookups as possible. However with a policy carefully optimized to exploit Column-based matching to its fullest, a truly amazing amount of processing time can be saved trying to find policy rule matches on the firewall.

But why exactly is "Any the enemy"? Suppose we have the following six rules at the top of a rulebase:

No.	Source	Destination	VPN	S
1	Admins	Corporate-GW	Any	
2	Any	Corporate-GW	Any	
3	Remote Access Users	Data Center LAN	RemoteAccess	
4	Corporate LANs / Branch Office LAN	Branch Office LAN / Corporate LANs	Site2Site	
▶ 5	InternalZone	Internet	Any	
6	attackers	Any	Any	

Figure 5-13: Sample Policy Demonstrating that "Any" is the Enemy

For this sample rulebase, suppose the destination IP for a new connection request is a DMZ address. Prior to starting a traditional "top-down, first-fit" evaluation of the rulebase for a new connection trying to find a match, the firewall performs Column-based matching first. It determines that since it is impossible for this connection to match rules 1-5 based on destination IP address, it doesn't need to try to match the connection against these rules at all. But why couldn't it exclude rule 6? Because rule 6 uses "Any" in its Destination field!

When the firewall is performing Column-based matching trying to exclude rules from further evaluation, which columns does it look at and in what order? Here they are:

1. Destination
2. Source
3. Service

So as you might suspect, avoiding a Destination of "Any" in as many rules as possible will maximize the number of rules that are excluded right at the beginning of the Column-based matching process. If the vast majority of rules are excluded based on the Destination field first, there are subsequently far fewer rules to examine with Column-based matching in the Source & Service fields. While avoiding the use of "Any" in the Source and Service fields can certainly help as well, trying to keep the Destination as specific as possible throughout your rulebase tends to yield the biggest "bang for the buck" as a result of your tuning efforts.

What about rules that use the object "Internet" or even negations of objects? Can Column-based matching still exclude these rules from a laborious top-down, first-fit match process? Yes! Only the object "Any" (which is not the same as "Internet") is your enemy from a policy tuning perspective when it comes to Column-based matching.

One interesting side effect of this new column-based policy evaluation technique is the possibility for what is known as an "early drop" to occur. Suppose that candidate traffic is being Column-matched against a rulebase and all rules with an Accept/Allow action were excluded. In other words, the only surviving rules after the Column-based evaluation had Drop/Block as an action. In that case the traffic will of course be dropped and logged, *but no matching rule number will be present in the log entry*. While we generally don't care about this situation since the packet was dropped anyway, the lack of a matching rule number causing the drop action can be a bit confusing when attempting to troubleshoot. This "early drop" behavior can be disabled if needed by toggling the `up_early_drop_optimization` kernel variable as specified here: sk111643: **Early Drop** - dropping connection before final rule match.

Network Policy Layer Recommendations

The policy tuning recommendations provided in the chapter thus far were general in nature and applied to all Access Control policy layers (and even the Threat Prevention policy layers covered in Chapter 9). In this section we will mainly focus on specific recommendations for the Network Policy Layer, which matches connections primarily by IP addresses and port numbers. In R77.30 management this is the policy under the "Firewall" tab of SmartDashboard.

If working with R77.30 management, create a Database Revision under the File...Database Revision Control menu that you can revert to should you make a critical mistake while optimizing your security policy! Policy revisions are automatically created in R80+ management. Follow these tips:

1. **If using Ordered layers in R80+ management, try to drop as much traffic as possible based on IP addresses and port numbers** (and potentially the Geo Policy as discussed earlier in this chapter) in the Network policy layer which is always evaluated first. If using Unified/Inline layers, only use IP addresses and services to match rules in the top layer, and invoke other blades such as APCL/URLF and Content Awareness inside sub-rules only. If using Unified/Inline layers, DO NOT specify application types such as "Facebook" or

"Twitter" in the top network layer; only specify services (port numbers) such as http and https there. Following these recommendations will ensure the maximum amount of traffic possible is dropped very early, well before any more performance-intensive blades are invoked for additional inspection.

2. **Try to put rules with the highest hit counts towards the top of the rulebase, while being careful not to compromise security**. This recommendation does not provide nearly the "bang for the buck" it used to due to the new Column-based Matching feature discussed earlier. If hit count data displayed seems inaccurate or incomplete, reviewing sk79240: **Hit Count** debugging is highly recommended. In R80+ management the Hit Count column is hidden by default, right click on any column title and check the box "Hits" to make it visible again. If your policy is extremely large, trying to scroll through and find the rules with the highest hit counts can be a bit of a challenge, as there is no way to sort the rules by hit count. However there is a shortcut you can employ: run the command `cpstat blades` on the firewall. This command will show the top hit rules in the currently installed policy in a very concise display.

3. **Create a rule to match and drop all broadcast traffic without logging it**.

WARNING: If DHCP or DHCP Relay is set up in the firewall's Gaia OS, this rule will prevent the various forms of DHCP from working properly. You will need to add an explicit rule permitting services dhcp-request & dhcp-reply prior to this new rule.

For example suppose the firewall has 4 interfaces:

eth0: 129.82.102.32/24
eth1: 10.1.1.1/24

eth2: 192.168.1.1/24
eth3: 172.16.16.1/16

Create five Node...Host objects that look like this:

OutsideBC: 129.82.102.255
DMZBC: 10.1.1.255
DMZ2BC: 192.168.1.255
InternalBC: 172.16.255.255
AllOnesBC: 255.255.255.255

Put all five Host objects in a Group called "Broadcast_Nets". Now create an early rule like this prior to the firewall Stealth Rule:

No.	Hits	Source	Destination	VPN	Service	Action	Track
⊟	Firewall Mgmt & Stealth Rule (Rules 1-3)						
1	⬛⬛	✳ Any	🔲 Broadcast_Nets	✳ Any	✳ Any	⬤ drop	− None

Figure 5-14: Broadcast Logging Suppression Policy Rule

Now all broadcast IP traffic that wouldn't be allowed to cross the firewall anyway will be silently discarded. Layer 2 MAC address broadcasts to ff:ff:ff:ff:ff:ff and multicast MAC addresses will still work, so protocols such as ARP and VRRP will be unaffected by this rule.

4. **Clean up garbage internal traffic** – While examining logs create a source filter matching only packets sourced from your internal network and DMZ(s). Add another filter in the Action column to only show Drop and Reject actions. Do you see internal systems constantly trying to connect somewhere using prohibited protocols (like NTP, DNS, NNTP, SNMP, and POP3/IMAP) that are being blocked by your security policy? Contact the administrators of those systems and tell them to either turn these features off, or modify them so they stop constantly trying to reach these prohibited services through the firewall. Typically there are

a handful of very bad offenders in this area, and once they clean up their act a surprising amount of policy evaluation and logging overhead can be saved on the firewall. If they refuse to clean up their act, or forcing them to do so would spark an OSI Layer 8 issue (company politics firestorm), check out the Rate Limiting feature discussed in Chapter 13 that can efficiently throttle their traffic with minimal firewall performance impact.

5. **Avoid using Domain objects to match domain name wild cards on R77.30 firewalls**. These consume a truly hideous amount of CPU overhead on an R77.30 firewall and impact SecureXL acceleration. While the implementation of Domain objects on an R80.10+ firewall has been substantially improved with a new FQDN function, they should still be avoided on general principle even though they no longer disable SecureXL Accept Templates (which are covered in Chapter 11). If you must use Domain objects in an R77.30 policy, place rules containing them as far down in the policy as possible. For more information about the new handling of Domain objects on an R80.10 firewall, see sk120633: Domain Objects in R80.10 and above and the CheckMates thread "FQDN in R80 Policy Access rule" here: https://community.checkpoint.com/thread/1379.

6. **Remove unused objects**. On R80+ management open the Object Explorer window and select "Unused Objects" instead of the default "All". (In the R77.30 SmartDashboard, right-click "Nodes" under "Network Objects" in the Objects Tree on the left-hand side of the R77.30 SmartDashboard and select More...Query objects. On the screen that appears, select "Unused Objects" for the Refined Filter...Refine By field). A list of all objects not referenced in any Policy will appear. Open each object listed for editing and check its NAT tab. If the NAT checkbox is not checked on the object it can be safely deleted. Deleting an object

without bothering to check its NAT tab can possibly break some of your NAT configuration, so be careful!

7. **Avoid Using Reject Actions**: The "Reject" action in a Security Policy rule should almost never be employed due to the extra overhead involved generating Negative Acknowledgements (NACKs); use a Drop action instead.

APCL/URLF Policy Layer Tips

In this section we will focus on specific recommendations for APCL/URLF policy layers, which match application types and/or URL categories. In R77.30 management this is the policy under the "Application & URL Filtering" tab of SmartDashboard. The overall goal for many of these recommendations is to ensure that traffic is not accidentally inspected by APCL/URLF when it should not be. Any connections that match an explicit Allow/Accept rule in an APCL/URLF policy are automatically ineligible for full acceleration by SecureXL on the firewall. For the most up-to-date best practices for configuring Application Control from Check Point, see: sk112249: Best Practices - Application Control.

1. Make sure the object "Any" is never specified in the Destination column of a policy layer performing APCL/URLF; in most cases you should be using object "Internet" instead. Keep in mind that if the "Interface leads to DMZ" checkbox is set on any interfaces of the firewall's topology, APCL/URLF will be applied to connections initiated from the internal network to those DMZs, not just to the Internet!

2. Avoid using "Any" directly in the Source column as well (or via the "Networks" tab of Access Role objects placed in the Source column); try to always specify explicit internal network objects and/or groups.

3. Limit actions can be specified in a rule matching applications and/or URL categories to throttle undesirable or bandwidth-hogging applications like this:

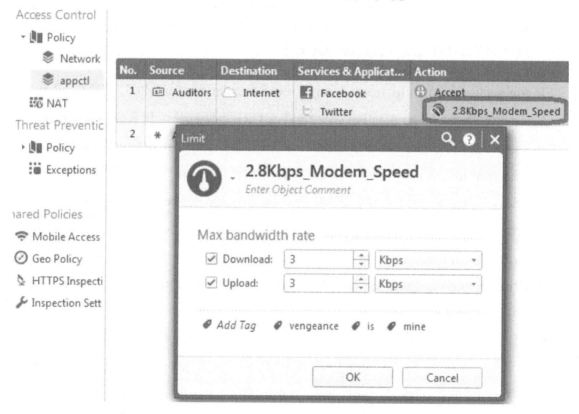

Figure 5-15: Setting APCL/URLF Bandwidth Limits

However keep in mind that Limits defined this way are shared per rule, and not per-user or even per-connection. In our example all users that are a member of the "Auditors" group, and match the rule, will share a whopping 3Kbps of bandwidth whenever they try to access Facebook or Twitter. The only way to do more granular limits is to break them up into separate rules, or enable the QoS blade which can perform per-connection or per-IP connection limits (but not per-user connection limits).

4. Be aware that bandwidth limits imposed on an Application/URL category will not survive a firewall failover in a High Availability situation. Existing connections with a limit imposed will survive the failover and continue, but the bandwidth limit will no longer be enforced for those existing connections by the cluster member taking over. New connections initiated that are subject to a Limit action will have those limits properly enforced on the newly active cluster member. See the following for more information: sk97775: Bandwidth Limit in Application Control does not survive cluster failover in ClusterXL High Availability mode.

5. When invoking APCL/URLF in a sub-rule using Inline layers, always evaluate the actual need for an explicit Accept logging cleanup rule in the sub-layer.

APCL/URLF Policy: Website Categorization Mode

A little-known fact about the Check Point URL Filtering solution (this does not include Application Control) is that URL categorization is completely cloud-based. In firewall versions since R75.40, there is no nightly download of a large URL database containing millions of sites and their categories; URL categorization is done by the firewall "on the fly" with the Check Point ThreatCloud. Website categorization results are cached in the memory of the firewall once they are received from the Check Point ThreatCloud. On the following screen in R80+ management is a controversial setting called "Website Categorization Mode":

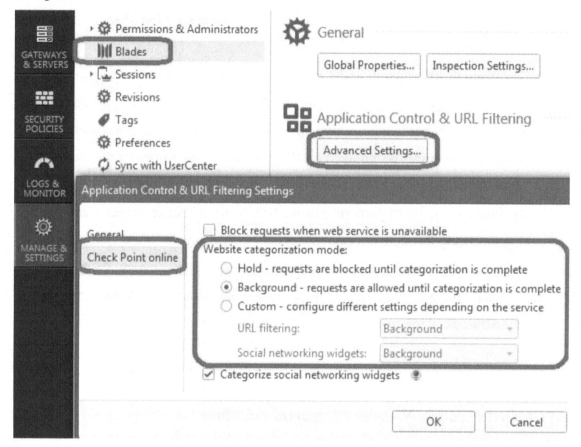

Figure 5-16: APCL/URLF Categorization Mode, Background or Hold?

(Under R77.30 management this screen is located on the Engine Settings screen under "Application & URL Filtering...Advanced") By default it is set to "Background", which is optimal from a performance perspective but not a security (and massive embarrassment) perspective. Consider this:

Your compliance officer has noted that by default when they visit a new, extremely obscure URL that no one in your company would ever visit, sometimes the site will come up the very first time they try it, even though it should be blocked. However if the page is refreshed after a few seconds it is then properly blocked, and remains blocked for everyone. Your compliance officer has indicated this is unacceptable and wants to ensure URL filtering is always enforced absolutely the first time, even if it causes additional browsing latency. How can you ensure this?

Due to the inherent nature of cloud-based lookups for URL categorization, there would normally be a delay when a user first tries to visit a website whose categorization result is not already contained within the firewall's cache. However by default the "Website Categorization Mode" is set to "Background – Requests are allowed until categorization is complete". This allows the user to always bring up a not-yet-categorized site quickly, without delay, even if it shouldn't have been allowed in the first place. Once the website categorization result has been received from the Check Point ThreatCloud, if the website is not allowed it will immediately start being blocked, and all users (including the original requester) will no longer be able to access it. But it came up that very first time, and the initial user could still see it (at least briefly).

This is one case where I feel security needs to trump performance, and all organizations should set "Website Categorization Mode" to "Hold-Requests are blocked until categorization is complete". Users will see a short delay when first attempting to connect to a non-cached site; but as long as your firewall is properly configured with good, quickly responding DNS servers and fast Internet connectivity, the delay is usually less than 1 second. Once the site is categorized and populated in the firewall's categorization cache, there will be no further user delays accessing the site.

R77.30 Only: APCL/URLF Policy Service Optimization

A little-known feature of the R77.30 APCL/URLF policy is the ability to specify APCL/URLF rules by Service (port number), as well as application. In R80+ management, the service can be easily specified in a policy layer that includes APCL/URLF. However the Service column in the APCL/URLF policy is hidden by default for R77.30 management. To display it right-click on the top of any APCL/URLF policy column and check "Service":

Figure 5-17: Adding Service Column to an R77.30 APCL/URLF Policy

Note that by default the Service for every APCL/URLF policy rule is "Any". When can these additional service criteria be employed to enhance firewall performance?

In the main security policy of every Check Point firewall is normally a generic rule that allows internal users to access the Internet. The main security policy must permit a connection to start (usually meaning a completed TCP 3-way handshake) before the APCL/URLF policy takes over, and tries to determine the application or URL category associated with a connection by inspecting packet data. Some organizations allow users to initiate a connection to the Internet on any TCP/UDP port, while other more security-conscious organizations only permit an approved list of ports such as 80, 443, 8080, 22, etc. Typically this approved list of ports is implemented in a group object called "allowed_ports", or something similar. The default Service for every APCL/URLF rule is "Any". If your organization only allows your users to initiate connections to the Internet on an allowed list of ports, you should most definitely leverage that existing group in the Service column of all APCL/URLF rules to help limit what traffic the APCL/URLF blade is required to inspect.

For extremely specific APCL/URLF rules, you may even be able to specify a single port number for known applications running on a well-known port. Not only does this keep the APCL/URLF policy from inspecting traffic it does not need to, but it allows for more efficient Column-based matching of APCL/URLF rules since the "wrong" port number on traffic being inspected can quickly and easily disqualify an APCL/URLF rule with a nonmatching port number. Detecting an application type or URL category takes a fair amount of CPU resources; however determining whether the destination port number matches during the APCL/URLF policy evaluation can be done very quickly and efficiently. For more information about matching a service, see sk90940: 'fw_worker' process consumes 100% CPU when Application Control blade is enabled.

Content Awareness Tips (R80.10 Firewall Only)

Following are recommendations when invoking the Content Awareness blade on an R80.10+ firewall, which can match both specific file types and sensitive/confidential data:

1. If trying to match both a file type and a specific content type in the same policy layer, place the rule matching the file type first, the follow it with the rule matching a particular type of content. This rule placement mirrors the order in which the firewall itself evaluates the content and is more efficient.
2. Using the Content Awareness feature does invoke a process space "trip" on the firewall as described in Chapter 10 for any data it needs to inspect. Make sure when invoking Content Awareness in your policy layers that it is confined only to traffic going to and from limited-bandwidth connections such as to the Internet. Specifically, try to avoid situations where Content Awareness is configured to inspect traffic travelling between two high-speed internal LAN networks.
3. If using Inline/Unified layers in your policy, avoid invoking Content Awareness matching in the top policy layer; keep Content Awareness matching confined to sub-layers only if possible.

NAT Policy Optimization

In general, NAT policies don't require a great deal of optimization. There are two techniques available for configuring NAT in a Check Point firewall policy:

- **Automatic NAT**: Selecting the NAT tab of a network object, configuring Static or Hide NAT, and specifying the NAT address to use. This technique will auto-create the needed NAT rules in the NAT policy.

- **Manual NAT**: Direct manipulation of the NAT policy by adding your own manual rules. This technique provides far more granularity for specifying precisely how NAT is to be performed by the firewall.

In general using the Automatic NAT setup technique is recommended. It will handle the majority of NAT scenarios well, and helps gloss over some of the internal details of how NAT works (such as having to deal with Proxy ARP). If the Automatic setup is handling all the NAT on your firewall, there is very little to do as far as optimization. A quick look at the NAT policy reveals that the order of automatically generated NAT rules cannot be changed (all automatic Static NATs will be followed by all automatic Hide NATs) and there is no "Hit Count" column.

NAT policy lookups always take place in the Firewall Path (F2F) unless NAT Templates are enabled (which are discussed in Chapter 11). If employing manual NAT rules on your firewall, based on some of the other recommendations in this chapter, your first inclination might be to move what you suspect (but cannot confirm) are the most commonly hit manual NAT rules towards the top of the NAT policy. However this will have practically no effect from a performance improvement perspective, due to the use of a NAT lookup cache by the firewall.

The NAT Cache

The first packet of a new connection accepted by the Network Access layer that involves NAT will always make a trip to the Firewall Path (F2F) by default, unless NAT Templates are enabled. Even if the firewall has a very large NAT rulebase, most of the time the firewall doesn't even have to evaluate it due to the NAT Cache Table **fwx_cache** which is enabled by default. Essentially the most common NAT rulebase hits are cached in a special state table that can determine the required NAT operation quite efficiently during future NAT lookups. The presence of this NAT caching mechanism is probably why hit counts are not available for NAT rules. Once the first packet of an accepted connection has been NATted, the NAT rulebase and its **fwx_cache** table is never consulted again for that particular connection, and as such the NAT applied to a connection's packets cannot ever change after the connection's first packet.

By default this NAT cache can contain up to 10,000 cached NAT entries (the cached entries are expired from the table after 30 minutes by default). Whenever an "Original Packet" NAT rule match occurs in the NAT rule base, the source, destination, and service port number associated with the matched NAT rule are cached in the **fwx_cache** table, along with the necessary NAT operation to be performed under "Translated Packet". If the same source, destination, and service port number show up for a new allowed connection, the NAT rulebase itself is never consulted, and the cached NAT operation is performed instead thus saving the overhead of a full NAT rulebase lookup.

So how many of the potential 10,000 NAT cache entries are in use on your firewall? Run the command **fw tab -t fwx_cache -s**:

```
[Expert@firewall:0]# fw tab -t fwx_cache -s
HOST            NAME            ID #VALS #PEAK #SLINKS
localhost    fwx_cache    8116    455   4518        0
[Expert@firewall:0]#
```

Figure 5-18: Displaying NAT Cache Statistics

#VALS indicates the number of current cached NAT entries and **#PEAK** indicates the peak number of entries in the table used since the firewall was last booted. If both **#VALS** and **#PEAK** are substantially less than 10,000, either you are not doing very much NAT on your firewall, or a maximal level of NAT caching is already occurring in the Firewall Path and there is nothing more to do.

However, what if **#PEAK** shows 10,000 exactly? First off, fear not. Using up all the entries in the NAT cache table does not cause an outage or otherwise impede traffic; it just results in more NAT rulebase lookups then there otherwise would be, which does impact performance. So how can we assess whether the NAT cache size should be increased?

As mentioned earlier, hit counts are not available for NAT rules. However you can poke around directly in the **fwx_cache** table on the live gateway to get an idea of which NAT rules are being used the most. The **fwx_cache** table does track the NAT rule number of cached entries; this lengthy command will show the top 20 most commonly cached/hit NAT rules:

```
fw tab -u -t fwx_cache|awk '{ print $3 }'|cut -c5-8|sort -n|uniq -c| \
sort -nr|head -20
```

(Note the '\' at the end of line 1 of this command is a backslash and allows us to continue the same command on a new line)

Hopefully you should now have a good idea of the most commonly hit rules in your NAT policy. But here comes the next big question: If the **#PEAK** value for the **fwx_cache** table is exactly 10,000, how much would potentially increasing the NAT cache size help? There is no direct way to answer this question, but there is a way to see how much CPU overhead the NAT cache is currently saving at its current size: we can simply turn it off and see what happens to CPU utilization on the firewall!

To accomplish this, run the command **mpstat 1** in a separate window. This command will show CPU utilization (user/sys/soft/hi as also shown in the **top** command) once per second. Let the command run for a while to get a good idea of the firewall's current CPU load. Now in a separate window disable the NAT cache on the fly with: **fw ctl set int fwx_do_nat_cache 0**. Observe the CPU utilization closely after the change. Does it go up, down or stay the same? You can probably draw your own conclusions about what to do given what you've observed thus far, but in general if the CPU load remains the same or drops (and earlier **#PEAK** showed exactly 10,000 or whatever the limit was set to) increasing the **fwx_cache** won't help. If however the overall CPU load went up, and especially if it went up a lot, increasing the **fwx_cache** size may help especially if you have a large NAT rulebase (1500+ rules).

Before considering an increase in the NAT cache size, make sure firewall has plenty of free memory (run **free -m** and look at the third line as detailed in the last chapter). The **fwx_alloc** table by default can have up to 10,000 entries, and it appears that each entry consumes about 50 bytes of memory, so the maximum amount of RAM that **fwx_alloc** can consume by default is 500,000 bytes (or about 500Kbytes). To increase the NAT cache size see sk21834: How to modify values of properties related to NAT cache table. If you have determined that you need to increase it, I'd recommend just doubling the **fwx_cache** size to start with – please resist the urge to crank it up to an obnoxiously high value as that can cause its own problems and actually hurt performance. After increasing the value run the commands shown earlier again to assess the impact of the change, and if it still needs to be increased try doubling it again. Just don't forget to turn the NAT cache back on by setting `fwx_do_nat_cache` back to 1 when you are done!

The 50K Hide NAT Connection Limit

When setting up a Hide NAT for a network object using the Automatic NAT setup technique, only a single IP address can be specified to hide behind regardless of whether the hiding IP address is one you've entered yourself or is just the address of the firewall itself. All forms of many-to-one Hide NAT operations (regardless of firewall vendor) remap the source port numbers in translated packets. This is performed to ensure that response traffic can be directed to the correct internal host that originally initiated the connection. Unfortunately there is a limited number of port numbers available: 65,535. Check Point firewalls by default use ports 10,000-60,000 for source port remapping of Hide NAT traffic. As a result, no more than 50,000 concurrent connections can be Hide NATted through a single hiding address.

So what happens when the $50,001^{st}$ connection utilizing the same external hiding address tries to start? It is dropped by the firewall (even if the security policy accepted it) with the dreaded "NAT Hide failure - there are currently no available ports for hide operation" error message appearing in the logs. New connections utilizing that same Hide NAT will continue to be dropped by the firewall until some ports "free up" for remapping. The perceived effect of this situation is absolutely terrible-looking firewall performance, as some connections seem to work and some seem to hang. This effect is quite pronounced with HTTP-based connections, as some parts of a web page seem to load fine while other elements of the web page remain blank or stall in the middle of rendering.

The typical way to deal with this limit was simply to use more external hiding addresses, and have some internal networks hide behind one outside address, while other internal networks hid behind a separate outside address. This configuration with 2 outside addresses would theoretically increase the total concurrent connections to 100k. But what if the first set of networks hits the 50k limit on their hiding address, could they "roll over" onto the other hiding address? Nope!

So right about now you might be wondering: how many concurrent connections are currently using a particular Hide NAT address on my firewall, and how close is that amount to the 50k concurrent connection limit? Assume the Hide NAT address in question is 203.0.113.1, convert it to hexadecimal (cb007101) and run this command:

```
fw tab -u -t connections | grep -ci cb007101
```

Divide the number reported by 2, and you have your answer. The result must be divided by 2 because each post-NATted connection is represented by 2 flows, one outbound (c2s) and one inbound (s2c).

Static vs. Dynamic Allocation of Hide NAT Ports per Firewall Core

In addition to the considerations listed above, enabling SMT/Hyperthreading (covered in Chapter 12) may cause NAT problems for an R77.30 or earlier gateway if the majority of the connections passing through the firewall are subject to Hide NAT. While enabling SMT/Hyperthreading can double the amount of available cores available for SND/IRQ and CoreXL Firewall Worker processing (the concept of Firewall Worker cores and CoreXL are covered in Chapter 7), the 50,000 source ports available for each external Hide NAT address are evenly divided amongst all the Firewall Worker cores for subsequent allocation. So for example on a 16-core R77.30 firewall with 12 Firewall Workers, for each Firewall Worker core only 4166 source ports per external Hide NAT address are available for source port remapping. With SMT enabled there are now 24 Firewall Workers and only 2,083 ports are available per core for remapping per external Hide NAT address. This is a rather low value, and new Hide NAT connections that fail to obtain a source port for remapping are simply dropped by the firewall, regardless of whether a security policy rule accepted them.

However R77.30 has an available built-in fix for the Hide NAT port allocation failures that are much more likely to occur when SMT/Hyperthreading is enabled. Ports used for Hide NAT source port reallocation can be dynamically pooled among the Firewall Worker cores, instead of being statically assigned. This new feature is not enabled by default in R77.30 and earlier. It involves setting the `fwx_nat_dynamic_port_allocation` variable from 0 to 1, which will dynamically pool source ports among all Firewall Worker cores. See sk103656: Dynamic NAT port allocation feature for instructions to set this variable on an R77.30 firewall.

In R80.10 gateway (whether upgraded from R77.XX or loaded from scratch) if there are 6 or more Firewall Worker cores configured, by default the `fwx_nat_dynamic_port_allocation` variable will be automatically set to 1, otherwise it will remain set to 0. Statistics can be dumped for the Dynamic Port Allocation feature by running this command:

```
fw ctl set int fwx_nat_dynamic_port_allocation_print_stats 1
```

These statistics including Hide NAT port allocation failures can then be viewed with the **dmesg** command.

Avoiding the Limit: "Many-to-fewer" NAT Configuration

If the number reported by the **fw tab** command earlier (divided by 2 of course) was uncomfortably close to the 50k Hide NAT limit discussed earlier, it possible to set up what I would term a "many-to-fewer" Hide NAT. As the name implies, it involves hiding internal networks behind more than one external IP address. Every external IP address added to the "fewer" side of the equation allows another 50,000 possible concurrent connections can be Hide NATed.

A "many-to-fewer" Hide NAT has been possible via manual NAT rules since around version R75. It is not really documented anywhere but it definitely does work; here is a quick outline of how to configure it; a screenshot of the key elements is provided at the end of this section:

1) Create a Manual NAT rule

2) In Original Source, put the inside network object (or a group of internal network objects) to hide

3) Translated Source of this manual NAT rule must be a IP Address Range object (a network object will not work), configured with the routable range of "fewer" addresses to hide behind

4) After adding the IP Address Range object in Translated Source it will by default be set to Static, right-click it and force Hide mode

5) If you are plucking these "fewer" outside addresses from your Internet-routable range of addresses located on the dirty subnet between the firewall's external interface and the Internet perimeter router, you must add manual static *proxy* ARPs for ALL addresses in the "fewer" range. Details on how to do this are contained in sk30197: Configuring **Proxy ARP** for Manual NAT. However if you are using R80.10+ firewall code, you can configure the firewall to automatically create proxy ARP entries for all your manual NATs. This feature is not enabled by default in R80.10+ but can be enabled as specified here: sk114395: Automatic creation of Proxy ARP for Manual NAT rules on Security Gateway R80.10.

WARNING: If the routable addresses are "plucked" as mentioned above, failure to add static proxy ARPs on the firewall for every single address in the "fewer" range will cause random-looking connectivity failures for some internal hosts and not others. These failures will be very difficult to diagnose; use the command **fw ctl arp** *to determine the IP addresses for which the firewall believes it needs to provide proxy ARP responses.*

Once the many-to-fewer NAT has been set up, internal hidden systems will always be assigned the same external IP hiding address from the "fewer" range. The selection of which "fewer" IP address to hide a particular internal host behind depends on that host's IP address. So for example if we are using 192.168.1.0/24 internally and hiding behind 203.0.113.17-203.0.113.20, internal host 192.168.1.3 might draw 203.0.113.18 for all its connections while 192.168.1.134 might draw 203.0.113.20 for all its connections. The "fewer" hiding address associated to an internal IP will never change (unless the "fewer" IP range itself changes). This address allocation behavior is briefly mentioned here: sk105302: Traffic NATed behind an Address Range object is always NATed behind the same IP address. Here is a screenshot showing the main elements of a "many-to-fewer" Hide NAT configuration:

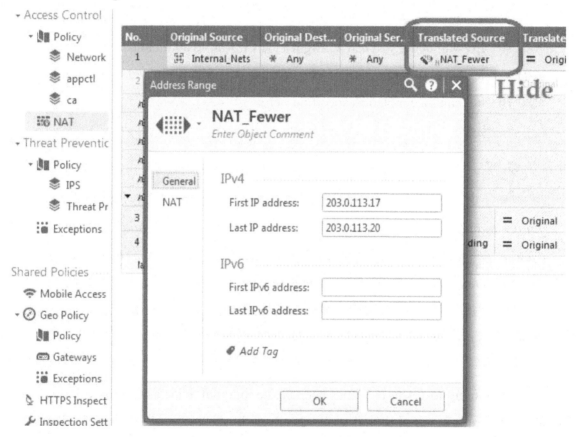

Figure 5-19: Many to Fewer Hide NAT Setup Example

Miscellaneous Policy Optimization & Visibility

This section covers a variety of topics that can provide more visibility into how the firewall is handling connections, and help the firewall play nice with some particularly cranky application-related network traffic.

Sending a TCP RST upon Connection Expiration

Some applications (such as web servers backending into a database server with a SQL connection) create a large number of TCP connections, yet never send any appreciable amount of data in them. All stateful inspection firewalls (including Check Point) enforce an idle timer on all open connections. Check Point's TCP connection idle timer is set to 60 minutes by default. Unfortunately when the Check Point TCP idle timer expires a TCP connection, by default that connection is silently removed from the firewall's state table, and no notification of any kind is sent to the two systems who established the TCP connection. When one of them attempts to send some data in the now-dead connection, it is promptly dropped by the firewall with a "TCP out of state" message. Regrettably some applications are just too stupid to quickly realize the connection is dead; they continue attempting to use it while their traffic continues to be dropped.

At some point, one or both of the end systems involved finally figures out their connection is truly and irrevocably dead, launches a new TCP connection that is immediately permitted by the firewall, and everything starts working again. Depending on how long it takes one or both sides to figure out what happened, the application may appear to be hung and the user's perception of overall application performance will be terrible. Undoubtedly the firewall will be blamed for the application's behavior, and once again the firewall administrators must exonerate themselves. There are three solutions to this problem:

1. Enable TCP keepalives on one or both of the systems participating in the TCP connections that keep getting idled out. The keepalives will need to be sent at least every 60 minutes. This is not a popular choice as it involves application system changes to fix what is perceived as a "firewall problem".

2. Increase the idle timeout for the Service object (SQL in our example) on the Advanced tab of the service object from the default of 60 minutes up to a maximum of 86400 seconds (24 hours) This will probably help but is not foolproof:

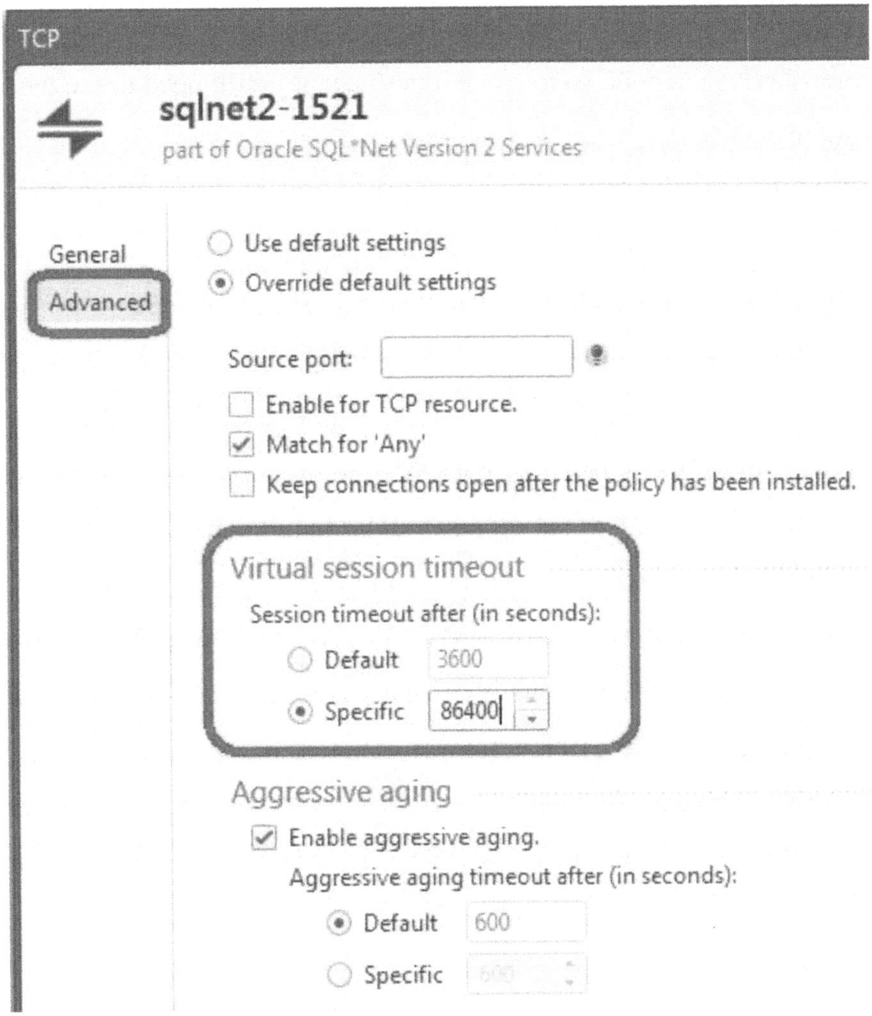

Figure 5-20: Session Timeout for TCP Services

3. Configure the firewall to send a TCP RST packet to both participants of a
    connection that has been idled out. Upon receipt of the TCP RST, both
    participants instantly realize their connection is gone and launch a new one
    immediately to recover from the situation. To enable this feature "on the fly", the

command is `fw ctl set int fw_rst_expired_conn 1`. This setting will not survive a reboot, so to make it permanent you'll need to see the following for more details: sk19746: How to force a Security Gateway to send a TCP RST packet upon TCP connection expiration.

4. In some cases however #3 will not fully remediate the situation, and you will be forced to go one step further with this: `fw ctl set int fw_reject_non_syn 1`. A classic example of an application that requires this firewall setting is SAP HANA traffic. This setting also handles client port reuse out of state errors when RST packets from the server to the clients get lost (e.g. due to policy install or packet loss). Bear in mind however that this setting is quite likely to make your friendly auditor/penetration tester upset with you, since the firewall will now issue a TCP RST for all received packets that are out of state and have the ACK flag set. An auditor running a TCP ACK `nmap` scan will have it light up like a Christmas tree with tens of thousands of ports showing up as filtered instead of closed. For this reason, using this setting is generally not recommended on an Internet perimeter firewall, but may be acceptable on some internal firewalls.

Enhanced Logging of Connection Timeouts

If you continue to have trouble with connections being idled out of the firewall's state table (and it is suspected the firewall is doing so inappropriately), you can configure the firewall to start creating extra log detail specifying when a connection was removed from the state table due to inactivity, and even whether it successfully established at all in the first place:

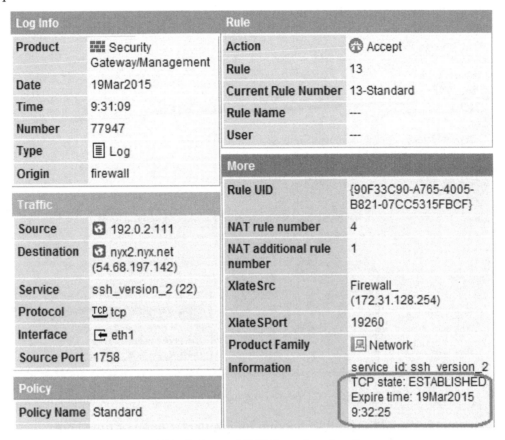

Figure 5-21: Enhanced TCP State Logging Example

Check out sk101221: TCP state logging. The command to enable this extra logging on the fly for R77.30 gateways is `fw ctl set int fwconn_tcp_state_logging` `x`. On firewall/cluster objects with a version of R80.10 or later, configuring TCP State Logging can now be performed directly on the firewall object from the SmartConsole as shown here:

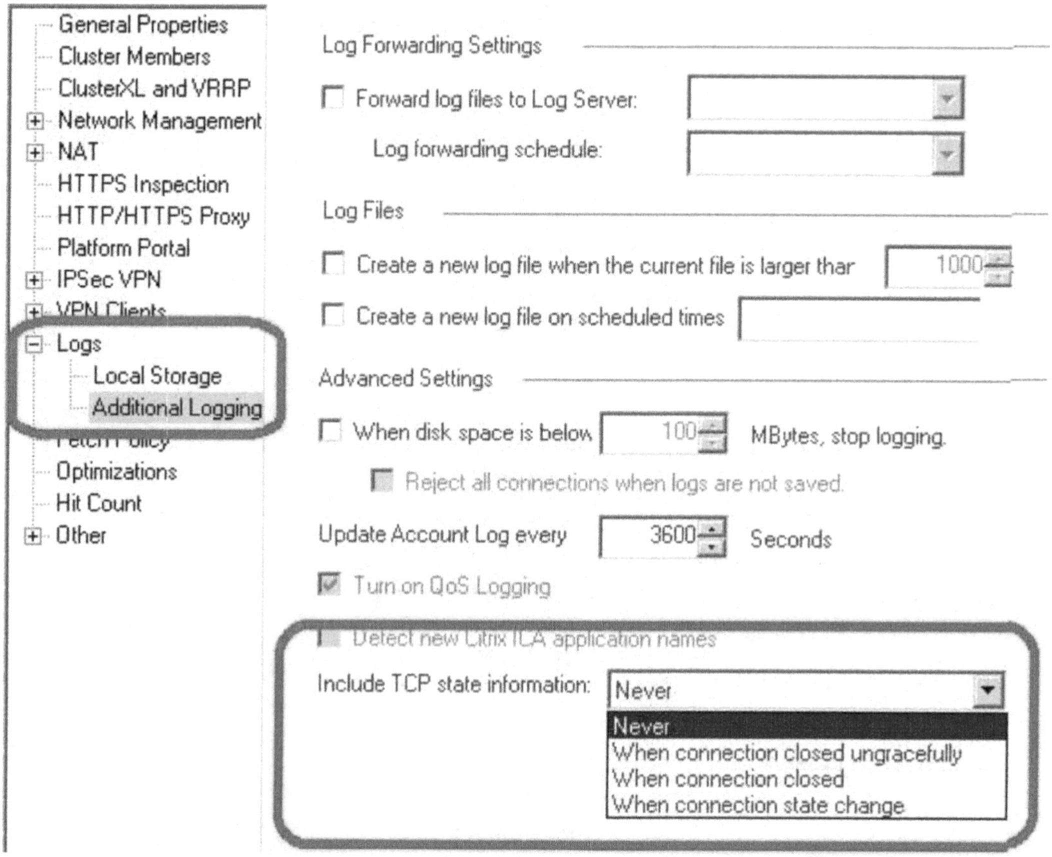

Figure 5-22: Enabling TCP State Logging from the R80+ SmartConsole

This feature is useful for troubleshooting intermittently hung or timed out connections that degrade application performance. If you'd like to obtain more information about the live contents of the firewall's connections table in a human readable format, including the current values of the connection idle timers, try the **fw ctl conntab** command:

```
[Expert@fw:0]# fw ctl conntab
<(outbound, src=[172.31.128.251,40870], dest=[8.8.8.8,53], UDP);
18/40  rule=0, service=domain-udp(333), Ifnsin=2, Ifnsout=2, conn
modules: RTM2>

<(inbound, src=[192.0.2.222,1247], dest=[146.20.132.177,80], TCP);
 3587/3600  rule=7, tcp state=TCP_ESTABLISHED, service=http(366),
Ifncin=1, Ifnsout=2, conn modules: NAT, RTM2, SeqVerifier>

<(inbound, src=[192.0.2.222,1059], dest=[23.35.204.171,80], TCP);
 3554/3600  rule=7, tcp state=TCP_ESTABLISHED, service=http(366),
Ifncin=1, Ifnsout=2, conn modules: NAT, RTM2, SeqVerifier>

<(inbound, src=[192.0.2.222,1162], dest=[74.125.124.113,80], TCP);
 3559/3600  rule=7, tcp state=TCP_ESTABLISHED, service=http(366),
Ifncin=1, Ifnsout=2, conn modules: NAT, RTM2, SeqVerifier>

<(inbound, src=[192.0.2.222,1474], dest=[172.217.1.70,443], TCP);
3572/3600  rule=7, tcp state=TCP_ESTABLISHED, service=https(368),
Ifncin=1, Ifnsout=2, conn modules: NAT, RTM2, SeqVerifier>
```

Figure 5-23: Using *fw ctl conntab* to View Connection Idle Timers

Accounting

An alternative to the TCP State Logging feature is using the "Account" option in the

Track column of the rule matching the problematic traffic. When this option is set for a

rule, an Accept entry is created at the start of the connection just as it is when the Track

column is set to Log. However once the connection finishes (FIN, RST, idle time out,

etc.) or every 60 minutes if the connection exists that long, the existing log entry is

converted from a "Log" type to an "Account" type. Additional information such as firewall routing egress interface, connection time, and number of bytes sent and received is added:

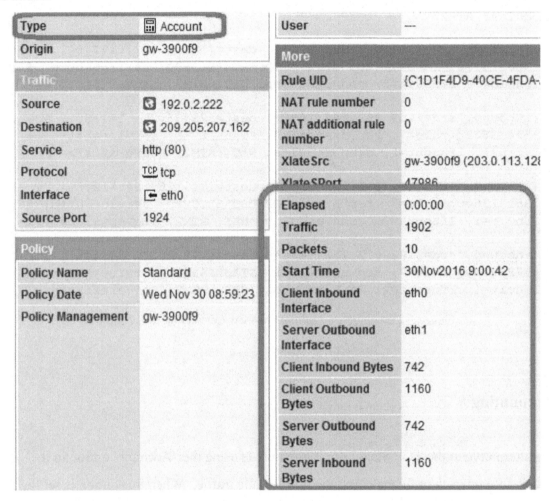

Figure 5-24: Additional Statistics Provided by the Accounting Log Option

While the Accounting option can be used to infer connection and session behavior, new to R80.10+ management is a feature called "Session Logging". When enabled, this feature will correlate multiple individual connections into a single "session" that has additional logging information provided. See the following thread at CheckMates called "Infinity R80.10 'Cool Feature of the Day' - Session logging" for more information about this great feature: https://community.checkpoint.com/thread/5164

Testing Policies: Packet Mode Searches & Packet Injector

So you've spent a lot of time optimizing your policy layers and they are looking great. But a user calls you and asks a seemingly innocuous question: "If I try to go from system 129.82.102.32 to system 2.3.2.2 for service FTP, will the firewall allow it?" There are thousands of rules in your policy, how are you going to find whether there is a matching rule for this type of traffic? The user could just try it of course, but suppose they can't yet because they are waiting on the network team to install the needed network ports. The go-live for these new systems is 3:00AM Sunday morning, so the user will just call you then if it doesn't work and have you add a firewall rule. Uh, no thanks. Let's find out right now and make the changes ahead of time if needed so we don't get woken up! There are two main ways to accomplish this: A packet mode search from the R80.10 SmartConsole or the packet injector tool.

For an example of how to conduct packet mode searches from the SmartConsole, consult the CheckMates article titled "Packet Mode, a new way of searching through your security policy in R80.10" available at this link:
https://community.checkpoint.com/thread/5233

While Packet Mode searches can tell you exactly how a policy will be applied, it cannot tell you how Gaia will route traffic associated with that connection. Even if your policy permits a certain connection, if the routing configured in Gaia is not correct the connection will fail. To test routing use the `ip route get` command from expert mode on the firewall like this:

```
[Expert@fw:0]# ip route get 129.82.102.32
129.82.102.32 via 172.31.128.1 dev eth1  src 172.31.128.251
    cache  mtu 1500 advmss 1460 hoplimit 64
[Expert@fw:0]#
```

Figure 5-25: Querying the Gaia Routing Table with *ip route get*

The second technique for testing policies is using the packet injector tool `pinj` to craft the exact traffic you want to test (complete with IP addresses and port numbers), then inject it into the firewall and watch what happens. Once successfully injected, the packet is treated like any other packet that arrived at the firewall and will be evaluated against policies, create the usual log entries, and if accepted will go through all four firewall processing points (iIoO). Very handy when you don't have access to the systems involved to launch test traffic, yet still want to see whether the firewall will handle certain traffic the way you expect. By using the `pinj` tool, not only will you be able to see if the packet was allowed by the firewall, but also exactly how Gaia routed it.

You can read more about the `pinj` tool and download it from here: sk110865: Check Point Packet Injector. Unfortunately at press time the `pinj` tool was only supported for R77.30 firewalls, and does not work at all in R80.10.

One other tool that can be used if `pinj` is unavailable is `tcptraceroute`; for our example we would invoke it as follows: `tcptraceroute -4 -T -p 21 2.3.2.2`:

```
[Expert@fw:0]# tcptraceroute -4 -T -p 21 2.3.2.2
traceroute to 2.3.2.2 (2.3.2.2), 30 hops max, 40 byte packets
 1  172.31.128.1 (172.31.128.1)  1.329 ms  1.453 ms  1.286 ms
 2  172.31.128.1 (172.31.128.1)  2.017 ms  0.989 ms  1.556 ms
 3  96.120.12.57 (96.120.12.57)  22.844 ms  24.485 ms  21.832
 4  ae-27-ar01.denver.co.denver.comcast.net (68.86.128.5)  24
```

Figure 5-26: *tcptraceroute* Example Usage

Note that traffic injected from the firewall itself with the **tcptraceroute** tool will only pass through the outbound INSPECT driver processing points (oO), and skip the inbound processing points (iI). Also note that an arbitrary source IP address (such as 129.82.102.32) cannot be specified with the **-s** option.

Access Control Policy Tuning: Key Points

- Properly defining your firewall's interface topology is crucial to proper application of the "Internet" network object and any Security Zone objects in use.

- Geo Policy is a highly underrated feature that can be used to drop large amounts of undesirable network traffic with minimal processing overhead, based on a source or destination geographic country.

- When employing policy layers under R80+ management, a "cleanup" rule does not always necessarily drop traffic.

- From a firewall performance tuning perspective, there are minimal differences between utilizing Ordered or Unified/Inline layers in a security policy under R80+ management.

- Avoid the use of object "Any" in as many columns of your policy layers as possible, but especially the Destination column to help maximize the performance gains provided by Column-based Matching and Early Drop.

- Utilize object "Internet" in APCL/URLF policies and try to avoid using "Any".

- A "many to fewer" manual Hide NAT can be configured to permit more than 50,000 concurrent connections in a single Hide NAT rule.

- Application connections that are timed out by the firewall can optionally receive a TCP RST notice from the firewall.

- Enhanced logging of TCP connections being idled out of the firewall's state table is available.

- Specifying "Accounting" in the Track column of a rule provides additional statistics about the matched connection, and can be used to infer how much data was sent (if any) in the connection and how the connection was routed.

CHAPTER 6
CLUSTERXL HA PERFORMANCE TUNING

Success is not final, failure is not fatal: it is the courage to continue that counts.

- Winston Churchill

Background

In today's increasingly cloud-based world, firewall failures cause unacceptable outages that can have far-reaching effects. ClusterXL permits the deployment of more than one firewall in a cluster, thus ensuring that if one firewall fails for any reason, another can immediately take its place and continue to pass traffic.

Using High Availability (HA) in a firewall implementation introduces a new set of challenges for ensuring optimal performance. Additional overhead is introduced to monitor and maintain cluster state, and also to synchronize state tables between cluster members for ensuring seamless failovers. In addition the relatively new Cluster Under Load (CUL) mechanism is enabled by default in R77.30 and later, and can have some surprising effects on cluster failover behavior if you aren't aware of it. However before diving into the optimization details, let's go ahead and deal with the big elephant in the room: active/standby (HA) vs. active/active (Load Sharing).

Firewall Clustering: High Availability vs. Load Sharing

The vast majority of Check Point firewall clusters deployed today are using ClusterXL High Availability, which is an active/standby model. A single active firewall processes 100% of the traffic load while the standby member (or members) processes 0% of the load, and merely takes state table synchronization updates from the active member. A common recommendation to increase overall firewall performance is to adopt an active/active model, which Check Point calls "Load Sharing" as shown here:

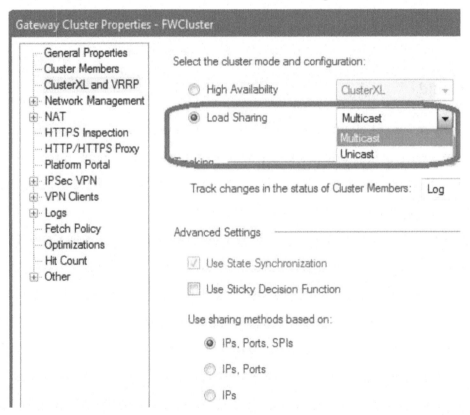

Figure 6-1: Firewall Cluster Load Sharing Options

Can migrating to a Load Sharing model increase overall firewall performance? Yes. Is it worth the additional complexity and troubleshooting murkiness? For most sites in the real world the answer is a resounding NO. "But wait aren't two heads better than one?" you ask. Your manager might also ask: "Why should our very expensive standby firewall just sit there and do nothing?"

To answer these questions let's examine the two supported modes of ClusterXL Load Sharing:

1. **Load Sharing Multicast** – This active/active clustering mode leverages multicast MAC addresses for efficient traffic distribution to all members of the firewall cluster. While it is the most efficient Load Sharing method and can definitely boost overall cluster performance and throughput, it relies on multicast MAC addresses, which are almost never handled properly by the switches and routers directly adjacent to the cluster. To make this Load Sharing technique work properly, extensive hardcoding of IP and MAC addresses may be necessary on all switches and routers that are adjacent to the firewall cluster. This dramatically increases configuration complexity by requiring substantial changes to the surrounding network that may not be obvious to another firewall administrator or third party. These hardcoded changes will almost certainly come back to bite you at the most annoying and inconvenient moment possible. In addition, frequently the "Sticky Decision Function" (SDF) must be enabled for certain features (such as the Mobile Access blade) to work properly when using this ClusterXL Load Sharing mode. Enabling SDF will kill almost all SecureXL acceleration on the firewall, resulting in degraded performance.

2. **Load Sharing Unicast** – This active/active technique avoids the hardcoded configuration morass imposed by the use of multicast MAC addresses, but the

method of traffic distribution amongst the cluster members is substantially less efficient. The Unicast traffic distribution method can even double the amount of traffic your network switches must carry when 3 or more cluster members are present! In a Load Sharing Unicast setup, one of the cluster members is elected the "Pivot" and will always initially receive all traffic bound for all cluster interfaces. In a 2-member Load-Sharing Unicast cluster by default the Pivot will redirect 70% of inbound traffic to the other cluster member for processing, and then process only 30% of the network load by itself. In a 3-member Load Sharing Unicast cluster, the Pivot inspects 20% of the network load and spends the rest of its time redirecting the remaining 80% of the traffic to the two other cluster members 40/40. In this scenario the firewall that has been elected the Pivot is little more than a glorified load balancer 80% of the time, with substantially increased switchport utilization to boot.

Based on the overall tone of the prior section, you probably have a sneaking suspicion that I am not a fan of Load Sharing. You would be correct. This isn't a specific beef with Check Point's implementation of Load Sharing; I also dislike active/active implementations on all other firewall vendors' products as well. Generally speaking, the complexity imposed by Load Sharing is not usually worth it in my opinion. From a design perspective if you still intend to push forward with a Load Sharing configuration, you are going to need at least 3 firewalls. If only two firewalls are used with Load Sharing and one of them fails, the remaining firewall may very well not be able to handle 100% of the load by itself and will buckle in quite noticeable ways. So you'll need a bigger firewall to address that possible contingency. But if you already have a bigger firewall, why not just do active/standby HA and save yourself the trouble of Load Sharing in the first place? *Load Sharing should not be employed for the sole purpose of allowing underpowered firewalls to perform acceptably.*

What about VRRP?

While this chapter focuses on ClusterXL which is by far the most common clustering technology engaged in new Check Point deployments, another option is available: Virtual Router Redundancy Protocol (VRRP). This popular clustering protocol was originally made available on the IPSO-based IP series appliances (formerly known as Nokia appliances), and VRRP is also supported with the Gaia operating system. Unfortunately VRRP has several drawbacks when compared to ClusterXL although VRRP still has its dedicated adherents:

- Cluster IP addresses must be separately set up in both the SmartConsole and Gaia web interface, and manually kept in sync with each other.
- Cluster split-brains (both HA members mistakenly being active/master at the same time) and routing "black holes" are much more likely due to a configuration mistake in a VRRP implementation.
- Monitoring of VRRP cluster state from the Check Point GUI tools such as SmartConsole & SmartView Monitor is limited; VRRP state monitoring must be performed from the firewall CLI or Gaia web interface.

ClusterXL and VRRP mostly provide the same features in regards to active/standby capabilities, but ClusterXL is dramatically easier to manage in day-to-day operation and far less error-prone from a configuration perspective. However VRRP does have two additional capabilities that ClusterXL does not, namely:

- VRRP can present more than one Cluster IP address (sometimes called a secondary address) on the same physical interface or logical subinterface, whereas ClusterXL can present only one. This is a relatively rare requirement though, since it usually indicates that more than one IP subnet is in use on the same VLAN/network segment, which is generally indicative of poor network design.
- VRRP can allow an external entity such as a load-balancing appliance or dynamic routing protocol to balance the traffic load between the cluster members; ClusterXL can only use its own load-sharing algorithms in Load Sharing mode.

If neither of these two use cases for VRRP applies in your environment, ClusterXL is strongly recommended. We will focus on ClusterXL for the remainder of this chapter as ClusterXL is much more commonly used than VRRP in most firewall deployments.

Performing Administrative Failovers the Right Way

Sometimes it is desirable to cause an administrative failover that does not involve unplugging network cables or causing other physical failures. There are two ways to perform this action, the right way and the wrong way:

1. **Right Way**: On the currently active member, from the gateway CLI type
   clusterXL_admin down

```
[Expert@fw:0]# cphaprob state

Cluster Mode:    High Availability (Active Up) with :

Number        Unique Address    Assigned Load    State

1 (local)    192.168.10.2      100%             Active
2            192.168.10.3      0%               Standby

Local member is in current state since Fri Oct 20 0:

[Expert@fw:0]# clusterXL_admin down
Setting member to administratively down state ...
Member current state is Down
[Expert@fw:0]#
```

Figure 6-2: Using *clusterXL_admin* to Initiate a Failover

This will install a new critical device (pnote) called "admin_down" in a failed state, which will cause an immediate failover to the standby member that has no such failure. The command **clusterXL_admin up** will restore normal operation, and may cause a failover back onto that member depending on the firewall's ClusterXL recovery settings.

2. **Wrong Way**: From the SmartView Monitor GUI, right-click the firewall and select "Cluster Member...Stop Member". Select "Cluster Member...Start Member" to restore normal operation on the cluster member:

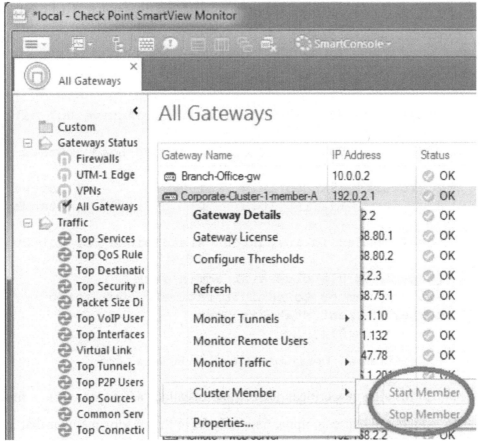

Figure 6-3: Using the SmartView Monitor GUI to Initiate a Failover

Why is using the `clusterXL_admin` command to induce an administrative failover considered the "right" way in my opinion? Both will cause a failover to occur as desired, *but if you happen to accidentally stop **all** cluster members from the SmartView Monitor, it will cause an outage.* If you accidentally run `clusterXL_admin down` on all cluster members, they end up with an "equal" failure (admin_down) and traffic continues to flow through the cluster without incident.

By default, when running the **clusterXL_admin down** command its effects will not survive a reboot; once the member boots back up the failed "admin_down" device will no longer be present, and the cluster member will resume normal operation. In some cases (such as during firewall upgrades), it is desirable to have this "admin_down" device persist across a reboot on a cluster member. This can be accomplished with the little-known **-p** option like this: **clusterXL_admin down -p**. Now the cluster member will not try to go active across reboots (unless it is the only working member of the cluster detected) until the command **clusterXL_admin up -p** is issued. Don't forget the **-p** option when issuing the "up" command in this case, or the "admin_down" device will come back to haunt you after a reboot!

While the content in this section may not have been directly related to performance tuning of the firewall, improper use of the SmartView Monitor to induce ClusterXL failovers can easily cause the absolute worst performance scenario possible: an outage.

Discovery: Firewall Cluster-Specific Performance Issues

Question: Are the members of the cluster healthy and running normally from a ClusterXL perspective?

Answer: Run **cphaprob stat** from all members of the cluster. The proper state reported by all firewalls should either be "active" or "standby". If you see any other states reported such as "ready" or "down", the cluster is not set up properly or experiencing an issue that should be corrected before proceeding. While further discussion of the "down" and "ready" states and how to correct them is beyond the scope of this book, the following SKs should help: sk42096: Cluster member is stuck in 'Ready' state and sk66527: Recommended configuration for ClusterXL.

The Magic MAC/Global Cluster ID

There is one situation you might see in a misconfigured cluster that is worth mentioning here however, as it can be so perplexing. When running the **cphaprob stat** command on all cluster members, both cluster members report they are the only cluster member present (i.e. the cluster members cannot "see" each other at all) and both of them also report they are "active"! How the heck can such a "split-brain" situation occur when setting up a new ClusterXL cluster?

This problem is related to the so-called "Magic MAC address" (yes that was its original name!), but it is now referred to as the "Cluster Global ID". On an R77.30 firewall, this value is set during the Gaia web interface First Time Configuration Wizard dialog in the Cluster Global ID field:

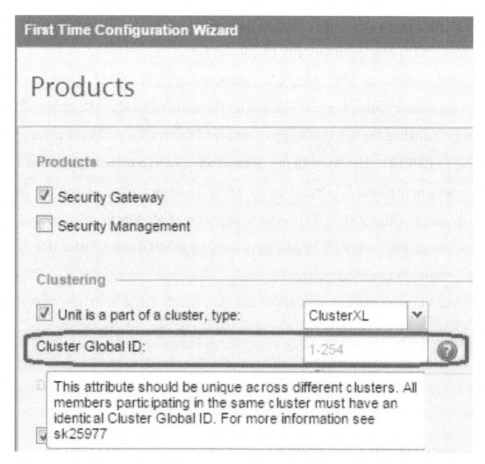

Figure 6-4: Setting the Global Cluster ID in R77.30

The command **cphaconf cluster_id set (Cluster ID Value)** can also be used to set this value. For an R77.30 firewall, the Cluster Global ID should be manually set to an identical value on all members of the same cluster, but be a unique value for different clusters. Failure to configure a matching Global Cluster ID value on the two R77.30 cluster members will cause the split-brain situation mentioned above. On R77.30 and earlier firewalls the Global Cluster ID value can be checked on each of the cluster members with the **cphaconf cluster_id get** command.

There is good news about this situation though for R80.10+ gateway: a matching Global Cluster ID is now automatically calculated for all cluster members through a process called "Automatic MAC Magic". This new feature is also designed to prevent conflicts with other existing firewall clusters on the same network. The status of this new feature (including the automatically calculated Global Cluster ID value) can be verified on an R80.10+ gateway with the **cphaprob mmagic** command. It can also be checked from a new ClusterXL-based screen of the **cpview** tool on an R80.10 gateway under "Advanced...ClusterXL". This new "Automatic MAC Magic" feature is also backwards compatible with R77.30 gateways that had their Global Cluster IDs configured manually in earlier versions.

One other situation that can sometimes inappropriately cause both members to go active is SecureXL being enabled on one member but disabled on the other, see: sk121753: Both ClusterXL High Availability members are Active.

Sync Network Health

Question: My firewall cluster is consuming huge amounts of CPU in sy/si space (as shown by the top command), and overall performance is sluggish. Is my state synchronization network healthy?

Answer: The sync network between the clustered firewalls is assumed to be quick and relatively error-free by the firewall's cluster state synchronization code. Sync network packet loss in excess of 2-3%, or latencies greater than 100ms (even if only transient), can cause cluster performance and stability issues. Run the command **fw ctl pstat** and examine at the last section labeled **Sync**:

```
Sync:
    Version: new
    Status: Able to Send/Receive sync packets
    Sync packets sent:
      total : 3549539, retransmitted : 1996
        retrans reqs : 8, acks : 4
    Sync packets received:
      total : 0,  were queued : 0, dropped by net :  8811
      retrans reqs : 8649, received 329 acks
      retrans reqs for illegal seq : 0
      dropped updates as a result of sync overload: 8610
```

Figure 6-5: Cluster Synchronization Network Statistics

Look at the total number of packets vs. those **retransmitted** or **dropped by net**. If greater than 1%, you may need to employ Selective Synchronization (which is discussed at the end of this chapter) or add another bonded physical interface to help carry the heavy state synchronization traffic. If problems are occurring in this area, you may also see syslog messages such as the following mentioned in this SK: sk23695: 'FW-1: State synchronization is in **risk**. Please examine your synchronization network to avoid further problems!' appears in /var/log/messages file.

Another useful command that can provide even more detail about the health of the sync network if needed is **cphaprob syncstat**. Synchronization statistics displayed by this command can also be reset on the fly by running **cphaprob -reset syncstat**.

If you elect to add a second sync network, bond it with another physical interface via the Gaia web interface (or clish) and declare the new bonded aggregate interface as "1st Sync" in the cluster object topology settings. DO NOT simply add a new non-bonded interface and declare it as "2nd sync" in the cluster topology, as this setup will severely degrade cluster performance. Check `netstat -ni` statistics as well for the physical sync interface(s) to ensure zero values for RX-ERR and RX-OVR.

For more information consult: sk34476: ClusterXL Sync Statistics - output of 'fw ctl pstat' command and sk34475: ClusterXL Sync Statistics - output of 'cphaprob syncstat' command.

CCP: Multicast vs. Broadcast

Question: When examining Control events in the SmartView Tracker/SmartLog or using the filter "type:Control" on the Logs & Monitor tab of the R80+ SmartConsole, I'm seeing constant messages about interfaces in the cluster flapping up and down, with occasional spurious failovers and degraded performance. What is wrong?

Answer: Check for a nonzero `carrier` value for the interface(s) reported to be flapping using the `ifconfig` command first, to ensure the NIC hardware itself is not changing link state because of a loose network cable or other physical issue.

If the interface is found to be stable and not losing link integrity, the switch attached to the firewall on that interface may not be reliably forwarding the cluster member's Cluster Control Protocol (CCP) traffic due to its multicast nature. As a result, the firewalls occasionally lose contact with each other and declare the interface between them to be "down", even though the physical interface itself is up, and general network connectivity between the two cluster members is actually fine on the "down" interface. The switch may need to have IGMP snooping configured to handle multicast traffic reliably. In addition some switches such as the Cisco Nexus 7000 will drop multicast traffic that uses a multicast MAC address, but does not also use a "traditional" Class D multicast IP address (224.0.0.0-239.255.255.255) which is the default behavior for ClusterXL. See the following SK to change this behavior: sk115142: Switch drops Check Point CCP packets when CCP is working in multicast mode.

As a last resort, the command **cphaconf set_ccp broadcast** can be executed on both cluster members to permanently change CCP traffic advertisements from multicast to broadcast. Note that setting CCP to broadcast will increase the amount of switch-flooded broadcast network traffic substantially on all clustered firewall interfaces, which should avoided unless absolutely necessary. See sk20576: How to set ClusterXL Control Protocol (CCP) in Broadcast / Multicast mode in ClusterXL for more information.

Other ClusterXL Problems

Question: I have an HA firewall cluster and I'm using 802.1q trunked interfaces with a mixture of tagged and untagged traffic on the same physical interface, and the network performance is terrible. Why?

Answer: Don't do this as it is not supported with ClusterXL. If you have an interface processing VLAN-tagged traffic, all traffic inbound to the interface should be tagged. There should not be any untagged (sometimes called native) traffic arriving at the interface. See sk101428: Poor performance on Unicast Load Sharing ClusterXL when using native/untagged VLANs.

Question: My cluster does not appear to be stable and fails over randomly for a variety of different reasons, which is impacting performance (and making stakeholders nervous).

Answer: When trying to troubleshoot intermittent or unexpected ClusterXL failovers, establishing exactly when failovers happened and whether they occurred in any kind of suspiciously predictable time interval can be quite time-consuming. Starting in R80.10, the output of the **cphaprob stat** command now displays how long that member has been in its current cluster state (i.e. how long since the last state change or failover).

In some cases, setting up real-time notifications to be sent whenever the cluster fails over can alert you to commence immediate troubleshooting. This is easily set up on the cluster object itself here:

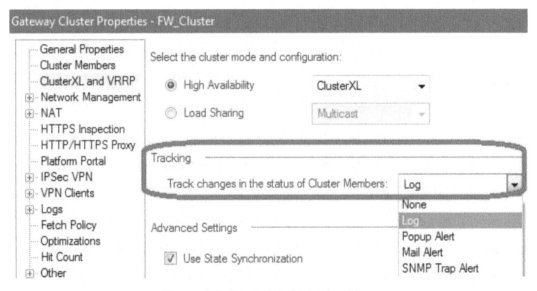

Figure 6-6: ClusterXL State Tracking

An undocumented clish command option introduced in R77.30 provides an easy way to see a concise history of when past failovers occurred: **show routed cluster-state detailed**:

```
gw> show routed cluster-state detailed

Cluster: Clustered
Master/Slave: Master
Sync IP: 192.168.212.73
Cluster Sync: Synchronized
Last Sent: INIT_STATE_FIN
Last Received: MASTER_INIT_STATE_REQ

Cluster VIPs
(long list of VIPs deleted)

Cluster Members: 2

Member ID Member Address
2 192.168.252.71

Cluster State Change History
Timestamp State Change Type
Jun 5 14:44:05 Slave to Master
Jun 5 14:44:00 Master to Slave
Jun 5 13:23:11 Slave to Master
Jun 5 13:23:03 Master to Slave
Jun 5 12:56:57 Slave to Master

Cluster Routed Pnote Change History
Timestamp Routed Pnote Event Description
Jun 5 14:44:05 OK Slave State Fin [OK]
Jun 5 14:44:00 PROBLEM DR Enabled; Master To Slave [Problem]
Jun 5 13:23:09 OK Slave State Fin [OK]
Jun 5 13:23:03 PROBLEM DR Enabled; Master To Slave [Problem]
Jun 5 12:56:55 OK Slave State Fin [OK]
Jun 5 12:56:50 PROBLEM DR Enabled; Master To Slave [Problem]
```

Figure 6-7: Viewing Failover Times with *show routed cluster-state detailed*

Once the timeline for unexpected failovers is established, there are a truly daunting number of individual SK articles that deal with cluster stability issues. Going through all of the possible situations is well beyond the scope of this book. The following two SKs can be quite helpful in this regard though: sk56202: How to troubleshoot failovers in ClusterXL and sk62570: How to troubleshoot failovers in ClusterXL - Advanced Guide.

Question: We suffered an upstream network failure that did not occur on the network/VLAN directly adjacent to the firewall. There was not a failover to the standby member (who had a working network path further upstream) because ClusterXL could not detect this indirect upstream network failure. Can we configure ClusterXL to monitor some upstream IP addresses, and cause a failover to occur when they can no longer be reached?

Answer: Yes! See sk35780: How to configure $FWDIR/bin/clusterXL_monitor_ips script to run automatically on Gaia / SecurePlatform OS.

Question: I've followed all the recommendations throughout this book and performance through my ClusterXL firewall cluster is still unacceptable! I'm suspecting that something is wrong with my ClusterXL setup, or perhaps even how the cluster is interacting with the surrounding network components. Is there any way to exonerate or further incriminate ClusterXL itself as the source of the problem?

Answer: Sure! During a maintenance window, gracefully power off the standby member of the cluster. Doing so creates a "cluster of one" and relieves the surviving firewall of a significant amount of performance-sapping duties such as state synchronization. If performance improves substantially during this period, it strongly indicates that some element of your ClusterXL setup is to blame, or how the cluster members are attached to your network and simultaneously interacting with it could be the culprit. If performance is still unacceptable, some element of your firewall's configuration other than ClusterXL or a problem in the surrounding network is causing the performance issue. If you've gone through all the recommendations in this entire book, the performance problem is much more likely to be somewhere in the surrounding network rather than the firewall cluster itself.

Troubleshooting "Slow" Failovers

Question: Whenever a failover occurs, all network traffic trying to pass through the firewall cluster comes to a screeching halt for about 15 seconds, and then resumes. When we experience multiple failovers in short time period this absolutely kills our network performance. What is going on?

Answer: There are several situations that can cause these "slow" failovers:

1. The default "dead" timer for ClusterXL is approximately 3 seconds. If the active member suffers a catastrophic failure (such as the power cord being pulled or a Gaia system crash/panic), the standby member must wait the dead interval before concluding the active member has failed and taking over. During that waiting period no traffic will pass through the cluster. However for administrative failovers using **clusterXL_admin** or other partial failures (such as a single network interface getting unplugged, or running a service-impacting command such as **fw unloadlocal**) failover to the standby should happen almost instantly with minimal packet loss.

2. If the active cluster member's CPUs are running at 80% utilization or higher, by default in R77.30 gateway and later the Cluster Under Load (CUL) mechanism is invoked, *which extends the ClusterXL dead timer from 3 seconds to 12 seconds*. The purpose of CUL is to avoid spurious and unnecessary failovers due to transient high CPU loads on the active cluster member. Needless to say if a catastrophic failure occurs on the active member while CUL is active, the standby member will have to wait four times as long before taking over. To determine if the CUL mechanism is currently (or previously) active on your cluster, run **grep cul_load_freeze /var/log/messages*** as CUL logs all information about

its operation to the gateway's syslog. Making sure your cluster members are properly tuned and optimized as outlined throughout this book can help keep your active cluster member well below 80% CPU utilization and avoid invoking CUL. More information about the CUL mechanism is here: sk92723: **Cluster** flapping prevention.

3. In some cases, the Spanning Tree Protocol (STP) algorithm on the switches adjacent to the firewall cluster may incorrectly sense a bridging loop when a failover occurs. As first mentioned in Chapter 2, by default the STP algorithm on the switch will block all forwarding to the problematic port for approximately 10-15 seconds in an attempt to break the bridging loop. On some Cisco switches, the LED for the switchport will visually glow amber instead of the usual green during this blocking period. This situation is much more likely to happen if the "Use Virtual MAC" option is set in the cluster object properties (it is disabled by default). Setting "portfast" mode on all switch ports attached to the firewall cluster will help avoid this situation and ensure a timely failover.

4. If the firewall cluster members themselves are participating in a dynamic routing protocol such as OSPF or BGP (and not just using static routes only), a slow failover could be indicative of routing table convergence problems in the network. In particular the Gaia option "Wait for Clustering" should be enabled on both cluster members, to ensure that any dynamic routing protocols on the firewall cluster members wait for the cluster to completely stabilize before commencing operation. The "Wait for Cluster" setting is enabled by default starting in R77.30, but if your firewall was upgraded from an earlier version it may not be enabled. See the following for more information about the "Wait for

Cluster" setting: sk92322: Neighborship for OSPF, BGP, RIP, and PIM in Gaia Cluster is formed with Physical IP addresses upon a reboot.

While the above list is by no means exhaustive, they are the most common causes of "slow" failovers that I've encountered in the real world.

To help minimize the number of failovers that occur, particularly when "slow" failovers are being experienced (regardless of the actual root cause), as a best practice it is strongly recommended to set the "Upon cluster member recovery" setting to "Maintain current active Cluster Member" as shown here:

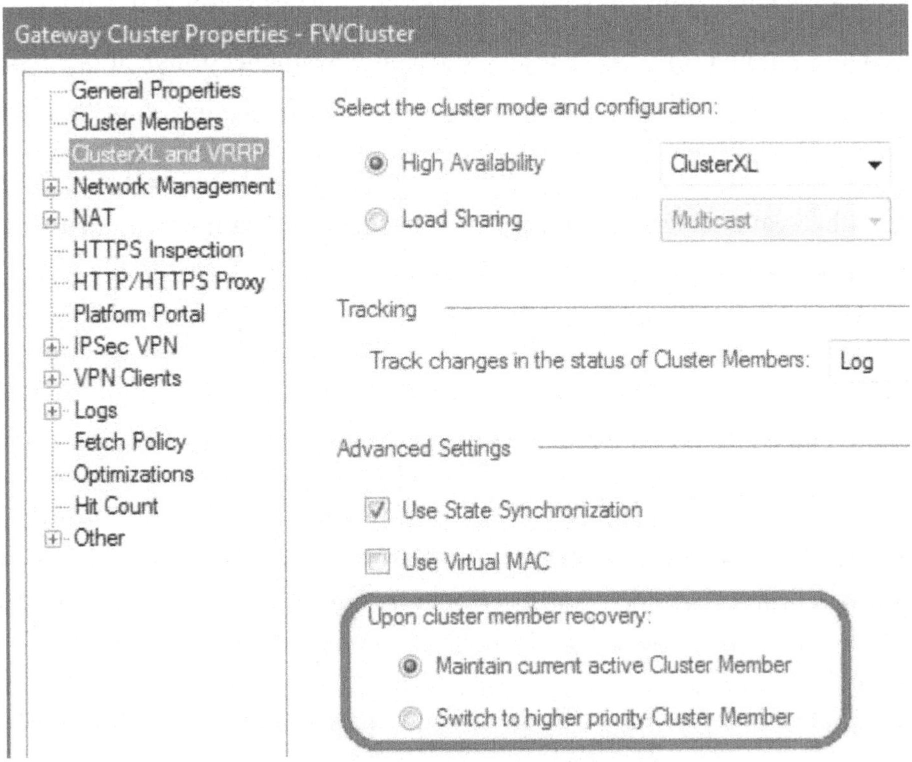

Figure 6-8: Cluster Member Recovery Setting

Selective Synchronization of Services

By default the members of a firewall cluster will synchronize the state of all connections between them. If the amount of sync traffic is so heavy that the firewall CPUs cannot keep up, processing time is wasted retransmitting and processing the lost sync updates. In most networks there are two protocols in particular that comprise at least 50% of state sync network traffic: HTTP and DNS. To determine if this is the case in your network, from SmartView Monitor (or `cpview`) execute the "Top Services" report in real-time while your firewall is in one of its busiest periods. Do protocols HTTP and DNS account for a very large number of new connections? It is possible to disable synchronization of HTTP and DNS between cluster members, which will dramatically reduce the amount of sync traffic and almost certainly make the sync network healthy again, albeit with one major consequence: If a failover occurs, any active HTTP or DNS connections will be unknown by the firewall taking over, and therefore be treated as "out of state" and subsequently dropped.

In most cases this is not a problem because if a HTTP connection or download stalls, by the time the user hits the refresh button the new firewall is fully operational and the web page rendering or file download picks up right where it left off. DNS uses the User Datagram Protocol (UDP) as its transport. UDP does not provide reliability anyway so DNS will just resend a query that appears to be lost. By that time the other firewall has taken over and the retransmitted DNS lookup succeeds.

However we can take Selective Synchronization a step further in a quite useful way. Suppose we have two types of HTTP traffic in our network:

- **Slackers**: HTTP connections initiated outbound to the Internet by our internal slacker user population, who is just screwing around on Facebook and not making the company any money

- **Money-making**: HTTP connections initiated inbound from the Internet to our web servers by paying customers, who want to pay us money on the final day of the calendar quarter and ensure our executives get their bonuses

Needless to say, for career security purposes we might want to preserve the latter HTTP connections across a failover (it is never a good idea to make a customer do anything extra like hit reload while in the process of spending money), but we don't particularly care about the outbound "slacker" HTTP connections in a failover scenario. Thankfully we can specify synchronization by individual service. So for our example we create two new service objects called "http_customer" and "http_slackers", and set both for destination port 80 on the "General" screen. While both services are set to match port 80, on the Advanced screen of the http_customer service we ensure that "Synchronize connection on cluster" remains checked, and on the service http_slackers that same option is UNchecked like this:

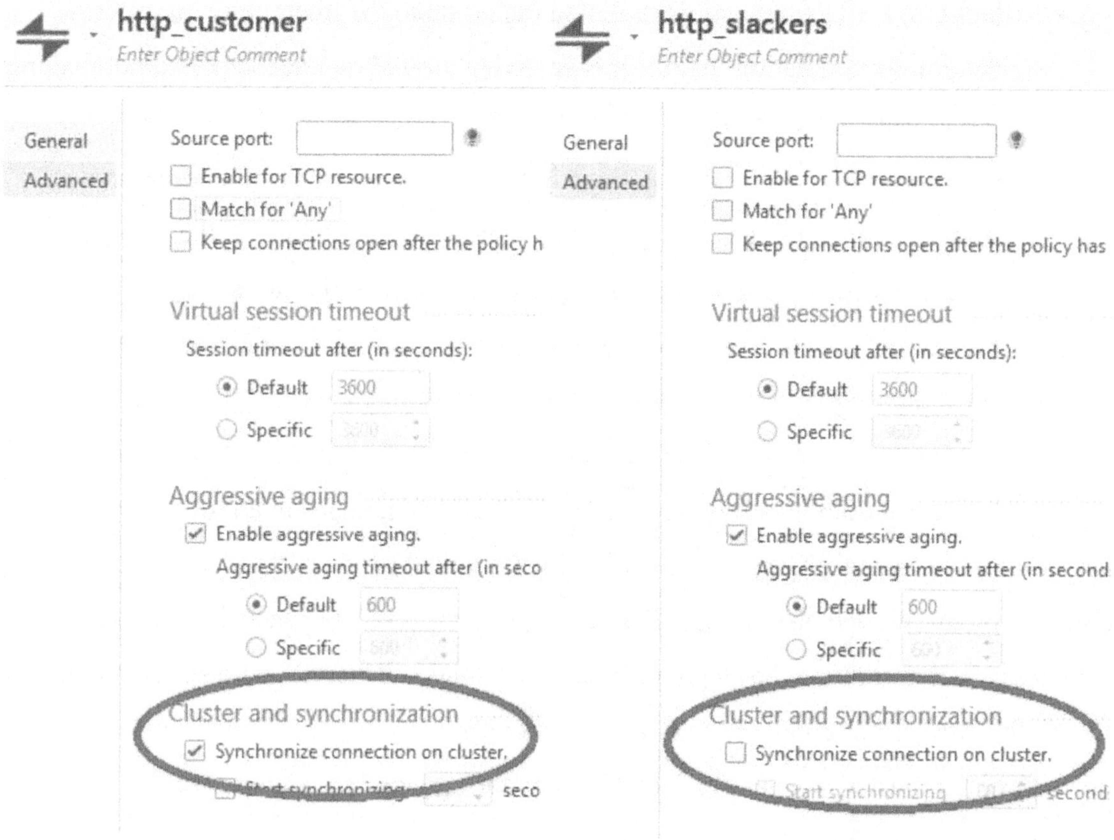

Figure 6-9: Selective Synchronization Service Setup

Also ensure the "Match for 'Any'" checkbox is cleared on both services as shown. In our rule base we create two separate rules leveraging these newly defined services:

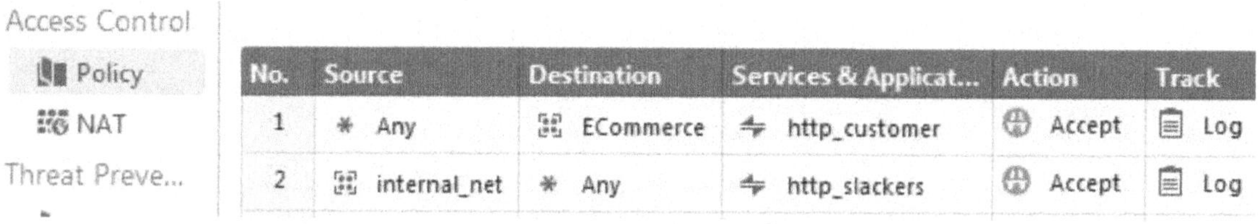

No.	Source	Destination	Services & Applicat...	Action	Track
1	✳ Any	⬚ ECommerce	⇸ http_customer	⊕ Accept	▤ Log
2	⬚ internal_net	✳ Any	⇸ http_slackers	⊕ Accept	▤ Log

Access Control
- 📘 Policy
- ▦ NAT
- Threat Preve...

Figure 6-10: Selective Synchronization Policy Rules

Now critical customer HTTP connections will survive a failover while the non-critical ones ("slackers") will not, all while significantly reducing the load on our sync network and improving the overall performance of the firewall.

You may have noticed the option for "Start Synchronizing" when examining the Advanced Properties of the HTTP and DNS services in our prior example. Don't use this setting for Delayed Synchronization, as there are many restrictions for this function to work correctly (and it is quite unlikely you will meet all these tangled requirements properly), namely:

- Applies only to TCP services whose 'Protocol Type' is set to 'HTTP' or 'None'.

- Delayed Synchronization is disabled if the 'Track' option in the rule is set to 'Log' or 'Account'.

- Delayed Synchronization is performed only for connections matching a SecureXL Accept Template.

Unless you've taken special care to ensure all of these conditions are true (some of them are discussed in later chapters), delayed synchronization won't work the way you expect, and your cluster sync interface will be as unhealthy as ever.

ClusterXL HA Performance Tuning: Key Points

- In most cases High Availability (active/standby) is recommended over Load Sharing (active/active).

- Use the `clusterXL_admin` command to perform administrative failovers; do not use the "Start/Stop Cluster Member" function of the SmartView Monitor GUI.

- Adhere to Check Point best practices for firewall cluster performance optimization. Ensure a healthy sync network and watch out for "Magic MAC" conflicts between multiple firewall clusters attached to the same VLAN.

- Some switches may not handle the stream of multicast CCP packets properly which will cause spurious failovers in the cluster. CCP may need to be set to broadcast mode to ensure reliable cluster behavior.

- "Slow" ClusterXL failovers that seem to take a long time and cause a short outage can be caused by a variety of factors such as STP/portfast, the Cluster Under Load (CUL) mechanism, and an unconverged firewall routing table.

- If the sync network between the cluster members is overloaded, selective synchronization of protocols such as HTTP and DNS between the cluster members can be employed.

CHAPTER 7
COREXL TUNING

Anyone can build a fast CPU. The trick is to build a fast system.

- Seymour Cray

Background

Now that we have ensured that the underlying network is cleanly delivering packets for inspection by the firewall, and gone through some basics of Check Point tuning, we are finally ready to undertake what will probably comprise the bulk of our efforts: CoreXL tuning followed SecureXL in later chapters. CoreXL is how Check Point firewalls leverage the processing power of multiple CPU cores on a firewall. Each available core on the system is ideally dedicated to only one of the two following functions:

1. Secure Network Dispatcher (SND) and IRQ (Interrupt Request) processing (this includes "Accelerated Path" processing discussed in Chapter 9). This function is also sometimes called a "dispatcher" in Check Point's documentation.

2. Firewall Worker INSPECT processing (this includes the Medium Path (PXL), Firewall Path (F2F) and the QXL paths discussed in Chapter 9). When running the `top` command, you will see numerous `fw_worker_X` processes in the output that represent the Firewall Worker cores.

This diagram shows the two types of core allocations and how they fit into the larger scheme of things:

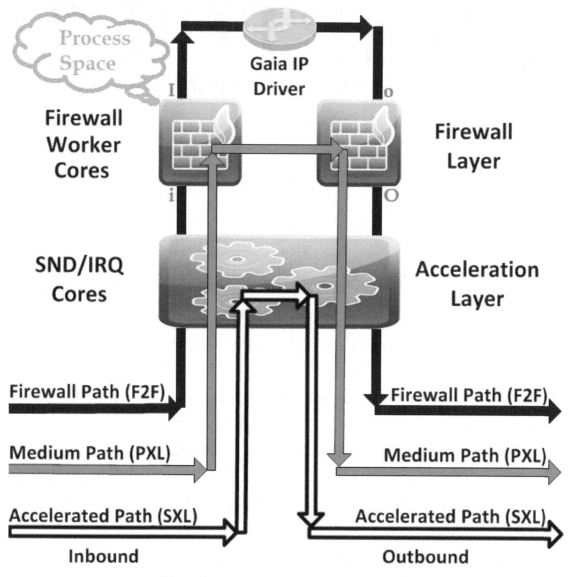

Figure 7-1: Firewall Traffic Processing Paths

Our main performance goal is the following: *CoreXL enabled with a sufficient number of cores allocated to SND/IRQ processing, with automatic interface affinity such that the RX-DRP rate is below 0.1% on all interfaces. RX ring buffers for all interfaces are set to the default. SecureXL is enabled with automatic interface affinity for all interfaces. All cores show at least 50% idle time during the firewall's busiest period.*

For the vast majority of networks this is the optimal configuration and what we will be shooting for. Is it possible that your firewall is oversubscribed and we cannot reach these goals? Yes! But more on that later.

Up to this point we have ensured the underlying Layer 1 network is cleanly delivering packets to our firewall, and packets are being sent and received reliably. We've also ensured that the Layer 2 components of your network are stable by examining the operation of the Spanning Tree algorithm on your switches, and we have profiled the CPU and memory utilization of the firewall so that we can accurately measure any gains obtained as a result of tuning. We have also made sure our policies are constructed in a way that maximizes the performance of rulebase lookups, and ensured that ClusterXL (if present) is operating properly and not causing performance issues.

At long last we have the requisite knowledge about your firewall setup acquired and we can start making dramatic CoreXL/SecureXL tuning adjustments. The changes up to now have been relatively minor in nature and correcting any existing network problems surrounding the firewall itself as well as some other optimizations. In this chapter we can finally discuss the final "Dark Triad" counter RX-DRP, which is by far the most insidious member of the Dark Triad since it is nonzero in most firewall deployments, and frequently misunderstood. However unlike the other two members of the "Dark Triad" (RX-OVR and RX-ERR), for which we target zero or an extremely low value as our goal, with RX-DRP we do not target (or expect) that the RX-DRP counter should always be zero or near zero. The reasons for this will become clear, however we must cover the basics of CoreXL first since it is inextricably linked to the RX-DRP counter.

Discovery & Analysis

Question: How many physical cores are there on my firewall?

```
grep -c ^processor /proc/cpuinfo
```

Question: Is CoreXL on?

```
fw ctl affinity -l
```

Question: Is SecureXL on?

```
fwaccel stat
```

Question: How are interface IRQs currently being processed?

```
cat /proc/interrupts
```

(You may need to make your screen very wide to avoid line wrapping)

Question: Is Multi Queue enabled? (Covered in Chapter 12)

```
cpmq get
```

Question: Is TCP Segmentation Offload (TSO) on?

(Note: The option after the `ls` command is a numeric 1)

```
ls -1 /sys/class/net|xargs -i -t ethtool -k {} |grep tcp| more
```

You should see **tcp segmentation offload: off** for all interfaces. If it is enabled on any interfaces it can cause network performance problems and should be disabled with the `ethtool -K (interface) tso off` command. See sk92524: Gaia Portal is not responding or times out after change of default gateway or default route and sk81100: SecurePlatform WebUI / Gaia Portal is slow or loads only partially when connecting to the machine through 10GB interface.

Question: Have RX ring buffers been adjusted from the default of 256 for 1Gbps interfaces or 512 for 10Gbps interfaces?

(Note: The option after the `ls` command is a numeric 1)

```
ls -1 /sys/class/net |grep -v ^lo|xargs -i ethtool -g {} |less
```

Question: Is Hyperthreading enabled?

```
cat /proc/smt_status
```

Question: Have manual interface affinities been specified?

```
cat $FWDIR/conf/fwaffinity.conf | grep -v "^#"
file $PPKDIR/boot/modules/sim_aff.conf
```

Phew, that was a lot of discovery! Our first priority is to focus on how interface IRQ interrupts are being processed on the firewall, as that is the most common cause of packet buffering drops and subsequent performance issues. Based on our discovery results above, let's look at the four possible configuration states of CoreXL and SecureXL. You need to determine which one of the following four combinations applies to your firewall:

Scenario 1: CoreXL on, SecureXL on

This is the default and therefore the most likely scenario in your environment for a multi-core firewall. `fw ctl affinity -l` returns output and `fwaccel stat` returns: `Accelerator Status : on`.

Scenario 2: CoreXL on, SecureXL off

`fw ctl affinity -l` returns output, but `fwaccel stat` returns `Accelerator Status : off`. SecureXL will need to be enabled for optimal performance of your firewall, unless you want to voluntarily go down the "rabbit hole" of manual interface affinities in Appendix A. Proceed to Chapter 9 to determine why SecureXL is off in your environment, and come back to this chapter once SecureXL has been enabled.

Scenario 3: CoreXL off, SecureXL off

If CoreXL is off (the `fw ctl affinity -l` command returns no output), this may well indicate that the system only has one core, or your configuration is subject to the VPN limitations discussed in the next chapter. Single core systems are not eligible to use CoreXL. Assuming you have 4 or more cores and the proper core licensing (only a concern for open hardware firewalls – Check Point appliances are always bundled with the proper core licensing), you will almost certainly want to enable CoreXL before proceeding. Be sure to check the CoreXL VPN limitations in the "CoreXL Unsupported VPN Features" section of the next chapter, and if they do not apply in your environment, run the command `cpconfig` on the firewall to enable CoreXL with the default settings, and reboot your firewall. If you have a 2-core system you'll need to see the "Special Case: 2 cores" section in this chapter, as CoreXL may have been deliberately turned off for performance reasons on a 2-core system.

Note: You may recall having to turn "something" off in the firewall that was breaking a critical application in your network. That "something" is almost certainly NOT CoreXL, it was probably SecureXL. Why this can sometimes occur with SecureXL is discussed at length in Chapter 9. Turn CoreXL back on please, unless you are utilizing one of the "CoreXL Unsupported VPN Features" described in the next chapter.

If SecureXL is also off, you will need to find out why. Proceed to the introduction of Chapter 9 to determine possible reasons why SecureXL has been explicitly disabled in your environment; it is enabled by default. Once SecureXL has been enabled return to this chapter.

Scenario 4: CoreXL off, SecureXL on

If CoreXL is off (the `fw ctl affinity -l` command returns no output), this may well indicate that the system only has one core, or your configuration is subject to the limitations discussed in the next chapter's "CoreXL Unsupported VPN Features". Single core systems are not eligible to use CoreXL. Assuming you have 4 or more cores and the proper licensing (only a concern for open hardware firewalls – Check Point appliances are always bundled with the proper core licensing), you will almost certainly

want to turn CoreXL on before proceeding. Be sure to check the CoreXL VPN
limitations in the "CoreXL Unsupported VPN Features" section in the next chapter, and
if they do not apply in your environment, run the command `cpconfig` on the firewall to
enable CoreXL with the default settings, and reboot your firewall. If you have a 2-core
system, you'll need to see the "Special Case: 2 cores" section in this chapter, as CoreXL
may have been deliberately turned off for performance reasons on a 2-core system.

*Note: You may recall having to turn "something" off in the firewall that was
breaking a critical application in your network. That "something" is almost certainly
NOT CoreXL, it was probably SecureXL. Why this can occur sometimes with SecureXL
is discussed at length in Chapter 9. Turn CoreXL back on please, unless you are
utilizing one of the "CoreXL Unsupported VPN Features" described in the next chapter.*

RX-DRP Analysis & Discussion

We dance round in a ring and suppose, but the secret sits in the middle and knows.

- Robert Frost

We finally come to one of the most misunderstood networking counters of all time, and
the final member of the RX "Dark Triad". First let's check the RX-DRP rate on our
firewall for our first interface **eth0**:

```
[Expert@firewall:0]# netstat -ni | grep eth0

Iface RX-OK RX-ERR RX-DRP RX-OVR  TX-OK TX-ERR TX-DRP TX-OVR
eth0   3701      0     93      0   4896      0      0      0
```

Figure 7-2: Examining RX-DRP Counter with *netstat -ni*

The main counters we want to inspect are RX-OK and RX-DRP. The `netstat -ni` command shows the values of these counters from when the firewall was booted (recall you can also use the `sar -n EDEV` command to get an idea of when the counters were actually incremented). Are they slowly but consistently accumulating over time, or do they burst suddenly during certain times of day?

In our example RX-OK is 3701, while RX-DRP is 93 on the eth0 interface. To compute the percentage drop rate, the calculation is (RX-DRP/RX-OK)*100. In our example: (93/3701) * 100 = 2.51%. Keep in mind that the drops we will examine here have nothing to with traffic being blocked by a Drop or Reject action in our firewall security policy. A more accurate term for these drops would be a "network buffering miss". You can view buffering misses on a Cisco router with the `show buffers` command; it is exactly the same concept.

One other somewhat unlikely thing to look for in a `netstat -ni` output when SecureXL is enabled is a nonzero TX-DRP counter. While rare, this can indicate that packets are being lost during the transmit operation. See sk75100: Drops on interface under load with SecureXL enabled for instructions to set the `sim_requeue_enabled` kernel variable. Complete all the SecureXL tuning adjustments covered later in this book before attempting to make this modification.

Generally speaking if the RX-DRP rate is greater than 0.1%, you should take action to mitigate the situation from a performance perspective. In my experience once the drop rate reaches 0.1% or higher, a noticeable impact to firewall throughput is encountered. 0.1% (1 in 1,000 packets are dropped) may seem to be a trivial amount of loss that would not substantially impact overall throughput. If the drops were evenly distributed (i.e. every 1,000th packet was dropped in a consistent fashion), it probably wouldn't have much of an impact at all. However in the real world these drops are almost never evenly distributed, and typically come in clumps that seriously damage overall network throughput. *Unlike the RX-OVR and RX-ERR counters discussed earlier, a zero RX-DRP rate is not our goal, and may not even be possible in most environments. You are probably more likely to hurt overall performance trying to tune the RX-DRP counters substantially lower than 0.1%.*

If no firewall interfaces are showing more than 0.1% RX-DRP (make sure the firewall has been up and running for at least 1 week to ensure good numbers - run the command **uptime** to check this), great! The rest of this section concerning RX-DRP tuning will mostly just be informational for you.

Network Buffering Misses

However if we have identified one or more interfaces with an unacceptable percentage of RX-DRPs, let's look specifically at what caused them. In our example interface **eth0** is showing an RX-DRP rate in excess of 0.1%. We can take a closer look with this command: **ethtool -S eth0**

Here are the particular fields in the output we are interested in that can possibly increment RX-DRP:

```
rx_missed_errors: 93
rx_fifo_errors: 0
rx_over_errors: 0
rx_length_errors: 0
rx_long_length_errors: 0
rx_short_length_errors: 0
```

A nonzero "missed" counter is by far the most common and indicates a ring buffer slot was not available to receive a frame. Seeing a nonzero counter in the other fields above is relatively rare. So we have determined that the RX-DRP rate is unacceptable, and we need to tune our firewall due to buffering misses. First off what is an RX-DRP exactly? Let's revisit "A Millisecond in the life of a Frame" from Chapter 1:

> **Stage 3**: The NIC kernel driver begins processing the hardware interrupt, retrieves the frame from the NIC's hardware buffer, and does various sanity checks on the frame. If the frame checks out, it places the frame into a reserved area in the host's RAM memory called a "receive socket buffer".

> **Stage 4**: The NIC driver populates an RX ring buffer slot with a descriptor referencing the location of the newly received frame in memory. Hardware interrupt processing is complete.

> **Stage 5**: The NIC driver schedules a soft interrupt (si/SoftIRQ) with the main CPU to retrieve frames via the RX ring buffer at its convenience.

The RX-DRP counter is incremented in Stage 4 when the NIC driver is *unable* or *unwilling* to place a descriptor in the RX ring buffer pointing to the frame it just received from the NIC's hardware buffer in Stage 3. *Unable* in this case means there is not a free RX ring buffer slot available. *Unwilling* means that a basic sanity check performed on the frame failed; this situation will be discussed in the "RX-DRP Revisited: Still Racking Them Up?" section at the end of this chapter. The "unable" scenario though is by far the most common and can dramatically impact the network performance of the firewall, so we will cover it at length. Regardless of whether the NIC driver is "unable" or "unwilling", the subject frame is discarded and will not be processed; all frames currently referenced in the ring buffer are not touched or overwritten. This is sometimes referred to as a "tail drop" queuing strategy. The most common cause of the drop: There is nowhere to put the frame's descriptor during hardware interrupt processing because the ring buffer is full. The crux of the issue is this: The SoftIRQ processing scheduled in Stage 5 did not empty frames quickly enough from the RX ring buffer before it overflowed and incoming frames were lost.

Remediating Network Buffering Misses

There are three methods to lower the RX-DRP rate if buffering misses are occurring:

1) **The best way:** Allocate more core processing resources for handling SoftIRQs in a timely fashion if available, this may also include enabling Multi-Queue as discussed in Chapter 12.

2) **Not desirable but unavoidable in some cases:** Increase the size of the RX ring buffer for more interface buffering capability.

3) **Unsupported and not recommended except in extreme circumstances:** Increase the CPU "budget" for processing frames during a single SoftIRQ processing run, by adjusting the undocumented `net.core.netdev_budget` Gaia kernel variable.

It's a Trap! Increasing Ring Buffer Sizes

Let's start with method #2 above: A common recommendation in the case of excessive RX-DRPs is to increase the size of the interface's RX ring buffer from its default of 256/512 frames of buffering, to some higher value (most NICs support a maximum ring buffer size of up to 4096 frames). However increasing the RX ring buffer size is simply addressing a symptom of the actual problem: not enough CPU resources are available to empty the RX ring buffer before it becomes full. The best solution is to allocate sufficient processing resources to empty the buffer in a timely fashion, without increasing the size of the ring buffer itself.

But with computers isn't more memory always a good thing? Doesn't that apply to ring buffers as well? With typical processing operations like executing code in an operating system, having more RAM is always better. Having to wait for data to be retrieved from a hard drive takes a relative eternity compared to how long it takes to retrieve it from RAM or a CPU's fast cache.

However this maxim does not apply in the case of buffer processing. The larger the buffer the more processing it takes to service that buffer, which will increase latency and jitter. To make matters worse, the excessive buffering and wild variances in packet delivery delay (called "jitter") can confuse TCP's congestion-avoidance mechanism on the communicating workstations causing them to "back off", which further reduces overall network throughput. It is not only real-time streaming applications such as voice and video that suffer when jitter is excessive. The decline in network throughput caused by oversized buffers is known as *BufferBloat*. To quote Wikipedia:

> **Bufferbloat** is a phenomenon in packet-switched networks, in which excess buffering of packets causes high latency and packet delay variation (also known as jitter), as well as reducing the overall network throughput. When a router device is configured to use excessively large buffers, even very high-speed networks can become practically unusable for many interactive applications like voice calls, chat, and even web surfing.

> Overly large buffers have been placed in some models of equipment by their manufacturers. In this equipment bufferbloat occurs when a network link becomes congested, causing packets to become queued for too long in those buffers. In a first-in first-out queuing system, overly large buffers result in longer queues and

higher latency, but do not improve network throughput and may even reduce goodput *to zero in extreme cases.*

Properly allocating CPU processing resources for SoftIRQ processing is vastly preferable to increasing network buffering. You can test for the presence of BufferBloat in your network, specifically in the "Network Buffer Measurements" report portion of this free testing tool:

> http://netalyzr.icsi.berkeley.edu

Remember, our performance goal is to properly allocate CPU resources such that SoftIRQ processing is handled in a timely fashion and the RX-DRP rate is 0.1% or less. In some limited cases, it may be desirable to increase the RX ring buffer size on a problematic interface when sufficient processing resources are simply not available due to the firewall being underpowered. *It is not always desirable (or possible) to have an RX-DRP rate of zero in all environments, and attempting performance tuning in this area when the RX-DRP rate is already less than 0.1% is just as likely to harm performance as it is to help it.*

Impact of Oversized Ring Buffers – An Example

You are probably thinking right about now: "Isn't all packet loss bad? Shouldn't we bend over backwards to prevent it at all costs?" NO! The "cost" in this case is actual degradation of overall network throughput, not just for connections trying to consume large amounts of network bandwidth, but for every packet attempting to traverse the firewall. The Wikipedia BufferBloat article does a good job of explaining this, but let's step through a quick example:

Two TCP-based streams are traversing the firewall. "Slowpoke" is only occasionally sending infrequent data but is delay-sensitive, while "Screamer" is not delay sensitive but has many terabytes of data to send. Screamer will flood the receiving interface's RX ring buffer with a huge number of frames as soon as it starts.

Suppose the inbound interface's RX ring buffer is set to the default of 256. Almost immediately Screamer overflows the RX ring buffer and experiences packet loss. Screamer's TCP sees the loss very quickly, and the TCP congestion control algorithm on Screamer *immediately backs off, sensing that the network is congested*. After backing off, Screamer's TCP will slowly attempt to send traffic faster and faster until loss is once again encountered. Screamer will very quickly settle down at the fastest speed possible that does not result in packet loss, thus ensuring the most efficient use of network resources for its connection, as well as for all other connections traversing the firewall. Jitter is very low and Screamer's TCP rarely has to make significant adjustments to its send rate. Should the lower bandwidth stream Slowpoke attempt to send a few packets during the much heavier stream Screamer's operation, the following is likely to be true:

- An RX ring buffer slot will very probably be available to receive Slowpoke's frame
- The delay incurred to get Slowpoke's frame read from the buffer and processed can be no more than the time it take to process between 1 and 254 frames from the ring buffer during SoftIRQ processing (1 in the best case, 254 in the worst case).

Now suppose the RX ring buffer has been cranked to the maximum of 4096 on the interface. The same scenario will now look like this:

Screamer does not overflow the RX ring buffer initially, and blasts frames at full speed until its TCP Send Window completely closes, consuming some but not all of the RX ring buffer capacity (the TCP Send Window is the amount of data a TCP Stream can send without having to receive an ACK from the receiver). Screamer's TCP does not see loss immediately, but a relatively long delay instead. Screamer's TCP must stop sending and wait until ACKs start coming back from the receiver before it can send more. As the ACKs start coming back, Screamer immediately sends as much data as it can until once again its TCP Send Window closes. The traffic pattern of Screamer in this case is quick, herky-jerky blasts of packets that start and stop repeatedly. Screamer's TCP sees potentially long & somewhat random-looking delays in the network (due to competition with other traffic and excessive buffering latency), thus causing it to back off much further than it should (due to the perceived performance inconsistency of the network). Should the lower-bandwidth stream Slowpoke attempt to send a few frames during all of this, the following is likely to be true:

- An RX ring buffer slot should be available to receive Slowpoke's packet, or it might get lost if Screamer is in the middle of a "packet blast".

- The delay incurred to get Slowpoke's packet read from the buffer is highly variable (1 in the best case, 4096 in the worst case). Jitter for Slowpoke (and any other streams crossing the firewall) is potentially up to *16 times higher* (4096/256 = 16) than the prior example, and Screamer will probably suffer due to the wild variances in queue processing delay as well.

This was a very simple example, but hopefully you can see why *it is almost never a good idea to crank the ring buffer in an attempt to avoid packet loss at any cost*. It is normal and expected for loss to occur when TCP streams attempt to consume too much bandwidth, so they will adjust to conditions in the network and ensure orderly access to the network for all connection streams. An excessive ring buffer size defeats that mechanism as network load increases. If you still need to increase ring buffer sizes anyway as a last resort (we will discuss this unhappy situation later), see sk42181: How to increase sizes of buffer on SecurePlatform/Gaia for Intel NIC and Broadcom NIC.

Seductive but Dangerous: Increase the SoftIRQ Budget

WARNING: Tampering with the `net.core.netdev_budget` *Gaia kernel variable is not documented by Check Point and not officially supported. Check Point's SND code running on the same SND/IRQ core as the SoftIRQ routines is almost certainly expecting a certain amount of access to core processing resources relative to those SoftIRQ service routines, and allocating a larger SoftIRQ CPU budget than provided by default may have unpredictable performance results.*

Now let's have a look at method #3 mentioned above: Increasing the CPU "budget" for processing frames during a single SoftIRQ processing run by adjusting the `net.core.netdev_budget` Gaia kernel variable. When a scheduled SoftIRQ processing run begins, packets are processed until one of the following three conditions occur, which will terminate that particular SoftIRQ run:

- All possible packets have been processed, and there are no more packets present in any interface ring buffer(s) being emptied by that CPU.

- A non-tunable absolute time limit of two "jiffies" has been reached. The actual duration of a "jiffy" is dependent on the CPU clock speed. This helps avoid improper monopolization of the CPU by the SoftIRQ routine.

- When the total budget (`net.core.netdev_budget`) for all interface(s) the CPU is assigned to empty has been reached. This default value of this variable is set to 300 frames.

In the last two situations listed above, the SoftIRQ processing run is terminated early before it has completely finished emptying the ring buffer(s), and it is forced to relinquish the CPU for other operations that wish to use it. How can we tell if either of these latter two situations has occurred on our firewall and in what quantity? Use the `cat /proc/net/softnet_stat | cut -c1-27` command, which displays all values in hexadecimal:

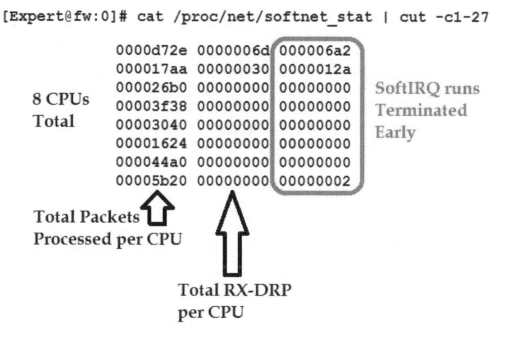

Figure 7-3: Checking for Early Termination of SoftIRQ Runs

The third column of the output is the important one in this context. If all you see in the third column is a bunch of zeroes on every line (each line represents one CPU), there is no need to tamper with the SoftIRQ budget. However if there are significantly large values present in the third column indicating numerous early terminations of SoftIRQ processing, it is highly likely that the second column is indicating a considerable number of RX-DRPs occurring as well. The RX-DRPs reported here are also visible with **netstat -ni**, but **netstat** reports total number of RX-DRPs *per interface*, while the statistics shown above display those same RX-DRP events *per CPU*.

Even if you see significant nonzero values in the third column, the right way to deal with this situation is to address the RX-DRPs first by allocating more CPU resources to SoftIRQ processing; this may also include enabling Multi-Queue as discussed in Chapter 12. Increasing the SoftIRQ budget should be a last resort.

Allocating More CPU Resources for SoftIRQ Processing

So we have observed an RX-DRP rate >0.1% on one or more interfaces. Next we need to determine if there are sufficient CPU resources allocated to handle network interface SoftIRQ processing on your firewall. We can then tune the firewall in productive ways that hopefully won't involve increasing RX ring buffer sizes or the SoftIRQ budget, both of which should always be considered a last resort.

Let's take a look at how we do that. Run `netstat -ni` on the firewall and note any interfaces that have nonzero RX-DRP counters. Compute the RX-DRP rate as demonstrated earlier; any interfaces showing an RX-DRP rate in excess of 0.1% are good candidates for tuning. Let's suppose that interfaces eth0 and eth1 are extremely busy and both exhibiting signs of excessive RX-DRPs. Let's look at how SoftIRQs are being processed for these interfaces with this command:

`cat /proc/interrupts`

(widen your terminal display to avoid line wrapping)

Look along the right-hand side of the output and find interfaces eth0 and eth1. On the same line with each interface, look back to the left and find any columns with nonzero counters. You see something like this:

```
[Expert@firewall:0]# cat /proc/interrupts
          CPU0        CPU1.......CPU7
   0:   105174136          0          0    IO-APIC-edge   timer
   1:         127          0          1    IO-APIC-edge   i8042
   4:         693        127        234    IO-APIC-edge   serial
   6:           5          0          0    IO-APIC-edge   floppy
   7:           0          0          0    IO-APIC-edge   parport0
   8:           3          0          0    IO-APIC-edge   rtc
   9:           0          0          0    IO-APIC-level  acpi
  12:         113          0          2    IO-APIC-edge   i8042
  15:          57          0         40    IO-APIC-edge   ide1
  59:          65          0          0    IO-APIC-level  uhci_hcd:usb1
  67:      344065        112        160    IO-APIC-level  ehci_hcd:usb2
  75:    25512470         49          3    IO-APIC-level  eth0, eth2
  83:    19342739        145          0    IO-APIC-level  eth3, eth1
 NMI:           0          0          0
 LOC:   102377029  102275417..102760638
 ERR:           0
 MIS:           0
[Expert@firewall:0]#
```

Figure 7-4: Examining SoftIRQ Processing Core Allocations

There are nonzero values for both interfaces in the CPU0 column, but very low numbers in the other columns (CPUs 1-7); this means that essentially all IRQ processing for both these interfaces is taking place on one core (CPU0).

But wait, look at all the other interfaces as well such as eth2 & eth3. Where are their IRQs being handled? Oops, looks like they are all getting handled on CPU0 as well. Clearly that one core is going to be very busy keeping up with SoftIRQ processing for all these interfaces. Let's take a look at the utilization on that core with the **top** command during one of your firewall's busiest periods. Hit "1" to show all the cores independently and focus on CPU0:

```
top - 05:25:43 up 1 day, 20:17,  2 users,  load average: 0.10, 0.11
Tasks: 90 total,  3 running, 209 sleeping,    0 stopped,   0 zombie
Cpu0  : 0.4%us, 3.3%sy,  0.0%ni, [0.1%id,] 0.5%wa,  0.0%hi, [95.7%si]
Cpu1  : 1.1%us, 1.3%sy,  0.0%ni, 97.6%id,  0.0%wa,  0.0%hi,  0.0%si,
Cpu2  : 0.1%us, 0.1%sy,  0.0%ni, 99.7%id,  0.0%wa,  0.0%hi,  0.0%si,
Cpu3  : 0.1%us, 0.1%sy,  0.0%ni, 99.8%id,  0.0%wa,  0.0%hi,  0.0%si,
Cpu4  : 0.1%us, 0.0%sy,  0.0%ni, 99.8%id,  0.0%wa,  0.0%hi,  0.0%si,
Cpu5  : 1.4%us, 1.2%sy,  0.0%ni, 97.3%id,  0.0%wa,  0.0%hi,  0.0%si,
Cpu6  : 0.1%us, 0.1%sy,  0.0%ni, 99.7%id,  0.0%wa,  0.0%hi,  0.0%si,
Cpu7  : 0.2%us, 0.1%sy,  0.0%ni, 99.8%id,  0.0%wa,  0.0%hi,  0.0%si,
Mem:   8028904k total,  2767664k used,  5261240k free,   272228k bu
Swap: 18900432k total,         0k used, 18900432k free,  1004720k ca

  PID USER      PR  NI  VIRT  RES  SHR S %CPU %MEM    TIME+  COMMAN
 6507 admin     15   0  122m  33m  23m S    1  0.4  2:08.70 dlpu
 6644 admin     15   0  175m  24m  16m S    1  0.3  0:41.59 cvpnd
    1 admin     18   0  1976  724  624 S    0  0.0  0:01.36 init
    2 admin     RT  -5     0    0    0 S    0  0.0  0:00.08 migrat
    3 admin     15   0     0    0    0 S    0  0.0  0:00.00 ksofti
    4 admin     RT  -5     0    0    0 S    0  0.0  0:00.00 watchd
    5 admin     RT  -5     0    0    0 S    0  0.0  0:01.25 migrat
```

Figure 7-5: High *si* Core Utilization Due to Excessive SoftIRQ Processing

See that? CPU0 is spending almost all of its time processing soft interrupts (si) and is even occasionally pegging at 100% (during which time RX-DRPs are sure to occur).

So our scenario is a very common one: an insufficient number of cores are allocated for SoftIRQ processing. Let's fix it. We want SecureXL enabled with automatic interface affinity, and CoreXL enabled with the proper number of cores for SND/IRQ processing. How we proceed will depend on how many cores are available on your system, so let's take a look at the default CoreXL allocations "out of the box".

Default Core Allocations & CPU Fast Caching

We have determined that we need to add more processing cores to handle SoftIRQ processing, which is a very common performance problem. In recent years processor speed has advanced much faster than RAM access speeds; a core may end up spending a great deal of its time in a blocked state waiting for access to the much slower RAM. The answer to this blocking problem is the use of fast memory caches located very close to the core itself. To take maximum advantage of the fast memory caches, we want an even number of adjacent cores performing the same function, if at all possible.

In some Intel architectures adjacent cores (i.e. Cores 0&1, Cores 2&3, etc) share Level 2 fast cache with each other, and sizable performance gains can be realized if the adjacent cores are serving the same function. The adjacent cores can more frequently pull their needed data from speedy Layer 2 cache, instead of waiting much longer for them to be retrieved from RAM or Level 3 cache (if present). Following this "adjacent cores" recommendation also maximizes the gains provided by a function called "prefetching" which is inherent in all modern processor architectures, which helps ensure that cores spend as little time as possible in a blocked state waiting for access to memory.

To underscore the gains that can be achieved with this adjacent cores technique and also trying to keep the core fast caches "hot" (i.e. continuously populated with the code and data the core needs to perform its useful work without waiting) as much as possible, consider the following: The CPU must retrieve executable code & the associated dataset into its Layer 1 (L1) cache for execution before it can begin processing. The following are approximations showing the difference between various access times for the different levels of memory storage on a system. Just for reference, a 2GHz processor has 2 billion (2,000,000,000) clock cycles per second:

- If data is in the L1 cache, the CPU can access it in about 1-2 clock cycles
- If data is in the L2 cache, the CPU can access it in about 10 clock cycles
- If data is in the L3 cache, the CPU can access it in about 50 clock cycles
- If data is in RAM, the CPU can get to it in about 100 clock cycles

- If the data must be retrieved from fixed disk storage, it will take between 100,000 and 10,000,000 clock cycles

Notice that having to access RAM takes many times longer than if the needed data was available from the core's L2 or L3 fast cache. Needless to say, it is desirable to have a pair of cores dedicated to one purpose (either SND/IRQ processing or a Firewall Worker instance) to maximize the chance that the various fast caches are "hot", instead of waiting up to 10 times longer for RAM access. If a single core is configured to perform both SND/IRQ and Firewall Worker functions, numerous L2/L3 cache "misses" will occur every time the processor switches contexts to execute the other function. The CPU must wait many times longer for the needed code and data to be retrieved from RAM before it can begin execution in the case of a cache miss. The amount of L1/L2 (and L3 if present) fast CPU cache on your firewall can be determined by running the **dmidecode -t cache** command on the firewall.

In quite a few performance tuning and deployment scenarios I've faced, there are not enough CPU cores allocated to SND/IRQ functions by default. These cores continually max out under heavy load, causing RX-DRPs to occur, thus constraining the amount of traffic that can reach the Firewall Worker cores, which as a result are almost never as busy as the SND/IRQ cores.

R80.10 "Taskset" Process Affinities

Manual process affinities (i.e. specifying which cores that firewall daemon processes are allowed to use) were only briefly mentioned in the first edition of this book, mainly in the context of adding a dedicated core for the **fwd** process to handle heavy logging. For this edition, manual affinity has been relegated to Appendix A, because the need to manually configure affinities has become somewhat rare in R77.30 and later. However there is one big exception for R80.10 and later. Compare the following two screenshots of the `fw ctl affinity -l -r` command output that were both taken on the same 8-core firewall. The first screenshot was taken while the firewall was running R77.30, while the second was acquired after that same firewall had been upgraded to R80.10:

```
[Expert@fwr7730:0]# fw ctl affinity -l -r
CPU 0:   eth0 eth1
CPU 1:
CPU 2:   fw_5
CPU 3:   fw_4
CPU 4:   fw_3
CPU 5:   fw_2
CPU 6:   fw_1
CPU 7:   fw_0
All:     cpsead mpdaemon rad status_proxy cpca cpstat_mo
```

```
[Expert@fwr8010:0]# fw ctl affinity -l -r
CPU 0:   eth0 eth1
CPU 1:
CPU 2:   fw_5
         rtmd fwd vpnd cpstat_monitor mpdaemon rad i
CPU 3:   fw_4
         rtmd fwd vpnd cpstat_monitor mpdaemon rad i
CPU 4:   fw_3
         rtmd fwd vpnd cpstat_monitor mpdaemon rad i
CPU 5:   fw_2
         rtmd fwd vpnd cpstat_monitor mpdaemon rad i
CPU 6:   fw_1
         rtmd fwd vpnd cpstat_monitor mpdaemon rad i
CPU 7:   fw_0
         rtmd fwd vpnd cpstat_monitor mpdaemon rad i
All:
```

Figure 7-6: Viewing *taskset* Affinity Changes between R77.30 and R80.10+

See the difference? In R77.30 and earlier gateway, firewall process daemons were allowed to execute on any open core that had available CPU slices, regardless of whether that core was allocated for SND/IRQ functions or as a Firewall Worker. However in R80.10 all firewall processes are only allowed to execute on a Firewall Worker core. This change in how process affinities are handled will occur automatically on an R80.10

firewall, regardless of whether it was upgraded from an earlier release or fresh-loaded from scratch. Physical cores dedicated to SND/IRQ functions will never have processes execute on them in this case.

Why was this affinity change made in R80.10? Almost certainly to keep the CPU fast caches as "hot" as possible for the SND/IRQ cores; this permits the relatively small SND/IRQ routines to take up increased residence in the CPU fast caches of the SND/IRQ cores, and not have those fast caches get constantly trashed by some wayward process looking for an open CPU. But just how "hot" can those fast caches get? The 13000 series and higher models of Check Point gateway appliances have at least 20MB of what Intel calls "SmartCache", which is essentially Layer2/Layer3 cache that is accessible to all cores. For comparison here is a table showing the resident memory size of the various R80.10 kernel drivers used for firewall traffic inspection & processing in the kernel:

Table 3: List of Check Point Firewall Kernel Modules

Function	Driver Name (lsmod)	Resident Code Memory Size
SND/IRQ	simmod/SND	~5.2 MB total
	NET_RX_SOFTIRQ	< 1MB total
	NET_TX_SOFTIRQ	< 1MB total
Firewall Worker	fw_X	40 MB per Firewall Worker
Monitoring Blade	rtm_X	3 MB per Firewall Worker
QoS/Floodgate	etm_X	3 MB per Firewall Worker
Route-based VPNs	vpntmod	50 KB
VRRP HA	vrrp_lkmmod	300 KB
IP/Net Control	ipsctlmod	100 KB

With 20MB or more of SmartCache available, the R80.10 SND/IRQ routines can easily take up near-permanent residence in fast cache, practically never have to wait around for access to the much slower RAM, and can't ever have their fast cache get polluted by pesky processes. When combined with fully accelerated and templated connections via SecureXL, truly staggering firewall performance levels are achievable on today's modern processor hardware.

Retrofitting "Taskset" Affinities to R77.30

So you are probably thinking right about now: that all this sounds great, but I have to upgrade to R80.10 to take advantage of this big performance boost? In actuality this enhancement can be retrofitted back to an R77.30 gateway like this with the

`taskset_us_all` command:

```
[Expert@fwr7730:0]# fw ctl affinity -l -r
CPU 0:   eth0 eth1
CPU 1:
CPU 2:   fw_5
CPU 3:   fw_4
CPU 4:   fw_3
CPU 5:   fw_2
CPU 6:   fw_1
CPU 7:   fw_0
All:     cpsead mpdaemon rad status_proxy cpca cpstat_monitor f
[Expert@fwr7730:0]# taskset_us_all -l 2-7
[Expert@fwr7730:0]# fw ctl affinity -l -r
CPU 0:   eth0 eth1
CPU 1:
CPU 2:   fw_5
         cpsead mpdaemon rad status_proxy cpca cpstat_monitor f
CPU 3:   fw_4
         cpsead mpdaemon rad status_proxy cpca cpstat_monitor f
CPU 4:   fw_3
         cpsead mpdaemon rad status_proxy cpca cpstat_monitor f
CPU 5:   fw_2
         cpsead mpdaemon rad status_proxy cpca cpstat_monitor f
CPU 6:   fw_1
         cpsead mpdaemon rad status_proxy cpca cpstat_monitor f
CPU 7:   fw_0
         cpsead mpdaemon rad status_proxy cpca cpstat_monitor f
All:
```

Figure 7-7: Retrofitting *taskset* Affinities to an R77.30 Firewall

Keep mind the following guidelines when performing this action:

1. Do not invoke the **taskset_us_all** command manually on R77.30 if your
   firewall has less than 6 cores. Doing so may cause an insufficient number of

cores to be available for use by processes, thus possibly starving those processes of enough CPU slices to operate normally. This "Fourth Path" performance-impacting situation is explored in Chapter 10.

2. Note that the list of processors (**2-7** in our example) provided to the **taskset_us_all** command are the physical core numbers (i.e. CPU X), *not* the Firewall Worker instance numbers (0-5 in our example).

3. While the **taskset_us_all** command takes effect immediately, it will not survive a reboot. To make this command permanent, add it to the **/etc/rc.local** file on the firewall. If you change the number of Firewall Workers after doing so, you will need to update the CPU numbers provided to the command in **/etc/rc.local**! At system startup R80.10 will dynamically determine which cores are dedicated to Firewall Worker operations and automatically assign process affinity to them.

4. Once the firewall has been upgraded to R80.10, remove the **taskset_us_all** command from **/etc/rc.local** if it was added there while the gateway was still running R77.30.

5. While this change will allow the SND/IRQ cores to run much more efficiently, it is likely to increase the load on the Firewall Worker cores, since they are now shouldered with the additional responsibility of allowing firewall processes to exclusively run on them. This can actually necessitate reducing the number of SND/IRQ cores which may now be more lightly loaded, which of course will subsequently allocate more Firewall Worker cores.

Specific Recommendations by Number of Cores

The following table contains the default core allocations "out of the box" when CoreXL is enabled, along with general guidelines that I use when deploying a new Check Point firewall. In cases where tuning adjustments are being made on an existing Check Point firewall, minimum idle percentages for the Firewall Worker cores are provided along with the same recommendations. There are always exceptions to the figures listed here, but in the vast majority of cases they have served me well as an initial starting point. Note that on open firewall hardware (such as a Dell or HP server), if the total number of cores exceeds the licensed number of cores, for purposes of CoreXL it will only "see" the licensed number of cores, and the remaining cores will be unusable. This behavior is covered in more detail in the upcoming "CoreXL Licensing" section.

Table 4: Recommended Core Allocations

Total # of Cores	Default SND/IRQ Cores	Default Firewall Worker cores	Minimum Idle%:Firewall Worker cores to add SND/ IRQ Cores	# of cores to reallocate to SND/IRQ if RX-DRP > 0.1%	Target Baseline Initial Configuration for new firewall
2	2	2	2/2 w/ CoreXL or 1/1 (CoreXL off)	2/2 w/ CoreXL or 1/1 (CoreXL off)	2/2 w/ CoreXL or 1/1 (CoreXL off)
4	1	3	40%	+1	2/2
6	2	4	35%	+1	3/3
8	2	6	35%	+1	3/5
12	2	10	30%	+2 or +3*	4/8 or 5/7*
16	2	14	25%	+2 or +4**	4/12 or 6/10**
20	2	18	25%	+2 or +4**	4/16 or 6/12**
24+	4	20	20%	+4 or +6***	6/18+***

* If 2 or more 10Gig+ interfaces are present and Firewall Worker aggregate idle is >45%, reallocate total of +3 cores to SND/IRQ
** If 2 or more 10Gig+ interfaces are present and Firewall Worker aggregate idle is >40%, reallocate total of +4 cores to SND/IRQ
*** If 4 or more 10Gig+ interfaces are present and Firewall Worker aggregate idle is >25% reallocate total of +6 cores to SND/IRQ.

If IPv6 is in use on the firewall, it must have its own dedicated worker cores separate from the IPv4 Firewall Worker cores. Keep the following guidelines in mind:

- There must be a minimum of two IPv6 Firewall Worker cores allocated if IPv6 is enabled on the firewall
- There cannot be more IPv6 Firewall Worker cores allocated than IPv4 Firewall Worker cores

Special Case: 2 Cores

Firewalls that have only 2 cores present, to some degree, are between a rock and a hard place when it comes to CoreXL. Use of 10Gbps interfaces (even if available) with a 2 core system is definitely not recommended. As shown in the table above, by default there are 2 cores allocated to Firewall Worker/INSPECT processing, and those same two cores are allocated to SND/IRQ processing as well when CoreXL is enabled. This lack of specialization in core functions will cause massive CPU fast cache thrashing as the two available cores switch back and forth from SND/IRQ functions to Firewall Worker/INSPECT functions. We have two possibilities available to us in this case:

- Default: CoreXL on, 2 SND/IRQ, 2 Firewall Workers
- Option: CoreXL off, 1 SND/IRQ, 1 Firewall Worker

It is not possible to leave CoreXL enabled yet reduce the number of Firewall Worker instances from 2 to 1 on a 2-core system. Your only choices on a 2-core system in regards to CoreXL are having CoreXL on or off (SecureXL is controlled separately). However if RX-DRP is >0.1% on any interfaces, and your firewall is configured with the default 2 SND/IRQ instances and 2 Firewall Worker/INSPECT instances, take some good performance and CPU utilization measurements, disable CoreXL using the `cpconfig` command, reboot the firewall, and measure performance again. When

CoreXL is disabled, all SND/IRQ processing is concentrated on Core 0, and a single Firewall Worker instance is placed on Core 1. In some environments this will provide a significant performance boost as the RX-DRP rate dives well below 0.1%, due to the massive increase in CPU fast cache hits on Core #0, since it is now specialized for SND/IRQ processing. However the clean delivery of packets may now throw a much higher load on the single remaining Firewall Worker instance, even though it has been relieved of the additional overhead of CoreXL. Contrary to what Check Point's documentation states, disabling CoreXL completely does not preclude the use of Medium Path processing (the Medium Path is discussed in Chapter 9).

If the RX-DRP percentage is below 0.1% on all interfaces, but the Firewall Worker core idle time is less than 50% during the firewall's busiest period, proceed to the SecureXL chapters to commence optimizations that will hopefully increase idle time on the Firewall Worker core before making any further CoreXL tuning attempts.

If RX-DRP is still in excess of 0.1% after disabling CoreXL, and SecureXL optimizations in later chapters have already been performed, this is one of the few situations where increasing the problematic interface's RX ring buffer size may be helpful, and is worth the potential trade-offs. Start by doubling the ring buffer size from its default of 256/512 on the problematic interface(s) using the clish command **set interface eth0 rx-ringsize X**. *Do not* blindly crank it to the maximum allowed value.

The goal is to tune the ring buffer size to be just big enough to handle the network load with an RX-DRP rate of <0.1% during the firewall's busiest period; arbitrarily cranking the buffer to maximum can actually cause additional overhead in the SND/IRQ core, and hurt overall throughput due to wild swings in jitter. If after increasing the ring buffer the RX-DRP rate is still >0.1%, double it again, and so on until the maximum is reached. If you reach the ring buffer maximum size for your NIC with an RX-DRP rate still greater than 0.1%, I regret to inform you that your firewall is not appropriately sized for your environment. You could try turning CoreXL back on after performing SecureXL tuning, but you are very likely to end up right back at the same conclusion: your firewall is oversubscribed for the network load it is being asked to process; time to get budgetary numbers in place for new firewall hardware. The Check Point `cpsizeme` tool can be quite helpful in determining how big of a firewall appliance you will need to purchase. See sk88160: The Check Point Performance Sizing Utility for more details.

Special Case: 4 Cores

By default a 4-core firewall has 1 core dedicated to SND/IRQ processing, and 3 cores allocated for Firewall Worker/INSPECT operations. Notice that cores 0 and 1 are performing different functions and will experience CPU fast cache thrashing "out of the box", while cores 2 and 3 are dedicated to Firewall Worker/INSPECT operations only and will run quite efficiently. This issue will be somewhat mitigated by the presence of L3 cache shared by all cores on newer CPU architectures (if present). Generally in this configuration the single core handling SND/IRQs will quickly become overwhelmed and begin accumulating RX-DRP's in excess of 0.1%, well before the idle percentage of the 3 Firewall Worker cores drops below 40%. The lack of sufficient processing resources on core 0 essentially limits how much data the Firewall Worker cores can receive and keeps their idle percentage high; it will almost certainly be above the required minimum specified in the table above. If RX-DRP's on one or more interfaces is in excess of 0.1%, it is a no-brainer on a 4-core system to reduce the number of Firewall Worker instances from 3 to 2. Adjacent cores 0 and 1 now will run much more efficiently just handling SND/IRQ operations, and there are still 2 Firewall Worker cores available as well.

With a 2/2 split it is fairly unlikely that RX ring buffer sizes will need to be increased with a 4 core system (unless the firewall is seriously overloaded), but increasing the interface ring buffer size can be justified in some cases. If you decide to increase the ring buffer size on an interface, try doubling it first. Start by doubling the ring buffer size from its default of 256/512 on the problematic interface(s) using the clish command **set interface eth0 rx-ringsize X**. *Do not* blindly crank it to the maximum allowed value.

If after increasing the ring buffer the RX-DRP rate is still >0.1%, double it again, and continue until the maximum is reached. If you reach the ring buffer maximum size for your NIC, I regret to inform you that your firewall may not appropriately sized for your environment, and it is probably time to get budgetary numbers in place for new firewall hardware. The Check Point **cpsizeme** tool can be quite helpful in determining how big of a firewall appliance you will need to purchase. See sk88160: The Check Point Performance Sizing Utility for more details.

If the idle percentage of the remaining Firewall Worker cores during the firewall's busiest period is still less than 50%, head to the SecureXL chapters for optimization steps to get that idle percentage up.

6-12 Cores Recommendations

Systems in this range by default have 2 SND/IRQ instances, with the remaining cores allocated as Firewall Worker instances. Unless there are 10Gbps interfaces present or numerous 1Gbps interfaces running at high sustained utilization (>90%), the default CoreXL settings will generally be sufficient. However if RX-DRP is over 0.1% on one or more interfaces, it is desirable to allocate more cores to SND/IRQ processing. In general it is not a good idea to increase RX ring buffers on a system with 6 or more cores; other tuning avenues will provide much better results.

It is desirable to have a single dedicated SND/IRQ core allocated to an individual 10Gbps or faster interface, if possible. In my experience, if a 10Gbps or faster interface has its own dedicated core for processing IRQs, it should be able to handle sustained throughput of at least 4-5 Gbps with an RX-DRP rate of less than the desired 0.1%. If after changing core allocation, `sim affinity -l` shows that one or more 10Gbps+ interfaces has its own dedicated SND/IRQ core to itself, but RX-DRPs since the change are still >0.1%, the interface(s) is/are a candidate for Multi-Queue (see Chapter 12). If after adding more SND/IRQ cores Firewall Worker core utilization becomes excessive, perform SecureXL tuning as specified in Chapter 9 before making any further CoreXL adjustments.

16-40 Cores Recommendations

By default systems with 16-20 cores have 2 cores allocated for SND/IRQ with the remainder assigned as Firewall Worker instances. Systems with 24 or more cores have 4 cores allocated for SND/IRQ, with the remainder assigned as Firewall Worker instances. Firewalls at this level pushing any significant amount of network traffic will almost always need more SND/IRQ cores allocated to obtain >0.1% RX-DRP, especially if numerous 10Gbps or faster interfaces are present. In general it is not a good idea to increase RX ring buffers on a system with 16 or more cores; other tuning avenues should provide much better results.

It is desirable to have a dedicated SND/IRQ core allocated to an individual 10Gbps or faster interface, if possible. In my experience, if a 10Gbps or faster interface has its own dedicated core for processing IRQs, it should be able to handle sustained throughput of at least 4-5 Gbps with an RX-DRP rate of less than the desired 0.1%. If after changing core allocation, **sim affinity -l** shows that one or more 10Gbps interfaces has its own dedicated SND/IRQ core, but RX-DRPs since the change are still >0.1%, the interface(s) is/are a candidate for Multi-Queue (see Chapter 12). If after adding more SND/IRQ cores Firewall Worker core utilization becomes excessive, perform SecureXL tuning as specified in Chapter 9 before making any further CoreXL adjustments.

Adjusting the Number of Firewall Worker Cores

The preferred method for adjusting the number of Firewall Worker cores (which directly impacts the number of SND/IRQ cores) is to run the **cpconfig** command from the CLI. Select the CoreXL menu selection and enter the number of desired Firewall Worker cores. Any cores not allocated as a Firewall Worker core will automatically be configured as a SND/IRQ core. The highest-numbered CPU cores will be automatically allocated as Firewall Worker cores, while the lowest-numbered CPU cores will be allocated as SND/IRQ cores. Here is an example on an 8-core firewall:

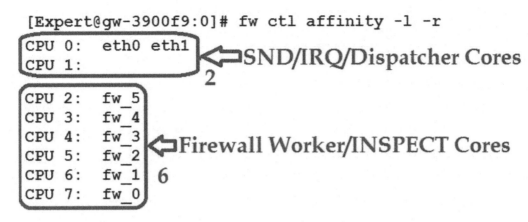

Figure 7-8: Viewing SND/IRQ & Firewall Worker Core Allocations

A reboot of the firewall will be required for any core allocation changes to take effect. If you have a firewall cluster, you must treat changing the core allocations the same way you would a version upgrade; do one member at a time, test under the new allocation, then change the other member's CoreXL allocation as shown here in **cpconfig**:

```
Configuring Check Point CoreXL...
====================================


CoreXL is currently enabled
       with 6 IPv4 firewall instances.

(1)  Change the number of firewall instances
(2)  Disable Check Point CoreXL

(3)  Exit
Enter your choice (1-3) : 1

This machine has 8 CPUs.

How many IPv4 firewall instances would
     you like to enable (2 to 8) [6] ?
```

Figure 7-9: Changing Firewall Worker Core Allocations with *cpconfig*

However on some systems there is an easier way. In the firewall's Gaia web interface, under Network Management...Performance Optimization the following screen *may* be available:

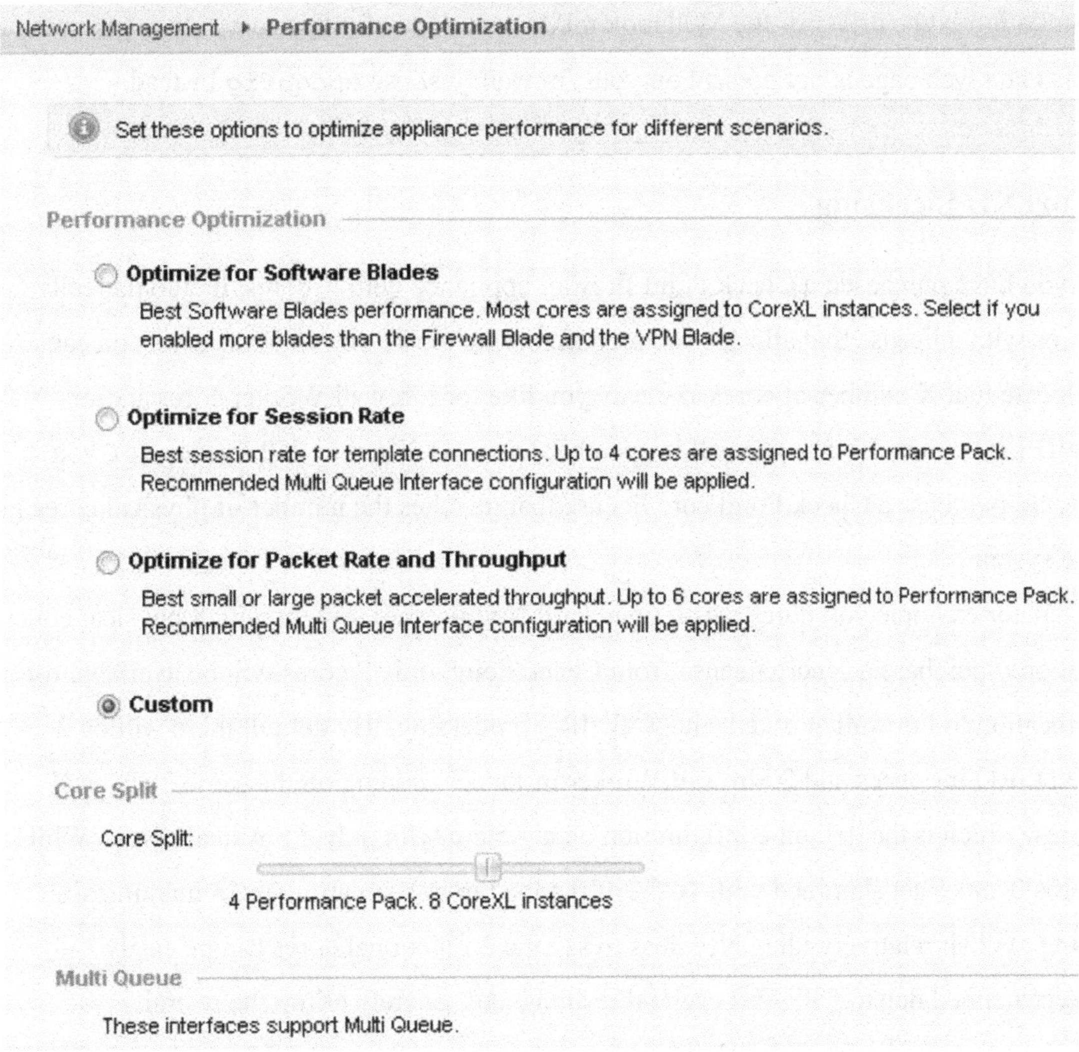

Network Management ▸ **Performance Optimization**

ⓘ Set these options to optimize appliance performance for different scenarios.

Performance Optimization

○ **Optimize for Software Blades**

Best Software Blades performance. Most cores are assigned to CoreXL instances. Select if you
enabled more blades than the Firewall Blade and the VPN Blade.

○ **Optimize for Session Rate**

Best session rate for template connections. Up to 4 cores are assigned to Performance Pack.
Recommended Multi Queue Interface configuration will be applied.

○ **Optimize for Packet Rate and Throughput**

Best small or large packet accelerated throughput. Up to 6 cores are assigned to Performance Pack.
Recommended Multi Queue Interface configuration will be applied.

◉ **Custom**

Core Split

Core Split:

4 Performance Pack. 8 CoreXL instances

Multi Queue

These interfaces support Multi Queue.

Figure 7-10: Changing Core Allocations via Gaia Web Interface

The slider can be used to adjust the number of Firewall Worker cores (which are
called CoreXL instances here; SND/IRQ cores are called "Performance Pack" on this
screen), and it will even show you the resulting number of SNQ/IRQ cores as well based
on the change! Unfortunately this screen may not be available on all firewall models;
your firewall must have at least six cores *and* must have at least one interface using

Intel's igb/ixgbe driver or the Mellanox mlx5_core driver for this screen to be present. If this Gaia web page is not present on your firewall, just use **cpconfig** instead.

CoreXL Licensing

If you have purchased a Check Point firewall appliance with X cores, it automatically ships with a license that allows you to configure up to X Firewall Workers. You can allocate that X number of cores any way you like for Firewall Worker cores and/or SND/IRQ cores. If your firewall is open hardware (Dell server, HP server, etc), you should purchase a Check Point core license that matches the number of physical cores in the system.

If for example you purchase an open hardware firewall system with 8 physical cores, but only purchase a 2-core license from Check Point, only 2 cores will be available for allocation to Firewall Workers and SND/IRQ processing. By default there will be 2 SND/IRQ instances and 2 Firewall Worker instances running on the same 2 physical cores, which is the default configuration on a system with only 2 physical cores. While cores 0 and 1 get slammed with 100% of the load in this situation, the remaining six cores will sit relatively idle. Needless to say the 2 functional cores can be easily overwhelmed due to CPU fast cache thrashing, and severely crimp the overall performance of the firewall. How do we see how many cores the firewall is licensed for? Run the command **fw ctl get int fwlic_num_of_allowed_cores**. Sample output is provided for an 8-core system that is fully licensed:

```
[Expert@fwr8010:0]# fw ctl get int fwlic_num_of_allowed_cores
fwlic_num_of_allowed_cores = 8
```

Figure 7-11: Checking CoreXL Licensing Status

You can also run `cplic print`. For open firewall hardware licenses look for "CPSG-C-XX-U" in the output; XX represents the number of cores your firewall is licensed for:

```
[Expert@firewall:0]# cplic print
Host                Expiration   Features
     .2.251         16Apr2015    CPSG-C-8-U CPSB-FW CPSB-VPN
 CPSB-IPSA CPSB-DLP CPSB-SSLVPN-U CPSB-IA CPSB-ADNC CPSG
-VSX-25S CPSB-SWB CPSB-IPS CPSB-AV CPSB-URLF CPSB-ASPM C
PSB-APCL CPSB-ABOT-L CK-
```

Figure 7-12: Example Open Hardware Firewall Licensed for 8 Cores

For most Check Point appliances you will see: CPAP-SGXXXX, where XXXX represents the model number which has a known number of cores:

```
[Expert@firewall]# cplic print
Host                Expiration   Features
     .48.10         never        CPAP-SG460X CPSB-FW CPSM-C-2
CPSB-VPN CPSB-NPM CPSB-LOGS CPSB-IA CPSB-SSLVPN-5 CPSB-ADN
C CPSB-ASPM CPSB-IPS-S1 CPSB-URLF CPSB-APCL-S1 CPSB-AV CK-
```

Figure 7-13: Example Check Point 4600 Appliance Licensed for 2 Cores

On a live firewall you can execute the `grep -c ^processor /proc/cpuinfo` command to see how may total cores are present. But what if you are looking to purchase a new Check Point firewall appliance? How can you find out how many cores it has? Check Point does not publish hardware specifications for their appliances, but well-known Check Point expert Tobias Lachmann compiled a list of user-reported core specifications for all of Check Point's firewall appliance models. While Tobias no longer maintains this list, Oliver Fink has taken it over at this URL:

https://lwf.fink.sh/category/security

The Trial License "Core Crunch"

This issue can be summed up quite succinctly with just one fateful screenshot:

```
[Expert@fw:0]# fw ctl affinity -l -r
CPU 0:   fw_3
CPU 1:   eth0 eth1
         fw_2            ???
CPU 2:   fw_1 fw_5
CPU 3:   fw_0 fw_4
All:     rtmd iwd vpnd cpstat_monitor fwm fgd50 mpdaemon rad ir
The current license permits the use of CPUs 0, 1, 2, 3 only.
```

Figure 7-14: Example Showing Effects of a Licensing "Core Crunch"

What the...? We can see that there are 4 processing cores total yet there are six Firewall Workers splattered all over the place. But how did it get this way? Some further investigation utilizing commands we covered earlier can help:

```
[Expert@fw:0]# grep -c ^processor /proc/cpuinfo
8

[Expert@fw:0]# fw ctl get int fwlic_num_of_allowed_cores
fwlic_num_of_allowed_cores = 4
```

Figure 7-15: Diagnosing a Licensing "Core Crunch"

Oops. This situation can occur on an open hardware firewall, which has more physical cores than permanently licensed cores. When this example firewall was first configured, it was using the built-in 15-day Trial Period license which permits an unlimited number of cores to be employed by CoreXL. Because there were 8 total cores present, the default allocation of 2 SND/IRQ cores and 6 Firewall Worker cores was initially set under the trial license. However once the permanent license for only 4 cores was applied and the firewall rebooted, there were still 2 SND/IRQ and 6 Firewall Worker cores allocated, and they all got "crunched" onto the 4 allowed cores as shown in the command output above. The SND/IRQ and Firewall Worker functions are tripping all over each other, and in some cases separate Firewall Workers are fighting each other for the same core! Needless to say the CPU fast caches will be getting mercilessly thrashed and overall firewall performance will be absolutely dismal.

To correct this particular situation described in our example: run **cpconfig,** allocate 3 Firewall Worker cores, and then reboot the firewall. However even after performing this step, as you might suspect the remaining 4 unlicensed cores will do practically nothing, while the 4 licensed ones are forced to carry the entire traffic load; core licensing limits *are* actively enforced by the Check Point code. This situation should never occur on a Check Point firewall appliance unless the wrong license is applied, as the license bundled with the appliance will always permit the same number of cores as actual physical cores.

CoreXL Firewall Worker Load Distribution

Run **fw ctl multik stat**. This shows the Firewall Worker cores and how many connections are being processed by each in the **Connections** column, along with **Peak** values. The connection numbers should be about the same for all Firewall Worker cores. In the next chapter we discuss a situation where the lead (lowest-numbered) Firewall Worker core on an R77.30 firewall could show abnormally high load compared to the other Firewall Worker cores, due to concentration of IPSec VPN operations on that core.

However there is one other situation that can cause a radical imbalance of processing
load between the Firewall Worker cores as seen here:

```
[Expert@firewall:0]# fw ctl multik stat
ID | Active  | CPU   | Connections | Peak

 0 | Yes     | 7     |         171 |       123
 1 | Yes     | 6     |          73 |       124
 2 | Yes     | 5     |         337 |       429
 3 | Yes     | 4     |          74 |        95
 4 | Yes     | 3     |       15110 |     17647
 5 | Yes     | 2     |          85 |       121
[Expert@firewall:0]#
```

Figure 7-16: Port Scans Causing Unbalanced Firewall Worker Core Utilization

In Chapter 4 an example was presented of how the firewall's connection table could
reach exhaustion: An auditor or penetration tester located on the inside of the network
running a port-scanning tool (like **nmap** or Nessus) is making thousands of connection
requests per second through the firewall. Almost all port-scanning traffic originated
from the Internet is dropped by the firewall, and thus never consumes an excessive
number of connection table slots. However when the scan is launched from inside the
trusted network, most of that traffic is probably going to be allowed, and thus the
connections table can rapidly fill up. However there is another effect that can occur in
this scenario when CoreXL is enabled: the vast majority of the scanning traffic can
become concentrated on a single Firewall Worker core, and not be distributed evenly.
How can this happen?

Suppose the auditor's port scan is targeting one system located in a DMZ from a
single inside workstation. The auditor begins sending thousands of connection requests
from the auditor's workstation to the IP address of the targeted server; all traffic is
sourced from one IP address and targeted against one destination IP address. On an

R77.30 firewall by default, when a SND/IRQ core receives a new connection request and needs to select an eligible Firewall Worker core to handle it, the SND/IRQ core runs a simple hash calculation involving only the source IP address and destination IP address of the new connection. Because there are thousands of connections going between the same two IP addresses, the SND/IRQ will always select the same Firewall Worker core for all the scanning connection attempts. This can severely degrade performance on the unlucky Firewall Worker core selected to handle this onslaught of connection requests arriving at LAN speeds.

The Dynamic Dispatcher (R77.30+)

R77.30 added the option to substantially improve Firewall Worker core load distribution via the Dynamic Dispatcher feature. This new Firewall Worker core load-balancing feature is disabled by default in R77.30 but enabled by default on R80.10 gateway. Use the command `fw ctl multik dynamic_dispatching get_mode` to check the status of the Dynamic Dispatcher on R80.10+. On R77.30 gateway the command to check the Dynamic Dispatcher status is `fw ctl multik get_mode`.

Instead of using just a hash of the source and destination IP address (and optionally the destination port number as well via the `fwmultik_hash_use_dport` kernel variable) as described above, the Dynamic Dispatcher constantly measures the CPU load of all Firewall Worker cores and allocates new connections to the most lightly loaded Firewall Worker cores. Note that the Dynamic Dispatcher only balances load among the Firewall Worker cores; this feature does *not* balance load between the various SND/IRQ cores. There is a very slight performance overhead imposed on the SND/IRQ cores by enabling the Dynamic Dispatcher, as the load measurement and dynamic allocation of new connections performed by the SND/IRQ cores is more complex than the old hash method. Once enabled, the Dynamic Dispatcher function is always active and attempting to balance load among all the Firewall Worker cores, regardless of the overall utilization level on the firewall. Keep in mind that the Dynamic Dispatcher is limited in its ability to deal with a so-called "elephant flow", which consists of a single connection sending a very large amount data at high speeds. All packets associated with that elephant flow must be handled by the same Firewall Worker core, to avoid potential out-of-order packet delivery.

If planning to enable the Dynamic Dispatcher on R77.30, ensure that you have loaded the latest Generally Available (GA) Jumbo Hotfix Accumulator before attempting to enable the Dynamic Dispatcher. The initial Dynamic Dispatcher R77.30 code suffered from various issues such as the ones below that were rectified in the subsequent R77.30 Jumbo HFAs:

- sk108432: Issues with traffic passing through Security Gateway with CoreXL Dynamic Dispatcher enabled

- sk108856: R77.30 cluster member might go Down after disabling CoreXL Dynamic Dispatcher only on one member

- sk108894: Difficulties in connecting to untrusted sites when both HTTPS Inspection and CoreXL Dynamic Dispatcher are enabled

- sk106665: VoIP traffic, or traffic that uses reserved VoIP ports is dropped after enabling CoreXL Dynamic Dispatcher

Enabling the Dynamic Dispatcher on R77.30 after loading the latest GA Jumbo HFA is about as close to a no-brainer as it gets, and I have not personally witnessed any situation where enabling the Dynamic Dispatcher caused problems with the firewall or the applications traversing it. But interestingly enough, there appears to be a real-time mechanism to partially disable the Dynamic Dispatcher on a per-port basis with these kernel variables that can be set or queried via the **`fw ctl set/get`** commands:

- **`dynamic_dispatcher_bypass_add_port`**
- **`dynamic_dispatcher_bypass_ports_number`**
- **`dynamic_dispatcher_bypass_remove_port`**
- **`dynamic_dispatcher_bypass_show_ports`**

These kernel variables did not exist in the initial R77.30 code release but seem to have been added in one of the R77.30 Jumbo HFAs; they also exist in the R80.10 firewall code. Be warned however that these variables are undocumented and tampering with them is most definitely not supported. But if certain applications are proven to be incompatible with the Dynamic Dispatcher for some reason, it is worth a call to the Check Point TAC to inquire about this hidden feature rather than disabling the Dynamic Dispatcher completely.

For more information see: sk105261: CoreXL Dynamic Dispatcher in R77.30 / R80.10 and above.

Priority Queuing (R77.30+)

Priority Queuing ensures that critical firewall control traffic is processed first in situations when a Firewall Worker core is running at 100% utilization. Unless a Firewall Worker core is running at 100% utilization, Priority Queuing will not be active. On an

R77.30 gateway, the Dynamic Dispatcher and Priority Queuing were inseparable; you could not enable one without enabling the other and vice-versa. By default both features were disabled on an R77.30 gateway, and I wholeheartedly recommend enabling them both on R77.30 gateway as long as the latest GA Jumbo Hotfix Accumulator has been loaded. The easiest way to check if Priority Queuing has become active on a firewall due to high load is via the **cpview** tool:

```
|------------------------------------------------------------
| CPVIEW.Advanced.PrioQ
|------------------------------------------------------------
| Overview SysInfo Network CPU Software-blades Advanced
|------------------------------------------------------------
| CPU-Profiler Memory Network SecureXL ClusterXL CoreXL PrioQ S
|------------------------------------------------------------
| Overview Instances
|------------------------------------------------------------
| PrioQ General Information
|
| PrioQ enabled                          0
| Number of active queues                8
| Queue length limit                   512
| packet limit/conn                    128
|
```

Figure 7-17: Checking Priority Queuing Status with *cpview*

On R80.10+ gateway the two features can be enabled and disabled separately with slightly different commands; by default the Dynamic Dispatcher and Priority Queuing are enabled on R80.10+ gateway. I haven't seen any problems caused by Priority Queuing in the real world so I'd recommend leaving it enabled. If Priority Queuing is enabled, you have the exciting ability to view the top connections by CPU usage. Run **cpview** and select CPU...Top Connections to see the top individual connections by CPU consumption. For the latest information about the Priority Queues consult: sk105762 - Firewall Priority Queues R77.30 / R80.10 and above.

RX-DRP Revisited: Still Racking Them Up?

So hopefully by now you have adjusted the number of Firewall Workers via **cpconfig** (almost certainly creating more SND/IRQ cores in the process), and there are now plenty of CPU resources to service SoftIRQs from the various NICs. You may have even already reached our goal of at least 50% idle on all cores during the firewall's busiest period, or even enabled the Multi-Queue feature described in Chapter 12; when enabled Multi-Queue allows more than one SND/IRQ core to process interrupts from a single interface.

Suppose that all SND/IRQ cores now stay well above 50% idle at all times on your firewall. But you make a disturbing discovery: the RX-DRP counter is still incrementing on one or more interfaces! Even more shocking, the RX-DRP counters seem to be incrementing regardless of the time of day or utilization level of the firewall and surrounding network! How can this be?

Earlier in the "RX-DRP Analysis & Discussion" section of this chapter we defined an RX-DRP as:

The RX-DRP counter is incremented when the NIC driver is unable or unwilling to place a descriptor in the RX ring buffer pointing to the frame it just received from the NIC's hardware buffer.

We covered the "unable" part of the equation pretty thoroughly earlier in this chapter; a full RX ring buffer not getting emptied fast enough by SoftIRQ processing. Now it is time to talk about the "unwilling" part. Recall Stage 3 from "A Millisecond in the life of a frame":

Stage 3: The NIC kernel driver begins processing the hardware interrupt, retrieves the frame from the NIC's hardware buffer, and does various sanity checks on the frame. If the frame checks out, it places the frame into a reserved area in the host's RAM memory, called a "receive socket buffer".

You are probably suspecting that the so-called "sanity check" on the frame failed for some reason and RX-DRP got incremented as a result. Exactly what constitutes a "sanity check" in this context? You might guess that the packet itself was corrupt with a CRC or framing error, but no! That situation is reflected in the RX-ERR counter discussed in Chapter 2, not RX-DRP. There are two main causes for a frame sanity check failure leading to an RX-DRP: a frame was received carrying an unknown or undesired protocol type, or VLAN-tagged traffic is being received from the network in an inappropriate manner. Let's examine each of these in detail, and how we can determine if these situations are present in your network.

RX-DRP Culprit 1: Unknown or Undesired Protocol Type

In every Ethernet frame is a header field called "EtherType". This field specifies the OSI Layer 3 protocol that the Ethernet frame is carrying. A very common value for this header field is 0x0800, which indicates that the frame is carrying an Internet Protocol version 4 (IPv4) packet. Look at this excerpt from Stage 6 of "A Millisecond in the life of a frame":

Stage 6: At a later time, the CPU begins SoftIRQ processing and looks in the ring buffer. If a descriptor is present, the CPU retrieves the frame from the associated receive socket buffer, clears the descriptor referencing the frame in the ring buffer, *and sends the frame to all "registered receivers"*, which will either be the

SecureXL acceleration driver (if SecureXL is enabled) or the Check Point INSPECT driver (if SecureXL is disabled). If a **tcpdump** capture is currently running, libpcap will also be a *"registered receiver"* in that case, and receive a copy of the frame as well.

During hardware interrupt processing, the NIC driver will examine the EtherType field and verify there is a "registered receiver" present for the protocol specified in the frame header. *If there is not, the frame is discarded and RX-DRP is incremented.* Example: an Ethernet frame arrives with an EtherType of 0x86dd indicating the presence of IPv6 in the Ethernet frame. If IPv6 has not been enabled on the firewall (it is off by default), the frame will be discarded by the NIC driver and RX-DRP incremented. What other protocols are known to cause this effect in the real world? Let's take a look at a brief sampling of other possible rogue EtherTypes you may see, that is by no means complete:

- Appletalk (0x809b)
- IPX (0x8137 or 0x8138)
- Ethernet Flow Control (0x8808) if NIC flow control is disabled
- Jumbo Frames (0x8870) if the firewall is not configured to process jumbo frames

The dropping of these protocols for which there is no "registered receiver" does cause a very small amount of overhead on the firewall during hardware interrupt processing, but unless the number of frames discarded in this way exceeds 0.1% of all inbound packets, you probably shouldn't worry too much about it.

But how can we find out what these rogue protocols are, and more importantly figure out where they are coming from? Run this **tcpdump** command to show every frame not carrying IPv4 traffic or ARP traffic based on the EtherType header field:

```
tcpdump -c100 -eni (iface) not ether proto 0x0800 and not ether proto 0x0806
```

(You will probably see BPDU spanning-tree advertisements from your locally attached switch in the output which is OK; these use a wide variety of EtherTypes that can't be easily filtered out).

RX-DRP Culprit 2: Unexpected or Invalid VLAN Tags

The following three situations can also cause RX-DRP to increment on an interface:

1. The firewall's interface is not configured for 802.1q VLAN tagging (it is just using a directly assigned IP address with no subinterfaces), yet is receiving VLAN-tagged frames from the switch. The tagged frames will be discarded and RX-DRP incremented.

2. The firewall's interface is configured for 802.1q VLAN tagging via subinterfaces for a quantity of known VLAN tags; however it is also receiving tagged traffic referencing an unknown VLAN tag. These frames will be discarded and RX-DRP incremented.

3. The firewall's interface is configured for 802.1q VLAN tagging via subinterfaces for a quantity of known VLAN tags, however it is also receiving untagged traffic (possibly from the "native" VLAN) and the leading/untagged physical firewall interface has no IP address configuration set. These untagged frames will be discarded and RX-DRP incremented.

Needless to say these situations indicate a misconfigured network; VLAN traffic is not being properly pruned by the switch attached to the firewall. Using various invocations of **tcpdump** we can determine the EtherType of invalid frames that are present and where they are coming from.

If you suspect Situation #1 is present, run:

```
tcpdump -c100 -eni (iface) vlan
```

This will display all VLAN-tagged frames (which shouldn't be arriving in the first place), along with the source MAC address of the device that sent them to the firewall.

If you suspect Situation #2 is present, the **tcpdump** syntax is a little more complicated, due to a quirk with how **tcpdump** handles multiple **vlan** expressions. First off you need to determine the list of VLAN tags that the firewall is properly configured to receive on the problematic interface. This can easily be accomplished with the **ifconfig -a** command, or from the Gaia web interface. Let's suppose the valid VLAN tags for an interface are determined to be 4, 8, and 96. To view all other possible VLAN tags arriving inappropriately, you'd think this command would do the trick:

```
tcpdump -c 100 -eni (iface) vlan and not vlan 4 and not vlan 8 and not vlan 96
```

This will not work the way you expect due to the above-referenced quirk in how **tcpdump** handles multiple vlan expressions. The following however will work and show us traffic associated with all VLAN tags, except the known valid ones (4, 8, and 96 in our example):

```
tcpdump -c 100 -eni (iface) vlan and not "(ether[14:2]&0x0fff = 4 \
or ether[14:2]&0x0fff = 8 or ether[14:2]&0x0fff = 96)"
```

(Note the '\' at the end of line 1 of this command is a backslash and allows us to continue the same command on a new line)

This will display all frames carrying an unexpected VLAN tag (which shouldn't be arriving in the first place), along with the source MAC address of the device that sent it to the firewall.

If you suspect Situation #3 is present, run the following command which will show all untagged traffic (which shouldn't be arriving in the first place):

```
tcpdump -c 100 -eni (iface) not vlan
```

Once again the situations described in this last section really shouldn't have much of a performance impact on the firewall (unless the quantity of this rogue traffic is ridiculously excessive), but are included for the sake of completeness and to further illustrate why we don't necessarily expect RX-DRP to always be zero in most real-world environments.

CoreXL Tuning: Key Points

- CoreXL and SecureXL should both be enabled for maximum firewall performance.

- The number of Firewall Worker cores you choose to allocate is one of the most important firewall tuning decisions you will make.

- An interface RX-DRP rate of <0.1% (not necessarily zero) should be targeted for all firewall interfaces.

- Network interface ring buffer size should only be increased in very specific cases to avoid BufferBloat.

- Allocating core functions in pairs (adjacent cores) helps maximize CPU fast caching.

- On R80.10+ gateway, by default firewall processes may only execute on cores assigned as Firewall Worker cores; processes may not execute on the cores assigned to SND/IRQ functions, which significantly increases SND/IRQ CPU fast cache utilization and overall firewall performance.

- Default core allocations will almost always need to be changed in the real world on larger firewalls, especially if numerous 10Gbps+ interfaces are present.

- The Dynamic Dispatcher and Priority Queuing features are enabled by default starting in R80.10, and should both be enabled on an R77.30 firewall assuming the latest GA Jumbo HFA has been installed.

- The RX-DRP counter can be incremented due to a misconfigured surrounding network, typically involving improper reception of 802.1q VLAN-tagged traffic or unknown Layer 3 protocols.

CHAPTER 8
COREXL VPN OPTIMIZATION

There are two types of cryptography in this world: cryptography that will stop your kid sister from reading your files, and cryptography that will stop major governments from reading your files.

- Bruce Schneier

*Note: If IPSec VPNs are used extensively on your Check Point firewalls, the new performance-related VPN features of R80.10 provide an **extremely** strong case for upgrading your firewalls to R80.10 if they are still running R77.30 or earlier.*

Introduction

There are a special set of considerations for Virtual Private Network (VPN) performance in the context of CoreXL. Upgrading to R80.10+ firewall code resolves many of them, but the limitations imposed by R77.30 and earlier are still documented here for completeness.

If you do a substantial amount of work with site-to-site IPSec VPNs on Check Point firewalls, I cannot recommend strongly enough taking the time to read through the following SK in its entirety: sk104760: ATRG: **VPN Core**. A bit lengthy to be sure, and it only contains a few performance-oriented tidbits scattered throughout, but it is absolutely invaluable for obtaining a good understanding of how IPSec VPNs really work on a Check Point firewall. Also to view the latest VPN-related performance tips from Check Point, be sure to check out sk105119: Best Practices - VPN Performance.

R80.10: MultiCore IPSec VPN & Route-based VPNs

While the vast majority of network connections can be efficiently balanced across the available Firewall Worker cores (Run the `fw ctl multik stat` command and look at the `Connections` column to see this in action), there is one glaring exception on R77.30 gateway and earlier: IPSec VPN handling. By default on R77.30, all IPSec-based and SSL VPN-based encryption and decryption can only take place on the lowest-numbered Firewall Worker core (`fw_0`).

I'm pleased to report though that the single-core IPSec VPN limitation in R77.30 gateway has at long last been resolved in R80.10+. IPSec VPN traffic is now balanced across all Firewall Worker cores by default on R80.10+ gateway. The commands `vpn tu tlist` and `vpn tu mstats` can be used to monitor the state of this new capability. While it is technically possible to switch off this MultiCore IPSec feature by setting the kernel variable `enable_ipsec_multi_core` to zero on R80.10+, doing so is not supported as explicitly stated here: sk118097: **MultiCore** Support for **IPsec** VPN in R80.10 and above.

R80.10 gateway also now supports the use of route-based VPNs and CoreXL together. Rarely used in the real world due to this longstanding CoreXL limitation, route-based VPNs utilize VPN Tunnel Interfaces (VTIs) and IP routing to determine what candidate traffic is "interesting" in regards to a VPN tunnel and needs to be encrypted. The overwhelming majority of Check Point IPSec VPNs currently are "domain-based", which means the VPN domain (formerly called "encryption domain") settings on the topology of the VPN endpoints determine which candidate traffic is "interesting" and requires encryption.

Route-based VPNs provide incredible flexibility in utilizing dynamic routing protocols such as OSPF through VPN tunnels, exchanging routing information with remote VPN sites, and even being able to dynamically adapt to network failures by changing firewall routes to avoid congested or inoperable network links. There is one caveat to be aware of however, the QoS blade is still not supported if VTIs are in use on a firewall, see: sk34086: QoS support on Virtual Tunnel Interfaces (VTI). Note that this limitation only applies to the QoS blade, and not to Limit actions specified in an APCL/URLF policy layer.

MultiCore SSL VPN

On an R77.30 firewall, part of this single-core VPN processing burden can be relieved by enabling a feature called "MultiCore SSL". Once enabled this feature allows SSL-based VPNs to be processed on many different Firewall Worker cores. See sk101223: MultiCore Support for SSL in R77.20 and above for more information about how to enable this feature.

MultiCore SSL is enabled on an R80.10+ firewall by default.

Recommended VPN Algorithms for Best Performance

The following sections detail which VPN algorithm settings should be used to maximize IPSec VPN performance without sacrificing security. Please note that these recommendations are made to improve performance, not necessarily provide the highest security possible for your VPN tunnels.

Unless stated otherwise, these recommendations apply to both R77.30 and R80.10+ gateways.

3DES vs. AES & AES New Instructions (NI)

Regardless of the code version you are utilizing on your firewall, the Advanced Encryption Standard (AES) algorithm is much more computationally efficient than 3DES. Converting existing tunnels from using 3DES to some form of AES (utilizing AES-256 for Phase 1, and AES-128 for Phase 2 is common) can help significantly reduce the load on the single VPN Firewall Worker core in R77.30, and also optimize any VPN processing that may be occurring on the SND/IRQ cores in the SecureXL Accelerated Path.

The 3DES algorithm was hurriedly introduced when it became clear that the 56-bit DES algorithm no longer provided a reasonable level of security. 3DES was originally designed to run directly on hardware, and performs poorly when virtualized in software on commodity processors such as Intel/AMD. The AES algorithm however was designed from the beginning to run efficiently on commodity processors, and tends to be at least 2-3 times faster than 3DES in the real world.

Another option worth investigation is the Intel AES New Instructions (NI) processor extensions, that can offload AES operations from the main CPU and into specialized hardware that is a part of recent Intel server-class processor architectures. Many Check Point appliance models can support AES-NI acceleration; however they must be running the Gaia OS in 64-bit mode (which requires a minimum of 6GB RAM) to take advantage of this feature. Generally speaking appliance model numbers 5600 and higher support AES-NI, *except* the 12200 model and the obsolete Power-1 9000/11000 series. The 3100 and 3200 firewall appliance models also support AES-NI.

Open hardware firewall processors that support AES-NI can also take advantage of AES acceleration as well; most server-class processing architectures manufactured after 2010 include support for AES-NI. However some vendors disable AES-NI support by default in the server's BIOS (consult your open hardware vendor's documentation if this is the case). Once again open hardware firewalls must be using the Gaia OS in 64-bit mode (which requires a minimum of 6GB RAM) to take advantage of AES-NI. Making the conversion for all tunnels from 3DES to AES, when combined with AES-NI hardware support, can yield truly amazing VPN performance improvements.

To check if AES-NI is present on the firewall and being utilized, run the command **dmesg | grep AES**.

If AES-NI support is present you will see the following:

```
VPN-1: AES-NI is allowed on this machine.  Testing hardware support.
VPN-1: AES-NI is supported on this hardware
```

If AES-NI support is not available you will see this:

```
VPN-1: AES-NI is not supported on this hardware.
```

For AES-NI capability testing to execute, and the above messages to be generated at all, the IPSec VPN blade must be enabled on the firewall. *Verifying AES-NI support is active (if supported) will at minimum quadruple AES encryption/decryption speed*, so if supported and active it is well worth your while to convert existing VPN tunnels away from 3DES and toward AES. Check Point has a great write-up on the relative performance levels of different encryption and hashing algorithms: see sk73980: Relative speeds of algorithms for IPsec and SSL. In addition, this SK extolls the virtues of using AES over 3DES for improved performance: sk98950: Slow traffic speed (high latency) when transferring files over VPN tunnel with 3DES encryption.

IPSec VPN Algorithms & SecureXL

Depending on how much of your network traffic is eligible for the SecureXL Accelerated Path (discussed in Chapter 9), some IPSec VPN processing can be offloaded into SecureXL via the SND/IRQ cores. If SecureXL is enabled on your firewall and you'd like to check if this is occurring run **fwaccel stats**. Nonzero or rapidly incrementing values in the **Accelerated VPN Path** section of the output indicate that SecureXL acceleration of IPSec traffic is occurring as shown here:

```
[Expert@fw:0]# fwaccel stats
Name                     Value   Name                     Value
--------------------     -------  --------------------     ------


Accelerated Path
-----------------------------------------------------------------
accel packets              0     accel bytes                0
conns created            389     conns deleted            243
C total conns             15     C templates                0
C TCP conns               13     C delayed TCP conns        0
C non TCP conns            2     C delayed nonTCP con       0
conns from templates       0     temporary conns          131
nat conns                  0     dropped packets            0
dropped bytes              0     nat templates              0
port alloc templates       0     conns from nat tmpl        0
port alloc conns           0     conns auto expired         0

Accelerated VPN Path
-----------------------------------------------------------------
C crypt conns              0     enc bytes                  0
dec bytes                  0     ESP enc pkts               0
ESP enc err                0     ESP dec pkts               0
ESP dec err                0     ESP other err              0
AH enc pkts                0     AH enc err                 0
AH dec pkts                0     AH dec err                 0
AH other err               0     espudp enc pkts            0
espudp enc err             0     espudp dec pkts            0
espudp dec err             0     espudp other err           0
```

Figure 8-1: Viewing IPSec VPN Acceleration Statistics

If this offloading causes a problem with some complex VPN traffic (pretty rare these days) all VPN traffic offloading into the Accelerated Path can be disabled with the **sim vpn off** command.

While offloading of eligible IPSec VPN traffic onto the SND/IRQ cores can improve overall VPN performance, the following algorithms are not implemented in SecureXL and will preclude SecureXL acceleration of all IPSec VPN traffic utilizing them:

- SHA-384 hashing algorithm
- AES-GCM-128
- AES-GCM-256

While the Galois/Counter Mode (GCM) versions of the AES algorithms combine integrity and encryption into a single operation that requires less CPU (and is even able to be accelerated directly in hardware with AES-NI), all traffic subject to these two GCM-based algorithms will be ineligible for processing in the SecureXL Accelerated Path and be forced into the Firewall Path (F2F). To be clear, the generic versions of the AES-128 and AES-256 algorithms *are* potentially eligible for processing in the Accelerated Path where they can take advantage of AES-NI as well.

Diffie-Hellman (DH) groups 19 & 20 that utilize Elliptic Curve cryptography incur less CPU overhead than the lower DH group numbers and are preferred from a firewall performance perspective. Diffie-Hellman groups 1-18 utilize Modular Exponential (MODP) cryptography which is substantially less efficient, and arguably less secure. For further information consult: sk27054: Defining Advanced Diffie-Hellman Groups for IKE in Site-to-Site VPN.

Another possible performance limitation is the use of NAT Traversal (NAT-T) for IPSec VPN traffic. When active, NAT-T provides an extra level of encapsulation for IPSec traffic to avoid violations of the IPSec ESP packet's digital signature by an intervening NAT device. While the additional overhead of essentially double-encapsulating VPN traffic is well-known (and should certainly be avoided whenever possible), there is a much less obvious but nonetheless significant performance impact possible. Unless the VPN traffic encapsulated with NAT-T is handled by SecureXL in the Accelerated Path, the NAT-T function itself cannot take place inside the kernel of the firewall at all. IPSec traffic subject to NAT-T handled in the Firewall Path (F2F) must make a trip into the "Fourth Path" for special handling via the **vpnd** daemon; any such transition between kernel space and process space on the gateway has extra overhead involved. This additional overhead will incurred for every single VPN packet subject to NAT-T that is not accelerated by SecureXL; the "Fourth Path" is covered extensively in Chapter 10.

Usage of NAT-T is not common with site-to-site VPNs, but is quite prevalent in Remote Access VPNs that utilize IPSec instead of SSL/TLS as a transport. NAT-T was only partially supported for IPSec site-to-site VPNs in firewall version R77.30, but is now fully supported in version R80.10 (but not enabled by default); see the following SK if you need to enable it: sk32664: Check Point Security Gateway initiating an IKE negotiation over **NAT-T**.

Low MTUs and PMTUD

A sub-1500 Maximum Transmission Unit (MTU) somewhere in the intervening network path between two firewalls attempting an IPSec VPN tunnel can wreak absolute havoc on VPN performance, because IP packet fragmentation cannot be performed on digitally signed IPSec traffic. The classic symptom: VPN performance for applications that frequently use maximum-size packets (such as file transfers & drive shares) is severely degraded; but small packets (like ping) work just fine through the VPN. The same large-packet protocols perform very well when being sent cleartext via the exact same network path.

If both sides of the VPN tunnel are a Check Point firewall, the recommended solution is to enable the "Permanent Tunnels" feature in the settings of the relevant VPN Community object for both firewalls. Doing so will cause the firewalls to perform tunnel testing with a Path Maximum Transmission Unit Discovery (PMTUD) probe upon initialization of the VPN to help determine if a low MTU value is present in the network path. If there is a low MTU present, both firewalls will reduce the size of their IPSec packets just enough to make them fit under the low MTU to keep large-packet performance from being impacted. Another frequently overlooked feature of Permanent Tunnels is the ability to have an Email or SNMP trap automatically sent upon tunnel failure; see sk25941: Configuring 'Mail Alerts' using **'internal_sendmail'** command:

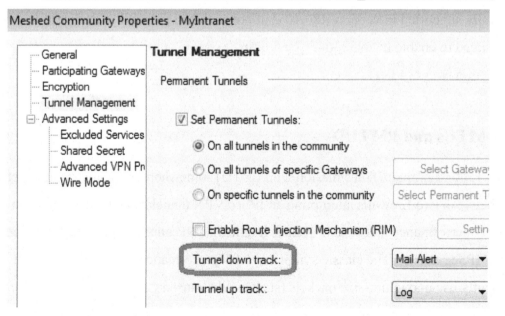

Figure 8-2: Notification Alert Options for VPN Tunnel Failures

If the Low MTU issue is seen in an interoperable VPN with a non-Check Point VPN peer, the Permanent Tunnels feature cannot be employed since it is proprietary to Check Point firewalls only. There are two options to rectify this interoperability situation:

- Enable and force IKEv2 on both ends; IKEv2 includes a built-in PMTUD mechanism.
- Enable TCP MSS Clamping: sk61221: How to control of the Maximum Segment Size (MSS) of TCP SYN and TCP SYN-ACK packets on Security Gateway. If SecureXL is enabled, the firewall must be running R77.20+ for clamping to work properly; see the following: sk101219: New VPN features in R77.20. Note that after upgrading the firewall to R80.10+ code, the behavior of MSS Clamping will change slightly and may require some adjustment to operate as expected; see the CheckMates thread called "R80.10 gateway, can't set sim_clamp_vpn_mss" accessible at this link: https://community.checkpoint.com/thread/6148 for the latest updates.

R77.30 Gateway IPSec VPN Performance Limitations

Note: This section does not apply to R80.10+ firewalls.

As mentioned earlier, on an R77.30 firewall, all IPsec-based encryption and decryption can take place only on the lowest-numbered Firewall Worker core (**fw_0**) by default:

```
[Expert@firewall:0]# fw ctl affinity -l
Mgmt: CPU 0
fw_0  CPU 7
fw_1: CPU 6
fw_2: CPU 5
fw_3: CPU 4
fw_4: CPU 3
fw_5: CPU 2
[Expert@firewall:0]#
```

Figure 8-3: Determining CPU Number of Lead Firewall Worker Core

As a result of this limitation, if there is a heavy amount of IPSec VPN-related traffic terminating on an R77.30 firewall, you may notice that the lead Firewall Worker core is showing very high utilization, thus crimping the VPN performance of the firewall. In addition to its IPSec VPN duties, the lead Firewall Worker core on R77.30 is also exclusively responsible for inspection of all VoIP protocols passing through the firewall, such as H.323/SIP/MGCP/SCCP. If there is a great deal of VoIP and VPN traffic passing through an R77.30 firewall, the lead Firewall Worker core will get very busy, and you will most definitely want to adhere to as many of the previously discussed CoreXL VPN optimization recommendations as possible.

If the single lead R77.30 Firewall Worker core automatically designated to handle all IPSec encryption and decryption is still experiencing an unacceptable level of utilization (less than 50% idle), even though AES encryption is in use and AES-NI support has been verified (or determined to not be possible on your firewall hardware), there is one more thing that we can do. The lead Firewall Worker core is not only responsible for all IPSec VPN operations, but by default it is also acting as a generic Firewall Worker core, handling its share of Medium Path and Firewall Path processing. You can verify this with the **fw ctl multik stat** command, and see the hundreds or thousands of connections the lead Firewall Worker core is processing in addition to its substantial IPSec duties:

```
[Expert@firewall:0]# fw ctl multik stat
ID | Active  | CPU     | Connections | Peak
-------------------------------------------------
 0 | Yes     | 7       |        2101 |     3153
 1 | Yes     | 6       |          73 |      124
 2 | Yes     | 5       |         337 |      429
 3 | Yes     | 4       |          74 |       95
 4 | Yes     | 3       |         110 |      147
 5 | Yes     | 2       |          85 |      121
[Expert@firewall:0]#
```

Figure 8-4: Unbalanced Distribution of Firewall Worker Core Load on R77.30

But what if **fw ctl multik stat** shows that practically all the traffic passing through an R77.30 gateway is being handled by the lowest-numbered Firewall Worker core, yet that firewall is not even a member of any VPN Communities and has no site-to-site VPNs configured for it at all? Needless to say this situation will cause truly abhorrent overall firewall performance on an R77.30 gateway and is a result of the situation described in this SK: sk117435: CoreXL FW Instance #0 is processing most of the traffic when VPN blade was enabled, but VPN encryption domain was not defined.

However assuming we do have one or more site-to-site VPNs configured on our firewall, there is a kernel variable called **fwmultik_dispatch_skip_global** that, when changed from its default of 0 to a value of 1 on R77.30 firewall, will instruct the IPSec Firewall Worker core to stop acting as a "generic" Firewall Worker core and to focus exclusively on IPSec operations, and nothing else. Needless to say this can dramatically reduce the overall utilization of the lead Firewall Worker core handling all IPSec operations, and free up CPU resources for timelier IPSec VPN processing.

This new kernel variable was actually introduced in R77 as part of SMT/Hyperthreading (covered in Chapter 12), so the information about this kernel variable is located here: sk93000: SMT (HyperThreading) Feature Guide. Do NOT attempt to set this kernel variable "on the fly" with the `fw ctl set` command; doing so is not supported. This kernel variable must be set in the `fwkern.conf` file and the firewall rebooted for the change to take effect. Keep in mind though that you are essentially reducing the effective number of Firewall Worker cores by one, so the general recommendation is to only consider setting this variable if you have at least 6 Firewall Worker cores and the aggregate idle percentage of all Firewall Worker cores prior to the change is greater than 30% during the firewall's busiest period. You can verify the new behavior after the reboot by running `fw ctl multik stat` again and noting the lower connection count passing through the lead IPSec Firewall Worker core; the only connections it processes now will be associated with IPSec VPN tunnels (and VoIP as mentioned earlier).

Also be aware that if SecureXL is enabled on R77.30, the lead Firewall Worker core will attempt to offload VPN traffic processing from itself into the SecureXL Accelerated Path serviced by the SND/IRQ cores. Needless to say this offloading can also significantly reduce the load on the lead Firewall Worker core. SecureXL and its optimization that allows this offloading to occur whenever possible is covered in later chapters.

Special Case: CIFS/SMB Performance over VPN

The well-known CIFS/SMB (Common Internet File System/Server Message Block) protocol frequently experiences degraded performance in the context of a site-to-site or

Remote Access VPN, but probably not for the reason you think. Commonly used for mounting drive shares (among other functions) in Microsoft Windows networks, CIFS/SMB version 1 was originally intended and optimized for use in a low-latency LAN environment. Part of this optimization was the requirement that for every certain amount of data sent (called an Application Block Size which ranges between 4KBytes-64Kbytes), an acknowledgement must be received from the peer before any more data can be sent. Note that this peer acknowledgement requirement is part of CIFS/SMB itself, and completely unrelated to the underlying transport protocol such as TCP window sizes or ACKs. The Network File System (NFS) protocol was also originally designed to run across a LAN with assumed low latency.

While this performance limitation of CIFS/SMB version 1 is not directly related to the use of a VPN, the networks employed by a VPN such as the Internet tend to have significantly higher latency than LAN or private WAN connections. There could be an impressive 10Gbit of Internet bandwidth between two sites on the Internet, but if the latency is 100ms or greater, CIFS performance across the VPN (or even in the clear) will be dismal no matter what you do.

While there is really no firewall tuning we can perform to improve this situation, there is something you can do: Try to force the systems involved to utilize SMB version 2.1 or higher which supports pipelining; many very old Windows systems still default to SMBv1. While the peer acknowledgement requirement still exists in SMB version 2.1 and later, pipelining allows multiple Application Blocks to be in transit between the peers simultaneously instead of just one block at a time. Ensuring the use of SMB version 2.1 or higher can provide dramatic CIFS/SMB performance improvements across a VPN or any other network with high latency.

One last tip related to CIFS/SMB performance: watch out for this issue which was fixed in R80.10: <u>sk109582: High CPU utilization on Security Gateway during Anti-Virus scan of large files transferred over CIFS/SMB2</u>.

CoreXL Unsupported VPN Features

CoreXL is not supported with the "Traditional" VPN setup mode on either R77.30 or R80.10+. The default mode for setting up Check Point VPNs is "Simplified" VPN Mode, which is fully compatible with CoreXL. Simplified mode utilizes objects called VPN Communities, and the "VPN" column will be present in the Security Policy Rule Base. Traditional Mode uses the "Encrypt" and "Client Encrypt" actions in the security policy rule base to build tunnels, and the VPN column will be absent in the policy.

Fortunately the R77.30 SmartDashboard provides a wizard to convert Traditional VPN Policies to Simplified under the menu "Policy...Convert...to Simplified VPN". If you have a Traditional Mode VPN, you must convert it to Simplified or you will be stuck having to disable CoreXL on your R77.30 firewall; as a result 100% of all Firewall Worker operations will be crammed on a single overloaded core, regardless of how many physical cores the firewall has. *Also note that the wizard to convert Traditional VPN policies to Simplified mode is not present in R80+ management. If you are planning to convert your VPN policies from Traditional to Simplified using the wizard, do it **before** upgrading to R80+ management.*

CoreXL cannot be enabled at all if a route-based VPN is in use on an R77.30 firewall; use of IKEv2 with route-based VPNs on an R77.30 firewall is also not supported. Both these limitations were resolved on the firewall in release R80.10.

CoreXL VPN Optimization: Key Points

- If a significant amount of IPSec VPN traffic is being handled by a pre-R80.10 firewall, upgrading to R80.10+ is strongly recommended for performance and functionality reasons.

- IPSec VPN processing for all tunnels can only take place on one Firewall Worker core on an R77.30 firewall.

- R80.10+ firewalls support MultiCore IPSec and Route-based VPNs by default even when used in conjunction with CoreXL.

- MultiCore SSL can substantially increase Remote Access VPN performance and must be manually enabled on an R77.30 firewall.

- The 3DES encryption algorithm should be avoided due to performance reasons; use the Advanced Encryption Standard (AES) algorithm instead, particularly if your firewall hardware supports AES-NI.

- Intervening sub-1500 MTUs present between firewalls attempting to pass IPSec traffic can kill VPN performance.

- Early versions of the CIFS/SMB protocol suite are intolerant of high-latency networks, and will exhibit terrible performance when used in a VPN across the Internet.

- Numerous R77.30 VPN performance and functionality limitations can be eliminated by upgrading your firewall to version R80.10+.

CHAPTER 9
SECUREXL THROUGHPUT ACCELERATION

Speed is a great asset; but it's greater when it's combined with quickness - and there's a big difference.

- Ty Cobb

Background

SecureXL. Mention this term to an experienced Check Point Firewall administrator and you might just see a pained grimace cross their face. Inquiring further, you are likely to get several stories about how the SecureXL feature caused a problem during a firewall cutover or upgrade. The problem was with one of the dreaded "legacy" enterprise applications that are hyper-critical, but are so old that no one left in your organization fully understands it, or frankly, even wants to touch it. SecureXL does have a well-deserved reputation for causing obscure problems that can only be solved by disabling SecureXL. I've been there myself many times, and can vividly remember back to the numerous times I had to disable it in frustration after a bleary-eyed night of troubleshooting.

I'm here to tell you: give SecureXL another chance!

SecureXL has been *significantly* improved in the R77 and later releases, and is much less likely to break those legacy applications; they may not still be around at your organization anyway! You may have a longstanding organizational policy of always disabling SecureXL on all your firewalls. That policy needs to be revisited; not only for the efficient processing of security enforcement operations in the SND/IRQ & Firewall Worker cores, but for the ability of the firewall to dynamically shift SoftIRQ processing in response to sudden changes in volume and direction of network traffic. This dynamic ability is known as "automatic interface affinity", and requires SecureXL to be enabled. Remember our stated goal, which is the best solution for the vast majority of sites:

> *CoreXL enabled with a sufficient number of processing cores allocated to SND/IRQ, with automatic interface affinity such that the RX-DRP rate is below 0.1% on all interfaces. RX ring buffers for all interfaces are set to the default. SecureXL is enabled with automatic interface affinity for all interfaces. All CPUs show at least 50% idle during the firewall's busiest period.*

Of course there can always be situations where SecureXL simply cannot be enabled for one reason or another. *However new in R75 and later is the ability to selectively disable parts of SecureXL, without turning it off completely.* If you still want to disable SecureXL entirely, yet ensure somewhat efficient processing of most network traffic, you will have to go down the rabbit hole of manual interface affinities discussed in Appendix A. In my view, this is not a desirable path to start down because it introduces additional complexity in your configuration that another firewall administrator (or consultant) may trip over. However a more serious drawback is the loss of the firewall's ability to dynamically shift SoftIRQ processing resources in response to changes in network traffic. While manually assigning interface affinities may work well right now, architectural or traffic pattern changes in the network (sometimes that may occur without your knowledge) can run afoul of your manual interface affinity configuration and suddenly cause RX-DRP rates well in excess of the targeted 0.1%. It is far more desirable to leverage automatic interface affinity, and let the firewall dynamically adjust its SND/IRQ processing resources on the fly without your intervention.

Selectively Disabling SecureXL

In a lonely corner of your state of the art computer room, there stands a defiant and hulking Behemoth of a computer system that scoffs at the shiny new servers and networking equipment surrounding it. The Behemoth has been around for longer than anyone can remember, and your organization pays an absolute fortune in support costs to maintain it. The Behemoth hasn't been manufactured in at least a decade, but cannot be replaced because it runs legacy software that is critical to the functioning of your organization. The legacy software and its Behemoth host care not about silly things like networking standards and RFCs, and have forced you to completely disable SecureXL in order to make the legacy software work correctly through the firewall.

The following pages discuss the case for re-enabling SecureXL if it has been disabled on your firewall due to application compatibility issues. Not sure how the heck I missed such a useful tip when preparing the first edition of this book, but there is a technique that allows SecureXL to be selectively disabled for certain IP addresses in R77 and later: sk104468: How to disable SecureXL for specific IP addresses. It involves a **table.def** file change on the Security Management Server with an **f2f_addresses** directive that can be made active with a simple firewall policy push. All traffic matching the IP addresses specified in this directive will always be sent to the Medium/Firewall paths for processing. It is also possible to disable SecureXL acceleration by port number using this technique but this option is rarely used. Unbelievably useful in environments where

SecureXL and all its benefits has to be disabled just to accommodate that one pesky system or application!

Suppose the Behemoth's IP address is 192.168.6.66 and we wish to disable SecureXL acceleration for all traffic to and from that system. First off, we need to determine the correct **table.def** file to edit on the Security Management Server. This information can be obtained from sk98339 - Location of 'table.def' files on Security Management Server. Here is a handy summary for the currently supported versions, note that both the version of the SMS and the firewall version are significant in determining the correct filename:

Table 5: Location of Correct *table.def* File for *f2f_addresses* Directive

SMS Version	Firewall Version	File Name
R77.30 (Gaia)	R77.30	`$FWDIR/lib/table.def`
R77.30 (Windows)	R77.30	`%FWDIR%\lib\table.def`
R80/R80.10	R77.30	`/opt/CPR77CMP-R80/lib/table.def`
R80/R80.10	R80.10	`$FWDIR/lib/table.def`

Always consult the SK referenced above to ensure the correct filename has not been changed since this book was published, or for any other version combinations not listed. *Changes made to* **table.def** *files may not survive a Security Management Server (SMS) upgrade, so don't forget to document these changes and check them after an upgrade!*

We then add the **f2f_addresses** directive in the proper **table.def** file as follows, don't forget to include commas between IP addresses if you are adding more than one:

```
/*
 * The following tables force TCP and UDP connections to be
 * forwarded to the firewall according to their tuples.
 *
 * src              Source IP address
 * dst              Destination IP address
 * dport            Destination port
 */
/* tcp_f2f_ports = { <dport> }; */
/* udp_f2f_ports = { <dport> }; */
/* tcp_f2f_conns = { <src, dest, dport> }; */
/* udp_f2f_conns = { <src, dest, dport> }; */

f2f_addresses =
{
192.168.6.66
};

voip_codecs_length_tab = { <0;420>      , /* G.711 (PCMU) */
```

Figure 9-1: Configuring *f2f_addresses* to Selectively Disable SecureXL

Save and exit the file, then reinstall policy to the firewall. Once complete, run the command **fw tab -t f2f_addresses** on the firewall to verify that the SecureXL exclusion for the configured IP address(es) is active. The excluded IP address(es) will be presented in hexadecimal:

```
[Expert@fw:0]# fw tab -t f2f_addresses
localhost:
-------- f2f_addresses --------
static, id 245
c0a80642
```

Figure 9-2: Verifying a SecureXL Exclusion on the Firewall

One less thing for the Behemoth to silently gloat about at your expense...

Use the `fwaccel stat` command to check whether SecureXL is enabled on your firewall. When attempting to re-enable SecureXL and retest your organization's critical applications, keep these other commands at the ready; FYI "SIM" stands for "SecureXL Implementation Module":

`sim vpn on|off` – By default SecureXL attempts to process some VPN traffic in the Accelerated Path in order to increase VPN performance whenever possible. Unfortunately in some older releases doing so could break certain VPN functionality; in particular, traffic that was required to be NATed before being placed into a VPN tunnel (not common but sometimes necessary due to RFC1918 private addressing overlaps between the two sites) would sometimes not function correctly when SecureXL was enabled. Disabling SecureXL would resolve the problem. The `sim vpn off` command tells SecureXL to stop attempting acceleration of any VPN traffic, but still allows automatic interface affinity and all the other advantages of SecureXL. After running this command, SecureXL must be gracefully restarted with the `fwaccel off;fwaccel on` commands in order for it to take effect. To make this change permanent across firewall reboots, add the line `sim_is_vpn_disabled=1` to file `$PPKDIR/boot/modules/simkern.conf` on the firewall.

`sim feature pbrroute on` – If SecureXL was originally disabled on the firewall because the Gaia Policy-Based Routing (PBR) function was actively being utilized, PBR's prior incompatibility with SecureXL was rectified on R77.30 but is not enabled by default. The above command will enable the use of PBR with SecureXL on an R77.30 gateway. SecureXL on an R80.10+ firewall already supports the use of PBR by default. For more information see sk109741: Packets are not routed correctly when PBR is configured and SecureXL is enabled.

Check for Manual Interface Affinity

So armed with the knowledge of how to selectively disable SecureXL if needed, hopefully you've decided to give SecureXL another shot. Any manual interface affinity settings you may have configured when SecureXL was disabled will be ignored after SecureXL is re-enabled, so we need to do a bit of discovery in this area first.

If SecureXL is already enabled on your firewall, be sure to check for any manual interface affinities that were previously set using **sim affinity -s** by running the command **file $PPKDIR/boot/modules/sim_aff.conf**. If the command returns **No such file or directory**, there are no manual interface affinities set via SecureXL and the desirable automatic interface affinity function is enabled. However if the command returns **ASCII text**, manual interface affinities have been previously configured via the **sim affinity -s** command. Assuming SecureXL is currently enabled on your firewall, you *probably* want to enable automatic interface affinity with the **sim affinity -a** command (which removes the **sim_aff.conf** file mentioned above and immediately enables automatic interface affinity), but I'd strongly advise paying a visit to Appendix A first to understand the ramifications of doing so.

If SecureXL is currently disabled on your firewall, examine the file **$FWDIR/conf/fwaffinity.conf**. If the only non-commented line (designated with a '#' character) you see is **i default auto** or **n temain 1 0** as follows then there aren't any manual affinities:

```
[Expert@fw:0]# cat $FWDIR/conf/fwaffinity.conf
# Process / Interface Affinity Settings
# ---------------------------------------
#
# Each line shoud contain:
# 1. A type - 1 character. "i" for interface, "n" for
process name, "k" for kernel instance.
# 2. An ID - interface name, process name, or kernel i
nstance number.

#    a. For interfaces, you can also write "default", a
nd the setting would apply to any interface not
#       mentioned in the file.
# 3. The desired affinity. Either:
#    a. One or more CPU numbers.
#    b. "all" - all CPUs are eligible.
#    c. "ignore" - do nothing for this entry.
#    d. "auto" - use any free CPU. A free CPU is one th
at doesn't appear in any line in this file,
#       and doesn't run a worker thread.
#
n temain 1 0
       OR
i default auto
[Expert@fw:0]#
```

Figure 9-3: Checking for Manual Interface Affinities in the fwaffinity.conf File

If you see any other non-commented lines here, you will want to head to Appendix A
and determine why manual affinities were defined in your environment. SecureXL will
default to automatic interface affinity when re-enabled (assuming the
$PPKDIR/boot/modules/sim_aff.conf file does not exist) and this is definitely the
preferred behavior, because it dynamically allocates SND/IRQ CPU resources to ensure
timely processing of packets from the interface ring buffers. A good explanation of

SecureXL automatic interface affinity can be found here: sk63330: Explanation about 'sim affinity -c' , 'fwaffinity_used_cpus' , 'fw ctl affinity -l -v'.

Now that you've been convinced that SecureXL is desirable and necessary due to my artful skills of persuasion, we will go into a brief overview of SecureXL. What does it do and how can it help firewall performance? Next we will talk about how to optimize the performance of your firewall with SecureXL, such that the processor load on the Firewall Worker cores can be significantly reduced. SecureXL is sometimes called "Performance Pack" or the "fastpath" in official Check Point documentation.

SecureXL Introduction

SecureXL has two main but separate functions:

> **Throughput Acceleration** (a.k.a. Packet Acceleration): The ability to expend less CPU by performing some security processing via a highly optimized Accelerated Path, thus increasing the overall throughput capability of the firewall.

> **Session Rate Acceleration** (a.k.a. Connection Rate Acceleration): The use of "Accept Templates" to expend less CPU when deciding whether to allow a new connection to be established. This portion of SecureXL will be covered in Chapter 11.

In almost all Check Point firewall appliance models up to and including the entire 23000 series, SecureXL simply exists as a highly optimized software kernel driver called the Acceleration Layer (or Accelerated Path) that runs on all cores designated for SND/IRQ processing. The Firewall Worker cores handle more intensive security inspection functions in the Medium and Firewall Paths. We will cover all three kernel processing paths in this chapter.

SecureXL Throughput Acceleration and SecureXL Session Rate Acceleration are two separate functions, but get mistaken for each other all the time; when running commands like **fwaccel stats -s** it is very easy to get confused about which feature each counter refers to:

```
[Expert@firewall:0]# fwaccel stats -s
Accelerated conns/Total conns : ███████████████████
Accelerated pkts/Total pkts   : 3847076259/3991577672 (96%)
F2Fed pkts/Total pkts   : 142170995/3991577672 (3%)
PXL pkts/Total pkts   : 2330418/3991577672 (0%)
[Expert@firewall:0]#
```

Figure 9-4: Viewing SecureXL Acceleration Statistics with fwaccel stats -s

Only the lines containing the string **Total pkts** refer to packets handled by SecureXL Throughput Acceleration. The single line containing **Total conns** only refers to packets handled by SecureXL Session Rate Acceleration, which will not be covered until Chapter 11. Most of the commands we will use to query the status of SecureXL will always report information concerning both portions of SecureXL; it is very important not to look at the wrong output during your SecureXL tuning endeavors. While **fwaccel stats -s** provides useful acceleration packet counters showing total number of packets processed in the various processing paths, you can also view live throughput numbers for each of the three paths in expressed in packets per second (pps) and Mbps. Run **cpview** on the firewall then select Advanced...Network...Path:

```
|-----------------------------------------------------------------
| CPVIEW.Advanced.Network.Path
|-----------------------------------------------------------------
| Overview SysInfo Network CPU Software-blades Advanced
|-----------------------------------------------------------------
| CPU-Profiler Memory Network SecureXL ClusterXL CoreXL PrioQ Streamin
|-----------------------------------------------------------------
| Path Direction Size BOTH_FIN
|-----------------------------------------------------------------
| Path distribution summary (available when SecureXL is on):
|
| Totals    SXL Mbps   SXL pps   PXL Mbps   PXL pps   FW Mbps   FW pps
| TCP              0         0          0         0         0        0
| UDP              0         0          0         0         0        0
| Other            0         0          0         0         2    3,164
|
| Protocol  SXL Mbps   SXL pps   PXL Mbps   PXL pps   FW Mbps   FW pps
| Other:-1         0         0          0         0         2    3,164
|
```

Figure 9-5: Viewing Live SXL/PXL/F2F Statistics with *cpview*

In the real world, SecureXL Throughput Acceleration tends to yield the majority of performance gains that can be extracted from SecureXL tuning, and thus will be covered first. SecureXL Session Rate Acceleration can definitely yield some nice gains as well, especially with Security or NAT polices that are extremely large. SecureXL Session Rate Acceleration will be covered in Chapter 11.

Throughput Acceleration

In essence Throughput Acceleration allows "shortcutting" across the firewall (and thus using less CPU resources) for connections crossing the firewall. This does not in any way reduce the security of the firewall's inspection, and is simply a more efficient way to process certain traffic. Consider this diagram:

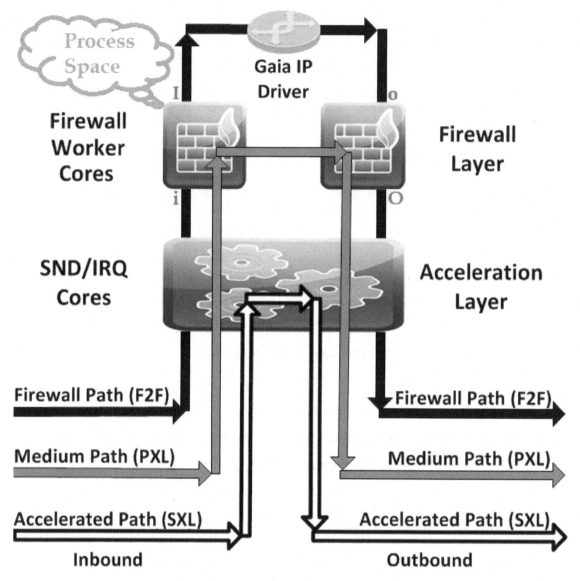

Figure 9-6: Firewall Traffic Processing Paths

When a packet arrives at the firewall and SecureXL is enabled, it arrives at the SecureXL Acceleration Layer (implemented on a SND/IRQ core), which tries to determine if it can process the packet itself with minimal processing required (in the

Accelerated Path), or if the packet needs to continue on to a Firewall Worker core for additional security processing via the Medium Path or Firewall Path. In some cases, packets must be sent into process space on the firewall for special handling; I have dubbed this performance-affecting situation the "Fourth Path" which will be covered in Chapter 10. Packets that can be handled exclusively by the Acceleration Layer will require much less CPU processing in order to be inspected and forwarded. Let's step through an example which does not assume that any SecureXL Session Rate Acceleration (also called "templating", which is covered in Chapter 11) is occurring.

1. An IP packet carrying a TCP segment with the SYN flag set arrives at the firewall. A new connection is attempting to start.

2. The packet is received by the SecureXL Acceleration Layer on a SND/IRQ core. This is a brand new connection, and as such it needs to be forwarded on to the Firewall Worker/INSPECT layer for full processing; however the Acceleration Layer does make a note in its state table about the properties of the packet, and on which interface it arrived.

3. The Firewall Worker/INSPECT driver receives the packet starting the new connection on the inbound side and evaluates it against the Security Policy. Let's suppose a rule is present matching the packet and the action is Accept; an evaluation is also performed against the NAT policy to determine if NAT needs to be applied to the packet.

4. The Firewall Worker/INSPECT driver forwards the packet to the Gaia IP routing driver for a forwarding decision.

5. The Gaia IP driver performs a routing table lookup and determines the packet's egress interface. The IP driver routes the packet towards that interface, and the packet is once again in the possession of the Firewall Worker/INSPECT driver on the outbound side.

6. The Firewall Worker/INSPECT driver performs any final processing required and releases the packet to the Acceleration Layer associated with the egress interface.

7. The SecureXL Acceleration Layer associated with the egress interface makes a note of where the packet was routed for egress, and simply forwards the packet to the egress network interface for transmission.

The second packet of the TCP three-way handshake (SYN-ACK) arrives at the firewall. The following occurs:

1. The SYN-ACK packet is received by the Acceleration Layer on an SND/IRQ core. It notes that the initial TCP SYN associated with this packet was seen earlier. If the connection is eligible for acceleration, after minimal security processing the packet is sent directly to the Acceleration Layer associated with the proper egress interface, thus skipping the Firewall Worker/INSPECT driver and Gaia IP routing completely.

2. The Acceleration Layer on the SND/IRQ core associated with the egress interface performs any final inspection operations and sends the packet to the egress interface for transmission.

All subsequent packets of this accelerated TCP connection will be handled solely by the Acceleration Layer and will not have to traverse the inbound Firewall Worker/INSPECT layer, the Gaia IP driver, or the outbound Firewall Worker/INSPECT layer. The optimized inspection operations required for this connection are performed exclusively by the Acceleration Layer (which runs on a SND/IRQ core in the kernel), thus saving valuable CPU processing time on the Firewall Worker cores. This is the essence of SecureXL Throughput Acceleration, and is quite desirable.

One important note: ICMP traffic (such as `ping`) and traffic to or from the firewall itself is never accelerated by SecureXL! To test for the presence of Throughput Acceleration you must use a stateful protocol such as TCP and the traffic must transit the firewall, the test traffic cannot be initiated from or sent to the firewall itself. Other protocols that can be accelerated by SecureXL are: UDP, PIM, GRE, and ESP. All other protocols are not eligible for Throughput Acceleration by SecureXL, and will always be handled by a Firewall Worker core in the Firewall Path. In addition, traffic received on a firewall interface that is set for Monitor Mode is completely ineligible for any acceleration by SecureXL as mentioned here: sk121792: Traffic coming through an interface configured in Monitor Mode is not fully accelerated by SecureXL.

Packet/Throughput Acceleration: The Three Kernel Paths

Properly tuning Packet/Throughput Acceleration tends to yield the "biggest bang for the buck" when it comes to the optimization effort involved in the real world. While Session Rate acceleration can help avoid computationally expensive rule base lookups at the start of the connection (such as at the start of a TCP 3-way handshake), Throughput Acceleration helps accelerate the packets associated with connections that actually carry data. Even small gains in performance tuning here add up into real, measurable improvement when thousands or millions of packets are involved.

Let's take a closer look at the **fwaccel stats -s** command output, and focus on the fields relevant to packet/throughput acceleration.

```
[Expert@firewall:0]# fwaccel stats -s
Accelerated conns/Total conns :
Accelerated pkts/Total pkts   : 9651006/71950385 (13%)
F2Fed pkts/Total pkts    : 4060369/71950385 (5%)
PXL pkts/Total pkts   : 58239010/71950385 (80%)
QXL pkts/Total pkts   : 0/71950385 (0%)
[Expert@firewall:0]#
```

Figure 9-7: Viewing SecureXL Acceleration Statistics with *fwaccel stats -s*

`Accelerated conns/Total conns`: Ignore this line for now; it is associated with SecureXL Session Acceleration which is covered in Chapter 11.

`Accelerated pkts/Total pkts`: This shows how many packets were able to be processed exclusively in the Accelerated Path via Throughput Acceleration discussed in the last section. The higher the percentage the better; generally shooting for a packet acceleration rate of 50% or higher is acceptable, 75% or better is ideal. Packets processed in this way were able to be "shortcutted" across the firewall with a minimum of processing and did not involve the Firewall Worker cores or Gaia IP routing at all. Due to this "shortcutting", packets handled by the Acceleration Layer will not show up in an `fw monitor` packet capture.

`F2Fed pkts/Total pkts`: This shows how many packets had to be forwarded to the Firewall Path on a Firewall Worker core and could not be accelerated at all. Generally we want this percentage to be as low as possible. Less than 20% is a reasonable target and less than 10% is ideal.

`PXL pkts/Total pkts`: This shows how many packets were not able to be completely handled by the Accelerated Path, but did not need to travel the full Firewall Path. PXL is known as the Medium Path, and is generally used to inspect traffic for IPS signatures but also involves the firewall features Application Control/URL Filtering, and the various Threat Prevention blades. Medium Path processing takes place on a Firewall Worker core. Contrary to what Check Point's documentation states, disabling CoreXL completely (sometimes desirable on a 2-core system as discussed in an earlier chapter) does not preclude use of the Medium Path.

`QXL pkts/Total pkts`: This line will only be displayed in version R77.10 and later. This counter measures packets subject to the QoS policy rulebase; to be clear this does not include Limit actions set in an Application Control/URL Filtering policy layer.

This counter and percentage will always be zero if the QoS feature is not enabled on the firewall. Let's look at sample `fwaccel stats -s` numbers from a live system:

```
[Expert@firewall:0]# fwaccel stats -s
Accelerated conns/Total conns :
Accelerated pkts/Total pkts   : 3847076259/3991577672 (96%)
F2Fed pkts/Total pkts    : 142170995/3991577672 (3%)
PXL pkts/Total pkts      : 2330418/3991577672 (0%)
[Expert@firewall:0]#
```

Figure 9-8: Viewing Heavy Use of Accelerated Path (SXL) with *fwaccel stats -s*

This output shows that from a packet acceleration perspective, 96% of the packets processed were exclusively handled by the Acceleration Layer, while only 3% traversed the Firewall Path. The Medium Path did not process even 1% of the packets. As stated earlier, if more than 75% of packets are traversing the Accelerated Path, there is very little to gain by further tuning efforts on the SecureXL Throughput Acceleration side of things. This is not typically what you will see on a system that has not been optimized, unless only the Firewall and VPN blades are active on the firewall and little else. Once again ignore the line containing "Total conns" for now; this is referring to Session Rate Acceleration. Let's look at another sample `fwaccel stats -s` output:

```
[Expert@firewall:0]# fwaccel stats -s
Accelerated conns/Total conns :
Accelerated pkts/Total pkts   : 9651006/71950385 (13%)
F2Fed pkts/Total pkts    : 4060369/71950385 (5%)
PXL pkts/Total pkts      : 58239010/71950385 (80%)
QXL pkts/Total pkts      : 0/71950385 (0%)
[Expert@firewall:0]#
```

Figure 9-9: Viewing Heavy Use of Medium Path (PXL) with *fwaccel stats -s*

This is much more typically what is seen in the real world. Notice that while 13% of packets took the Accelerated Path and 5% traversed the Firewall Path, a whopping 80% took the PXL path (also known as the Medium Path). Packets on the Medium Path are not completely handled by the Acceleration Layer, but do not take the complete Firewall Path either; however all Medium Path processing does take place on a Firewall Worker core. The features that tend to prevent traffic from taking the Accelerated Path and pull it into the Medium Path (PXL) are: IPS, Application Control/URL Filtering and the various Threat Prevention blades. *Note that any traffic subject to the HTTPS Inspection feature will always be handled in the Firewall Path (F2F); we will cover HTTPS Inspection tuning in Chapter 10.*

On almost all firewall hardware, SecureXL is implemented as a highly optimized kernel software driver executing on all SND/IRQ cores. However on 21000 series appliances equipped with an optional Security Acceleration Module [SAM] card, traffic processed in the SecureXL Accelerated Path is completely handled in the dedicated SAM hardware, without ever touching the main processor cores (or the system bus) at all. For example, if traffic eligible for SecureXL acceleration arrives on one NIC port of a 21000 SAM card and needs to be sent out another NIC port on the 21000 SAM card, *the embedded hardware in the SAM card itself performs all the necessary inspection and forwards it out the destination NIC port, without ever tapping any main CPU or system bus resources at all.* Near wire-speed, highly predictable forwarding latencies can be achieved in this scenario, *but only if SecureXL is enabled and tuned properly.* If utilizing a SAM card, the following SKs are required reading for proper optimization:

- sk107157: ATRG: Security Acceleration Module (SAM) card
- sk93036: Known Limitations of Security Acceleration Module (SAM) on 21000 Appliance
- sk94484: Accelerating traffic with the Security Acceleration Module (SAM) while also using non-accelerated blades.

Our optimization efforts in this chapter will focus on four primary objectives:

1. **Accelerated Path Optimization**: Attempt to process as much traffic as possible in the Accelerated Path. This is where we will see the most dramatic performance gains if done properly, so we will cover it first.

2. **Medium Path CPU Usage Optimization**: For traffic that takes the Medium Path, try to expend the minimum amount of CPU time necessary to process packets. Tuning here can definitely be beneficial, but the performance gains will not be as dramatic as moving traffic into the Accelerated Path.

3. **Firewall Path Optimization**: Discussion of what kind of traffic ends up in the Firewall Path, and what (if anything) we can do about it. Traffic processed in the Firewall Path consumes the most overhead of the three kernel paths, so we want to avoid it as much as possible.

4. **Awareness of the "Fourth Path"**: How trips up into process space on the firewall can impact performance. This concept is discussed in Chapter 10.

Just one clarification: As we proceed in the next section, you may get the impression that the Medium Path is "bad", as we make attempts to keep traffic from entering it whenever possible. Nothing could be further from the truth. If there is one path that we want to avoid, it is the Firewall Path (along with the possibility of process-based inspection in the Fourth Path), which consumes the most CPU processing resources on a Firewall Worker core. The Medium Path is a kind of compromise between the Firewall Path and the Accelerated Path that advanced firewall features will utilize for so-called "Deep Inspection" or "Active Streaming" of packets, without incurring the full overhead of the Firewall Path.

Accelerated Path Optimization

First off, traffic in the Medium Path has been designated as requiring additional inspection that the Acceleration Layer cannot completely provide. What features can cause traffic to be diverted to the Medium Path? Let's see:

- IPS (by FAR the most common reason)
- Anti-Bot
- Anti-Virus
- Threat Emulation
- Threat Extraction
- Application Control/URL Filtering

In Chapter 5 we covered optimizing your firewalls Network Access policy layers, which included APCL/URLF and Content Awareness. The great news is that a lot of necessary groundwork for optimizing the Threat Prevention (TP) features has already been accomplished based on the recommendations in Chapter 5. Properly setting up your firewall's network topology, ensuring the external interface(s) are properly defined, and optimization of Column Matching/Early Drop were all covered in Chapter 5. So if you've skipped ahead to this chapter with the intent of optimizing your Threat Prevention policies, I'd strongly recommend going back to Chapter 5 and ensuring the optimizations listed there have been accomplished first.

If none of these advanced features are enabled on your gateway, you may find that easily 90% of traffic is already taking the Accelerated Path! If you only have IPS enabled on your gateway, and none of the other TP features enabled, it is pretty clear which feature is causing the majority of traffic to take the Medium Path. But what if you have IPS and Application Control/URL Filtering in use? I can tell you right now that IPS is the most common reason that traffic is forced into at least the Medium Path. Even if you have the controversial IPS feature "Bypass under Load" enabled, and the bypass has been activated by heavy load on the firewall, all traffic subject to IPS inspection will still take the Medium Path. Traffic subject to IPS inspection will not suddenly become eligible for the Accelerated Path when the bypass becomes active.

Quickly Assessing IPS/Threat Prevention Performance Impact

WARNING: The commands listed in this section will disable some or all of the Threat Prevention (TP) features, potentially exposing your organization to attacks. Do not forget to turn these IPS/Threat Prevention features back on when you are finished!

This is one of those rare situations where we can actually get a preview of the potential performance gains that are possible with proper TP tuning. Try a little experiment: during your firewall's busiest period, in one terminal window run `cpview` then select "Advanced...Network...Path" to perform real-time monitoring of path selection by the firewall. In another terminal window run the `ips off` command and watch the percentages of traffic in each of the three paths start to change! If IPS was the only listed feature that was originally enabled, you should see a dramatic swing away from the Medium Path into the Accelerated Path, and a subsequent drop in CPU utilization on the Firewall Worker cores displayed in the output of `top`. If you have one or more of the other TP features or APCL/URLF enabled, the swing will probably still occur, but not be nearly as dramatic. This experiment should give you a good idea of how much traffic the IPS feature is pulling into the Medium and/or Firewall Paths. Don't forget to turn IPS back on with the `ips on` command when you are done!

If you are using some combination of the other Threat Prevention blades (Anti-Virus, Anti-Bot, Threat Emulation and/or Threat Extraction) we can perform a test similar to the one in the last paragraph to see how these blades impact path selection and firewall performance. Run `cpview` and select "Advanced...Network...Path", get a good look at the statistics being reported and overall CPU load, then run the command `fw amw unload` on the firewall. This command will disable all Threat Prevention blades except IPS, and you can immediately observe how much these Threat Prevention blades have impacted the firewall's path selection & CPU utilization similarly to what was observed with IPS. You can use the command `fw stat -b AMW` to verify the disabled state of the various Threat Prevention blades. Don't forget to turn Threat Prevention back on with the `fw amw fetch local` command!

An interesting experiment to be sure, but we had to turn off the IPS and/or Threat Prevention blades to see those big gains! How can we tune these features to not have such a big impact?

IPS: R77.30 vs. R80.10 Firewall

Before we proceed, we need to have a little chat about how IPS is related (or not) to Threat Prevention policies depending on the version of code on your firewall (not on the Security Management Server).

R80.10 and later gateways have the IPS function fully integrated into the main Threat Prevention policy layer. Instead of having to set the "IPS Protection Scope" and configure specific IPS exceptions, the Threat Prevention policy layer columns "Protected

Scope", "Source", and "Destination" can be used to explicitly specify which IPS profile should be applied to network traffic matching these columnar criteria. Exceptions can still be added to the Threat Prevention policy layer, but they can potentially apply to the entire Threat Prevention policy, not just to the IPS feature. Some items that were previously listed as IPS Protections under pre-R80 management are now separated into the "Inspection Settings" portion of the R80/R80.10 SmartConsole. Changes to these "Inspection Settings" values require a Network Access policy reinstallation to take effect because they have been separated from the Threat Prevention policy layer:

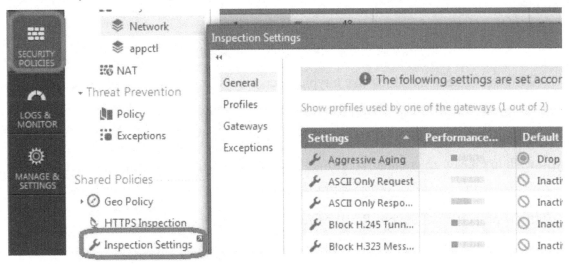

Figure 9-10: R80+ Management Inspection Settings

In the R80+ SmartConsole, IPS Profiles are no longer directly assigned to R80.10+ gateways on the firewall object; this action is performed in the Threat Prevention policy alongside all the other Threat Prevention blades. However for pre-R80 firewalls, IPS Profiles are assigned in a special IPS "rulebase" that becomes visible if you have at least one pre-R80.10 firewall defined with the IPS feature enabled:

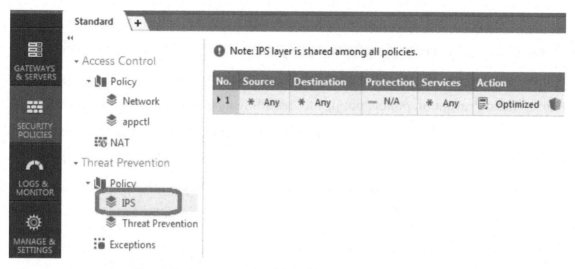

Figure 9-11: Special IPS "Policy" for pre-R80 Firewalls

While this screen may look like a typical security policy, you'll rapidly find that it is not once you start working with it. For example, the Source, Destination, Protection/Site, and Service fields cannot be edited at all for pre-R80 gateways! Should you wish to take more granular control of how IPS protections are applied to network traffic on an R77.30 gateway, you will be quite limited.

In the properties of the pre-R80.10 firewall object on the IPS screen, you can select "Protect internal networks only" or "Perform inspection on all IPS traffic". The former setting will only apply IPS protections against traffic that is heading to a non-External (i.e. Internal) interface of the gateway as defined in the gateway's topology. The latter setting will apply IPS Protections to all traffic regardless of where it is headed. Which direction the inspected connection was originally initiated (i.e. inbound or outbound) does not impact how this setting is applied. This setting will be discussed more extensively in the next section.

You can define IPS exceptions for a single IPS Profile or multiple profiles. With an IPS exception rule, traffic matched by Source, Destination, and/or Service can be excluded from all IPS enforcement or a subset of IPS enforcement. The subset could be a single protection or multiple protections. For pre-R80 gateways the IPS "policy" in the R80+ SmartConsole is really just a place to define which IPS Profile is assigned to a gateway, and to create IPS exceptions. R80.10 firewalls have their IPS settings consolidated in the much more flexible main Threat Prevention policy, along with all the other Threat Prevention features Anti-Virus, Anti-Bot, Threat Emulation & Threat Extraction.

There are three main ways to limit the amount of traffic that IPS inspection directs into the Medium (and possibly Firewall) Paths:

- IPS Protection Scope setting (pre-R80 gateways only)
- Signature Performance Impact Rankings
- Avoiding IPS Signatures known to disable acceleration

IPS Protection Scope Setting (pre-R80.10 Firewalls Only)

This is a pretty easy one. In the SmartDashboard, edit your firewall/cluster object and open the IPS screen:

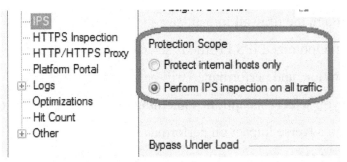

Figure 9-12: IPS Protection Scope Screen on an R77.30 Firewall Object

There are two settings under Protection Scope for pre-R80.10 firewalls:

Perform IPS Inspection on all Traffic – This is typically the default setting on an R77.30 gateway. All traffic regardless of direction has IPS inspection applied. This includes traffic passing from one internal network (like a DMZ) to another, as well as connections to or from External interfaces. "Internal" in this context means any interface defined as Internal on the firewall/cluster object's topology screen in the SmartDashboard:

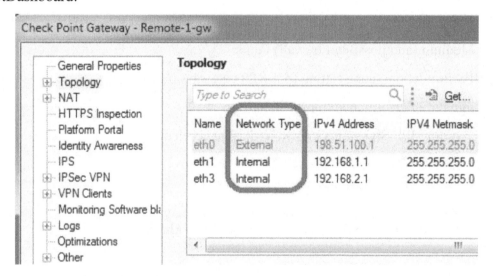

Figure 9-13: R77.30 Firewall Interface Topology Screen

This is the default setting for IPS Protection Scope; it will probably force almost all traffic passing through the firewall into at least the Medium Path unless the Default_Protection/Optimized IPS Profile is selected. Very little traffic will be subject to throughput acceleration, and performance will be negatively impacted. There is even a warning issued if you select this option; something to the effect of "Turning on this option may have an adverse impact on performance".

Protect Internal Hosts Only – When selected for an R77.30 gateway, IPS protections are only applied to packets traveling to a network defined as "Internal".

"Internal" in this context means any interface defined as Internal in the firewall/cluster object's topology anti-spoofing screen (and includes DMZs as well). This also includes traffic passing from one Internal network (like a DMZ) to any other Internal network.

It does not matter whether the connection was originally initiated from an External or Internal interface; any packet attempting to leave the firewall towards an Internal interface will have IPS protections applied. Traffic whose destination is an External interface (typically going to the Internet or perhaps a site-to-site VPN utilizing the Internet) will not have IPS protections applied with **Protect Internal Hosts Only** set.

From purely a security perspective, one could argue that **Perform IPS Inspection on all Traffic** is always the right setting for pre-R80.10 firewalls (it is the default after all!). Of course we want the IPS to prevent attacks against our internal and DMZ systems. But what about traffic leaving your network bound for a system on the Internet? What about traffic entering a VPN tunnel bound for a business partner or vendor across the Internet? Shouldn't your firewall ensure that possible attacks emanating from your internal network don't target your partners? One could assert that the remote parties should take steps to protect themselves, but try telling that to a key business partner whose network just got crushed by a worm or attack launched from inside of your own network! Also consider the positioning of the subject firewall in your network; the correct setting is likely to be different for a firewall deployed on the perimeter of your organization, as opposed to another firewall buried deep inside your internal network with no direct Internet access.

As with any topic in network security, it is a matter of trade-offs. As we all know, the answer to many security-related questions will very frequently begin with: "Well that depends...". This may frustrate upper management decision-makers, but ensures excellent job security prospects for security administrators. Leaving the default setting

Perform IPS Inspection on all Traffic enabled is pretty common in most environments on pre-R80.10 firewalls, however if your Firewall Worker cores are perpetually overloaded and you can't allocate any more Firewall Workers due to a shortage of cores, consider setting **Protect Internal Hosts only** for IPS inspection.

Signature Performance Impact Rankings

Regardless of firewall code version, all individual IPS Protections have their own individual Performance Impact ranking of Very Low, Low, Medium, High, or Critical. But what do these rankings mean in the context of the three kernel processing paths discussed so far? Based on my lab observations and real-world experience, I've determined the following:

- IPS Protections with a "Very Low" or "Low" Performance Impact are processed 100% in the Accelerated Path
- IPS Protections with a "Medium" Performance Impact are processed at least 90% in the Medium Path
- IPS Protections with a "High" Performance Impact appear to be processed about 50% in the Medium Path and about 50% in the Firewall Path (*Note that all imported SNORT IPS signatures are automatically assigned this ranking and are therefore ineligible for handling in the Accelerated Path*)
- IPS Protections with a "Critical" Performance Impact are processed 100% in the Firewall Path.

Needless to say active IPS Protections with a Performance Impact of Medium, High, or Critical can dramatically impact how much traffic can be processed in the Accelerated Path. The default IPS profile assigned to a firewall "out of the box" is a built-in profile called "Default_Protection" on an R77.30 or earlier SMS; the equivalent default on an R80+ SMS is called "Optimized". All signatures enabled in these profiles can be handled 100% in the Accelerated Path. In independent testing by NSS Labs, the Default_Protection/Optimized IPS profile was found to be approximately 86% effective in stopping attacks, while the other included IPS Profile "Recommended_Protection" (named "Strict" in R80+ management) stopped 99% of attacks. However the Recommended_Protection/Strict IPS profiles do enable numerous protections with Performance Impact rankings of Medium, High, and Critical.

Let's determine what IPS profile your firewall is using, so we can assess how much of each type of IPS Protection is present. On an R80+ SMS managing R77.30 or earlier firewalls, the IPS profile name assigned can be found in the SmartConsole by going to the Security Policies...Threat Prevention...Policy...IPS screen. From the IPS tab in the R77.30 SmartDashboard, select Gateways and you should see the IPS Profile in use by the firewall. Let's assume the assigned profile name is "MyProfile".

For R80.10+ firewalls being managed by an R80.10+ SMS, IPS optimizations are performed in the main Threat Prevention policy covered later in this chapter.

Go to the IPS Protections screen and click the top of the "Performance Impact" column to sort your view by this column, until you see a large number of signatures with Performance Impact "Critical". Now look at the column titled "MyProfile" and you will see the individual IPS Protection settings for the profile in use by the gateway. All IPS Signatures with a Performance Impact of "Critical" should be displayed first:

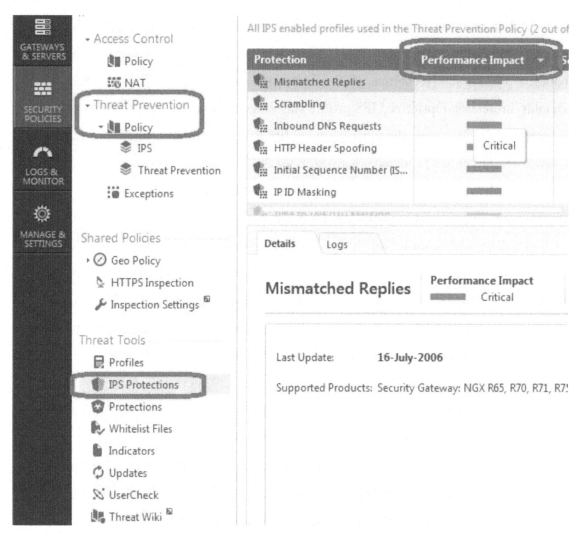

Figure 9-14: Sorting IPS Signatures by Performance Impact

For R77.30 SmartDashboard, this screen is accessed by selecting the IPS tab along the top of the screen, clicking "Protections", and sorting the list by "Performance Impact".

For any signature set for an action of Detect or Prevent for the firewall's profile, quickly evaluate the relevance of this signature to your environment; a signature with a

Confidence Level of only "Low" or "Medium" indicates it is much more likely to generate false positives, which can be a compelling reason to disable that particular signature. Treat signatures set for "Detect" instead of "Prevent" with extra prejudice. Surprisingly, having an IPS signature set to Detect actually consumes *more* CPU than having it set to Prevent. An action of "Prevent" immediately kills the offending packet and drops/stalls the rest of the connection if it is TCP-based. (Some IPS signatures actually perform a "Reject" by also sending a TCP RST to both endpoints of the connection – whether an IPS Protection invokes this reject action as opposed to just a drop action is not user-tunable) A setting of Detect just logs the finding and allows the connection to continue, thus consuming far more CPU as it continues to monitor the live connection looking for the same or additional threats.

Notice that you can double-click any IPS Protection and go to its Description tab to read more about the signature. Is it looking for an attack against an Oracle database, but the only database product used in your entire organization is Microsoft's SQL Server? Also consider the Severity rating if the IPS Protection in question: Is the performance impact Critical but the Severity of the attack Low or Medium? That should factor into your decision about whether having that signature enabled is worth the overhead incurred. You can directly right-click the Prevent/Detect action in the MyProfile column and select "Inactive" to disable the signature. Continue down the list until you reach the end of signatures designated with a Critical performance impact. As of this writing there were about 226 of these, so be patient.

After taking a break (and clicking File...Save if using the R77.30 SmartDashboard to ensure your work was saved), continue with all signatures ranked with a High performance impact. There will be about 500-600 of these, so once again, be patient. In my experience the best "bang for the buck" is obtained by evaluating just the Critical and

High impact signatures, and deactivating the ones you don't need to minimize the amount of traffic sent to the Medium and Firewall Paths, especially if the signature only has a Confidence Level of "Low" or "Medium". Remember that changing a signature action from Prevent to Detect does not save any CPU, and can actually cause a slightly higher load on the firewall's CPU. Setting an IPS signature to Inactive will of course reduce CPU load the most. You are more than welcome to continue this process with signatures rated as "Medium-High" and on down the line, but you will soon reach diminishing returns for your efforts, as the number of signatures to evaluate per performance rating category rapidly increases.

Avoiding IPS Signatures Known to Disable SecureXL

There are several signatures in particular that are known to force massive amounts of traffic into the Medium Path or even the Firewall Path in some cases:

- IP ID Masking/Fingerprint Scrambling
- Time to Live (TTL) Masking/Fingerprint Scrambling
- TCP SYN Attack Configuration
- ASCII Only Response Headers
- Small PMTU
- Network Quota (check out the "Rate Limiting" feature in Chapter 13 for a much more efficient way to enforce quotas)
- ClusterXL Load Sharing Sticky Decision Function (SDF), which only applies to Load Sharing Multicast ClusterXL deployments

Check the configuration of these signatures and SDF if applicable; you will almost certainly want to set these to Inactive, as they tend to disable SecureXL for all traffic subject to them to varying degrees.

Threat Prevention Policy Rule Optimization

The optimization procedure for the Threat Prevention policy (which specifies Anti-Virus, Anti-Bot, Threat Emulation, & Threat Extraction operations regardless of gateway version) is very similar to APCL/URLF policy optimization covered in Chapter 5. For R80.10+ firewalls being managed by an R80.10+ SMS, IPS is also controlled directly from the same Threat Prevention policy as all the other Threat Prevention blades, and provides many more useful avenues for IPS optimization. If your firewall is still running version R77.30 or earlier, your ability to improve IPS performance by limiting its enforcement to only certain traffic will be severely restricted.

R80.10+ firewalls are allowed to have more than one Threat Prevention policy layer active at the same time. If this is the case, all separate Threat Prevention policy layers are evaluated simultaneously, the first rule matching the traffic is selected in each layer, and then the most restrictive action based on the match(es) are performed. To be clear, the order of most restrictive action to least restrictive is: Prevent, Ask, Detect, and finally Inactive. Only one rule (the first one found) from each individual Threat Prevention policy layer can be matched.

Following are some general tips for constructing your Threat Prevention policies, but the real power tool for Threat Prevention policy optimization is the proper use of so-called "null" profiles which are covered in a later section. The general goal for Threat Prevention policy rule optimization is to only apply the specific Threat Prevention features where they are needed, which is typically for traffic crossing a network boundary into a more or less trusted area. Threat Prevention (TP) capabilities in general impose significant overhead on the firewall, and accidentally applying full Threat Prevention capabilities against network traffic crossing between two internal networks at multi-gigabit speed is undesirable for obvious reasons. In addition, proper Threat Prevention policy rule construction can ensure as much traffic as possible is eligible for handling in the Accelerated Path by SecureXL:

- Make sure the topology of the firewall's interfaces is properly and completely defined so the object "Internet" and DMZ networks are calculated correctly. This topic was covered in Chapter 5.

- Try to use the most specific "Protected Scope" in the Threat Prevention policy as possible. Any object you configure in the "Protected Scope" column will have its traffic inspected based on the Threat Prevention policy rule, regardless of whether the protected object initiated the connection or not. Use of "Protected Scope" is different from the Access Control policy layers where the Source object defines who originally opened the connection.

- If you want to limit enforcement of Threat Prevention protections based on the direction of connection initiation to make less traffic subject to scanning and increase firewall performance, it is possible to unhide the Source and Destination columns of the Threat Prevention policy and configure them accordingly. It is also possible to unhide the "Services" column and explicitly configure it to only match against certain port numbers as shown:

Figure 9-15: Unhiding Columns in the Threat Prevention Policy

However for simplicity's sake and to ensure full coverage of network traffic it is generally recommended to utilize Protected Scope whenever possible instead.

Instead of a Protected Scope of "Any", use negations of groups, networks and/or host objects if at all possible. Recall the catchphrase from Chapter 5: "Any is the Enemy"! Try to avoid setting a Protected Scope of "Any" in a Threat Prevention rule column unless:

- The Source and Destination fields are being employed for more granular control in lieu of only using a Protected Scope definition (which is left set to "Any"); in that case make sure the *neither* the Source *nor* the Destination field are set to Any.

- Additional criteria for Protected Scope are included in the profile settings for the Anti-Virus and Threat Emulation blades. *However watch out for having a Protected Scope column of "Any" in a Threat Prevention rule that is utilizing a profile with IPS, Anti-Bot, or Threat Extraction enabled.* Anti-Virus and

Threat Emulation have their own Protected Scope settings embedded in the profile properties (which are covered in the next section), while the other three blades do not and will be applied to very large amounts of traffic if the rule's Protected Scope is left set to Any.

- The profile specified in the Action field of the rule is being used to disable most or all Threat Prevention blades from inspecting traffic matching the rule as detailed below.

- Just as in the APCL/URLF policy layer, there is no "implicit drop" at the end of the TP policy, so an explicit "Accept" cleanup rule at the bottom of the TP policy is not necessary for proper operation. The presence of such a rule at the end of the Threat Prevention policy will guarantee that virtually zero network traffic will be handled in the Accelerated Path by SecureXL.

Threat Prevention Profile Optimization

While the Threat Prevention policy rules specify what traffic should be matched and inspected by the various components of Threat Prevention, the all-important profile specified in the Action column of the matching rule controls the behavior of the individual Threat Prevention features. The profile options most directly relevant to firewall performance will be highlighted and discussed in the upcoming sections of this chapter. The settings shown in the screenshots will generally be the defaults set "out of the box", and we will be working with the built-in R80+ profile called "Optimized". Be on the lookout for settings relevant to firewall performance that have been changed in your local environment from the default settings as we continue.

General Policy Profile Optimization

When editing a Threat Prevention profile, the "General Policy" screen is probably one of the most important when it comes to performance optimization. For traffic matching a Threat Prevention rule invoking a profile such as "Optimized" in the Action field, we can control which individual TP features will inspect the traffic. Keep in mind though that unless the referenced feature is actually enabled on the firewall object under General Properties...Network Security, that feature will not be applied to traffic traversing that particular firewall. Running the command **enabled_blades** from an expert mode prompt on the firewall is another quick way to determine which features are active.

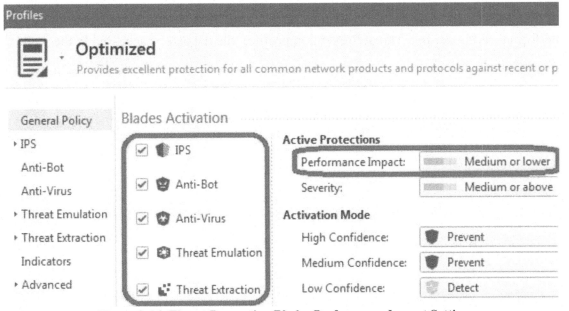

Figure 9-16: Threat Prevention Blades Performance Impact Setting

If a Threat Prevention rule matches candidate traffic and one or more of the features shown are not checked in the profile settings, that feature's protections will not be applied to the traffic at all. This assumes only one Threat Prevention policy layer is present, but if there is more than one Threat Prevention layer present, the most restrictive action of any matching rule in multiple Threat Prevention layers is selected. If the candidate traffic does not match any Threat Prevention rule in any Threat Prevention policy layer, the default action is Accept (which will not be separately logged) and acceleration of that traffic by SecureXL is possible.

The next important field, Performance Impact, specifies in general what protections should be applied for the 5 Threat Prevention blades based on their potential performance impact. You might assume that this setting only governs the IPS feature, but it controls what elements of *all* the different Threat Prevention features will be active. The following table shows what type of protections are enabled by the different settings for Performance Impact in a Threat Prevention profile; this list can be accessed in the R80+ SmartConsole from Security Policies...Threat Prevention...Threat Tools...Protections:

Table 6: Performance Impact Summary of TP Protection Categories

Protection	Blade(s)	Engine	Performance Impact
IPS	IPS	Signatures	Varies
Reputation IPs	Anti-Bot	Reputation	Low
Reputation URLs	Anti-Bot	Reputation	Low
Reputation Domains	Anti-Bot	Reputation	Low
Mail Activity	Anti-Bot	Mail Outbreaks	Low
Viruses	Anti-Virus	Signatures	Low
URLs w/ Malware	Anti-Virus	Reputation	Low
File Types	Anti-Virus	File Type	Low
Malicious Activity	Anti-Virus & Anti-Bot	Signatures	Low-69% Medium-27% High-4%
Unusual Activity	Anti-Bot	Behavioral Patterns	Low-54% Medium-8% High-38%
Exploit Detection	Threat Emulation	Exploit Detection	Low –33.3% Medium-33.3% High-33.3%
Links Inside Mail	Anti-Virus & Anti-Bot	Reputation	Medium
Unusual Activity	Anti-Virus	Behavioral Patterns	High
Unusual Activity	Anti-Virus	Behavioral Patterns	High

This table comes in quite handy when trying to determine how to configure the Performance Impact setting, based on what features your organization plans to use.

IPS Profile Optimization (R80.10+ firewall only)

This section assumes the Threat Prevention layer will be applied to an R80.10+ firewall. As far as the profile settings for IPS above, the most useful screen from an optimization perspective (beyond what has already been covered in this chapter) is Additional Activation...Protections to Deactivate:

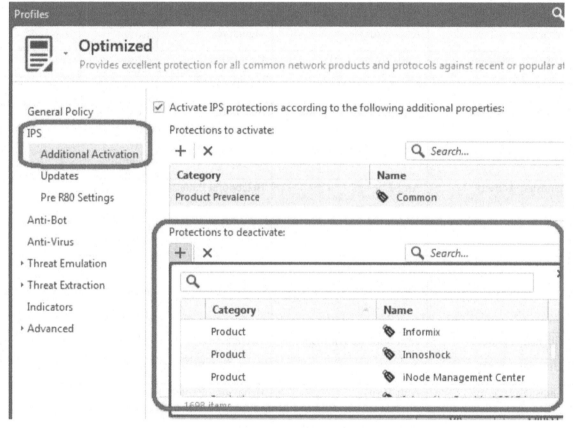

Figure 9-17: IPS Product/Vendor Deactivation Categories

This is a very long list, but the most useful categories are "Product" and "Vendor". By deactivating huge numbers of IPS signatures covering vendors and products you know for a fact aren't in use within your organization, the total number of IPS signatures being searched for by the firewall can be substantially reduced. This will save large amounts of CPU processing resources in the Medium Path.

Anti-Bot/Anti-Virus Profile Optimization

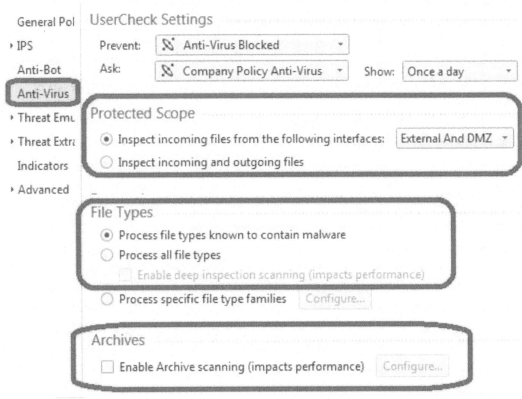

Figure 9-18: Anti-Virus Performance Settings

Note that in the Anti-Virus profile settings, we have the opportunity to specify even further restrictions on the Protected Scope of traffic subject to Anti-Virus scanning. Obviously there must have been a match on the Protected Scope column of the rule invoking this profile first for these additional scope restrictions to be imposed. However bear in mind that your firewall topology must be properly defined as covered in Chapter 5 for the terms "External" and "DMZ" to have any useful meaning here.

The "File Types" settings shown in the screenshot are the default and should be left alone for performance reasons. Files subject to deep inspection scanning (if enabled) will also cause a trip to process space on the firewall, which is referred to as the "Fourth Path" and covered in Chapter 10.

Enabling Archive Scanning may have a dramatic impact on firewall performance as this function is handled by the **dlpu** process on the firewall in the "Fourth Path". If unacceptable performance is encountered scanning archive files and/or excessive amounts of CPU are being consumed by the **dlpu** and/or **rad** processes on the firewall, see the following for more information: sk94056: When Anti-Virus and Anti-Bot blades are enabled, RAD process and DLPU process consume CPU at high level. The obvious security trade-off here is that if archive files are simply allowed without being scanned, they could contain threats that the firewall will not block.

One last tip: If you are using a firewall version prior to R80.10, at press time there was a performance problem with Anti-Virus and Anti-Bot on an R77.30 or earlier gateway detailed here: sk106062: CPU load and traffic latency after activating Anti-Bot and/or Anti-Virus blade on Security Gateway. This problem was fixed in R80.10+ gateway.

Threat Emulation/Threat Extraction Profile Optimization

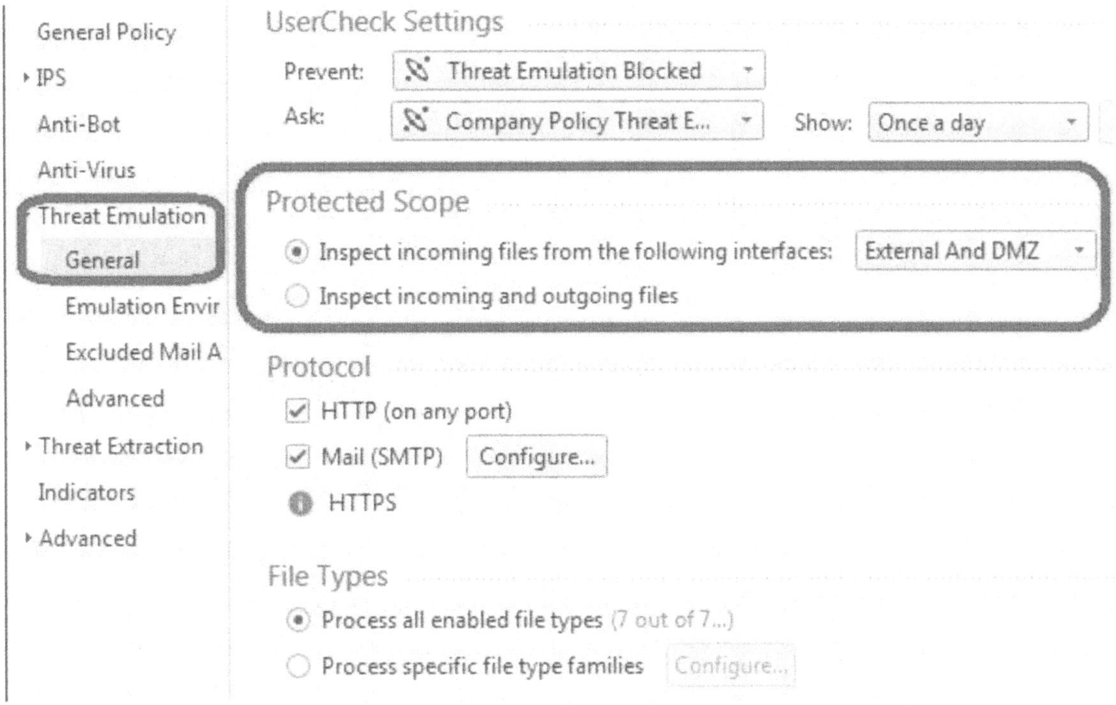

Figure 9-19: Threat Emulation Performance Settings

Similarly to the Anti-Virus blade, for the Threat Emulation feature above we have the ability to further clarify the Protected Scope beyond what was matched in the Threat Prevention policy's Protected Scope column. As before, the firewall's topology must be properly defined as covered in Chapter 5 for the terms "External" and "DMZ" to have any useful meaning here.

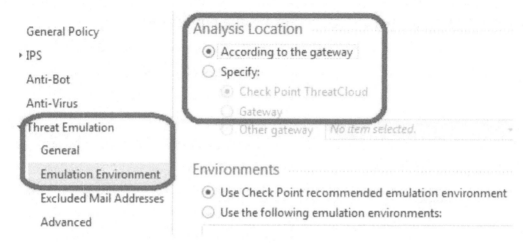

Figure 9-20: Threat Emulation Analysis Location

While emulation of suspect executables can potentially be performed somewhere other than the Check Point ThreatCloud, it can cause highly variable emulation performance to occur without careful tuning. If you choose to perform emulation locally, there are some limitations to be aware of:

1. By default if the CPU cores allocated for emulation are more than 90% busy, no more emulation VMs will start until the CPU load drops below that value, thus potentially causing a large backlog of emulation requests.

2. Do NOT check the "Disable static analysis" checkbox shown on the following page's screenshot. Doing so will cause every single file encountered to be sent for emulation (even if it has been emulated previously), and should only be enabled in a lab environment or under the guidance of Check Point TAC.

3. By default the emulation VM processes may not consume more than 70% of the system's RAM. If there is not enough RAM available, startup of new emulation sessions will be delayed. A runaway memory leak in an unrelated process on the emulation system can potentially delay or bring emulation to a complete halt.

The Check Point ThreatCloud is most commonly employed for emulation services; dedicated Threat Emulation appliances are also available for purchase from Check Point.

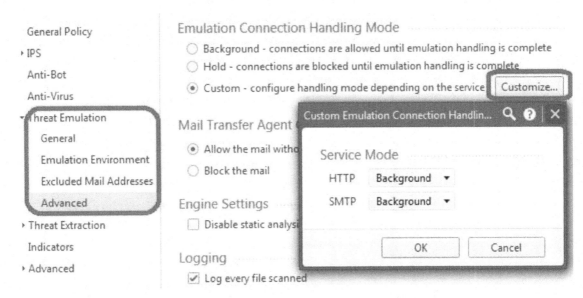

Figure 9-21: Threat Emulation Handling Mode

Emulating files can cause a long delay that will be noticeable for users. The default value for "Emulation Connection Handling Mode" shown above is typically Background which is appropriate for most environments, especially when combined with the use of the Threat Extraction feature to quickly deliver a sanitized copy of the documents to end users while file emulation is still processing.

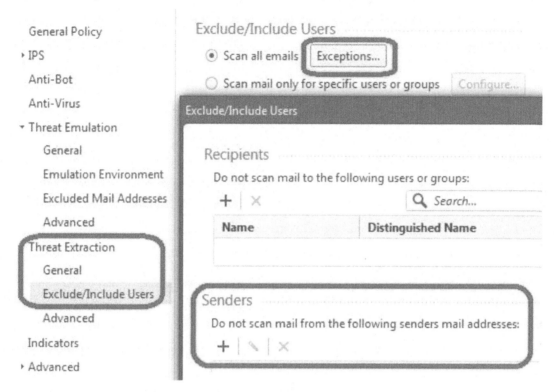

Figure 9-22: Excluding Email Users from Threat Extraction

For the Threat Extraction blade settings shown above, be sure to exclude service accounts and other system accounts that send large amounts of email from being processed by this feature, such as system/network status notifications, meeting reminders, and other bulk automated email messages.

Testing Threat Prevention Policy & Profile Optimizations: CheckMe

A classic problem with Threat Prevention policies has always been how to test them, particularly after making major changes. The test virus EICAR and test malware WICAR are frequently employed for this purpose, but there is a much easier way

provided by Check Point known as CheckMe. Simply visit http://www.cpcheckme.com
from a web browser and start the assessment:

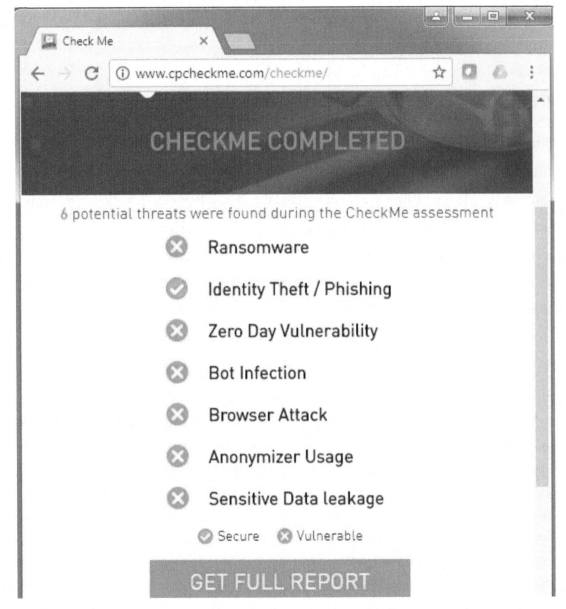

Figure 9-23: CheckMe Assessment Results

This tool can provide quick verification that your Threat Prevention policy/profile optimizations have not impacted the firewall's enforcement of Threat Prevention protections in any unexpected ways. More info: sk115236: CheckMe - Instant Security Check.

Medium Path CPU Usage Optimization

Up to this point we have examined the IPS Protection Scope (R77.30 gateway only) that limits the amount of traffic that needs to be processed by IPS, and therefore be directed to at least the Medium Path. We've optimized the Threat Prevention policy to make as much traffic eligible for the Accelerated Path and checked performance-affecting Threat Prevention profile settings. Hopefully you've now seen more traffic taking the Accelerated Path, and noticed a corresponding drop in Firewall Worker core utilization. Some further improvement in Firewall Worker core utilization can be obtained by trying to reduce the amount of CPU expended while in the Medium Path, and there will be a few back-door opportunities to potentially get more traffic into the Accelerated Path as well.

There are two major ways to accomplish this optimization, each with their own pros and cons:

1. Matching traffic in a Threat Prevention policy rule that invokes a profile disabling the inspection performed by one or more Threat Prevention features

2. Creating Threat Prevention and/or IPS exceptions

Threat Prevention: Profile-based Disabling vs. Exceptions

Let's visually inspect what each of these techniques actually looks like before diving in. In our following example the dreaded "Behemoth" system mentioned in the section "Selectively Disabling SecureXL" earlier in this chapter is (surprise surprise) running afoul of various Threat Prevention features. False positives are blocking critical traffic to and from the Behemoth, due to its appalling lack of respect for networking and application standards adhered to by the whole world. After getting thoroughly excoriated by an executive for your sheer incompetence in allowing your firewall to block critical production traffic, you decide to disable all Threat Prevention features for all traffic going to and from the Behemoth. Look at the following two screenshots:

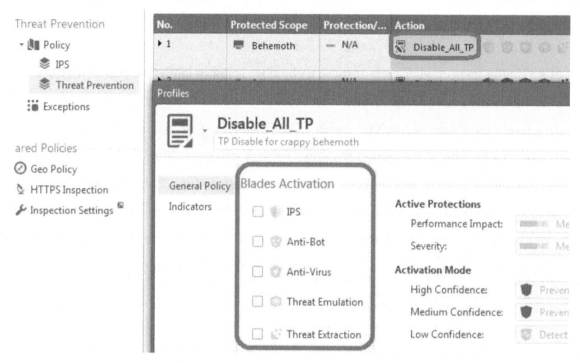

Figure 9-24: "Null" Threat Prevention Profile Example

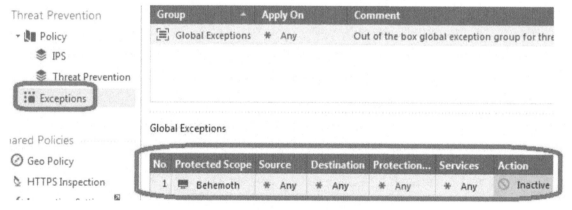

Figure 9-25: Threat Prevention Exception Example

While both the methods shown for disabling all Threat Prevention protections for the Behemoth will accomplish the stated goal, generally speaking only one of them will make traffic to and from the Behemoth potentially eligible for handling in the Accelerated Path, while the other one will have no effect on path selection by the firewall but will save a bit of CPU in the Medium Path. Can you guess which one is preferable from a performance tuning perspective?

When a Threat Prevention exception is defined as shown in the latter screenshot, it only impacts the *decision* rendered by the various Threat Prevention blades: is this traffic hostile or not? Using an exception as shown in our example still causes the Behemoth's traffic to traverse at least the Medium Path, and does not make the traffic eligible for handling in the Accelerated Path at all. This stated behavior is not a hard and fast rule for all TP blades in every situation and on every firewall code version, but should be assumed in the majority of real-world traffic situations.

In the former screenshot a Threat Prevention rule matched the Behemoth's traffic as a Protected Scope, and invoked a profile called "Disable_All_TP" which had all five Threat Prevention blades unchecked (a "null" TP profile). On an R80.10+ firewall, this technique signals to SecureXL that absolutely zero handling by Threat Prevention is necessary, and SecureXL may be able to handle the traffic in the Accelerated Path. Even if the example traffic to and from the Behemoth still requires handling the Medium Path because it is being inspected by other features such as APCL/URLF, significant CPU time is saved in the Medium Path as a result of skipping all Threat Prevention inspection completely. The amount of traffic that can potentially be handled in the Accelerated Path using this null profile technique is far higher on an R80.10+ gateway than an R77.30 or earlier gateway due to ongoing firewall code improvements.

One other wrinkle to keep in mind though: What about multiple Threat Prevention layers for R80.10+ firewalls? In most configurations I've seen, there is only one Threat Prevention policy layer in a policy package, or at least there is a typical Threat Prevention policy layer and a "special" separate IPS policy layer for R77.30 and earlier gateways. The previous example assumes that only one Threat Prevention policy layer exists, but what happens if there is more than one?

If there are multiple Threat Prevention policy layers present, they are all evaluated simultaneously, with no more than one rule matched per individual TP policy layer. Multiple matches will always choose the most restrictive action. In our example, if traffic to and from the Behemoth matches a rule in more than one TP policy layer, the Disable_All_TP profile will probably not be applied, as it is almost certainly less restrictive than the match in the other TP policy layer. On the other hand, Global Exceptions are just that: applied globally across all TP policy layers. So as long as there is only one TP policy layer (not including the "special" IPS layer for R77.30 gateways) the Disable_All_TP profile will be applied as expected to the Behemoth's traffic. *Watch out though when you first add a second TP policy layer, as it may start overriding null TP profiles that were defined in your original TP policy layer!*

Use Cases for Threat Prevention Exceptions

As mentioned in the last section, using so-called "null" TP profiles are preferred from a performance optimization perspective. When you are aiming to make certain traffic immune to TP inspection in a broad, wide-ranging way, null TP profiles are the way to go. However if you need to make precise, very specific exceptions to how TP is applied to certain traffic, trying to do so in the main TP policy is a very clumsy way to do it. This situation is perfect for Global Exceptions, which can allow you to exempt certain traffic from being checked for a single IPS Protection if you desire, while maintaining the protected afforded by other IPS signatures and the rest of TP. If you still aren't convinced to use null TP profiles whenever possible, check this out:

> *Even if a TP Global Exception excludes all traffic from all Threat Prevention inspection (including IPS), various protections will still be enforced anyway such as the IPS Protections HTTP Header Patterns, ASCII only response, ASCII only request, HTTP URL Patterns and CIFS File Name Patterns. This behavior was a known limitation for R80.10 gateway at press time (IDs 02518174 & 02515164/02513631).*

Exceptions: Inter-DMZ Interaction & DMZ Backend Connections

Look at the Network Access policy layer permitting interaction between the various DMZ networks, and also connections that are allowed to be initiated from the DMZ(s) to the internal network. What kind of traffic is allowed? Does it consume large amounts of bandwidth?

One could potentially create a TP exception for at least some connections initiated from a DMZ system to another DMZ, or even connections initiated from a DMZ system to the internal network. A classic and very tempting example is network backups. Every night gigantic amounts of data traverse the firewall sourced from DMZ systems heading for the backup server, which could be located in another DMZ or perhaps somewhere on the internal network. Exempting this traffic from TP processing with an exception is tempting, and could potentially save a lot of CPU overhead in the Medium Path.

Careful here! Remember that systems located in DMZ networks are only semi-trusted; they were probably placed in a DMZ because they are undertaking some kind of risky processing that involves interactions with potentially hostile systems on the Internet. If you were to create an exception for this traffic, and an attacker (or malware) was to compromise that DMZ system, they/it would be free to attack the backup server at will, and the firewall's TP inspection would be none the wiser. The risk here is that an attacker could repeatedly initiate connections to the backup server and experiment until a compromise was achieved – and the various Threat Prevention blades would be completely oblivious to it because of the exception. There would be no assurance that the connection attempted was made by the legitimate backup program on the DMZ server, rather than some kind of installed attack tool.

One good option: If the DMZ system currently initiates the connection to the internal backup server, see if you can flip that around. Can the backup server initiate the connection to the DMZ server and do the backup that way? It would be much safer to exempt a connection initiated from the internal network to the DMZ from TP processing. While an attacker with a foothold on a DMZ server could still try to attack the backup server via the connection already initiated from the internal network to the DMZ server, the attacker would no longer have the ability to launch new attacks at their leisure against the backup server located in the internal network.

Carefully consider the risks before creating exceptions which blind TP to connections initiated from a semi-trusted system located in a DMZ, especially when connecting to the internal trusted network!

Exceptions: Internal to DMZ Connections

In most network architectures the internal network is far more trusted than a system that resides in a DMZ. There are numerous opportunities to create exceptions and achieve an extremely high "bang for the buck" factor when it comes to saving processing overhead in the Medium Path. In the prior section, significant caution was advised in blinding Threat Prevention to inspection of connections initiated from a DMZ. Not nearly as much caution needs to be exercised when the internal trusted network initiates a connection to a semi-trusted DMZ. In particular if network backup connections, Microsoft Active Directory replications, and/or VMware vSphere replications are initiated from the trusted network to DMZ systems, exceptions for these specific traffic types can provide a handsome increase in firewall performance. So for an internal backup server initiating connections to DMZ servers for the purpose of backups, the relevant Exception would be as follows:

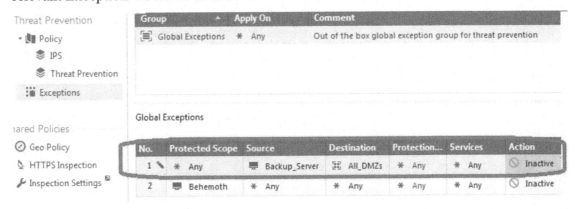

Figure 9-26: Exception for Heavy Backups Traffic

Run "**top**...1" on your gateway and observe the current Firewall Worker core utilization. Install policy with the newly created exception. Depending on how much traffic is matching the new exception, you may see CPU utilization drop on the Firewall Worker cores, where TP processing occurs.

R77.30 IPS Engine Settings vs. R80+ Inspection Settings

The transition to R80+ management includes a significant revamping of the IPS blade. Some items that were previously listed as IPS Protections on the "Engine Settings" screen under the IPS tab in the R77.30 SmartDashboard, are now separated out into the "Inspection Settings" portion of the R80+ SmartConsole. From a performance tuning perspective, watch out for the circled settings and whether they are enabled:

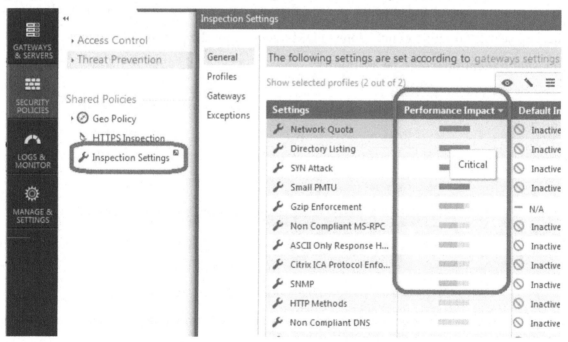

Figure 9-27: Inspection Settings Performance Impact

Changes to these "Inspection Settings" values in the R80+ SmartConsole only require a Network Access policy reinstallation to take effect, because they have been separated out from the IPS feature and the Threat Prevention policy layer.

IPS Profiling: Find CPU-hogging IPS Protections

So you've used IPS exceptions to limit the amount of CPU expended in the Medium Path and disabled IPS signatures with a Critical/High performance impact that are not relevant to your environment. You've even optimized the Threat Prevention policy for your R80.10+ gateway in regards to IPS. You've checked the Engine/Inspection Settings related to IPS as well. But there still seems to be an awful lot of CPU being expended on the Firewall Worker cores in the Medium and Firewall Paths, as shown by **top**...1. Running the "quick assessment" test mentioned earlier in this chapter shows that IPS is definitely the feature consuming inordinate amounts of CPU, and you can't seem to nail down which IPS Protection is causing it.

Check out these SKs: sk110737: IPS Analyzer Tool - How to analyze IPS performance efficiently and sk43733 - How to measure CPU time consumed by IPS protections. The procedures documented in these SKs demonstrate how to gather CPU usage statistics for the individual IPS Protections and identify the "hog". The instructions vary considerably depending on the code versions in use and whether your environment is standalone or distributed, and as such are beyond the scope of this book.

Firewall Path Optimization

You've followed all the recommendations so far in this chapter, but when you run an `fwaccel stats -s` command the percentage of traffic taking the Firewall Path is still stubbornly high (>20%)! There will always be some processing occurring in the Firewall Path on a typical firewall. We spent a lot of effort trying to get traffic out of the Medium Path and into the Accelerated Path whenever possible, but what should we do when traffic seems to be stuck in the Firewall Path constantly? First off, up to 20% of total traffic taking the Firewall Path is generally fine (the average is about 5-10% on well-tuned firewalls from what I've seen), but what kind of situations can cause >20% of traffic to keep taking the Firewall Path? We will cover some of the more common causes in the following sections, however keep in mind that Check Point is constantly optimizing their code in an attempt to have as much processing as possible occur in the Medium and Accelerated paths and avoiding the high-overhead Firewall Path. You may upgrade your firewall code at some point in the future and find that stubbornly high Firewall Path utilization has suddenly disappeared!

One quick note before we begin: traffic entering a firewall interface configured for "Monitor Mode" is never eligible for acceleration by SecureXL and will always go F2F, see the following for more detail: sk121792: Traffic from an interface configured in Monitor Mode is not fully accelerated by SecureXL.

IP Fragmentation: Nemesis of SecureXL

You would think in today's world of high-speed Internet access, and with the massive proliferation of the various Ethernet standards, that just about every network in the world would have a Maximum Transmission Value (MTU) of at least the Ethernet default of 1500. Unfortunately you would be wrong. Sub-1500 MTU values were very common in the early days of the Internet due to dial-up connectivity and the SLIP/PPP protocols (default MTU 576 in most cases). Varying MTU values on different networks are dealt with by a process called IP fragmentation. Packets that are larger than a target network's smaller MTU value are fragmented into 2 or more pieces by an intervening router, and the fragment(s) successfully traverse the rest of the network path to the end receiver. It is the end receiver's responsibility to reassemble the fragments back into the original packets and process them. As we saw in Chapter 8's "Low MTUs and PMTUD" section, digitally signed traffic (such as IPSec) cannot be fragmented in transit, since it would violate the ESP packet's digital signature.

However there is a truly insidious effect on firewall performance when a fragmented packet arrives at the firewall: *All received packets that have been fragmented are ineligible for SecureXL Throughput Acceleration (Accelerated Path) or the Medium Path; they will always take the Firewall Path. This limitation still exists in R80.10 gateway.* You can execute the optimization strategies stated earlier in this chapter all you want, but fragmented packets will always end up in the Firewall Path no matter what you do. Check Point firewalls perform a process called "virtual defragmentation" to ensure that a single attack has not been split into multiple packets for purposes of evading detection, and this virtual defragmentation process can only occur in the Firewall Path.

The only exception to this is the Check Point 21000 series appliance with an optional SAM card installed; if present the SAM card can perform virtual defragmentation in a highly accelerated fashion. Fragmentation can degrade firewall performance if a large percentage of received traffic is fragmented, and there is very little you can do about it directly on the firewall itself. However if a connection is eligible for Medium or Accelerated Path processing, and one or some of that connection's packets are fragmented, only the fragmented packet(s) will be handled in the Firewall Path. The remainder of the connection's packets can still be handled in the Medium or Accelerated Path; the mere presence of a fragmented packet in a connection's stream does *not* doom the remainder of the connection to languish in the Firewall Path, regardless of future packet fragmentation status.

If you suspect fragmentation is occurring, we can confirm this from the firewall using various tools. There is very little you can do about fragmented packets arriving from the Internet (unless your organization's own Internet perimeter router is the one doing the fragmenting), but you should try to avoid this situation on any networks under your administrative control. To figure out how many fragments the firewall is receiving, run these commands:

fw ctl pstat and **fwaccel stats -p**

```
Fragments:
          0 fragments, 0 packets, 0 expired, 0 short,
          0 large, 0 duplicates, 0 failures
```

Figure 9-28: Fragmentation Statistics Displayed by *fw ctl pstat*

```
[Expert@firewall:0]# fwaccel stats -p
F2F packets:
--------------
Violation                 Packets    Violation                 Packets
--------------------      -------    --------------------      -------
pkt is a fragment          4896      pkt has IP options              0
ICMP miss conn                6      TCP-SYN miss conn            3688
TCP-other miss conn         146      UDP miss conn              194417
other miss conn               0      VPN returned F2F                0
ICMP conn is F2Fed            0      TCP conn is F2Fed           38783
UDP conn is F2Fed          6694      other conn is F2Fed             0
uni-directional viol          0      possible spoof viol             0
TCP state viol              405      out if not def/accl             0
bridge, src=dst               0      routing decision err            0
sanity checks failed          0      temp conn expired               0
fwd to non-pivot              0      broadcast/multicast             0
cluster message               0      partial conn                    0
PXL returned F2F              0      cluster forward                 0
chain forwarding             0      general reason                  0
[Expert@firewall:0]#
```

Figure 9-29: Displaying Count of Fragmented Packets with *fwaccel stats -p*

If the fragment numbers seem high, run this tcpdump command to see all fragmented packets and figure out where they are coming from:

```
tcpdump -eni any '((ip[6:2] > 0) and (not ip[6] = 64))'
```

Any traffic appearing in this output is fragmented; notice that the -e option will also show you the source MAC address of the entity that sent the fragmented packet to the firewall, in order to help you trace the fragmented packet back to its origin. The only way to correct this situation is to ensure a consistent MTU value is in use throughout your internal and DMZ networks. In the real world when a large amount of internal traffic is improperly fragmented, it is usually due a misconfigured MTU on a router somewhere. I've seen correcting an internal MTU issue such as this make a *huge* difference in firewall performance. Of course there are situations where low MTUs are legitimately present due to legacy private network connections to partners or vendors (i.e. 56Kbps lines, dialup lines & ISDN).

If you are concerned about fragments impacting the performance of the firewall, it is possible to forbid IP fragments from crossing the firewall at all.

If a large portion of your network's legitimate production traffic is fragmented, forbidding fragments on the firewall will cause a massive outage. Run the `tcpdump` *command mentioned earlier and MAKE SURE that you don't have legitimate production traffic in your network that is fragmented before you decide to try forbidding IP fragments!*

Fragments can be disabled in the R77.30 SmartDashboard under the IPS tab...Protections...IP Fragments...(IPS Profile in use by your firewall)...Forbid IP Fragments checkbox. In R80+ management the setting is located under "Inspection Settings":

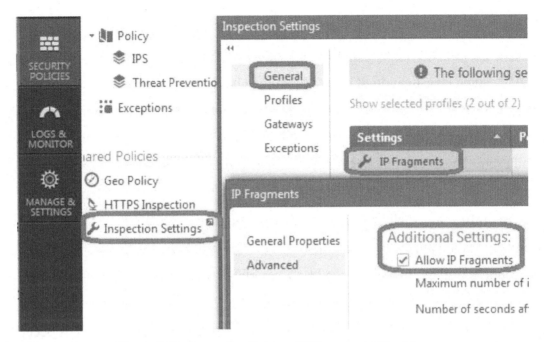

Figure 9-30: Inspection Settings IP Fragments Checkbox

One last time: be careful with this one! You can cause a huge outage by unchecking the box!

Case Study: Oracle Database Traffic & IP Fragmentation

An Oracle user reports terrible database performance through a Check Point firewall. When running performance benchmarks of Oracle traffic through the firewall, one of the Firewall Worker cores hits 100% utilization and overall throughput is only a small percentage of the available LAN bandwidth. The commands `fwaccel stats -p` and `fw ctl pstat` report huge numbers of fragmented packets traversing the firewall.

After some investigation, it is found that the Oracle database product has a critical setting known as "Session Data Unit" or SDU. By default, Oracle sets this value to 2048 which is obviously higher than the typical Ethernet MTU of 1500. Unfortunately this default setting will result in massive IP fragmentation of traffic leaving the Oracle database server. If this traffic attempts to traverse a Check Point firewall, none of the database traffic will be eligible for SecureXL Throughput Acceleration and will always take the Firewall Path (F2F). If the involved traffic is contained within a single TCP connection traversing two high-speed LAN interfaces, one unlucky Firewall Worker core will rapidly hit the wall as far as performance is concerned. The Dynamic Dispatcher cannot mitigate this situation in this particular case, because the heavy traffic is occurring inside a single TCP connection (sometimes referred to as an "elephant flow"), whose processing cannot be performed by more than one Firewall Worker core.

The fix to get rid of this packet fragmentation? Set the Oracle SDU value to 1460. But why not set it to 1500? The 40 byte differential accounts for the presence of IP and TCP headers which total about 40 bytes. After applying this Oracle SDU setting change, firewall performance was substantially increased due to the lack of packet fragmentation.

Which Path is a Certain Connection Using, and Why?

Suppose a certain connection traversing the firewall is experiencing a latency or functionality issue. It could well be one of those dreaded "legacy applications" that nobody wants to think about or interfere with, similar to the "Behemoth" discussed earlier in the book. In the usual finger-pointing that ensues, the firewall will of course be blamed first, and must be cleared of any wrongdoing. You check the firewall logs and everything looks fine, with only Accept/Allow actions for the connection in question; no drops/blocks from APCL/URLF, IPS, Threat Prevention or any other blades are present. You have run a **tcpdump** or **fw monitor** and have verified basic network connectivity and two-way packet flow for the subject connection. As the firewall administrator, you may now be wondering: which of the three paths (Accelerated, Medium, or Firewall) is this problematic connection being processed in? In the past, SecureXL was well-known for sometimes breaking legacy application connections in non-obvious ways when using the Accelerated Path; disabling SecureXL (thus eliminating the Accelerated Path completely) was the only way to make the legacy application work again.

First off ensure that the connection is actually live and passing traffic. Seeing an "Accept" action for the connection in the logs only means the connection started, and was accepted by the firewall. It does not mean that it is still active at this very moment. Next determine the source and destination IP addresses of the problematic connection (suppose the source is 192.168.1.100 and the destination is 129.82.102.32 as an example). If your firewall is running the R77 release or later, go ahead and run the following command to view the SecureXL connections table:

```
fwaccel conns | grep 192.168.1.100 | grep 129.82.102.32
```

WARNING: Running the **fwaccel conns** *command on a firewall using code older than release R77 can cause performance issues to suddenly start occurring on the firewall during the command's execution. See* sk97772: "Soft lockup" on multiple CPU cores occurs when running 'fwaccel conns' / 'fwaccel conns -s' or while running 'cpinfo' on Security Gateway running on Gaia OS.

Look at the **Flags** column for our subject connection. If the only flag shown in the row of periods is an **F**, the connection is being handled in the Firewall Path. If both an **F** and an **S** are present, the connection is being processed in the Medium Path. If all you see is a row of periods (with no letters displayed) the connection is being handled in the Accelerated Path. The SecureXL connections table can also be viewed in its raw form with the **fw tab -t cphwd_db** command.

If a **F** and/or **S** is present in the connection's flags, we can use the **sim dbg** command to see precisely why packets associated with this connection have been punted out of the Accelerated Path (Check Point calls this a SecureXL "violation") and into the Medium or Firewall Paths.

WARNING: Enabling debugging on a live production firewall can have serious performance impacts if done improperly. While throughout the book we have generally wanted to run commands during the firewall's busiest period, for this procedure you may want to wait until after hours.

The following technique can be used to determine why this connection (or an inordinate amount of traffic in general) seems to be constantly stuck in the Firewall and/or Medium Paths. First we need to set a filter for our debugging. This is very important to keep the debug output from overwhelming us, and possibly impacting firewall performance. Only one filter can be active at a time. Here is how to set it for our example:

```
sim dbg -f 192.168.1.100,*,129.82.102.32,*,6
```

This filter will match all TCP traffic sourced from 192.168.1.100 to 129.82.102.32 on any source port and any destination port. Make this filter as specific as possible for your environment! If you can add a destination port number in lieu of the second asterisk, do it! Note that this example filter will not show reply traffic sourced from 129.82.102.32 back to 192.168.1.100. Run the **sim dbg list** command and verify the filter is displaying correctly:

```
sim dbg -f 192.168.1.100,*,129.82.102.32,*,6
sim dbg list

Module: mgr

Module: adp


Filter: <192.168.1.100, 0, 129.82.102.32, 0, 6>
```

Figure 9-31: Path Determination Setup Using *sim dbg*

Double-check the filter. Triple-check it! Make sure the targeted connection is passing traffic and commence the debug like this:

```
sim dbg -m pkt + pxl + f2f; sleep 15; sim dbg resetall
```

Note that we are running the debug for only 15 seconds, and then turning it back off automatically. This "dead man's switch" approach to debugging ensures that the firewall will recover itself without your intervention, should it be suddenly bogged down by an improperly filtered debug. Now look in **/var/log/messages**:

```
[fw4_0];get_conn_flags: ISP redundancy is set on for the
connection -> F2F;
```

In this example the traffic was subject to the ISP Redundancy feature which was set for Load Sharing mode, which will force all traffic into the Firewall Path (F2F) for all its processing. What else can cause excessive amounts of traffic to be directed into the

Firewall Path? See sk32578: SecureXL Mechanism for the authoritative and current list.
When reading this SK, remember that the section titled "Traffic Acceleration" refers to
Throughput Acceleration as covered in this chapter, and the "Connection establishment
acceleration" section refers to "Session Rate Acceleration", which is not covered until
Chapter 11.

In a lab environment where traffic traversing the firewall can be strictly controlled in
a testing scenario, a quick and easy way to get an idea of why traffic keeps getting punted
out of the Accelerated Path is to run the command:

```
watch -d -n1 fwaccel stats -p
```

Now initiate application traffic and see what SecureXL "violations" get highlighted:

```
Every 1.0s: fwaccel stats -p

F2F packets:
--------------
Violation              Packets   Violation              Packets
------------------     -------   ------------------     -------
pkt is a fragment            0   pkt has IP options           0
ICMP miss conn               7   TCP-SYN miss conn         4173
TCP-other miss conn        146   UDP miss conn           200603
other miss conn              0   VPN returned F2F             0
ICMP conn is F2Fed           0   TCP conn is F2Fed        40282
UDP conn is F2Fed         6723   other conn is F2Fed          0
uni-directional viol         0   possible spoof viol          0
TCP state viol             421   out if not def/accl          0
bridge, src=dst              0   routing decision err         0
sanity checks failed         0   temp conn expired            0
fwd to non-pivot             0   broadcast/multicast          0
cluster message              0   partial conn                 0
PXL returned F2F             0   cluster forward              0
chain forwarding             0   general reason               0
```

Figure 9-32: Watching *fwaccel stats -p* for SecureXL Violations

The violation counters displayed here are not formally documented anywhere but hopefully they are self-explanatory enough to give you an idea of what is happening. For more information also consider the `fwaccel stats` command with no other command-line arguments, which will give even more detailed packet statistics for the Accelerated Path, Accelerated VPN Path, Medium Path (PXL), Accelerated QoS Path (QXL) and the Firewall Path (F2F).

SecureXL Throughput Acceleration: Key Points

- SecureXL should be enabled for maximum performance; SecureXL can be selectively disabled for certain IP addresses if needed to ensure application compatibility.

- SecureXL Throughput Acceleration permits optimized handling of existing connections in three possible kernel-based paths: SXL, PXL and F2F.

- Use of the IPS and Threat Prevention features is the most common reason that traffic cannot be exclusively handled in the Accelerated Path.

- IPS Performance Impact rankings directly indicate whether traffic can be handled in the Accelerated, Medium or Firewall Path.

- Avoid using "Any" in the Protected Scope column of the Threat Prevention policy if possible.

- Firewall Worker CPU load can be dramatically lowered by "null" Threat Prevention profiles and Global Exceptions.

- Ideally no more than 20% of traffic should be handled in the Firewall Path on a properly tuned firewall.

- The `fwaccel conns` command can be used to determine conclusively which kernel-based processing path (SXL, PXL, or F2F) is handling a certain connection.

- The `sim dbg` command can (carefully) be used to determine why large amounts of traffic or certain connections seem to be constantly stuck in the Firewall or Medium Paths.

CHAPTER 10
THE FOURTH PATH: PROCESS SPACE TRIPS

The journey, not the destination matters...

- T.S. Eliot

Note: The phrase "Fourth Path" used in this chapter is the term I chose to describe certain process space operations on the firewall, and is not a term that is used or endorsed by Check Point.

Background

I want to be absolutely clear right from the start: *Some firewall inspection operations being performed by processes running in process space instead of inside the Gaia kernel is not necessarily a bad thing, even with the performance impact it causes.* On a firewall that has been properly sized and tuned, trips up into process space are not a big deal and cause a barely noticeable degradation in performance. However on a firewall that has not been properly tuned based on the recommendations in this book, or on a firewall that is severely overloaded, the place that performance problems tend to appear initially are firewall operations that involve a trip up into process space.

Reading this section, you may get the impression that trips up into process space on a Check Point firewall are some kind of horrible design flaw specific to Check Point that can never be corrected. Nothing could be further from the truth. Once of the best things about the Check Point firewall (and the reason a book like this could *never* be written for any other vendor's firewall) is that its administrators have full access to the underlying Gaia/Linux operating system via expert mode. As a result Check Point administrators can observe the internal workings of the firewall to whatever degree of intimacy desired, and leverage all the great Unix/Linux tools developed over the last 40+ years. Other firewall vendors deliberately lock their administrators out of the firewall's underlying operating system, and confine them to a command shell equivalent to clish that only lets firewall administrators see what those vendors want them to see. Are process space trips like this happening on other vendor's firewalls? Almost certainly, but those vendors are simply not allowing you see it (and probably a lot of other "inconvenient" things going on under the hood as well). Recall this diagram of the three kernel paths shown earlier which shows the Firewall Path (F2F), and a link up into process space (i.e. the "Fourth Path") for certain firewall operations we will discuss in this chapter:

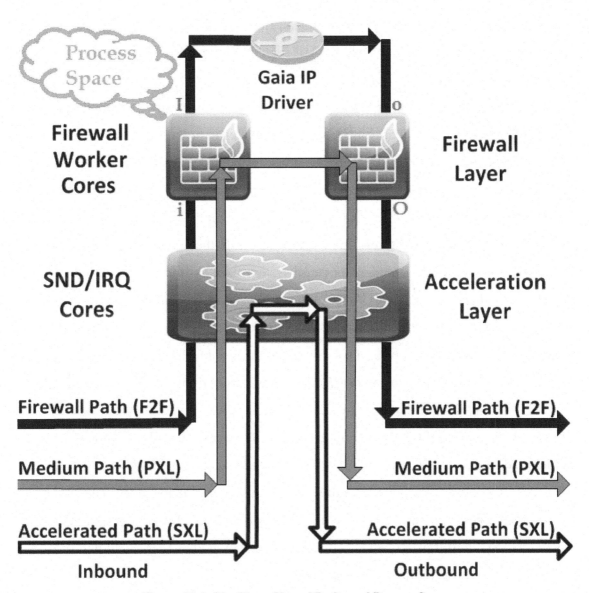

Figure 10-1: The Three Kernel Paths and Process Space

Why is being aware of Check Point firewall functions that cause trips up into process space (sometimes referred to as "folding") of such importance from a performance tuning perspective? There are three reasons:

The first reason is related to a fundamental tenet of any operating system: to interact with the underlying system hardware, code that executes in process space must interface with the kernel layer to do so. The big advantage is that process code needs no direct knowledge of the underlying system hardware components, and can run on just about any combination of hardware without needing to be recompiled. Another advantage is that the process can horribly screw up or otherwise crash, the kernel will automatically clean up the big mess left behind, and overall system stability is ensured.

The second reason is that this interfacing between processes and the kernel imposes significant overhead, much more than is caused by kernel drivers/modules accessing the underlying hardware themselves. This overhead becomes much more pronounced on smaller firewalls with less than 8 cores, and even on larger firewalls that are overloaded.

The third and final reason to be aware of firewall process space trips: kernel code always has the power of CPU preemption compared to a process; if both a process and a kernel module have work to do and they both want to use the same CPU to do it, the process will lose every time and have to wait for the kernel code to finish. The amount of time the process will have to wait for the CPU could be an arbitrarily long time (relatively speaking) if overall CPU utilization by kernel modules is very high due to an overloaded or improperly tuned firewall.

The vast majority of Check Point firewall processing takes place in the Gaia kernel utilizing custom kernel code developed by Check Point. Most traffic is entirely inspected within the kernel by Check Point's kernel code, and also handled by other drivers entirely within the kernel as well, such as IP and the various Ethernet NIC drivers. When no trips to process space are required, processing traffic completely within the kernel in the SXL, PXL, and F2F paths can be done at truly incredible speeds. So why does a Check Point firewall perform some of its inspection operations in processes instead of the kernel?

Many new Check Point firewall features, when first introduced, are initially implemented as processes. Over time, some or all of those functions are moved down into the Check Point kernel code for more efficient handling. The main reason this is done is to ensure stability of the firewall: if new code implemented as a process happens to crash, the kernel just cleans up the mess and the process is automatically restarted. However if that new code was to crash inside the kernel, the entire Gaia operating system would crash and the whole firewall would reboot.

Some features though are never migrated down into the kernel and remain implemented in a process indefinitely. A classic example is the handling of IKE Phase 1 and Phase 2 negotiations with a VPN peer gateway. While mainline IPSec encryption and decryption is fully handled in the kernel, IKE negotiations are still handled by a daemon called **vpnd** on the firewall even though the IPSec VPN features have been around since the 1990s. Why?

A quirk of the IKE negotiation protocol is that a significant amount of processing (including a very computationally expensive Diffie-Hellman key calculation) occurs in IKE Phase 1 *before the VPN peer is even authenticated*. This is what I would term a "potentially unsafe" operation being undertaken by the firewall. Could the unauthenticated peer we are negotiating with have hostile intent, and be sending us maliciously crafted packets with the intent of causing a DoS or even flat-out crashing us? *Yes!* If the crash occurs in a process, the kernel simply cleans up the carnage and the process is restarted. However if this "potentially unsafe" operation causes a DoS or unexpected failure down in the kernel, the entire firewall could be slowed or even crashed completely.

One final use case for executing a firewall function in a process instead of the kernel: firewall interaction with outside servers including the Check Point ThreatCloud. A process is well-suited to "waiting around" for a response from an external server, while it is generally counterproductive to have kernel code do so. So for example if a URL needs to be categorized and the needed information is not already cached, the kernel can put the subject connection on hold and pass the site categorization request to a process (**rad**), and the kernel can then resume processing of other network traffic. When the categorization result is finally returned, the kernel is notified with the results and takes the appropriate action on the held connection. This is much more efficient than having kernel code "waiting around" for this categorization response, as we want the kernel code to immediately get back to what it is supposed to do: inspect and move packets through the firewall in an expeditious fashion.

So to summarize, be aware of the following in regards to process space trips occurring on the firewall before proceeding to the next section:

- On a firewall that has been properly sized and tuned, trips up into process space are not a big deal and cause a barely noticeable degradation of performance
- The kernel provides an abstraction layer between a process and the underlying hardware, and can clean up the mess left behind by a crashed process
- Extra processing overhead is incurred by trips to process space while inspecting traffic, and the effect can be more noticeable on smaller firewalls (<8 cores)
- If a CPU is heavily loaded and executing in mostly system/kernel space, processes trying to use that same CPU can experience delays of an indeterminate length

- Newer Check Point features are frequently implemented as processes, and those features may eventually be moved down into the kernel for increased efficiency

- Firewall processes also handle "potentially unsafe" situations where a hostile peer may try to crash or otherwise DoS the firewall

- Firewall processes are also employed to send requests to external servers such as the Check Point ThreatCloud, and "wait around" for a response which permits the kernel to resume processing other traffic; when the response arrives it is then sent back to the kernel code that requested it

Process Space Trips: The List

Now that we've established the basics of process space trips on a Check Point firewall, let's get into exactly what features and options will incur a trip up out of the kernel on an R80.10 firewall. Bear in mind that the features and settings about to be presented here are situations that can potentially cause a performance impact to live traffic that will be noticed by users. This is by no means a complete list of every possible function handled by processes on the firewall, but a list of situations that can cause noticeable performance impacts to live user traffic due to a process space trip.

As an example of a process space function that does not directly impact user traffic: by default the Application Control (APCL) blade will contact the Check Point ThreatCloud every 2 hours to see if there are any application pattern updates. This procedure is executed in process space on the firewall, but even if a new update is available and needs to be installed, this update procedure does not in any way directly impede or delay user traffic. However be aware that whenever a signature update is applied to APCL/URLF and/or certain Threat Prevention blades, SecureXL will be automatically restarted; this may cause a transient spike in Firewall Worker core utilization as mentioned here: sk121712: SecureXL restarts periodically when Application Control & URL Filtering / Anti-Bot / Anti-Virus blade are enabled.

On the other hand, if HTTPS Inspection is enabled on the firewall and a user initiates a new connection to a website subject to this feature, a trip occurs and the process-space daemons **wstlsd/pkxld** are called upon to handle the initial HTTPS negotiation and asymmetric key calculations on the user's behalf. The user must wait for these operations to complete in the processes before the HTTPS site will begin to appear in their browser; after negotiations are complete HTTPS encryption/decryption then occurs from that point in the F2F path which is fully implemented in the kernel. If the **wstlsd/pkxld** processes are trying to use a CPU that is heavily loaded in kernel/system space, they will be forced to wait for the CPU before they can complete the HTTPS negotiation that the user is waiting on. Depending on how long the processes have to wait, the user may see a blank screen and a long delay when first trying to connect via HTTPS to a secure website, but then the page renders quickly and subsequent navigation of the same HTTPS site performs very well. If the user goes to a completely different HTTPS site and the high CPU situation is still present, the user will potentially see an initial site loading delay once again. HTTPS Inspection optimization will be covered in more detail later in this chapter.

Once again, the processes listed below are involved with trips up to process space that can potentially start delaying live user traffic flows in noticeable ways. A particular focus here is traffic that is obtaining good performance fully inside the kernel, but then is potentially degraded by a trip up into process space on the firewall.

The following situations are specifically excluded from this table:

- Trips that start "down" from process space into the kernel. Examples would be presenting the login portal for the Mobile Access Blade, displaying the Identity Awareness Captive Portal, and showing UserChecks. While these portal pages are indeed handled by firewall processes, and delays experienced by users waiting for the appearance of these various portal pages can certainly be annoying, they are relatively infrequent events that do not directly impact firewall throughput.

- Trips that can delay emails sent/received with SMTP are not included, since these delays are not normally noticed by users, unless the delays are ridiculously excessive in which case other problems are usually present.

One last note: the "Likely Reason" for the trip stated in the following table is my personal opinion, and does not necessarily reflect the views of Check Point. Any blades not listed in this table do not cause process space trips:

Table 7: Summary of Process Space Trip Events

Blade	Process(es)	Purpose	Likely Reason
Firewall	`fwd`	Process a DNS lookup for a Domain Object	Unsafe, Waiting
IPSec VPN	`vpnd`	IKE P1/P2 negotiations, non-accelerated NAT-T traffic, Visitor Mode traffic	Unsafe, Waiting
APCL**	`rad`	Non-cached site names classified as applications	Waiting
URLF**	`rad`	Non-cached site names classified as URL category	Waiting
DLP	(multiple)	Practically all process-based	Unsafe, Waiting
Anti-Bot	`rad`	Reputation check for non-cached IP address entries	Waiting
Anti-Virus	`dlpu, rad`	Archive/MD5 File Inspection	Unsafe
Threat Emulation***	`dlpu, ted`	Unknown executable detonation – Increases substantially if "static analysis" is disabled	Unsafe, New Feature, Waiting
Threat Extraction	`scrubd, scrub_cp_ file_convertd`	Remove any active content from documents	Unsafe, New Feature
Identity Awareness****	`pdpd`	Form user-to-IP mapping for use with Access Role objects	Unsafe, Waiting
Content Awareness	`dlpda,cp_file _convertd`	"DLP-lite" and file-type identification	New Feature
HTTPS Inspection	`wstlsd, pkxld`	Initial HTTPS negotiation, asymmetric key calculation	Unsafe, Waiting

** For APCL/URLF: Only if "Website Categorization Mode" is set to "Hold" on this screen:

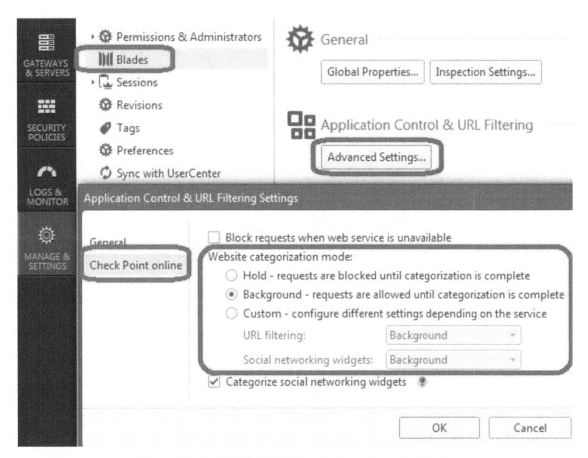

Figure 10-2: APCL/URLF Website Categorization Mode

*** For Threat Emulation, only if "Emulation Connection Handling Mode" is set to "Hold" under Threat Emulation...Advanced on the relevant Threat Prevention profile as shown here:

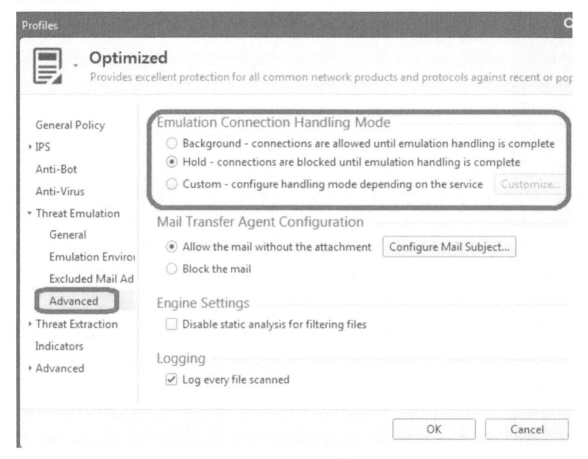

Figure 10-3: Threat Emulation Handling Mode Profile Setting

**** While insufficient CPU cycles being available for the firewall's Identity Awareness process **pdpd** does not directly impact a user's traffic performance, timely formation of user to IP address mappings via AD Query can fall behind, and the user can be initially denied access to privileged resources due to a lack of identity. This situation can be avoided in R80.10+ by using the separate Identity Collector software to "outsource" the formation of user-to-IP mappings away from **pdpd** on the firewall. See sk108235: Identity Collector - Technical Overview.

Special Case: DNS and the rad Daemon

The Resource Advisor Daemon (**rad**) is a key process for many of the commonly used blades listed in the table above. The **rad** process handles interaction between the firewall and the Check Point ThreatCloud for dynamic lookups of content such as URLs; as such it needs reliable access to the Internet and timely DNS responses to avoid potential delays of user traffic. To ensure that all DNS servers defined in Gaia are reachable and delivering timely responses (which **rad** actively depends on), run this quick test:

1. On the firewall from expert mode, run **cat /etc/resolv.conf** and note the DNS servers listed there. For our example the listed DNS servers will be 8.8.8.8 and 4.2.3.2.

2. Now make sure that all DNS servers listed are reachable and responding promptly with the **nslookup** command like this:

```
[Expert@fw:0]# nslookup
> server 8.8.8.8
Default server: 8.8.8.8
Address: 8.8.8.8#53
> www.shadowpeak.com
Server:         8.8.8.8
Address:        8.8.8.8#53

Non-authoritative answer:
www.shadowpeak.com        canonical name = shadowpeak.com.
Name:    shadowpeak.com
Address: 97.74.144.158
> server 4.2.3.2
Default server: 4.2.3.2
Address: 4.2.3.2#53
> www.shadowpeak.com
;; connection timed out; trying next origin
;; connection timed out; no servers could be reached
```

Figure 10-4: Verifying DNS Responsiveness for the *rad* Daemon

See that? Looks like the second DNS server's IP address has a typo (it should be 4.2.2.2), get that fixed! Make sure all DNS servers in the firewall's list are correct and responding promptly, or DNS resolution delays experienced by the **rad** daemon could pass through to user sessions.

As mentioned numerous times throughout this book, it is very important to have the most recent GA Jumbo Hotfix Accumulator loaded on your firewall to obtain the latest performance fixes, and the critical **rad** process is no exception. Still not convinced? Well then feel free to check out these performance-related problems with the **rad** daemon that can be easily avoided by loading up the latest GA Jumbo HFA:

- sk103422: Resource Advisor (RAD) does not reuse connections (opens new connection for each request)
- sk106170: Random issues with HTTP web browsing - traffic latency increases, and at some point web browsing stops working
- sk111578: RAD daemon might shutdown due to SIGPIPE signal, which causes functionality issues with various Software Blades that rely on this daemon

If the Website Categorization Mode has been set to Hold, and an unacceptable level of latency is encountered by users subject to the features that depend on the **rad** daemon (and you've tested the firewall's DNS connectivity as detailed above), additional statistics can be gathered from the **rad** process for further troubleshooting. The command is **rad_admin stats on (urlf|appi|malware|av)**. Then to view ThreatCloud interaction statistics after having enabled them, run **cpview** and select Advanced...RAD:

```
|-------------------------------------------------------------.
| CPVIEW.Advanced.RAD
|-------------------------------------------------------------.
| Overview SysInfo Network CPU Software-blades Advanced
|-------------------------------------------------------------.
| CPU-Profiler Memory CoreXL PrioQ Streaming RAD
|- More info available by scrolling up ----------------.
| RAD Statistics Up Time        3 days, 05:53:51
|
| Name                          APPI    AB     AV   URLF
| Found in LDB                  N/A    N/A    N/A     0
| Sent to Site                  N/A    N/A    N/A     0
| Round Trip (ms)               N/A    N/A    N/A     0
| Hit Count                     N/A    N/A    N/A     0
| Miss Count                    N/A    N/A    N/A     0
| Error Count                   N/A    N/A    N/A     0
| Cache Size (bytes)            N/A    N/A    N/A     0
| Max Cache Size (bytes)        N/A    N/A    N/A     0
| Cache Total Host Records      N/A    N/A    N/A     0
| Max Cache Total Host Records  N/A    N/A    N/A     0
| Avg Family Size               N/A    N/A    N/A     0
| Max Family Size               N/A    N/A    N/A     0
|- More info available by scrolling down --------------.
```

Figure 10-5: *rad* Daemon Statistics

One other situation involving the **rad** daemon to watch out for: if URL Filtering is enabled and the **rad** daemon seems to be constantly consuming large amounts of CPU time, it is possible that the URL Filtering cache is constantly overflowing. This cache is sized at a maximum of 20,000 entries by default (which is usually sufficient for up to 1,000 users) and if it overflows, *the entire cache will be cleared thus causing a big flurry of URL Filtering lookups to the Check Point ThreatCloud by the **rad** daemon as it repopulates the cache*. If the cache is constantly overflowing this can lead to persistently high CPU usage by the **rad** daemon, and cause noticeable user web traffic delays if the

Website Categorization Mode is set to "Hold". The current URL Filtering cache utilization can be checked with this command: **fw tab -t urlf_cache_tbl -s**

```
[Expert@fw:0]# fw tab -t urlf_cache_tbl -s
HOST          NAME            ID #VALS #PEAK #SLINKS
localhost   urlf_cache_tbl   89   934    0       0
[Expert@fw:0]#
```

Figure 10-6: Checking URL Filtering Cache Utilization

The URL Filtering cache size should not be increased from the default of 20,000 unless you are certain this overflow situation is occurring in your firewall. To modify the URL Filtering cache size, consult: sk90422: How to modify URL Filtering cache size?.

HTTPS Inspection

HTTPS Inspection is a feature that allows the firewall to perform a successful "man in the middle" attack against your own internal users' HTTPS-secured connections to the Internet. It can also be configured to inspect inbound HTTPS traffic to your DMZ servers. Once successfully configured, this feature allows the firewall to inspect HTTPS-encrypted traffic with all the capabilities that can typically be employed against cleartext traffic (APCL/URLF, Threat Prevention, etc.) that is passing through the firewall.

Due to its rapidly increasing popularity, and tending to be on the front lines of potential process space trip delays experienced by users, this section will explore HTTPS Inspection optimization in detail. This discussion is not intended to provide an introduction to the HTTPS Inspection feature, its basic operation or the overall organizational & legal ramifications of deploying it on your firewall. If you haven't yet set up HTTPS Inspection or have little experience working with it, reading the following two SKs first is strongly recommended before proceeding: sk65123: **HTTPS Inspection FAQ** and sk108202: Best Practices - **HTTPS Inspection**.

As mentioned earlier in this book, HTTPS Inspection on a gateway always takes place in the Firewall Path (F2F) and is not eligible for Throughput Acceleration by SecureXL at all. In addition certain operations such as HTTPS negotiations (`wstlsd`) and asymmetric key calculations (`pkxld`) trigger a process space trip on the firewall.

The Impact: Enabling HTTPS Inspection

Enabling HTTPS Inspection on your firewall incurs a potential "double whammy" as far as performance is concerned.

First off for each HTTPS connection request received from a user, the firewall essentially is having to proxy that HTTPS connection, and now must handle the initial HTTPS negotiations & key calculations for two separate secure connections, as well as symmetric encryption and decryption of data for both connections.

Second, traffic that was previously not subject to inspection by various firewall blades such as Threat Prevention and APCL/URLF because it was encrypted with HTTPS, can now be decrypted then fully inspected by potentially many more blades, thus incurring even more overhead on the firewall.

The use of the term "double whammy" is particularly appropriate here, because when sizing a new firewall for purchase that intends to utilize the HTTPS Inspection feature, the general recommendation is to basically double the size of the firewall. In the real world I have found this recommendation to be spot-on. So if based on a customer's requirements the Check Point Appliance Sizing Tool recommends firewall hardware capable of 200 SecurityPower Units (SPU), double it to 400 SPU if HTTPS Inspection will be extensively used. SPUs are part of Check Point's proprietary benchmarking system used to rate the speed of different firewall appliance hardware.

HTTPS Inspection Performance Recommendations

Following are general recommendations for minimizing the performance impact and delay experienced by users when HTTPS Inspection is active:

1. Make sure Gaia is running in 64-bit mode which requires a minimum of 6GB RAM. The edition of Gaia can be checked with the clish command **show version os edition**. If Gaia is using 64-bit mode and HTTPS Inspection is enabled, a special 64-bit companion process to the **wstlsd** processes called **pkxld** is spawned:

```
[Expert@fw:0]# ps -ef | egrep -e "wstlsd|pkxld"
admin    22361  6721  0 08:34 ? 00:00:00 wstlsd 0 0
admin    22362  6721  0 08:34 ? 00:00:00 wstlsd 0 1
admin    22363  6721  0 08:34 ? 00:00:00 wstlsd 0 2
admin    22364  6721  0 08:34 ? 00:00:00 wstlsd 0 3
admin    22366  6721  0 08:34 ? 00:00:00 wstlsd 0 4
admin    22367  6721  0 08:34 ? 00:00:00 wstlsd 0 5
admin    22380 22363  0 08:34 ? 00:00:00 /opt/CPshrd-R80/bin/pkxld
```

Figure 10-7: *pkxld* and *wstlsd* on a 64-bit Firewall with Six Worker Cores

The **pkxld** process leverages the 64-bit mode of the processor and various performance-enhancing processor extensions to dramatically speed up key calculations when the initial connection to an HTTPS site is made. Because the user must wait for this calculation to complete in process space before the HTTPS web page will begin to appear, ensuring 64-bit mode is active can have a noticeably positive impact on a user's experience.

2. Make sure AES-NI is being properly detected and utilized on the firewall as specified in the Chapter 8 section "3DES vs. AES & AES-NI". If Gaia is running in 64-bit mode the **pkxld** process can take advantage of the AES-NI capability which can improve AES operations 4-10X. When considering a new firewall that will implement HTTPS Inspection, choose firewall hardware containing a processor architecture that supports AES-NI. Generally speaking appliance model numbers 5600 and higher support AES-NI, *except* the 12200 model and the obsolete Power-1 9000/11000 series. The 3100 and 3200 appliance models also support AES-NI.

3. Make sure there is adequate idle time available on the Firewall Worker cores during the firewall's busiest period. For every Firewall Worker core configured one **wstlsd** process is spawned, which handles the initial HTTPS negotiation (and key calculations if Gaia is running in 32-bit mode) for all inspected HTTPS connections on that particular Firewall Worker core. If all the cores assigned to Firewall Workers (R80.10+ firewalls) or all cores on the entire system (R77.30 firewalls) are consistently running at more than 85% utilization in kernel space (sy/si/hi), the **wstlsd** processes will probably be starved for CPU. As a result, sites subject to HTTPS Inspection will suffer slow initial page loads.

4. Some Check Point administrators try to mitigate the overhead of full-fledged HTTPS Inspection by using the "Categorize HTTPS Sites" function. This feature performs a URL categorization of the Site Name/Subject in the Internet web server's SSL certificate, and blocks the HTTPS negotiation from completing if the categorization result is a prohibited type of site. Using this function will *not* avoid a process space trip, because the initial HTTPS negotiation is still performed by the `wstlsd` daemon, even if the protected content of an approved HTTPS connection itself will not be decrypted by the firewall. When full HTTPS Inspection is enabled on a firewall, the globally set "Categorize HTTPS Sites" function will no longer be performed on that particular firewall. Traffic matching a Bypass action in the HTTPS Inspection policy for that firewall will also not be categorized, even if "Categorize HTTPS Sites" is still checked.

5. As mentioned numerous times throughout this book in regards to policy optimization, try to avoid the use of "Any" in the Source, Destination, and Service fields of the HTTPS Inspection policy. Similarly to the Access Control and Threat Prevention policies, failure to heed this recommendation can result in massive amounts of LAN-speed traffic suddenly becoming subject to HTTPS Inspection inadvertently, which can potentially crater the performance of even the largest firewalls. Proper use of object "Internet" and negations of host/network objects and groups in the Source and Destination fields of the HTTPS Inspection policy can help keep this highly unpleasant situation from occurring.

6. If using a pre-R77.30 firewall, before attempting to enable HTTPS Inspection, upgrading to at least R77.30 and installing the latest GA Jumbo Hotfix Accumulator is strongly recommended. There were numerous performance

enhancements to the HTTPS Inspection feature introduced in R77.30 and its subsequent Jumbo Hotfix Accumulators.

7. The features, capabilities and performance of HTTPS Inspection are more or less the same between R80.10 and R77.30 (with the latest GA R77.30 Jumbo HFA loaded of course). However R80.10+ is strongly preferred for firewalls with 8GB of RAM or less due to the various HTTPS Inspection memory consumption optimizations introduced in that version, especially if SMT/Hyperthreading will be enabled which itself substantially increases memory consumption. See the following for more information about these R80.10 memory usage optimizations: sk120131: Memory utilization in R80.10 Security Gateway / StandAlone.

8. Be aware that when APCL/URLF Limit actions are specified restricting bandwidth for application traffic rules subject to HTTPS Inspection, under certain circumstances the effective throughput can be much lower than the amount of bandwidth specified in the Limit action. See the following for more information: sk70600: Connectivity issues when configuring **Application Control limit** and enabling HTTPS Inspection.

9. If attempting to perform benchmarking of HTTPS Inspection on a Check Point firewall, be sure to enable HTTPS Inspection in "Test Mode" as detailed here: sk104717: HTTPS Inspection Enhancements in R77.30 and above. HTTPS Inspection Test Mode compensates for non-uniqueness quirks in HTTPS load-testing traffic, and helps ensure accurate performance results.

10. If attempting a kernel debug of traffic subject to HTTPS Inspection due to performance problems, the actual decrypted data will not be shown in the debug results which can hinder troubleshooting efforts. To make the decrypted data appear in the kernel debug itself execute the following commands:

```
fw ctl set int https_inspection_show_decrypted_data_in_debug 1
fw ctl set int ssl_inspection_extra_debug 1
```

If you use these settings for illegal and/or immoral purposes, you are a very bad person and should be ashamed of yourself.

The Fourth Path - Process Space Trips: Key Points

- On an overloaded firewall, situations requiring a process space trip on the firewall are likely to cause noticeable levels of delay.

- Traffic subject to HTTPS Inspection is always handled in the Firewall Path (F2F).

- Some firewall functions are implemented in processes for one or more of the following reasons: to ensure firewall stability, to handle situations that require waiting for a response from external server, and/or because they are newly implemented features.

- The `rad` process is critical to the proper functioning of numerous blades.

- Slow or unreachable DNS servers configured on the firewall can cause sizable delays of user traffic.

- The main recommendations to ensure acceptable HTTPS Inspection performance are: make sure Gaia is running in 64-bit mode, ensure the firewall is not overloaded, and avoid using "Any" in the HTTPS Inspection policy.

- Firewalls with 8GB of RAM or less benefit extensively from HTTPS Inspection memory optimizations introduced in code version R80.10.

CHAPTER 11
SECUREXL SESSION RATE ACCELERATION

It's hardware that makes a machine fast. It's software that makes a fast machine slow.

- Craig Bruce

Background

In Chapter 9 we noted that the first packet associated with the TCP 3-way handshake usually goes through the entire Firewall Path. Once SecureXL "learned" the new connection, and the second packet of the TCP 3-way handshake (SYN-ACK) was received, that connection and all its subsequent packets were potentially eligible for Throughput Acceleration and could be handled exclusively by the Accelerated Path. This assumes of course, that the traffic was not subject to additional inspection by the APCL/URLF or Threat Prevention features, in which case the Medium Path would be employed. Recall this diagram that shows the various paths:

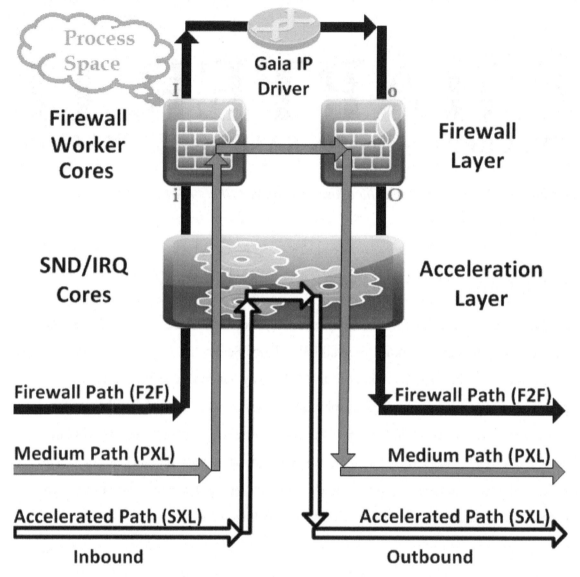

Figure 11-1: Firewall Traffic Processing Paths

However upon receipt of the first packet of a new connection (most of the time a TCP SYN), one of the most computationally expensive operations possible has to be undertaken in the Firewall Path by a Firewall Worker core: Security Policy rulebase evaluation. In other words a Firewall Worker core must decide if the connection should be allowed to start based on the Security Policy. In modern production environments, security rules can easily number into the hundreds or thousands, and on R77.30 the Firewall Worker core must sequentially search through the Security and NAT rulebases looking for a match in a "top-down, first-fit" fashion. R80.10+ gateways use Column-based matching as detailed in Chapter 5, but there can still be a fair amount of overhead involved finding a rule match. As policy size continues to grow, regardless of the technique used by the firewall to find a rulebase match, the amount of CPU processing required will increase. Firewalls that experience extremely high new connection rates wind up expending an inordinate amount of CPU time in the Firewall Path, determining if the connections should be allowed via evaluation of the Access Control policy layers.

Once the TCP SYN has been accepted and forwarded, the Acceleration Layer can potentially take over and move subsequent packets associated with that connection in a highly efficient fashion via the Accelerated Path. Wouldn't it be great if we could somehow streamline the process of handling that first packet in the Firewall Path, which is tying up so much of the CPU on our Firewall Worker cores performing policy lookups? The answer is SecureXL Session Rate Acceleration.

When Session Rate Acceleration is active, the Acceleration Layer will still initially forward new connection requests to the Firewall Path, but it will also try to form what is known as an "Accept Template" for the connection request that it just passed to the Firewall Path. As an example, the Accept Template below records the following eight attributes about the connection in the Acceleration Layer's template cache:

Source IP Address: 192.168.1.100
Destination IP Address: 129.82.102.32
Source Port Number: 1050
Destination Port Number: 80
IP Protocol Type: 6 (TCP)
Ingress Interface (determined by Acceleration Layer on inbound side): eth0
Egress Interface (determined by Acceleration Layer on outbound side assuming
the packet was allowed): eth1

The initial TCP SYN for that new connection will still traverse the Firewall Path, and once the SYN-ACK packet is received by the Acceleration layer, it will either process it via the Accelerated Path on the SND/IRQ cores, or send it for Medium/Firewall Path processing on the Firewall Worker cores if required.

However now suppose another new connection request arrives inbound at the Acceleration Layer. The Acceleration Layer will consult its Accept Template table. Does this new connection's attributes match 7 of the 8 elements of any current entries in the Accept Template table? Let's suppose the new connection request looks like this:

Source IP Address: 192.168.1.100
Destination IP Address: 129.82.102.32
Source Port Number: 2055
Destination Port Number: 80
IP Protocol Type: 6 (TCP)
Ingress Interface (determined by Acceleration Layer on inbound side): eth0
Egress Interface (determined by Acceleration Layer on outbound side): eth1

Compare this with the attributes of our first connection. See how only one field is different (the source port number) for this connection? That is good enough for an Accept Template match, because if SecureXL Session Rate Acceleration can "mask" or disregard just one of the fields, it can match a prior templated connection. The SYN packet and the rest of the TCP three-way handshake *is now handled exclusively by the*

Acceleration Layer. There is no need to do a Security Policy rulebase lookup in the Network Access layer. The connection's packets are allowed and throughput accelerated on the Accelerated Path or sent to the Medium/Firewall Path for processing immediately.

Essentially the Acceleration Layer is assuming that since the first connection was accepted by the Firewall Path, the second connection which was almost exactly the same should be permitted as well, with the same routing. Notice how we just avoided performing a security policy evaluation in the Network Access policy layer for the second connection, which once again is one of the most computationally expensive operations a firewall has to perform. The maximum number of Accept Templates that can be created in the Acceleration Layer by default is equal to 25% of the connections table size. Accept Templates also have an idle timeout of 100 seconds by default.

You may be saying to yourself: "Well gee, how many subsequent connections are only going to have ONE thing different and be able to match on an Accept Template like that?" Actually there are two protocols famous for rapid-fire, short-lived connections that only have one thing change between the different connections (usually the source port): HTTP and DNS. These two protocols alone can easily be responsible for 40% of the new connections created on a firewall, which will of course require constant Network Access policy lookups.

Discovery

Question: What is your firewall's new connection rate?

Answer: During your firewall's busiest period, bring up the SmartView Monitor, highlight the firewall in question, and select "Network Activity":

firewall
IP Address: 192.0.2.251
Version: R77.20
OS: Gaia Kernel Version: 2.6
Up Time: 1 days and 1 hours
System Information, Network Activity Licenses

General Info

Name	Value
Bytes Throughput (Bytes/Sec)	849228
Accepted Packet Rate (Packets/Sec)	1044
New Connections Rate (New Connections/Sec)	29
Concurrent Connections	489

Figure 11-2: Viewing New Connections Rate in SmartView Monitor

After about 10 seconds or so you should see the connection rate in the "New Connections Rate" field. Alternatively, to view the firewall's New Connection Rate (Connections/sec) from the CLI, run the **cpview** command and select "Network".

How do we best take advantage of the SecureXL Session Rate Acceleration feature? Session Rate Acceleration does require some tweaking and tuning of policies in order to obtain its full benefits. But hopefully now that you've obtained a basic understanding of how it works, the tuning process will be made easier.

Question: Are Session Rate Acceleration Accept Templates being formed for my firewall's security policy?

Answer: Run the command **fwaccel stat**:

```
[Expert@firewall:0]# fwaccel stat
Accelerator Status : on
Accept Templates   : enabled
Drop Templates     : disabled
NAT Templates      : disabled by user

Accelerator Features : Accounting, NAT,
                       HasClock, Templa
                       Sequencing, TcpS
                       DelayedNotif, Tc
                       WireMode, DropTe
                       Streaming, Multi
                       Nac, Asychronich
Cryptography Features : Tunnel, UDPEnca
                        3DES, DES, CAST
                        ESP, LinkSelect
                        EncRouting, AES
[Expert@firewall:0]#
```
Figure 11-3: SecureXL Accept Templates Fully Enabled

If all you see on the **Accept Templates** line is **enabled**, congratulations! No further tuning of your security policy is needed; all Network Access layer policy rules with an "Accept" action are eligible for Session Rate Acceleration by SecureXL. You are far more likely to see Accept Templates fully enabled like this on an R80.10+ firewall than an R77.30 firewall due to the many improvements to SecureXL templating in the R80.10 release; more on those improvements later.

However you are much more likely to see something like this in the command output, especially if the firewall is version R77.30:

```
[Expert@fw:0]# fwaccel stat
Accelerator Status : on
Accept Templates    : disabled by Firewall
                      Layer Network disables template
                      offloads from rule #7
                      Throughput acceleration still enabled
Drop Templates      : disabled
NAT Templates       : disabled by user
NMR Templates       : enabled
NMT Templates       : enabled

Accelerator Features : Accounting, NAT, Cryptography, Routi
                       HasClock, Templates, Synchronous, Id
                       Sequencing, TcpStateDetect, AutoExpi
```

Figure 11-4: SecureXL Accept Templates Partially Disabled

This means that rules 1-6 with an Accept action in your security policy are eligible for Session Rate Acceleration/templating. On R80.10+ firewalls an additional message **Throughput acceleration still enabled** will appear in the output in this case, clarifying that SecureXL Throughput Acceleration (covered in Chapter 9) is unaffected by this condition. Rule 7 is configured in such a way that it is not eligible for templating. *As a result, all rules after rule 7 are also not eligible for templating.* In a later section we will look at what can cause a rule (#7 in our example) to disable templating, and how to modify or work around rules of this nature.

Question: How many of my firewall's current connections were allowed by Accept Templates?

Answer: Run **fwaccel stats -s**:

```
[Expert@firewall]# fwaccel stats -s
Accelerated conns/Total conns : 3910/4297 (90%)
Accelerated pkts/Total pkts   :
F2Fed pkts/Total pkts   :
PXL pkts/Total pkts   :
QXL pkts/Total pkts   :
[Expert@firewall]#
```

Figure 11-5: Showing a High % of Templating Optimization with *fwaccel stats -s*

The only part of the output we want to examine for this chapter is the **Accelerated conns/Total conns** line; all other parts of the output refer to Throughput Acceleration which was covered in Chapter 9. **Accelerated conns/Total conns**: shows how many of the current connections in the firewall's state table were able to start completely inside the Acceleration Layer via Session Rate Acceleration; the higher the percentage the better. Generally a connection acceleration rate of 50% or higher is desired; 75% or better is ideal. Connections accelerated in this way avoid a very computationally expensive security policy rulebase lookup in the Network Access policy layer. In our sample output, 90% of the current connections being tracked in the firewall's state table were permitted by Accept Templates. This is excellent, and if the Accelerated conns percentage on your firewall is 75% or higher, there is no real need for any further Session Rate Acceleration tuning.

However you are much more likely to see something like this:

```
[Expert@firewall:0]# fwaccel stats -s
Accelerated conns/Total conns : 310/4297 (7%)
Accelerated pkts/Total pkts   :
F2Fed pkts/Total pkts   :
PXL pkts/Total pkts   :
QXL pkts/Total pkts   :
[Expert@firewall:0]#
```

Figure 11-6: Showing a Low % of Templating Optimization with *fwaccel stats -s*

This is a firewall in dire need of Session Rate Acceleration tuning, which is covered in the next section. Generally speaking our target is an **Accelerated conns** rate of at least 50%, preferably 75% or higher.

Question: How many Accept Templates have been created by SecureXL Session Rate Acceleration?

Answer: Run **fwaccel templates -s**:

There are 105 templates in SecureXL templates table

This is just a number for later comparison to evaluate the effectiveness of our Session Rate Acceleration tuning efforts; make a note of the value currently returned by your firewall for later reference. In an upcoming section we will go through how to tune your policy to optimize the formation of SecureXL Accept Templates. However there is a little something you need to be aware of before we proceed.

Anti-Bot: Slayer of SecureXL Templates

After a grueling policy tuning session based on the recommendations later in this chapter, at long last **fwaccel stat** finally reports **Accept Templates: enabled**. Victory! You crack open a container of your favorite beverage and start running **fwaccel stats -s** to bask in the glory of your great accomplishment. You start wondering just how high the SecureXL templating percentage can go, but there is something horribly wrong. The templating rate (**Accelerated conns**) is ZERO. Confused, you keep running the command over and over. No change, still zero. What the...?

If you have Anti-Bot enabled on the firewall, all traffic subject to inspection by that blade will be ineligible for SecureXL templating (but Throughput Acceleration will be unaffected). If you are seeing a template rate of zero in this case, you are probably applying the Anti-Bot blade to all traffic crossing the firewall with a Protected Scope of "Any" in the relevant Threat Prevention policy rule. In Chapter 9 there were numerous warnings about avoiding the use of "Any" in the Protected Scope field for this very reason (among many others).

The cause of this issue is that a key component of Anti-Bot is IP address reputation. However if a connection is fully templated by SecureXL and a rulebase lookup never occurs in the Firewall Path, the Anti-Bot feature (which lives in the Medium and Firewall Paths) will never see the start of the connection and be able to determine the reputation of the IP addresses involved. If Anti-Bot cannot see the connection start, it cannot stop it until it reaches the Medium or Firewall Path when data begins to flow in the connection, assuming it ever does due to the possibility of being fully throughput accelerated in the SXL Path. As of R80.10, there does not appear to be a notification mechanism between SecureXL and the Anti-Bot feature, so as a result templating cannot be allowed at all for new connections subject to Anti-Bot inspection. This limitation does not appear to be documented anywhere that I can find, but certainly confused the heck out of me the first time I encountered it.

Obviously the solution is to be a bit more careful with how Anti-Bot is applied in your Threat Prevention policy; details are located in Chapter 9.

Policy Tuning to Maximize SecureXL Templating

In the prior section we saw something like this when running `fwaccel stat`:

```
[Expert@fw:0]# fwaccel stat
Accelerator Status : on
Accept Templates  : disabled by Firewall
                    Layer Network disables template
                    offloads from rule #7
                    Throughput acceleration still enabled
Drop Templates    : disabled
NAT Templates     : disabled by user
NMR Templates     : enabled
NMT Templates     : enabled

Accelerator Features : Accounting, NAT, Cryptography, Routi
                       HasClock, Templates, Synchronous, Id
                       Sequencing. TcpStateDetect. AutoExpi
```

Figure 11-7: SecureXL Accept Templates Partially Disabled

Clearly there is something in security policy rule 7 that is disabling Accept Templates from that point in the policy. But what is it?

| 7 | 🖧 int_nets | 🔢 All_DMZs | ✳ Any | DCE ALL_DCE_RPC | 🌐 Accept |

Figure 11-8: Security Policy Rule Utilizing a Service that Disables Templating

Consider the following rulebase conditions below that can cause this to occur. Note that running R80.10+ on your firewall eliminates almost all of these templating limitations, and the best part is you don't have to do anything special to take advantage of them other than upgrade your firewall to R80.10!

- Rules with RPC/DCOM/DCE-RPC services
- Certain rarely used complex services (i.e. http_mapped, ftp_mapped) and services of type Other with a custom matching condition
- Rules with User, Client or Session Authentication actions. (These are legacy functions that have been supplanted by Identity Awareness).
- Rules containing service "traceroute" (resolved in R80.10+)

- Rules containing services dhcp-request/dhcp-reply (resolved in R80.10+)

- Time objects (resolved in R80.10+ by NMT Templates)

- Dynamic objects (resolved in R80.10+ by NMR Templates)

- Domain objects (resolved in R80.10+ by NMR Templates - *Don't use domain objects on R77.30 gateway or earlier as they can cause terrible firewall performance!*).

It is quite possible that the rule disabling the formation of Accept Templates in SecureXL is utilizing one of the object types listed above. First off, do you still need that rule? What is its hit count? If it is zero, try disabling the rule, reinstalling policy, and running `fwaccel stat` again. Now see which rule (if any) is disabling templating. If you are able to repeat this procedure enough times until `fwaccel stat` reports:

`Accept Templates : enabled`

You are good to go, and all rules in the Network Policy layer with an "Accept" action can be fully templated; now check how many more templates have now been created with the `fwaccel templates -s` command. However if you cannot simply delete or disable the rule halting template formation since it serves a critical function, you basically have two options. (The screenshots coming up will still be from SMS version R77.30, as it is far more likely that the following techniques will be required if that version is still in use on your firewall)

1. Move the offending rule as far down as possible in your rule base so that the many more rules above it will become eligible for templating; in particular try to move the offending rules below all rules with high hit counts if you can. If using R80.10+ on your firewall, the biggest situation to worry about is the presence of

RPC/DCOM/DCE-RPC services in your policy; move these rules as far down as possible in your policy. Moving rules around always has the potential to cause rule hiding conflicts during policy verification, so you may need to experiment a bit.

2. Move the rules with the highest hit counts towards the top of your rule base. Doing so will not only make these rules eligible for templating, but will also help optimize policy lookups in the Firewall Path on R77.30 firewalls when an Accept Template is not present. While this second technique will tend to yield the biggest bang for the buck from a performance perspective, unfortunately the rules with the highest hit counts tend to be very general rules that use large networks or "Any" in the Source, Destination, and/or Service fields of the rule. Attempting to move these rules higher in the rulebase, as it is currently configured, is quite likely to generate an avalanche of rule hiding errors during policy verification.

One way to get around this is to determine what specific elements of the Source, Destination, and/or Service fields of the highly utilized general rule causes the most hits. As an example, towards the end of most rulebases there tends to be a rule that lets all internal users out to the Internet, and it looks something like this:

Figure 11-9: Typical Outbound Internet Access Policy Rule

Attempting to move this rule near the top of your policy (perhaps just after the firewall stealth rule) is almost certain to cause a flurry of rule hide errors that will prevent you from installing the policy. This is typically due to the Service field being set to

"Any", or a large number of approved ports. However suppose you determine that the top services utilized by users accessing the Internet in the SmartView Tracker/SmartLog for this rule are http, https, and ssh. If you have the Monitoring blade license, you can easily determine this in the SmartView Monitor by running a "Top Services" real-time report or a historical SmartView Monitor "Top Services" report for the last week.

Now you create a new "split" rule right below the firewall's stealth rule like this:

2	▭	✳ Any	🖳 Firewall_	✳ Any	✳ Any	⬤ drop	📄 Log
⊟	SecureXL Templating Optimized Rules	(Rules 3-6)					
3	▭	🖧 Internal_Nets	✳ Any	✳ Any	TCP http TCP https TCP ssh	⊕ accept	📄 Log

Figure 11-10: New Templating Rule Splitting Services Out from a Lower Rule

The original generalized rule is left at the bottom of the rulebase, untouched other than removing the services http, https and ssh from the Approved_Ports group. Now the vast majority of outbound Internet traffic can be templated by Session Rate Acceleration, and, as an extra bonus, the R77.30 top-down policy evaluation in the Firewall Path is much more efficient! There may be a few service conflicts between your new rule and lower rules, but they are likely to be quite manageable compared to leaving the Service field as "Approved_Ports" in this new upper rule! Depending on the rule you are attempting to split out in this fashion, you may also need to substitute something more specific than "Any" in the Source and/or Destination fields.

Following is an example rulebase showing a practical application of these techniques:

Policy

No.	Hits	Source	Destination	VPN	Service	Action	Track
−		**Firewall Mgmt & Stealth Rule** (Rules 1-2)					
1	▭▭▭	▦ Admin	▭ Firewall_	✳ Any	TCP ssh TCP https	⊕ accept	▤ Log
2	▭▭▭	✳ Any	▭ Firewall_	✳ Any	✳ Any	◉ drop	▤ Log
−		**SecureXL Templating Optimized Rules** (Rules 3-6)					
3	▭▭▭	▱ Internal_Nets	✳ Any	✳ Any	TCP http TCP https TCP ssh	⊕ accept	▤ Log
4	▭▭▭	✳ Any	▣ Web_Server	✳ Any	TCP http TCP https	⊕ accept	▤ Log
5	▭▭▭	✳ Any	▣ Mail_Server	✳ Any	TCP smtp TCP POP3S TCP IMAP-SSL	⊕ accept	▤ Log
6	▭▭▭	▣ Web_Server	▣ DB_Server	✳ Any	TCP sqlnet1 ▦ sqlnet2	⊕ accept	▤ Log
−		**Rest of Policy for rarely-hit rules** (Rules 7-19)					

Figure 11-11: Policy Showing New Section for Optimized SecureXL Templating

We have created a "SecureXL Templating Optimized Rules" section of the policy for rules with high hits counts near the top of our policy. Ideally any rule with a high hit count (which will visually show a red or orange bar in the "Hits" field) should be moved into this section of the policy. Rules that are too nonspecific for relocation that high in the rulebase should have portions of them split into a higher rule in the rulebase, as shown earlier.

Now look at how many hits are occurring against the original generalized rule towards the bottom of your policy. It should be reduced significantly; open the SmartView Tracker/SmartLog and only look at traffic matching the lower generalized rule. If you see lots and lots of matches against the lower rule for a service that happens to still be matching against this rule's "Approved_Ports" Service field, consider "splitting" that service off into the upper rule you created earlier! Deal with any rule hiding errors as needed. Rinse and repeat until the vast majority of hits are occurring on the upper optimized rules in the "SecureXL Templating Optimized Rules" section of the rulebase.

If something still seems to be disabling Session Rate Acceleration templating in your rulebase, consult sk32578: SecureXL Mechanism for the current and authoritative list of situations that cause this to occur. Be sure to look at the **Acceleration of connections (templates)** section of the SK, not the part covering the "Acceleration of packets"! As noted earlier, upgrading your firewall to R80.10+ relaxes the templating rules significantly, but watch out for Anti-Bot! Don't forget to check how many more templates have been formed with the `fwaccel templates -s` command compared to what we saw earlier, once the policy optimizations or firewall upgrade to R80.10+ is complete.

Other Situations That Can Disable Session Acceleration

Some individual connections matching a security policy rule cannot be templated, but their presence does not disturb the templating process of subsequent rules. This is a major source of confusion when tuning SecureXL Session Rate Acceleration. As an example the service FTP is commonly cited as "disabling acceleration". This does *not* mean that use of the FTP service in a rule will disable templating of all subsequent rules beneath it; it simply means that the individual FTP connection itself cannot be templated, and will incur a full security policy rulebase lookup in the Firewall Path. Subsequent rules beneath the rule referencing the FTP service can still be templated. What other types of connections cannot be individually templated?

- VPN traffic cannot be individually templated. Connections that are encrypting into a VPN tunnel outbound, or decrypting from a VPN tunnel inbound, are not eligible for Session Rate Acceleration via Accept Templates. (In a prior chapter we also noted that most VPN traffic is not eligible for Throughput Acceleration either, and on an R77.30 firewall must take the Firewall Path on the lowest-numbered Firewall Worker core)
- Complex connections (FTP, H323, etc.) cannot be individually templated. "Complex Connections" are generally defined as protocols that dynamically open data ports on the fly.
- Non-TCP and Non-UDP traffic (including ICMP & GRE traffic) cannot be individually templated. Only TCP connections and UDP traffic are eligible for templating.

Once again, the presence of these situations in your security policy rulebase does not disable templating of subsequent rules; it just precludes the use of templating for these individual connections.

NAT Templates

NAT rulebase templating ability was introduced relatively recently in release R75.40. We spent a fair amount of time earlier in this chapter optimizing the templating process for the main Security Policy (called the Network Policy Layer in R80+ management). Hopefully you were able to increase the "Accelerated conns" percentage displayed by `fwaccel stats -s` to at least 50%, preferably more than 75%. However if all those connections are subject to NAT, what about NAT rulebase lookups for all of these connections? These NAT lookups are still processed in the Firewall Path unless NAT Templates are enabled in SecureXL.

However unless *at least 50%* of connections are able to be templated (`Accelerated conns/Total conns`) *AND* at least 50% of traffic is being handled in the Accelerated Path (`Accelerated pkts/Total pkts`) as shown by `fwaccel stats -s`, there is little to gain by enabling NAT Templates and potentially a lot to lose. NAT Templates can only be enabled and disabled via the `fwkern.conf` file and a firewall reboot, so if problems start to occur after enabling NAT Templates an outage will be required to turn them back off unless you have a firewall cluster. Enabling NAT Templates also seems to increase the likelihood of problems with other parts of the firewall, including SecureXL randomly disabling itself:

- sk113398: Dynamic Dispatcher 'instance mismatch' drops on ports 80 and 443
- sk100467: "Accelerator Status : off by Firewall (too many general errors (N) (caller: ...))" in the output of "fwaccel stat" command
- sk106709 - SecureXL instability when SecureXL NAT Templates are enabled and Hide NAT is configured on VSX
- sk111015 - Traffic outage on ClusterXL after enabling both CoreXL Dynamic Dispatcher and SecureXL NAT Templates
- sk117332 - Cluster member with enabled SecureXL crashes during policy installation due to issues in SecureXL NAT Templates

So should you enable NAT Templates? I can only speak from my own experience, but I've rarely if ever needed to enable them. The fact that NAT Templates are still disabled on R80.10 firewalls by default would seem to confirm my hesitancy to enable them. If the tuning techniques detailed throughout this book are properly implemented, I've always been able to obtain good performance with an acceptable amount of headroom for future growth, without needing NAT Templates in almost all cases. In my opinion, enabling NAT Templates is usually past the point of diminishing returns when it comes to most firewall performance optimization efforts, especially if the vast majority of traffic inspection is occurring in the Medium Path, which is quite typical in the real world. Throughout the book I've emphasized a best "bang for the buck" approach that maximizes performance gains, without extensive effort or venturing into obscure or esoteric areas. Most of the sizable performance gains have probably been realized by this point of the book, unless there are special circumstances present.

Should you still wish to enable SecureXL NAT Templates, consult sk71200: SecureXL NAT Templates. Once again, unless *at least 50%* of connections are able to be templated (**Accelerated conns/Total conns**) *AND* *at least 50%* of traffic is being handled in the Accelerated Path (**Accelerated pkts/Total pkts**) as shown by **fwaccel stats -s**, there is probably little to gain by enabling NAT Templates. Also be aware of the following, some of which was already mentioned in this chapter:

- Enabling NAT Templates involves a change to the **fwkern.conf** file on the firewall, which is used to specify custom kernel variable values in the Check Point code. This file will typically not survive a version upgrade on the firewall, and must be manually reconfigured once any upgrade is completed. A reboot of the firewall is required to make any **fwkern.conf** changes active; needless to say this will cause an outage unless you have a firewall cluster.

- If NAT Templates cause an issue, the only way to turn them back off is to edit the **fwkern.conf** file and reboot the gateway; once again this process will cause an outage unless you have a firewall cluster.

- Once enabled, statistics involving NAT Templates can be viewed with the **fwaccel stats** command.

SecureXL Session Rate Acceleration: Key Points

- SecureXL Session Rate Acceleration is a completely separate function from Throughput Acceleration via the three kernel paths.

- Session Rate Acceleration uses Accept Templates to accelerate the start of a new connection and avoid a computationally expensive security policy rule base lookup in the Network policy layer.

- Traffic subject to inspection by the Anti-Bot blade cannot be Session Rate Accelerated (templated) at all.

- The R80.10+ firewall code includes numerous Session Rate Acceleration improvements that make all rules in a Network policy layer far more likely to be completely eligible for templating.

- Security policy rule base optimization in the Network Access policy layer may be required to get the most out of Session Rate Acceleration.

- NAT Templates can be enabled to permit SecureXL templating of NATed connections; however the performance gains will be minimal if most packets are processed in the Medium and/or Firewall Paths on the firewall.

CHAPTER 12
MULTI-QUEUE & SMT/HYPERTHREADING

The more real people I get to know, the more I am convinced the simpler the solution, the better the solution.

- William J. Bernstein

Introduction: Multi-Queue

In Chapter 7, there was an extended discussion about the most insidious member of the so called RX "Dark Triad": the RX-DRP counter. All too frequently, an unacceptably large number of incoming packets would be dropped by the firewall. Not because they violated a security policy, but because there was an insufficient amount of CPU resources allocated for timely servicing of network interface ring buffers. After thoroughly dissecting the network buffering mechanism and how the RX-DRP counter indicated a problem was occurring, we saw that it was a "no brainer" to reallocate more CPU cores for SND/IRQ processing to ensure timely servicing of network buffers, with an RX-DRP rate of less than 0.1% as our goal.

Enabling Multi-Queue and/or SMT/Hyperthreading is NOT a no-brainer!

Neither of these features is enabled by default, and for good reason. If these features are enabled indiscriminately, the complexity of the firewall configuration can be increased for no tangible benefit. Inevitably this complexity will come back to bite you at the most inconvenient (and potentially career-limiting) moment possible. Complexity is the enemy of security, and networks in general. Few things make my blood boil more as a consultant than seeing unnecessary complexity introduced into a design that provides no measurable, tangible benefit. Just because you *can* do something and it "sounds cool" doesn't mean you *should*.

Enabling these features inappropriately can do much more than just increase complexity; *they can actually degrade firewall performance*.

With all that said, Multi-Queue and SMT/Hyperthreading are great features that can significantly boost firewall performance, under the right set of circumstances. In this chapter we will explore what set of circumstances lend themselves to activating these features, and how best to do so in your network. If one or both of these features is enabled but no tangible gains are achieved, my overwhelming recommendation is to turn them back off!

Note: The procedure described in sk63128: How to assign RX and TX of 10 Gb interface, which uses IXGBE driver, to different CPU cores was a primitive way to spread interface buffer processing overhead across more than one core, and a precursor to the introduction of the Multi-Queue feature. Don't use this primitive workaround, use Multi-Queue instead.

Discovery: Multi-Queue

Recall a key component of our stated goal for performance optimization was stipulating a network interface RX-DRP rate of less than 0.1%, and that all cores are at least 50% idle during the firewall's busiest period. If your firewall has already reached that goal, there will probably be no tangible benefit to enabling Multi-Queue other than possibly increasing the processing "headroom" available to the firewall for weathering a Denial of Service attack. Proceed if you wish, but please heed the earlier warnings about increasing the complexity of the firewall unnecessarily.

Question: Is Multi-Queue already enabled on any interfaces of my firewall?

Run `cpmq get`

Question: Is SecureXL enabled?

Run `fwaccel stat`

Question: Do I have any interfaces using the igb/ixgbe/mlx5_core drivers that are eligible for Multi-Queue?

(Note: The option after the `ls` command is a numeric 1)

```
ls -1 /sys/class/net | grep -v ^lo | xargs -i ethtool {}
```

Question: Do all my interfaces have an RX-DRP rate less than 0.1%?

Run `netstat -ni`. Divide RX-DRP by RX-OK and multiply by 100 to obtain the RX-DRP percentage.

Question: How many cores does the firewall have?

```
cpstat -f cp os | grep -i CPUs
```

Your firewall must have at least 2 cores to use Multi-Queue, and the underlying hardware must support IRQ Swizzling; however enabling Multi-Queue on a 2-core firewall is virtually unheard of, and on a 4-core firewall it will probably provide minimal performance benefits. Multi-Queue is primarily employed on firewalls with 6 or more cores.

Analysis: Multi-Queue

If you have skipped to this chapter to enable Multi-Queue without performing the steps laid out in all the earlier chapters, it is very important to tune the firewall as described in all prior chapters before evaluating the need for Multi-Queue. After performing those optimizations you may realize you don't need Multi-Queue at all! Keep the firewall configuration as simple as possible please!

If you have reached this point, the firewall has probably been tuned to the best of your abilities, however you are still suffering an RX-DRP rate of >0.1% on one or more of your interfaces, or you were not able to obtain our stated goal of 50% idle on all cores during the firewall's busiest period. This is generally indicative of three situations:

1. There are plenty of cores allocated to the SND/IRQ function, the interface in question may even have been allocated its very own dedicated core for SoftIRQ processing (`sim affinity -1`), and that core's only job is to do nothing but empty that single interface's RX ring buffer. However the single dedicated core either has substantially less than 50% idle time available during the firewall's busiest period, and/or the RX-DRP rate is still >0.1%. This situation is not too common with 1Gbps interfaces (if it is, there is probably something else wrong such as the firewall being severely overloaded), but this situation can easily occur

on a busy 10Gbps+ interface. *Multi-Queue will most definitely help in this scenario, and the performance gains can be impressive.*

2. You've gone through all the tuning procedures in the earlier chapters, but you just don't seem to have enough cores available to allocate for SND/IRQ processing. Ideally each of the 10Gbps+ interfaces has its own dedicated core for SoftIRQ processing, but trying to allocate enough SND/IRQ cores to accomplish this subsequently overloads the remaining reduced number of Firewall Worker cores. There may even be 1Gbps interfaces racking up too many RX-DRP errors in this case. Examine the processor utilization of the SND/IRQ cores (`sim affinity -l` followed by "`top`...1"). If during the firewall's busiest period the SND/IRQ cores are averaging 25-50% idle (or you see large disparities in idle percentages amongst the SND/IRQ cores), *Multi-Queue can definitely provide some tangible gains in this scenario, but keep in mind that the firewall is moderately overloaded, so be sure to temper your expectations.*

3. If all the SND/IRQ cores have less than 25% idle time available during the firewall's busiest period and you can't reallocate more cores to SND/IRQ due to high Firewall Worker core utilization, the firewall is severely overloaded and Multi-Queue is not likely to make much of a difference; overall firewall performance will probably get worse if you turn it on. Proceed in this case at your own risk.

When Multi-Queue is disabled (which is the default), there is only one queue and associated ring buffer for each active network interface, and only one SND/IRQ core is allowed to process that particular ring buffer. Note that there is only one queue per *physical* interface. An interface with only one IP address assigned to it receiving untagged traffic, and another interface trunking 500 VLANs via 802.1q, both look exactly the same from an interface buffering perspective: one queue. Multi-Queue allows more than one queue per physical interface for up to 5 separate physical interfaces at once; bonded/aggregate interfaces are supported as well.

When Multi-Queue is enabled for an interface, by default multiple SND/IRQ cores may now process packets from that interface instead of just one. This is accomplished by creating multiple parallel queues for the same interface; the number of queues created is equal to the total number of SND/IRQ cores allocated (subject to some limits discussed below). So if you have a 16-core system with a 4/12 split, enabling Multi-Queue on an interface creates 4 parallel queues for that single interface, one per SND/IRQ core. As traffic arrives on the Multi-Queue-enabled interface, a hashing algorithm runs in the NIC driver to decide which of the 4 available queues should receive the packet for processing. It is always desirable to "stick" packets associated with a certain connection (or network stream) to the same queue every time. Failure to do so could result in out-of-order delivery of packets, which is an unmitigated disaster from a performance perspective when TCP is involved.

The hashing algorithm that "sticks" a single connection's packets to the same queue every time imposes some slight additional overhead on the SND/IRQ cores. In most cases this is more than made up for by relieving the single-core processing bottleneck on a very busy 10Gbps+ interface. However if all the SND/IRQ cores are already overloaded, enabling Multi-Queue (with its additional hashing mechanism overhead) *can actually make overall firewall performance worse*.

By default enabling Multi-Queue will create as many parallel queues for an interface as there are SND/IRQ cores. However if the interface in question is using the Intel igb driver (typically associated with older Intel 1Gbps NICs), there is a maximum limit of 4 queues that can be created for that interface, regardless of the number of SND/IRQ cores. As a result, a maximum of 4 SND/IRQ cores will be able to process a single interface's frames with the igb driver.

For the 3000/5000/15000/23000 series of firewall appliances, there is an additional limitation for the on-board (built-in) NICs; they utilize the igb driver yet due to a NIC hardware limitation, can only have a maximum of two parallel queues per interface. As such, it is recommended to avoid using the onboard NICs on these appliances to handle heavy traffic loads that might require Multi-Queue functionality. For more information see sk114625: Multi-Queue does not work on 3200 / 5000 / 15000 / 23000 appliances when it is enabled for on-board interfaces.

For newer Intel interfaces using the ixgbe driver (typically 10Gbps+ NICs), the limit per interface is 16 parallel queues. In the past, only the NICs manufactured by Intel supported Multi-Queue on Gaia. However the 15000/23000 series of appliances now have a 40Gbit fiber expansion card available which is manufactured by Mellanox (driver name displayed by `ethtool -i` is "mlx5_core") that also supports Multi-Queue. Just be aware that these NIC cards are relatively new and have not been as thoroughly vetted as the Intel NICs, and of the following limitation: sk112517: 40 GbE fiber cards on 15000 / 23000 appliance stop working after installing Take 128 and above of R77.30 Jumbo Hotfix .

A few general notes about Multi-Queue:

- SecureXL MUST be enabled to use Multi-Queue.
- Multi-Queue can be enabled on no more than 5 physical interfaces at one time, regardless of NIC hardware and driver types.
- If the number of Firewall Worker cores is changed (which will cause the number of SND/IRQ cores to change), boot the firewall into the new core configuration,

run the command **cpmq reconfigure,** and then reboot the firewall again to properly reconfigure Multi-Queue for the new core configuration. You cannot skip the intermediate reboot, and must reboot the firewall twice.

- It is possible to change the number of parallel queues per interface manually with the **cpmq set rxnum** command, so that it no longer matches the overall number of SND/IRQ cores. This may be useful in some limited circumstances to exclude some of the SND/IRQ cores from being asked to process Multi-Queue traffic from certain interfaces, thus freeing them up for other operations.

- Only enable Multi-Queue on the interfaces that need it, due to the slight additional overhead imposed on the SND/IRQ cores required to "stick" connections to the same queue. Good interface candidates for Multi-Queue either have an RX-DRP rate >0.1%, or have substantially less than 50% idle on their corresponding SND/IRQ core during the firewall's busiest period.

- If the overwhelming majority of traffic is handled by only two interfaces on the firewall (and especially if they are 10Gbps or higher), enabling Multi-Queue for those two interfaces is strongly recommended.

Enabling Multi-Queue

Note: If you have skipped to this section because you are gung-ho about indiscriminately enabling Multi-Queue because it "sounds cool", please stop and read everything in this chapter prior to this section to ensure you completely understand the possible ramifications of what you are about to do.

Once you have determined which interface(s) need some SoftIRQ processing help via Multi-Queue, run the command **cpmq set**. You will be presented with a list of interfaces that are eligible for Multi-Queue operation. Select the interface(s) you determined earlier for Multi-Queue operation and exit. Once changes are complete, you will need to reboot the firewall to make them effective. After reboot run **cpmq get** to verify that Multi-Queue is enabled on the interface(s) desired. Run **top**...1 and recheck the processing load on all SND/IRQ cores; it should now be far more balanced.

However on some systems there is a much easier way to enable Multi-Queue. In the firewall's Gaia web interface under "Network Management... Performance Optimization" the following screen *may* be available:

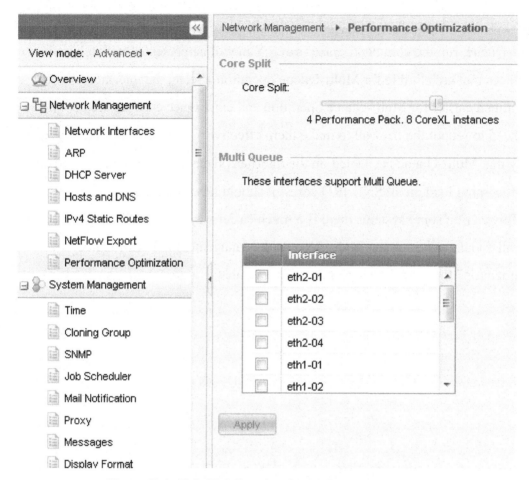

Figure 12-1: Gaia Web Interface Multi-Queue Setup Page

At the bottom of the screen is a list of all network interfaces that are eligible for use with Multi-Queue; simply check the box next to the interfaces you wish to enable and click OK. A reboot is still required for the changes to take effect. Your firewall must have at least six cores *and* must have at least one interface using Intel's igb or ixgbe driver (or the Mellanox mlx5_core driver) for this screen to be available. If this web page is not present on your firewall, just use the `cpmq set` command instead.

Multi-Queue: RX-DRP Still Incrementing Regularly?

If you've enabled the Multi-Queue feature and ensured that all SND/IRQ cores are at least 50% idle at all times, RX-DRPs should happen very rarely. If however you notice they are still racking up on a regular basis even when the firewall is not busy at all (but performance is still excellent overall), there is probably a misconfiguration in your network switches that should be corrected. Consult the "RX-DRP Revisited: Still Racking Them Up?" section of Chapter 7.

Introduction: SMT/Hyperthreading

In the first edition of *Max Power*, SMT/Hyperthreading was referred to as "Hyperspect" which is an outdated term. That first edition also took a fairly hard line against enabling SMT, unless it was conclusively shown that the vast majority of firewall traffic was being handled in the Medium Path (PXL). It was also stated that enabling SMT under any other circumstances was just increasing complexity for a questionable gain in performance, and that SMT had not been extensively deployed by many Check Point customers in the real world. My stance on SMT has softened somewhat since then, *but assuming you have reached our stated goal of 50% idle on all cores during the firewall's busiest period with an RX-DRP rate of less than 0.1% on all interfaces, you really don't need to enable SMT, even if your firewall supports it.*

However for the new series of 5800/5900/15400/15600/23500/23800 appliances, Check Point now recommends enabling SMT as a best practice regardless of the percentage of PXL traffic, assuming they are running at least take 132 of the R77.30 Jumbo HFA on the firewall (or R80.10+). Apparently the reason for this recommendation is that Check Point has performed all their quality assurance testing on these specific hardware models with SMT enabled, as opposed to it being disabled for all their testing on prior models.

I'm not quite ready to state that enabling SMT/Hyperthreading on a firewall that supports it is a "no-brainer" just yet, but we are getting close.

Discovery: SMT/Hyperthreading

Question: Is SMT (Simultaneous multithreading) enabled?

Answer: Run `cat /proc/smt_status`. Three results are possible:

1. `Unsupported` – Your firewall appliance does not meet at least one of the many requirements for SMT/Hyperthreading detailed below.

2. `Soft Disable` – Your firewall appliance hardware supports SMT/Hyperthreading, but it has not yet been enabled from `cpconfig`.

3. `Enabled` – SMT/Hyperthreading is enabled. The default for Check Point appliances is disabled, so SMT/Hyperthreading was explicitly enabled at some point.

SMT/Hyperthreading support was introduced in the R77 release and allows a Check Point firewall appliance to take advantage of Intel's CPU Hyperthreading feature (technically called Simultaneous multithreading or SMT) in certain processor architectures. Until the release of version R77, SMT/Hyperthreading was always disabled on all Check Point appliances, and Check Point strongly recommended always disabling Hyperthreading in the BIOS on open hardware firewalls, so as to avoid conflicts with CoreXL. While Intel claims as much as a 50% performance boost can be obtained by enabling Hyperthreading, Check Point states that a more realistic expectation of the gains obtained on the firewall is in the 20-30% range.

Hopefully you have already completed the tuning procedures described in all the chapters leading up to this one. If you have skipped to this section because you just want to enable SMT/Hyperthreading without being aware of the possible ramifications, you need to STOP and complete all the tuning procedures in the prior chapters. It is likely that after proper tuning you may find you don't need to enable SMT/Hyperthreading at all! If you have completed all the prior tuning procedures in this book, read on.

Before delving any further into SMT, we must first visit the long list of requirements that all must be met to leverage this feature. They are:

1. Only certain higher-end Check Point appliance model numbers support SMT. Generally speaking appliance model numbers 5800 and higher support SMT/Hyperthreading, *except* the 12200 model and the obsolete Power-1 9000/11000 series.

2. The firewall appliance must be running Gaia in 64-bit mode with code level R77 or later to enable SMT, and must have a minimum of 8GB RAM. All current Check Point appliances whose processor architectures support SMT ship with at least 8GB of RAM included, except the 12400 and 12600 appliances.

3. CoreXL must be enabled. The maximum number of Firewall Worker cores that can be configured (regardless of whether SMT is enabled or not) is limited to 32 for the R77.30 release. For R80.10+ gateway, this limit has increased to 40.

4. Run **free -m** on the candidate firewall. The number in the "free" column on the "-/+ buffers/cache" line of the output should be at least 3072 for firewalls with up to 12 total cores, and at least 6144 for firewalls with more than 12 cores.

If there is insufficient free memory, firewall performance will be severely impaired by virtual memory paging and swapping if you attempt to turn SMT on.

5. Due to memory limitations (and a possible dramatic performance impact), features that are contraindicated for enabling SMT are: the older DLP blade (*not* Content Awareness), Anti-Virus (Traditional Mode Only), and Security Policy rules that utilize legacy resource objects.

6. Do not enable SMT on a 15000/23000 series appliance using the relatively new 25G/40G/100G Mellanox NIC hardware as doing so was not supported at press time. See sk116742: Installing and Configuring Dual 25G/100G I/O card in 15000 and 23000 Appliances for updates.

7. SMT has never been officially supported on any open firewall hardware, and this restriction continues into the R80.10 code release.

8. The software features that tend to benefit most from SMT are the so-called "next-generation firewall" ones that perform quite a bit of traffic pattern matching and Active Streaming in the Medium Path (PXL), such as Application Control, URL Filtering, and Threat Prevention. Note that "traditional" Firewall Security Policy/NAT functions do *not* benefit from SMT. Enabling SMT on a firewall that does not utilize any of the "next-generation firewall" features listed above is likely to actually degrade firewall performance and capacity in ways that are sure to surprise you (rather unpleasantly I might add).

9. The QoS feature that is part of the Advanced Networking blade is not supported with SMT. This limitation does not apply to the 5800/15400/15600/23500/23800 appliances specifically using at least Take 138 of the R77.30 Jumbo Hotfix Accumulator (or R80.10+). This restriction does *not* include Limit actions implemented in an APCL/URLF policy layer for any appliance model.

Analysis: SMT/Hyperthreading

Once SMT is enabled, there are essentially twice as many cores available for configuration as SND/IRQ or Firewall Worker cores. Remember the recommendation from the CoreXL chapter to allocate cores by function in adjacent pairs to maximize CPU fast memory cache access? That recommendation is even more important when SMT is enabled. You should *never* set two adjacent cores to perform different functions when SMT is enabled. For the record, adjacent cores would be 0+1, 2+3, 4+5, etc. These so-called "adjacent cores" are not really two separate cores when SMT is enabled; they are just two logical threads on the *same physical core*. If possible, is *strongly preferable* to allocate core functions in blocks of 4 cores (for example 0,1,2,3 and 4,5,6,7) to maximize CPU L2 fast cache sharing between the 2 physical (4 logical) adjacent cores when SMT is enabled.

R77.30 Special Case: IPSec VPNs & SMT/Hyperthreading

Recall from Chapter 8 that all IPSec VPN traffic is confined to only one Firewall Worker core on R77.30 firewalls, regardless of whether CoreXL is enabled or not. R80.10+ firewalls support MultiCore IPSec VPNs by default and are not subject to this limitation. However this presents a special problem when SMT is enabled in R77.30; by default the poor single logical core that is tasked with all IPSec VPN operations now has to share resources with another Firewall Worker instance trying to run on the same physical core. Only being able to use one core for all IPSec VPN operations in R77.30 was bad enough, but this situation is now exacerbated with SMT enabled.

Thankfully there is a workaround for R77.30; simply set the `fwmultik_dispatch_skip_global` kernel variable to a value of 2 as described in:

sk93000: SMT (**Hyperthreading**) Feature Guide. When set to 2, this variable stipulates that the single core tasked with handling IPSec VPN traffic will only concern itself with handling IPSec VPN traffic (it doesn't also try to act like a generic Firewall Worker core as well) AND that the adjacent core (really just another logical thread on the same physical core) just sits idle and does not do anything at all. This configuration helps avoid thread contention and CPU fast cache thrashing on the physical core that is dedicated to processing IPSec VPN operations. Once again, R80.10+ firewalls are not subject to this limitation due to the new MultiCore IPSec feature, so if you have upgraded your gateway to R80.10+ make sure to unset `fwmultik_dispatch_skip_global` if you have manually configured it.

Enabling SMT/Hyperthreading

Note: If you have skipped to this section because you are gung-ho about indiscriminately enabling SMT, please stop and read everything in this chapter prior to this section to ensure you completely understand the possible ramifications of what you are about to do.

To enable SMT/Hyperthreading:

1. Run `cpconfig`, select the `Configure Hyper-Threading` menu option and select "yes". If this option does not appear in the `cpconfig` menu, your firewall does not support SMT; see the list of requirements earlier in this chapter.

2. On R77.30 or earlier gateways extensively utilizing IPSec VPNs, set kernel variable `fwmultik_dispatch_skip_global` to 2 as mentioned earlier. This step is unnecessary on R80.10+ firewalls.

3. Reboot the firewall.

4. If you have Multi-Queue enabled on any interfaces, run `cpmq reconfigure` and reboot the firewall again. *Note: The reboot in step 3 cannot be skipped prior to running* `cpmq reconfigure`, *you must reboot first before running this command.*

5. After reboot, run `fw ctl affinity -l -a -r` and `sim affinity -l` to verify the new core configuration.

6. If Multi-Queue is enabled, run `cpmq get` to verify proper Multi-Queue operation.

Multi-Queue & SMT/Hyperthreading: Key Points

- It is not quite a "no brainer" to always enable SMT/Hyperthreading; doing so indiscriminately can actually hurt firewall performance and increase complexity.

- Multi-Queue allows more than one SND/IRQ core to process SoftIRQ interrupts for an interface and is particularly useful for 10Gbps+ interfaces.

- When enabled, Hyperthreading leverages the SMT function of Intel processor architectures to double the total number of cores available.

- Traditional firewall processing performance is not enhanced by enabling SMT/Hyperthreading.

- So-called "next-generation firewall" features that are heavily dependent on Medium Path processing benefit the most from Hyperthreading.

- Numerous memory and hardware requirements must be met for the firewall to be eligible to use SMT/Hyperthreading.

- R77.30 firewalls that process large amounts of IPSec VPN traffic and plan to enable SMT/Hyperthreading should be upgraded to R80.10+.

CHAPTER 13
INCREASING FIREWALL RESISTANCE TO DOS ATTACKS

Elliot: *This was a RUDY (R-U-Dead-Yet) attack. This is awesome.*
Gideon: *Awesome? You think this is awesome? This is killing us, Elliot.*

Mr. Robot, episode "Eps1.0_hellofriend.mov"

Background

Our stated goal of 50% idle on all CPU cores during the firewall's busiest period, and an RX-DRP rate <0.1% goes a long way towards increasing the firewall's resistance to a Denial of Service (DoS) attack, by ensuring a large amount of processing "headroom" is available. Features listed in this chapter can help significantly increase the firewall's resistance to a DoS attack. These features are primarily designed for use in mitigating a DoS attack from the Internet, but particular capabilities (such as Rate Limiting described below) can sometimes be useful to throttle an internal system or network that is consuming too many connections in the firewall's state table, or sending extremely heavy bursts of packets through the firewall that are detrimental to overall performance. Enabling the Multi-Queue feature (covered in the previous chapter) can also provide some benefits in a DoS scenario by distributing the processing of network interface SoftIRQs across multiple cores.

For the latest Check Point firewall DoS mitigation strategies, see sk112241: Best Practices - DDoS attacks on Check Point Security Gateway.

Aggressive Aging

A good starting point for the real world is to ensure that "Aggressive Aging" is enabled on your firewall at all times. The other remaining features listed below tend to be deployed in direct response to an observed or expected DoS attack. In R77.30 the "Aggressive Aging" capability is implemented as an IPS signature that can be found under the IPS tab of SmartDashboard under "Protections". A valid IPS license/contract is required. Make sure that the IPS profile assigned to your gateway has the Aggressive Aging signature enabled.

On R80.10+ firewalls, Aggressive Aging has been separated from the IPS blade and is part of the Inspection Settings component of the Access Control policy layers as shown here:

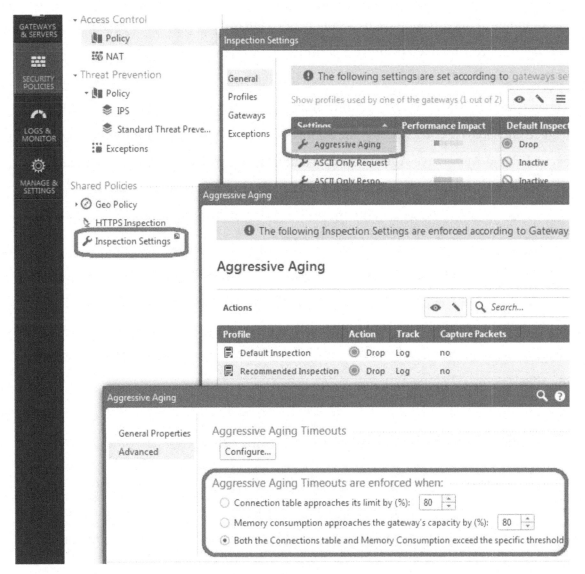

Figure 13-1: Aggressive Aging

If Aggressive Aging is enabled, by default if the amount of RAM consumption and connections table capacity reaches 80% on the firewall, the oldest idle connections in the firewall's connections table will be expired early in an attempt to keep the firewall from running out of free RAM memory or connection table capacity. Should the firewall run out of either of these resources, new connections attempting to start through the firewall will be dropped, and overall firewall performance will suffer. Aggressive Aging actions will be logged by default; you could even set up an email alert or SNMP trap from the "Track" menu of the Aggressive Aging signature to alert you in real time when the trigger thresholds are reached and the feature activates. Whenever a threshold is exceeded and Aggressive Aging becomes active, messages such as **FW-1: Capacity Problem detected: Connections Table/Memory Consumption has exceeded XX%** will be written the firewall's syslog and/or appear in the firewall's traffic logs viewable in the SmartConsole GUI.

This alerting setup can be a great "canary in the coal mine" notification that your firewall is suddenly approaching its capacity limits due to an unexpectedly large amount of legitimate connections, or the commencement of a DoS attack that may necessitate enabling some of the other features listed below, depending on the nature and scope of the attack.

Firewall Enhanced Durability/Heavy Load QoS

Originally introduced in R60, this capability is seldom used these days due to the newer, more robust anti-DoS features that have been introduced. This HLQoS feature consists of the **sim hlqos** and **sim tmplquota** set of commands. See the following for more information: sk33239: What are Enhanced Durability features?.

Drop Templates & Drop Optimization

Drop Templates were introduced in R70 as a technique to directly insert "fast drop" rules into the Accelerated Path to more quickly & efficiently discard offending traffic; these "fast drop" rules have absolutely nothing to do with the main Security Policy's rules visible in the SmartDashboard/SmartConsole. Unless Drop Templates are in use, only *accepted* traffic is able to be accelerated by SecureXL Session Rate Acceleration templates. Traffic that does not match an Accept Template will have to be forwarded to the Firewall Path for the Security Policy evaluation and subsequent drop to occur. This will of course incur far more CPU overhead than immediately dropping the traffic directly in the Accelerated Path instead. Drop Templates can be added and modified from the CLI using the `sim dropcfg` command. In versions R70-R75.30, a well-hidden Global Properties checkbox called "enable_drop_templates" was used to toggle the entire Drop Templates feature off and on for all managed firewalls.

For various reasons the original Drop Templates feature was not very well-known, and caused numerous problems when it was implemented by firewall administrators. The problems were severe enough that the "enable_drop_templates" checkbox disappeared from the Global Properties in version R75.40, never to be seen again. The implementation of Drop Templates was thoroughly overhauled and reborn in R76; Check Point retroactively withdrew official support for Drop Templates in all versions prior to R76: sk66402: SecureXL **Drop Templates** are not supported in versions lower than R76.

As part of the overhaul of Drop Templates, a new feature called "Drop Optimization" was introduced. As opposed to the static nature of Drop Templates that were created and removed manually by the firewall administrator using the CLI command `sim dropcfg`, Drop Optimization utilizes various default thresholds that dictate when to start forming dynamically created Drop Templates, and when they should be automatically removed. Enabling Drop Optimization is performed on the firewall object here:

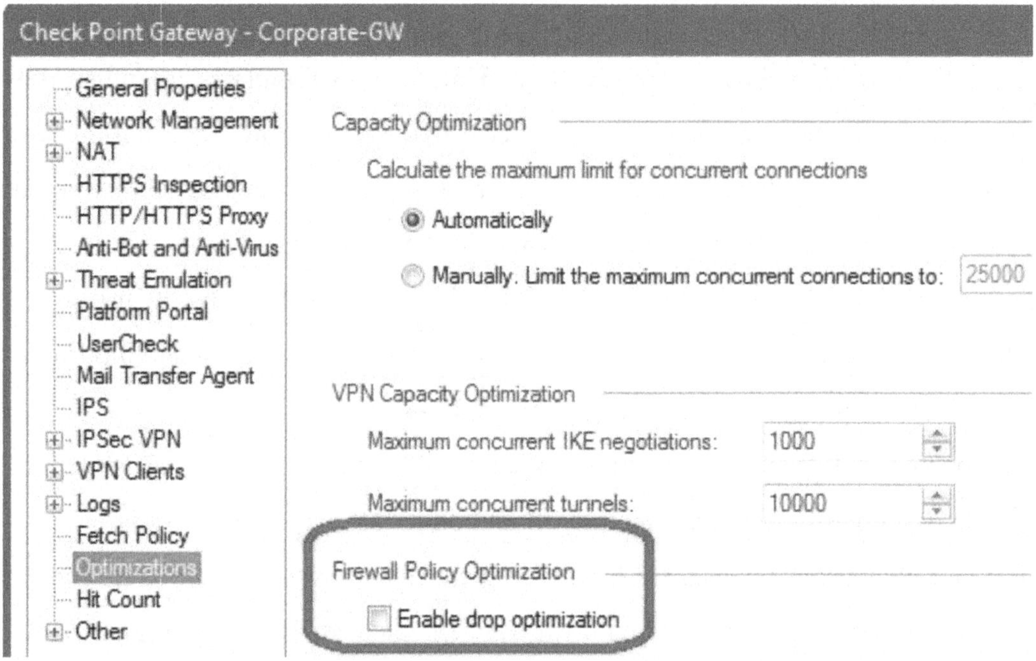

Figure 13-2: Checkbox to Enable Drop Optimization on Firewall Object

When Drop Optimization is enabled, the default thresholds dictate that if more than 101 drops per second occur on an individual Firewall Worker core, the feature activates. Drop Templates for the offending traffic are automatically formed and inserted into the SecureXL Acceleration Layer; drops begin occurring immediately in the Accelerated Path with no need to visit the Firewall Path, thus saving valuable CPU resources on the Firewall Worker cores.

Once the overall number of drops declines to less than 20 per second (based on the default thresholds), the Drop Optimization feature deactivates and all the dynamically created Drop Templates are removed from the Accelerated Path. Drops now occur once again in the Firewall Path, with full logging if specified in the Track column of the security policy rule matching and dropping the traffic.

So the inevitable question: Should you enable Drop Optimization on your firewall? It is not enabled by default (including in R80.10), but Drop Optimization should probably be turned on in most environments that are running at least version R77.30. However consider the following before enabling Drop Optimization:

- The dynamic nature of Drop Optimization may instill a false sense of security initially, then cause intermittent problems later. Example: Drop Optimization is enabled in the SmartDashboard/SmartConsole and policy is pushed to the firewall. The current drop rate is not high enough for dynamic Drop Template formation; you execute your test plan and everything seems OK. However later the drop rate rises to the point where drop templates start being dynamically formed. At that time you start noticing various network issues that were not present before; traffic discarded by Drop Templates is *not* logged. Logging of traffic discarded by drop templates can be enabled by setting kernel variable **sim_track_dropdb** to 1; (See: sk67861: Accelerated Drop Rules Feature in R75.40 and above), but this will cause significant logging overhead and negate many of the Optimized Drops performance improvements.

- SecureXL can start dynamically dropping traffic without your intervention or knowledge based on traffic conditions. Thankfully by default a firewall log entry will appear whenever Drop Optimization reaches its activation threshold, and again when it falls below its deactivation threshold. While continuously active, Drop Optimization will also issue another log entry every 5 minutes by default providing statistics about the number of packets dropped. Be on the lookout for these log entries in the firewall's traffic logs should you start encountering unexplained problems at some point after enabling Drop Optimization. Once again, individual logs showing exactly what was matched by the drop template (source IP, destination IP, service, etc) will *not* be provided by the Drop Optimization feature when it is in an active state.

- If you suspect traffic is currently being discarded by Drop Templates, you can run the command **fw ctl zdebug -T drop**, which will show in real-time all packets being dropped by the firewall (including Drop Templates); the drop reason in the zdebug output in this case will be stated as **Attack Mitigation**. The command **sim dropcfg -l** will also show any active drop templates on the firewall that were created by Drop Optimization if it is currently active.

SecureXL "Penalty Box" Mechanism

Introduced in R75.45, and when enabled with the **sim erdos** command, this feature will begin dropping all traffic from a source IP address that is causing more than 500 security policy or IPS-related drop actions per second by default. The offending source IP address is placed in the "penalty box" for a default of 180 seconds:

```
Usage: sim erdos <options>
  -h                  - this help message
  -x <0/1>            - enforce only on external interfaces
  -v <0/1>            - enforce on VPN traffic
  -m <0/1>            - monitor only
  Penalty box:
  -e <0/1>            - enable/disable
  -t <seconds>        - time a host is penalized
  -d <violations>     - rate of allowed violations per address
  -l <0/1>            - log when a host is put in the penalty box
  -k <0/1>            - log dropped packets
  Misc:
  -z                  - zap the statistics
  -f <0/1>            - enable/disable drop all fragments
  -o <0/1>            - enable/disable drop all IP options
```

Figure 13-3: SecureXL Penalty Box Options

During the penalty box period, all traffic from the source IP address is discarded by the SecureXL Acceleration Layer and never even reaches the Firewall Path. See the following for more information: sk74520: What is the SecureXL penalty box mechanism for offending IP addresses?.

Rate Limiting for DoS Mitigation/Network Quota

Introduced in R76 and further enhanced in R77.10, this incredibly useful and underrated feature consists of the Suspicious Activity Monitoring (SAM) commands **fw samp** and **sim_dos**. It allows the creation of flexible, fast-acting SAM rules that limit the number of new connection requests, concurrent connections, overall number of packets, and/or overall number of payload data bytes that can be consumed by a source (or destination) IP address, network or geographic country. Here we see the usage for the **fw samp add quota** command:

```
[Expert@firewall:0]# fw samp add quota
add quota: bad number of arguments
NAME: fw samp add quota - add a rule with quota limits
USAGE:
  fw samp add ... quota [flush true]
      [source-negated true] source SOURCE
      [destination-negated true] destination DESTINATION
      [service-negated true] service SERVICE
      [LIMIT-NAME LIMIT-VALUE] ...
      [track TRACK]
OPTIONS:
  flush: load quota rules
  SOURCE: range, cidr, cc or asn,...
  SERVICE: IPPROTO[/PORT-[PORT]],...
  LIMIT-NAME: concurrent-conns, new-conn-rate, pkt-rate,
          byte-rate, concurrent-conns-ratio,
          new-conn-rate-ratio, pkt-rate-ratio,
          byte-rate-ratio
  TRACK: source or source-service
[Expert@firewall:0]#
```

Figure 13-4: Rate Limiting Options of *fw samp add quota*

Definitely a bit intimidating, as there are over 20 different arguments and matching criteria available, so let's go ahead and step through a quick example.

Your new internal auditor, Jim Profit, has discovered the wonders of the **nmap** and Nessus attack tools, and is thoroughly enjoying blasting your underpowered firewall with ridiculous amounts of port scan traffic aimed at your organization's various DMZ networks. Jim's internal workstation has a static IP address of 192.168.48.96 and is targeting various destination DMZ networks that can be summarized as 172.17.8.0/22. You want to let Jim do his job (as no one *ever* wants an auditor upset with them), but you need to ensure acceptable firewall performance for everyone else. You decide to limit Jim's workstation to 100 new connection requests per second. The command to do this would be:

```
fw samp add -a d -l r -n Limit_Jim_Profit_PortScanning quota \
source cidr:192.168.48.96/32 destination cidr:172.17.8.0/22 service any \
new-conn-rate 100 flush true
```

(Note: the '\' character at the end of lines 1 & 2 of this command is a backslash and allows us to continue the same command on a new line)

Key arguments for our sample **fw samp add** command:

    -a d (action drop)

    -l r (regular logging)

    -n Limit_Jim_Profit_PortScanning (name of rule)

    new-conn-rate 100 (limit new connection rate to 100/sec)

    flush true (make this new Rate Limiting rule take effect immediately)

We can check the status of our rules with the command **fw samp get**:

```
[Expert@firewall:0]# fw samp get
Get operation succeeded
operation=add uid=<550f8baf,00000000,fb0200c0,00007fb2>
target=all timeout=indefinite action=drop log=log
name=Limit_Jim_Profit_PortScanning source=cidr:
192.168.48.96/32 destination=cidr:172.17.8.0/22
service=any new-conn-rate=100 flush=true req_type=quota
[Expert@firewall:0]#
```

Figure 13-5: Using *fw samp get* to Examine Rate Limiting Rules

We can check the status of enforcement with **cat /proc/ppk/dos**:

```
[Expert@firewall:0]# cat /proc/ppk/dos
Memory:
==========================
allocations (small)      :     11
allocations (big)        :     24
allocations (total)      :     35
bytes (small)            :    856
bytes (big)              :  24532
bytes (total)            :  25388
failed (small)           :      0
failed (big)             :      0
Objects:
==========================
Rules                    :      4
Rule sets                :      2
Policies                 :      1
Tracked objects          :      0
Fragments                :      0
States                   :      1
Policy id                :      3
Active                   :   true
Monitor only             :  false
External only            :  false
Max log rate             :    100
[Expert@firewall:0]#
```

Figure 13-6: Checking Rate Limiting Enforcement with *cat /proc/ppk/dos*

But we have done all this, and Jim is still laughing gleefully as he pummels our firewall with well over 100 connection requests per second! Why isn't our new quota working? Remember these quotas were originally designed to blunt the effects of DoS attacks, which tend to arrive most often on the external interface(s) of the firewall. By default these quotas will only be enforced on the firewall's external interfaces. To enforce our quota on all firewall interfaces (and abruptly halt Jim's grating laughter), run the **sim_dos ctl -x** 0 command.

Should all heck suddenly break loose when messing around with these Rate Limiting features due to a misconfiguration, the following command will save your bacon by instantly placing all enforcement of these features into Monitor-only mode: `sim_dos ctl -m 1`. After correcting the issue, run `sim_dos ctl -m 0` to disable Monitor-only mode and resume Rate Limiting enforcement.

As demonstrated in our example, this feature can be useful to throttle an internal system (such as an internal auditor running a port scan) or network that is consuming too many connections in the firewall's state table, or sending extremely heavy bursts of packets through the firewall that are detrimental to overall firewall performance. These special rules are not really part of the firewall's main security policy, but can efficiently drop traffic in the Acceleration Layer well before it ever reaches the Firewall Worker cores. This feature is somewhat similar to the IPS "Network Quota" protection, *however a serious downside to using the IPS "Network Quota" feature is that all traffic subject to this IPS Protection will be ineligible for any SecureXL acceleration whatsoever, and will always take the Firewall Path.* The Rate Limiting feature discussed in this section is not subject to this performance limitation and is fully implemented in the Accelerated Path. For more information see the "Rate Limiting for DDoS Mitigation" section of R77 Security Gateway Technical Administration Guide.

Finally, should you find your network sustaining a confirmed DoS attack, the invaluable document DDoS Protections on the Security Gateway Best Practices Guide is available on Check Point's website and can be quite helpful. However if DoS attacks are becoming a regular and increasingly annoying occurrence for your organization, be aware that Check Point does sell dedicated DDoS Protector appliances.

Increasing Firewall Resistance to DoS Attacks: Key Points

- Drop Optimization and Drop Templates can be employed to efficiently drop traffic in the Accelerated Path, without an expensive rule base lookup in the Firewall Path.

- Various features such as Aggressive Aging, Heavy Load QoS, and the SecureXL "Penalty Box" mechanism are available to strengthen the firewall's defenses against DoS attacks.

- The SecureXL-based Rate Limiting capabilities of the `fw samp` command are quite extensive and should always be used instead of the IPS Signature "Network Quota".

CHAPTER 14
DIAGNOSING INTERMITTENT PERFORMANCE ISSUES

Humans have a phrase: "What is past, is prologue." Minbari also have a phrase: "What is past, is also sometimes the future."

Babylon 5, episode "Z'ha'dum"

Introduction

Ah...the dreaded "intermittent network performance issue" that strikes fear into the heart of firewall and network administrators everywhere. Users complain that the network is slow during what appear to be random periods, and you can seem to find no pattern to the slowdowns or any correlation to increased network and/or firewall load. In other cases, performance was reported to be slow at some point in the past, but it seemed to clear up "all by itself". If you've worked in Information Technology for any significant length of time, you are painfully aware that when problems occur and then seem to disappear with no explanation, they will inevitably return at the most utterly inconvenient and highly annoying moment possible.

Regardless of whether the issue is a one-time event in the past or a seemingly random recurring issue, of course the firewall will be blamed and the poor firewall administrator will be required to exonerate themselves. A typical Network Management System

(NMS) that polls network devices and receives event traps from them using a protocol such as Simple Network Management Protocol (SNMP), can be invaluable in tracking down these types of issues and their cause. But look out: some NMS's can get overly aggressive with their SNMP and ICMP polling of DMZ systems and actually cause performance issues on the firewall. Check out the Rate Limiting feature described in Chapter 13 if needed to help keep the NMS from pounding the firewall too hard.

In this chapter we will examine what you have to work with when trying to diagnose past and/or intermittent performance problems, and it is not possible (or infeasible) to catch the problem "in the act". While we will tend to follow the philosophy espoused by the progression of chapters in this book and work our way up from the bottom of the OSI stack, there are certain things to check that have a high "bang for the buck" value when it comes to quickly finding a problem's root cause. In those cases we will employ some shortcuts to save troubleshooting time.

While the tools and techniques presented in this chapter can certainly be useful when trying to diagnose things that are intermittently (or permanently) broken and not working at all, our focus will be situations where everything is still working but is just much slower than usual. The root cause can most certainly be someplace external to the firewall itself; however our main concentration will be exonerating or further implicating the firewall in regards to the performance issue.

What Changed & When?

Did the performance problem start immediately (or start randomly happening) after something was changed in the firewall or surrounding network? First off, make sure you have a very good idea of when the problem started and how often it tends to occur (if

applicable). Does it seem to affect everywhere in your organization or just certain parts?
Does it tend to happen in the middle of day when everyone is at their desks, or in the
middle of the night when typically only automated processes like backups are executing?
Be sure to establish clear answers to these questions: Where? When? Who? How?
Doing so will help lead us to the answer for "Why?" which is what we seek. And then of
course the big question: does the problem seem to impact traffic that does not pass
through the firewall at all? If the answer to that last question is yes, the problem is
probably not something directly related to the firewall.

If you are clearly able to establish when the performance problem first started (and
when it has recurred if applicable), your initial step is to see if something was changed on
the firewall that may have induced this behavior to start occurring. There are two main
areas to check for configuration changes made on the firewall: the Gaia OS and the
Check Point policy/object configuration.

For the Gaia OS, look at the syslog files on the firewall in **`/var/log/messages*`**.
All changes made to the Gaia OS configuration via clish or the Gaia web interface are
logged there. If a firewall cluster is present, make sure you look in the syslog of the
firewall that was active when the problem happened. Based on the timestamps within,
proceed to the log entries just before the problem started. Here is an example which has
been edited for brevity:

```
Nov 19 09:57:49 2017 fw xpand[5899]: log info: objectName: Static Rou
tes,administrator: admin, operation: Set Object, facility: Cli messa
ge: Gateway  192.168.66.0/24 is set to 1.2.3.4
Nov 19 09:58:01 2017 fw xpand[5899]: log info: objectName: DNS,admini
strator: admin, operation: Set Object, facility: Cli message: Tertia
ry DNS server is set to 8.8.8.8
Nov 19 09:59:00 2017 fw xpand[5899]: log info: objectName: Static Rou
tes,administrator: admin, operation: Delete Object, facility: Web-UI,
 message: Deleted gateway 1.2.3.4 for 192.168.66.0/24
Nov 19 09:59:00 2017 fw xpand[5899]: Configuration changed from local
host by user admin
Nov 19 09:59:04 2017 fw clish[12216]: cmd by admin: Processing : expert
   (cmd md5: b9b83bad6bd2b4f7c40109304cf580e1)
```

Figure 14-1: Finding Gaia Configuration Changes in Syslog

In the screenshot above, we can see that all Gaia OS changes are logged and the **facility** field specifies whether clish or the Gaia web interface was used to make the change. Be extremely wary of transitions into an expert mode shell by an administrator (as seen on the last line), as any changes made to the system in expert mode are not logged. However most changes made from expert mode will be overwritten when the firewall is booted, so a firewall reboot is worth a try if you see suspicious expert mode usage by another administrator (or yourself!) around the time the problem started. This assumes of course the firewall has not been rebooted since the expert mode session was logged, and the problem is still occurring.

To see if any changes were made to the Check Point configuration around the time of the problem starting, audit logs can be very helpful. The following screenshots show how to access the audit logs on both R77.30 and R80+ management:

Figure 14-2: The R77.30 Audit Log

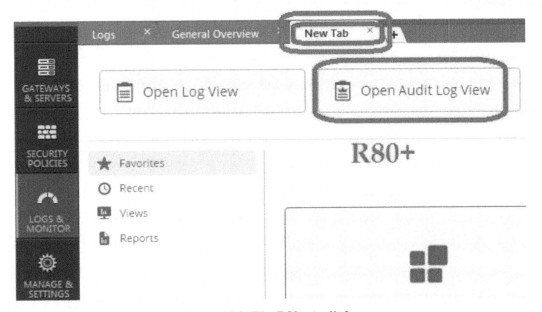

Figure 14-3: The R80+ Audit Log

Time	A.	T...	Admin...	Operation	Object Type
Yesterday, 6:14:30 AM		🗐	admin	✕ Delete Rule	Access Control Rule
Yesterday, 6:12:30 AM		🗐	admin	☀ Create Layer	Access Control Rulebase
Yesterday, 6:12:30 AM		🗐	admin	☀ Create Layer	Access Control Rulebase
Yesterday, 6:12:30 AM		🗐	admin	☀ Create Layer	Access Control Rulebase
16 Nov 17, 7:05:09 PM		🗐	kelly	✎ Set Object	
16 Nov 17, 7:05:09 PM	✔	🗐	lauren	⏷ Install Policy	AMW
16 Nov 17, 7:05:09 PM		🗐	kelly	✎ Set Object	
16 Nov 17, 7:05:08 PM		🗐	justin	☀ Create Object	GatewayStaticProfilesCon·
16 Nov 17, 7:05:08 PM		🗐	justin	☀ Create Object	GatewayStaticProfilesCon·
16 Nov 17, 7:05:08 PM		🗐	justin	☀ Create Object	GatewayStaticProfilesCon·
16 Nov 17, 7:05:08 PM	✔	🗐	brandon	⏷ Install Policy	AMW

Figure 14-4: R80+ Audit Log Entries Example

Pay particular attention to when policy was reinstalled to the firewall experiencing the issue, and the published changes that came just prior, as the policy installation action may have installed several different published sessions and their associated changes!

Syslog – A Frequently Effective Shortcut

As shown the last section, the syslog log files on the firewall can be helpful when trying to quickly determine if problematic changes were made to the Gaia OS configuration. However many other messages are logged via syslog for both the Gaia OS and the Check

Point inspection code that can be quite informative. As such we will be taking a bit of a shortcut here and investigating syslog messages early in our efforts, which can indicate problems practically anywhere on the firewall.

Unfortunately so many messages can be redirected to these syslog files that they can overflow, and the oldest message files will be rolled off and automatically deleted. This effect can cause older syslog log files you are seeking to be unavailable, which is frustrating to say the least. However there is a solution to ensure that these logs will always be available for retroactive inspection: configure the firewall to automatically forward all its syslog logs via the Check Point logging mechanism to the Security Management Server for storage. Now even syslog files that have rolled off on the firewall will still be available, and you'll even be able to use the great search capabilities of R77.30 SmartLog or the Logs & Monitor tab of the R80+ SmartConsole! *Setting syslog logs to be automatically forwarded to your Security Management server for all your firewalls is highly recommended* if you don't already possess some kind of external syslog monitoring product such as Splunk; the procedure to do so is detailed here: sk102995: How to export **syslog** messages from Security Gateway on Gaia OS to a Log Server and view them in SmartView Tracker.

When looking at syslog entries, any suspicious log entries occurring around the time of the problem starting or recurring are definitely worth your time to investigate. Here is a partial list of the most typical messages you might see and their meanings: sk33219: Critical error messages and logs. However the log messages you might encounter here are nearly limitless, so you'll almost certainly be performing SecureKnowledge and Internet searches in an attempt to determine what the messages mean, and what you should do about them. The Check Point TAC can also be quite helpful in this regard, as well as CheckMates (community.checkpoint.com) and CPUG (cpug.org).

Historical Statistics Granularity – cpview vs. sar

Sar and cpview are wonderful tools that can be run live to examine real-time statistics with a very high degree of granularity. When running these tools in live mode, the minimum granularity for the sar command is 1 second, while cpview can have a refresh rate set as low as 0.1 second. This level of granularity should be more than sufficient for just about every situation you wish to observe, no matter how fleeting it may be.

However when using these tools in historical mode, the available granularity is significantly reduced. By default sar only reports historical statistics every 10 minutes, and the numbers reported for variable items such as CPU usage are averaged inside that 10 minute period. The cpview daemons that record its history data take a sampling of variable statistics every 30 seconds, then record the average of those two samplings once a minute. While the granularity offered by cpview in history mode may appear more than sufficient, there are some limitations to keep in mind. A huge spike in CPU utilization that lasts 20 seconds, but is not occurring during one of the cpview historical sampling captures every 30 seconds will not show up at all, while being easily detectable from cpview in live mode. Obviously for accumulated data values that only increase, such as network counters that track total numbers of packets sent and received, the granularity limitations are not as important. While sar does average its data points over a 10-minute interval, limitations abound here too. For example in sar's 10-minute measuring interval if all a firewall's cores are 99.9% idle for 9 minutes and then 100% utilized for 1 minute, sar will report overall average CPU utilization during that period as only 10%, which is technically accurate but misleading.

So we can see thus far that **cpview** does offer superior historical granularity when compared to **sar**, so we will generally prefer **cpview** whenever possible. However there are some statistics not available in **cpview** that only **sar** can provide, and we will utilize **sar** in those cases. Both tools automatically record their historical data by default, and **cpview** data is kept for 30 days on the firewall. **Sar** keeps its historical data for only 7 days, however this can be increased by editing the **/etc/sysconfig/sysstat** file.

cpview's historical data is stored in a database format, and can only be viewed directly from the CLI by using the **cpview** utility itself. However the historical data stored by **sar** can not only be queried with the **sar** command itself, but a readable text copy of all **sar**'s historical values for a particular day is also stored in the file **/var/log/sa/sarXX**, where XX is the day number of the month. (Note that the very similar looking filename **/var/log/sa/saXX** is what the **sar** command itself queries when executed in historical mode and is not directly human-readable). The **sarXX** file is great for searching with **grep** or just for perusing around the date and time of a performance problem, and is essentially the equivalent of running **sar -A** (show all statistics) for that date.

Running sar and cpview Historical Reports

The best way to illustrate how to run historical reports is with an example: Suppose the date is November 20, 2017. You've received reports stating that on November 19th at about 2:00pm, while you were offsite attending a very informative CheckMates user community event, degraded performance was experienced on the network. Generally speaking you'll want to begin examining historical data taken about 30 minutes before the issue began, get a quick feel for how everything was behaving before the issue started, then step forward into the problem period to see how things changed. The `cpview` command to run for our example would be `cpview -t Nov 19 2017 13:30:00`:

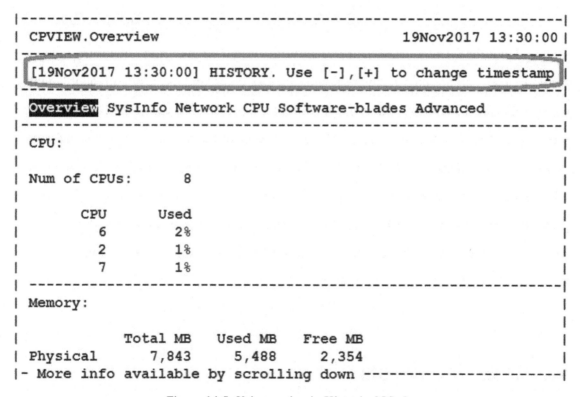

Figure 14-5: Using *cpview* in Historical Mode

The circled status bar in `cpview` will be colored green (not shown) thus indicating that `cpview` is in history mode and is not currently showing live statistics. Now press the "+" key to begin stepping forward, minute by minute. The beauty of this approach is that you can visit any page in **cpview** at whatever point in time you are currently viewing.

For the **sar** command, we might start by checking core utilization starting at 1:30pm on November 19th with this command:

`sar -f /var/log/sa/sa19 -s 13:30:00 -P ALL`

```
fw# sar -f /var/log/sa/sa19 -s 13:30:00 -P ALL
Linux 2.6.18-92cpx86_64 (fw)      11/19/17

13:30:01 CPU %user %nice %system %iowait  %idle
13:40:02 all  0.46  0.30    0.31    0.00  98.93
13:40:02   0  0.21  2.35    0.19    0.02  97.23
13:40:02   1  0.01  0.00    0.01    0.00  99.99
13:40:02   2  0.58  0.00    0.36    0.00  99.06
13:40:02   3  0.67  0.00    0.48    0.00  98.85
(snip)
13:50:01 all  0.66  0.30    0.34    0.00  98.70
13:50:01   0  0.11  2.34    0.17    0.02  97.36
13:50:01   1  0.12  0.00    0.06    0.00  99.83
13:50:01   2  0.63  0.00    0.55    0.01  98.81
13:50:01   3  0.54  0.01    0.42    0.00  99.03
(snip)
14:00:01 all  0.74  0.30    0.44    0.01  98.52
14:00:01   0  0.57  1.28    0.40    0.03  97.73
14:00:01   1  0.00  1.07    0.02    0.00  98.91
14:00:01   2  0.87  0.00    0.53    0.01  98.59
14:00:01   3  0.95  0.00    0.41    0.00  98.64
(snip)
14:10:01 all  0.44  0.30    0.31    0.00  98.95
14:10:01   0  0.21  2.34    0.18    0.02  97.25
14:10:01   1  0.00  0.01    0.01    0.00  99.98
14:10:01   2  0.59  0.00    0.47    0.00  98.93
14:10:01   3  0.57  0.00    0.46    0.00  98.97
```

Figure 14-6: Using *sar* in Historical Mode

We can see overall and individual core utilization just prior to the problem period and continuing into the problem period. Later in this chapter we will use both of these tools to help determine why performance was degraded.

SmartView Historical Reports

Included for completeness is the little-known capability of the R77.30 and R80+ SmartView Monitor GUI to provide historical network & CPU activity reports. While the available granularity of these reports falls off considerably after 24 hours has passed, they can be useful to establish visual trends over a long period for items such as firewall CPU utilization and network activity. There are a couple of prerequisites that must be met for these SmartView Monitor reports to be available:

- The Security Management Server must have a Monitoring blade (CPSB-MNTR) license present.
- The "Monitoring" checkbox must be set on the firewall object for which you want to run the reports (and policy must have then been installed to the firewall) in order for the firewall kernel module `rtm` to be loaded and commence gathering the needed statistics.
- On the "Monitoring software blade" screen of the firewall object, make sure all checkboxes are selected to maximize the amount of historical data available. (Note that this screen will not be present at all unless the "Monitoring" checkbox is set on the firewall object)

Right-click "Custom" in the SmartView Monitor as shown to get started:

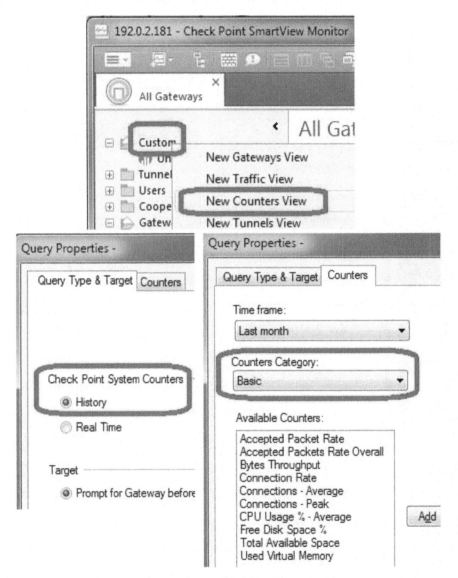

Figure 14-7: SmartView Monitor Historical Reports

Many elements of these SmartView Monitor Traffic/Counters reports (subject to the prerequisites mentioned earlier) can also be accessed from the R80+ SmartConsole:

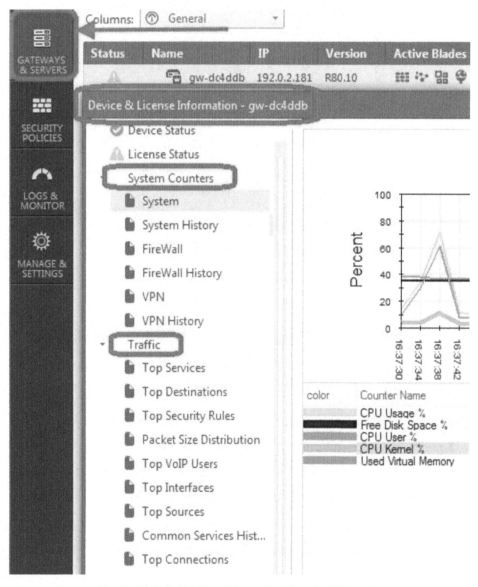

Figure 14-8: R80+ SmartConsole Historical Reports

For R80+ management, assuming SmartView is licensed and enabled on the Security Management Server, an additional historical network activity report is also available from the SmartConsole:

Figure 14-9: R80+ SmartView Historical Network Activity Report

Gaia System & Network Checks

Our two main weapons for examining Gaia system/network statistics are **cpview** and **sar**. The historical statistics presented by these tools are distinct from each other, and gathered in very different ways as discussed earlier.

For this stage of our investigation, we will focus on the historical CPU, memory, and network utilization of the firewall in our quest to locate the performance problem.

Spikes in any of these statistics around the time of the performance issue should most definitely be investigated further. The following table summarizes the useful options we can pass to **sar**, the equivalent screen in **cpview** (if applicable), and the preferred tool:

Table 8: *sar* vs. *cpview* for **Viewing Historical Data**

sar Option	**cpview** Screen	Preferred Tool & Notes
-n DEV	Network.Interfaces.Traffic	**cpview** - Both tools show similar network traffic statistics, but cpview has better time granularity; SmartView Monitor reports can also be used to graph this data
-n EDEV	Network.Interfaces."Errors and Drops"	**sar** - Shows network error counters incremented per 10-minute interval, cpview shows only running error totals
-P ALL	CPU	**cpview** - Both tools show similar CPU utilization data, but cpview has better time granularity; SmartView Monitor reports can also be used to graph this data
-r	Overview."Memory"	**sar** - Shows more detailed memory stats including memory allocated for buffering/caching; SmartView Monitor reports can also be used to graph this data
N/A	Overview."Network"	**cpview** - Check for sudden increases in new "Connections/sec", "Concurrent connections" & "Packets/sec"
-A	**-p**	Dump all possible data/screens once

Check Point Firewall Software Checks

If after examining the historical Gaia system and network statistics in the last section, the cause of the poor performance has still not been identified, it is time to examine the Check Point firewall software side of things. Typically performance problems will not be indicated by an explicit drop/block/reject log entry in the firewall logs, however try invoking these log filters in SmartLog (R77.30) or the "Logs & Monitor" SmartConsole tab (R80+) around the time of the performance issue and see if anything interesting pops up:

- **type:Control**
- **type:Alert** (R77.30 SmartLog only)
- **type:"System Alert"** (R80+)
- **"Aggressive Aging"** (shows if Aggressive Aging was invoked due to high load)
- **"Quota"** (to check if a network bandwidth/connections quota was exceeded)

The following screenshot shows the **type:Control** filter in action:

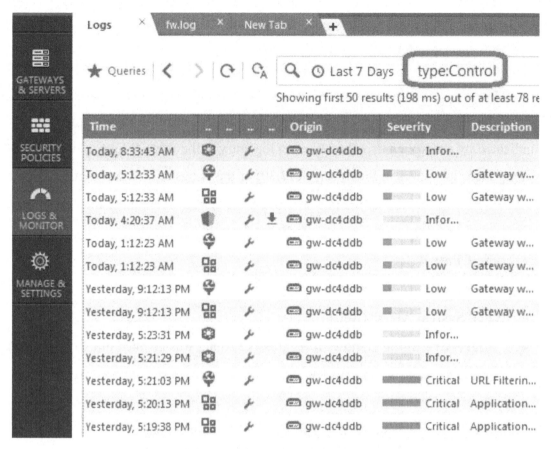

Figure 14-10: Using the "type:Control" Log Filter

As mentioned in the prior section, also be sure to visit the `cpview` screen "Overview.Network" around the time of the issue, to ensure there was not a sudden spike in concurrent or new connections.

If ClusterXL is in use on the firewall, was there a failover (or series of failovers) around the time of the issue? While not necessarily the root cause of the performance problem, unexplained failovers around that time should be investigated, even if it is determined that they were merely a symptom of the real problem. The undocumented clish command `show routed cluster-state detailed` command mentioned in

Chapter 6 can provide a convenient timeline of the most recent failovers, and the **type:Control** log filter mentioned earlier can provide more information about the cause of the failover. On an R80.10+ firewall, the **cphaprob stat** command will also report the time and date of the last failover; the "Advanced.ClusterXL" screen of **cpview** can also provide this information.

The **cpwd_admin list** command covered in Chapter 4 should also be run to determine if any critical firewall processes crashed and were restarted around the time of the problem. For certain processes there is a log file available which may prove helpful if one of these processes is logging any errors just before terminating abnormally:

- **fwd**: **$FWDIR/log/fwd.elg**
- **fwm**: **$FWDIR/log/fwm.elg**
- **vpnd**: **$FWDIR/log/vpnd.elg**
- **cpd**: **$CPDIR/log/cpd.elg**

There are other ***.elg** log files in the firewall's **$CPDIR/log** and **$FWDIR/log** directories that may prove useful as well.

Diagnosing Intermittent Performance Issues: Key Points

- As a first step, make sure something wasn't changed in the Gaia or Check Point firewall configuration around the time the issue started.

- Examining the syslog entries on the firewall can be an effective shortcut in various troubleshooting situations.

- Using `cpview` and `sar` in historical mode are the two main tools employed to diagnose past or intermittent firewall performance issues.

- The SmartView Monitor GUI and the SmartView component of the R80+ SmartConsole can be used to graph some network and system utilization data.

- The `cpview` and `sar` tools each have their own pros and cons as far as amount of data presented and available levels of time granularity.

- Log filters such as **type:Control** can be used in the Check Point logs to search for more detail about intermittent issues, such as the reason for a ClusterXL failover.

CHAPTER 15
FINAL THOUGHTS - RINSE AND REPEAT

Isn't that what you do, don't you take your net and throw it out into these far-out places of quantum physics and systems theory? And don't you find that the only thing you ever catch is your own self back again?

- Thomas Harriman, *Mindwalk*

Congratulations. You should now see the kind of performance you expect from your firewall, or at least understand why it can't be achieved. But what if you still aren't getting the needed performance? You were able to reach our goal of 50% idle on all cores and less than 0.1% RX-DRP on all firewall network interfaces. But you still don't seem to be getting the performance you expect from the firewall and surrounding network!

In Chapter 1 we talked about the "art and science" of performance tuning. Prior to executing the tuning recommendations in this book, there was a good chance that the firewall was the bottleneck in your network. Hopefully now it isn't.

In many of my "firewall performance tuning" consulting engagements I am forced to go well beyond just the firewall when trying to optimize overall performance. Why? Because now that the firewall has been optimized, the main bottleneck has moved elsewhere in the environment! This is the curse of performance tuning: it never ends. Remember in Chapter 1 how you spent so much time discovering the network path leading up to the firewall and beyond it? You were probably cursing my name at some point as you traced cables through a rat's nest of copper, and probably discovered all kinds of in-line appliances such as IPSs, Web Filters, and DDoS protection appliances, as well as the core components of your network such as switches and routers.

Well here is where all that work pays off: even if you are now getting the network performance you expect (but especially if you aren't), you need to go back and recheck the health of all those network devices you discovered in the "Network Device Health Check" section of Chapter 1. Any overloaded networks? Buffering misses? Pegged CPUs? About a third of the time after completing the firewall performance optimization for a customer, I discover another device in the customer's network is now buckling under the new load.

Who are the usual suspects? That old Cisco DMZ switch with firmware from the late 90's causing random spikes in latency. An inline load balancing appliance that now can't keep up with the network buffering requirements and is dropping packets. An IPS appliance whose CPU was close to being saturated before the firewall's optimization, but is now solidly slammed at 100%. Some unidentifiable, brightly colored appliance with pretty blue LEDs whose NICs are suddenly starting to hang up and reset themselves at random intervals.

All this caused by ensuring clean, efficient processing of traffic through the firewall! You never thought of yourself as an artist when you went to work in IT did you? Welcome to the modern "art and science" of performance optimization. Good luck!

APPENDIX A – MANUAL AFFINITY

This is your last chance. After this, there is no turning back. You take the blue pill - the story ends, you wake up in your bed and believe whatever you want to believe. You take the red pill - you stay in Wonderland and I show you how deep the rabbit hole goes.

-Morpheus, *The Matrix*

Background

You probably don't want to be here in the land of the "red pill" with manual affinities. If you have followed the "blue pill" recommendations outlined in the preceding chapters, you have probably been able to squeeze at least 75% of the ultimate maximum performance from your firewall unless your environment has a very unique setup or requirements. If you have reached this part of the book and need to work with manual affinities, one of the following 3 situations is probably present:

Scenario 1: Lab Benchmarking

You are doing firewall performance benchmarks in a lab or as part of a firewall "bake off" situation and need to extract every last ounce of performance from the firewall. Since you are working in a lab environment, there is no need to worry about impacting production traffic; you can experiment all you want without your manager running down the hall asking you what the heck is going on with the firewall. This is definitely a legitimate situation that can become highly educational once you start manually tinkering with all the components we have discussed. Using Multi-Queue (if available) and allocating the proper number of SND/IRQ cores should preclude the need to increase interface RX ring buffer settings; be warned that doing so may actually *decrease* measured throughput. Also creating sufficiently diverse traffic paths in a lab testing scenario for benchmarking can be problematic; be sure to consult the "CoreXL Firewall Worker Load Distribution" section of Chapter 7 to avoid saturating a single core during your performance testing.

Scenario 2: Firewall Moderately Overloaded

Core idle percentages are in the 20-49% range during your production firewall's busiest period; all the recommendations in the book have been followed, yet you still can't quite seem to reach our stated goal: 50% idle on all cores during the firewall's busiest period with an RX-DRP rate of less than 0.1%. Core idle percentages in the 20-49% range are still quite acceptable in most environments and afford a decent amount of firewall processing "headroom" to deal with unexpected but relatively brief traffic spikes. Manual affinities can definitely be employed in an attempt to get those idle percentages to go higher, but all you are really doing in this case is giving the firewall more processing headroom. Because the firewall is not heavily overloaded and pegging out at 100% CPU very often (if at all), your manual affinity efforts are not likely to net much of a tangible performance gain in this case. But getting that extra headroom may help you sleep a little better at night, and even buy you some extra time in a rapid growth situation to get next year's budget numbers together for a firewall hardware upgrade.

Scenario 3: Firewall Severely Overloaded

Core idle percentages are less than 20% across the board during the firewall's busiest period; all the recommendations in the book have been followed, yet you still can't seem to get anywhere near our stated goal: 50% idle on all cores during the firewall's busiest period with an RX-DRP rate of less than 0.1%. You are definitely in the danger zone here; an unexpected but sustained increase in network traffic, tepid DDoS attack, or viral YouTube cat video could easily start spiking individual cores to 100% (thus engaging Priority Queuing if enabled), and the overall network throughput will begin to decrease in noticeable ways. Manual affinities can help you pull the firewall back from the edge of the abyss slightly in this case, but keep in mind that all the "quick and easy" performance gains have probably already been obtained earlier in this book. Also keep in mind that if you make a mistake or incorrect assumption during your manual tuning efforts, the impact is quite likely to be dramatic, and may even culminate in what looks to your stakeholders like a firewall outage. Proceed with caution, and it is probably time to get budgetary numbers in place for new firewall. The Check Point `cpsizeme` tool can be quite helpful in determining how big of a firewall appliance you will need to purchase. See sk88160: The Check Point Performance Sizing Utility for more details.

Manual Affinities allow you to take very granular control of how cores are assigned to three basic Check Point firewall functions:

1. **Interface Affinity** – What SND/IRQ cores are assigned to process SoftIRQs and the Accelerated Path for an interface's inbound frames as described earlier in "A Millisecond in the Life of a Frame".

2. **Process Affinity** – What cores are assigned to run various daemon processes on the firewall? Examples include the Check Point `fwd`, `vpnd`, `rad`, and `cpd` daemons. This also includes various generic Gaia/Linux processes.

3. **Kernel Affinity** – Which specific cores will be designated as SND/IRQ cores and which specific cores which will be designated as Firewall Worker cores?

Both interface affinity and kernel affinity have been discussed previously in this book, while process affinity has not (other than the "R80.10 Taskset Process Affinities" section in Chapter 7). Manual process affinity is generally the least important affinity from a performance perspective in most cases. In some cases it may be necessary to assign manual process affinities to the daemon processes associated with various firewall features in order to ensure adequate performance.

Discovery

Question: Is SecureXL enabled?

Answer: Run command: `fwaccel stat`

Question: What are my current interface, process, and kernel affinities right now?

Answer: `fw ctl affinity -l -a -v` and `sim affinity -l`

The kernel and interface affinities listed should not be a surprise if you've gone through this entire book; but what about the process affinities? You probably see a long list of firewall processes with **any** after them on R77.30. "Any" means that if that process wakes up and needs to use a CPU, a core that is not currently busy will be assigned to handle the process. It could be a SND/IRQ core or it could be a Firewall Worker core; however on R80.10+ firewalls a process can only utilize cores allocated for Firewall Worker functions. But doesn't that violate one of our key principles about trying to prevent CPU fast cache thrashing?

Technically yes it does, however one thing you may have noticed when running **top** on your firewall is that the vast majority of traffic processing via the Accelerated, Medium and Firewall Paths occurs in the kernel of the firewall. On the third line of the **top** output, kernel processing includes the **sy**, **wa**, **hi**, **si**, and **st** percentage variables. The **us** and **ni** variables represent process space daemon processing, while **id** is of course the CPU idle time left over.

On a typical firewall, most processing occurs in the kernel, with very little going on in process space other than the **fwd** daemon receiving logs from the kernel and forwarding them to the Security Management Server over the network. Exceptions to this were explored in Chapter 10. Certain features such as DLP, Anti-Virus, Threat Emulation, Identity Awareness, and Anti-spam/Email are partially or fully handled by processes (in lieu of the kernel) to maintain the stability of the firewall. If these features are active, process space daemon processing may be much more prevalent than stated. One common optimization made with manual affinities in the past on R77.30 was to put all busy daemon processes on their own dedicated single core (or 2 cores), so that they won't occasionally step in on the SND/IRQ and/or Firewall Worker cores, thus avoiding CPU fast cache misses.

Manual Affinities & SecureXL

The procedure for configuring manual interface affinities will heavily depend on the answer to one key question: Is SecureXL (also called Performance Pack) enabled or not? If SecureXL is enabled (which hopefully it is based on our discussion at the beginning of Chapter 9), the command **sim affinity** will be the primary technique used to set manual interface affinities. If SecureXL is disabled, the **fw ctl affinity** command must be used instead. In the following sections we will also examine the **$FWDIR/conf/fwaffinity.conf** file and its applicability to setting permanent manual affinities.

Manual Interface Affinity with SecureXL Enabled

The **sim affinity** command is used to set manual interface affinities when SecureXL is enabled. *Attempts to set manual interface affinity via the* **$FWDIR/conf/fwaffinity.conf** *configuration file will be thoroughly ignored when SecureXL is enabled.* First check the current interface affinities with the command **sim affinity -l**:

```
[Expert@firewall:0]# sim affinity -l
eth0 : 0
eth1 : 1
eth2 : 0
eth3 : 1
[Expert@firewall:0]#
```

Figure A-1: Checking Automatic Interface Affinities

You should see a list of all physical interfaces and to which core their SoftIRQ processing is assigned. If the default automatic affinity is currently in effect, the interfaces will be assigned to various SND/IRQ cores (assuming there is sufficient traffic passing through the firewall). If the traffic levels are extremely low (such as in a lab environment), you may see all interfaces still assigned to CPU 0. Rest assured that the interface SoftIRQ processing will start being distributed across multiple SND/IRQ cores when the firewall's traffic load increases sufficiently. If you wish to set manual interface affinities run **sim affinity -s**:

```
[Expert@firewall:0]# sim affinity -s
Usage : For each interface enter one of the following:
Return             - To keep the default values (appearing in [ ])
all                - To allow all processors for this interface
List of processors - A list of processor numbers between 0 and 7

eth0 [0] :

eth1 [1] :

eth2 [0] :

eth3 [1] :
[Expert@firewall:0]#
```

Figure A-2: Setting Manual Interface Affinities when SecureXL is Enabled

Once this command is run, you will be prompted with each of the firewall's physical interfaces, one by one. The prompt will show the core number currently assigned to the interface. You may press <RETURN> to accept the current value, enter a new core number, or enter "any" (not recommended). If you enter a new core number, ensure that it is indeed a non-Firewall Worker core with the **fw ctl affinity -l -a -v** command. Accidentally assigning SoftIRQ processing for an interface to an existing

Firewall Worker core will dramatically impact performance in a negative way. Setting "any" for a manual interface affinity can also have a dramatically negative performance impact for the same reason, and should be avoided. Changes made here take effect immediately and will survive a reboot; the modified settings are stored in the `$PPKDIR/boot/modules/sim_aff.conf` file on the firewall. Run `sim affinity -l` again to verify the changes. Keep in mind that once you set manual interface affinity for a particular interface, it is no longer eligible to be moved around by automatic affinity on the SND/IRQ cores in response to a change in firewall network load. All other interfaces that do not have a manual interface affinity set can still have their SoftIRQ processing moved around as needed by SecureXL automatic interface affinity.

Manual Interface Affinity with SecureXL Disabled

When SecureXL is disabled, the `fw ctl affinity` command can be used to change interface affinities "on the fly"; however these affinity changes will not be persistent across a reboot. The `$FWDIR/conf/fwaffinity.conf` file must be modified to make any manual affinities persist across a firewall reboot when SecureXL is disabled. Begin by checking the current interface affinities with the `fw ctl affinity -l -a -v` command:

```
[Expert@firewall:0]# fw ctl affinity -l -v -a
Interface eth0 (irq 75): CPU 0
Interface eth1 (irq 83): CPU 1
Interface eth2 (irq 75): CPU 0
Interface eth3 (irq 83): CPU 1
Kernel fw_0: CPU 7
Kernel fw_1: CPU 6
Kernel fw_2: CPU 5
Kernel fw_3: CPU 4
Kernel fw_4: CPU 3
Kernel fw_5: CPU 2
Daemon cpca: CPU all
Daemon status_proxy: CPU all
Daemon cplmd: CPU all
Daemon fwd: CPU all
Daemon in.asessiond: CPU all
Daemon in.geod: CPU all
Daemon mpdaemon: CPU all
Daemon cpd: CPU all
[Expert@firewall:0]#
```

Figure A-3: Checking Interface, Kernel, and Process Affinities

Suppose we wish to change interface eth0 from its current CPU core 0 to core 1. The preferred technique is to add the following line to **$FWDIR/conf/fwaffinity.conf** file:

```
i eth0 1
```

Run the command **$FWDIR/scripts/fwaffinity_apply** to make the affinity change specified in the **fwaffinity.conf** file take effect immediately; this setting will also survive a firewall reboot. Alternatively the following command will take effect immediately, but not survive a firewall reboot:

```
fw ctl affinity -s -f -i eth0 1
```

```
[Expert@firewall:0]# fw ctl affinity -s -f -i eth0 1
eth0: CPU 1 - set successfully
[Expert@firewall:0]# fw ctl affinity -l -v -a
Interface eth0 (irq 75): CPU 1
Interface eth1 (irq 83): CPU 1
Interface eth2 (irq 75): CPU 1
Interface eth3 (irq 83): CPU 1
Kernel fw_0: CPU 7
Kernel fw_1: CPU 6
Kernel fw_2: CPU 5
Kernel fw_3: CPU 4
Kernel fw_4: CPU 3
Kernel fw_5: CPU 2
Daemon cpca: CPU all
Daemon status_proxy: CPU all
Daemon cplmd: CPU all
Daemon fwd: CPU all
Daemon in.asessiond: CPU all
Daemon in.geod: CPU all
Daemon mpdaemon: CPU all
Daemon cpd: CPU all
[Expert@firewall:0]#
```

Figure A-4: Setting Manual Interface Affinity When SecureXL is Disabled

Making quick, experimental changes to affinities using the **fw ctl affinity** command as shown above is useful in a non-production lab environment, but the former technique of modifying **fwaffinity.conf** and applying the change via the **fwaffinity_apply** command is the preferred method on a production firewall. It takes a bit longer to set it up this way, and you are more likely to spot a mistake in the configuration before your changes are made active.

Manual Daemon Process & Kernel Affinity

Daemon process & kernel manual affinity is much more rarely employed than manual interface affinity. (Note than on an R80.10 firewall, the "taskset" command affinities discussed in Chapter 7 will automatically assign all firewall processes to the Firewall Worker cores only) The most common use case for manual process affinity in the real world is to allocate a dedicated core for the **fwd** process, if there is a heavy amount of logging being performed by the firewall and logs are being lost. The presence of numerous **Log buffer is full** messages in the firewall's **/var/log/messages** file can indicate this situation is occurring; prior to CoreXL's introduction in R70, this situation was typically rectified by increasing the log buffer size as specified in sk52100: /var/**log**/**messages** files show - '**Log** buffer is full'. However on an overloaded firewall utilizing CoreXL, allocating **fwd** its own dedicated core can solve the problem as well. In my experience, a firewall should probably have at least 8 cores to consider this course of action for the **fwd** or other daemons.

There are two techniques available for making process and kernel affinity changes:

1. Change the **$FWDIR/conf/fwaffinity.conf** file and run
    $FWDIR/scripts/fwaffinity_apply

2. Change them "on the fly" with the command **fw ctl affinity -s -f -k** (for kernel affinities) or **fw ctl affinity -s -f -n** (for Check Point process affinities).

The best way to see this in action is to provide an example. We have an eight-core system with a 4/4 split (4 SND/IRQ cores and 4 Firewall Worker cores). We have 4 active network interfaces that are currently being serviced by the 4 SND/IRQ cores. Process affinities are still the default of "Any". We want to move all interface SoftIRQ processing to Cores 0 and 1 only, put all daemon processes on Cores 2 & 3, and leave the 4 Firewall Worker cores on Cores 4-7. The SND/IRQ and Firewall Worker cores will now no longer be impeded by random interruptions from daemon processes needing to use their CPU. First off, we run **fw ctl affinity -l -a -v**:

```
Interface eth0 (irq 75): CPU 0
Interface eth1 (irq 83): CPU 1
Interface eth2 (irq 88): CPU 2
Interface eth3 (irq 97): CPU 3

Kernel fw_0: CPU 4
Kernel fw_1: CPU 5
Kernel fw_2: CPU 6
Kernel fw_3: CPU 7

Daemon in.geod: CPU all
Daemon cpca: CPU all
Daemon status_proxy: CPU all
Daemon in.asessiond: CPU all
Daemon fwd: CPU all
Daemon mpdaemon: CPU all
Daemon vpnd: CPU all
Daemon rtmd: CPU all
Daemon cpd: CPU all
```

We have now verified the current configuration and obtained a current list of the daemon processes that will need to be called out for core reallocation.

Method 1: Add following lines to `$FWDIR/conf/fwaffinity.conf` then run `$FWDIR/scripts/fwaffinity_apply`:

```
i   eth0   0
i   eth1   0
i   eth2   1
i   eth3   1
n   in.geod   2 3
n   cpca   2 3
n   status_proxy   2 3
n   in.asessiond   2 3
n   fwd   2 3
n   mpdaemon   2 3
n   vpnd   2 3
n   rtmd   2 3
n   cpd   2 3
```

Notice how we specified more than one core (2 and 3) for the process affinities; either core is eligible to process activity from the named daemon in that case. Generally you should not specify more than 1 core with manual interface affinities, as it will not balance SoftIRQ processing between the two nominated cores as you would expect; one core will be chosen and it will process 100% of the SoftIRQ load. Use Multi-Queue instead (covered in Chapter 12), if you wish to balance SoftIRQ processing between 2 or more SND/IRQ cores for a single interface. Notice we did not specify any kernel instances with a **k** operand; specifying the number of Firewall Worker instances with **cpconfig** and letting them occupy the highest-numbered cores while divvying up the lowest-numbered cores without overlap via **fwaffinity.conf** or **fw ctl affinity** should be sufficient for almost all environments. I have never had a need to assign a kernel instance to a very specific core; simply adjust the total number using the `cpconfig` command.

Method 2: Run the following commands. They will take effect immediately, but not survive a reboot (ideal for lab experimentation!):

```
fw ctl affinity -s -f -i eth0 0
fw ctl affinity -s -f -i eth1 0
fw ctl affinity -s -f -i  eth2 1
fw ctl affinity -s -f -i eth3 1
fw ctl affinity -s -f -n in.geod 2 3
fw ctl affinity -s -f -n cpca 2 3
fw ctl affinity -s -f -n status_proxy 2 3
fw ctl affinity -s -f -n in.asession 2 3
fw ctl affinity -s -f -n fwd 2 3
fw ctl affinity -s -f -n mpdaemon 2 3
fw ctl affinity -s -f -n vpnd 2 3
fw ctl affinity -s -f -n rtmd 2 3
fw ctl affinity -s -f -n cpd 2 3
```

Run `fw ctl affinity-1 -a -v` and we now see the following:

```
Interface eth0 (irq 75): CPU 0
Interface eth1 (irq 83): CPU 0
Interface eth2 (irq 88): CPU 1
Interface eth3 (irq 97): CPU 1
Kernel fw_0: CPU 4
Kernel fw_1: CPU 5
Kernel fw_2: CPU 6
```

```
Kernel fw_3: CPU 7
Daemon in.geod: CPU 2 3
Daemon cpca: CPU 2 3
Daemon status_proxy: CPU 2 3
Daemon in.asessiond: CPU 2 3
Daemon fwd: CPU 2 3
Daemon mpdaemon: CPU 2 3
Daemon vpnd: CPU 2 3
Daemon rtmd: CPU 2 3
Daemon cpd: CPU 2 3
```

Atrocious Affinity Archetype

A great way to understand something like manual affinity is to look at an absolutely atrocious example of how it can be abused. A customer complained of terrible firewall performance. They had SecureXL turned off for legitimate application compatibility concerns, so they configured manual interface affinities. The firewall had eight 1Gbps network interfaces in use and eight physical cores. CoreXL was configured with 8 Firewall Worker cores (alarm bells should already ringing in your head if you've read this whole book). I had to choose my words carefully to keep the engagement professional when I saw their **fwaffinity.conf** file:

```
i eth0 0
i eth1 1
i eth2 2
i eth3 3
i eth4 4
```

```
i eth5 5
i eth6 6
i eth7 7
```

Needless to say they were having a few performance problems due to CPU fast cache thrashing and non-specialization amongst the cores (as every single one of them was handling both SND/IRQ tasks and Firewall Worker tasks). To add insult to injury, RX-DRP was well above 0.1% on their three busiest network interfaces. After running a **netstat -ni** command, we determined that the busiest interfaces descending order were: **eth7, eth6, eth0, eth1, eth2, eth4, eth3, eth5**. We reduced the number of Firewall Worker cores from 8 to 4 with **cpconfig**, (thus allocating 4 dedicated SND/IRQ cores on cores 0-3, and 4 Firewall Workers on cores 4-7) and modified **fwaffinity.conf** as follows:

```
i eth7 0
i eth6 1
i eth0 2
i eth1 3
i eth2 3
i eth4 2
i eth3 1
i eth5 0
```

(Note: Interfaces were listed in **fwaffinity.conf** file in decreasing order of utilization for illustration purposes, but the actual order of entries in the file itself does not influence the final applied configuration)

The four busiest interfaces were assigned first to Cores #0 -3 in order by utilization. Next the least busy interface (**eth5**) was paired with the busiest interface (**eth7**) on Core #0, the second busiest interface (**eth6**) was paired with the second least-busy interface (**eth3**) and so on. After booting the firewall to make the new number of Firewall worker cores take effect and having the new configuration in the **fwaffinity.conf** file get applied, overall firewall performance was greatly improved with RX-DRP well below 0.1% on all interfaces.

APPENDIX B - ADDITIONAL RESOURCES & INDEXED CLI QUICK REFERENCE

The following is a summary of this this book's performance-related CLI commands in a quick reference format. It is by no means intended to replace Check Point's outstanding collection of CLI reference documents and Advanced Technical Reference Guides (ATRGs) related to firewall performance, the most prominent of which are these:

- R77 Command Line Interface (CLI) Reference Guide
- R80.10 Performance Tuning Administration Guide
- sk98348: Best Practices - Security Gateway Performance
- sk33781: Performance analysis for Security Gateway NGX R65 / R7x
- sk98737: ATRG: **CoreXL**
- sk98722: ATRG: **SecureXL**
- sk93000: SMT (HyperThreading) Feature Guide
- Check Point Advanced Technical Reference Guides

In addition a great video series on the Check Point Support Channel at YouTube called "Security Gateway Performance Optimization" is available here:

https://www.youtube.com/user/checkpointsupport

If perusing the electronic PDF copy of this book, page numbers listed in the following index are clickable and will instantly take you to that page.

Network/System Commands – Gaia OS & Firewall

`arp -an | wc -l`

Display current number of IP to MAC address mappings
Pages: 68, 69

`cat /etc/resolv.conf`

Display currently configured DNS servers
Page: 355

`cat $FWDIR/conf/fwaffinity.conf | grep -v "^#"`

Check for manual interface affinity (SecureXL disabled)
Page: 201

`cat /proc/interrupts`

Display current CPU allocation for SoftIRQ processing per interface
Pages: 200, 216

`cat /proc/ppk/dos`

Display current Rate Limiting statistics
Page: 417

`cat /proc/smt_status`

Display SMT/Hyperthreading enabled/disabled
Pages: 201, 400

`cat /proc/net/softnet_stat | cut -c1-27`

Display SoftIRQ processing statistics
Page: 214

`cat /proc/sys/vm/zone_reclaim_mode`

Display Gaia memory zone reclaim setting
Page: 88

`cligated`

SecurePlatform dynamic routing configuration
Page: 52

`clusterXL_admin down`

Set ClusterXL member down to cause failover
Pages: 177, 178, 189

`clusterXL_admin down -p`

Set ClusterXL member down to cause failover (persistent – survive reboot)
Page: 179

`clusterXL_admin up`

Set ClusterXL member up
Page: 177

`clusterXL_admin up -p`

Set ClusterXL member up (persistent – clear previous **down -p**)
Page: 179

`cpconfig`

General Check Point configuration tool
Pages: 203, 204, 229, 234, 235, 238, 241, 247, 400, 404, 455, 456, 458

`cpd_admin debug on|off`

Debug cpd process
Page: 83

cphaconf cluster_id get

    Get Magic MAC/Global Cluster ID
    Page: 181

cphaconf cluster_id set (Cluster ID Value)

    Set Magic MAC/Global Cluster ID
    Page: 181

cphaprob mmagic

    Magic MAC/Global Cluster ID settings (R80.10+)
    Page: 182

cphaconf set_ccp broadcast

    Change CCP mode from multicast to broadcast
    Page: 185

cphaprob stat

    View ClusterXL state
    Pages: 179, 180, 186, 439

cphaprob syncstat

    View detailed ClusterXL state sync counters
    Page: 183

cphaprob -reset syncstat

    Reset ClusterXL state sync counters
    Page: 183

cplic print

    Check current firewall licenses
    Page: 239

`cpm_debug.sh -t <TOPIC> -s <SEVERITY>`

Debug cpm process
Page: 83

`cpmq get`

View Multi-Queue interface status
Pages: 200, 391, 397, 405

`cpmq reconfigure`

Apply Multi-Queue changes for new core allocations
Pages: 396, 405

`cpmq set`

Change Multi-Queue interface status
Pages: 397, 398

`cpmq set rxnum`

Set maximum number of interface RX queues
Page: 396

`cpsizeme`

Measure sizing requirements of current firewall
Pages: 231, 232, 445

`cpstat blades`

View rules with top 10 highest hit counts
Page: 138

`cpstat -f cp os | grep -i CPUs`

Determine total number of CPUs
Page: 391

cpstat -f power_supply os

Check firewall power supply status
Page: 37

cpstat -f sensors os

Check firewall voltage/temperature sensors
Page: 35

cpview

View firewall performance statistics in real-time
Pages: 81, 85, 98, 100, 102, 182, 246, 282, 293, 357, 372, 428, 429, 436, 438, 439

cpview -p

Print all cpview statistics
Page: 100, 436

cpview -t

View historical firewall performance statistics
Pages: 20, 430

cpwd_admin list

View start times of firewall processes monitored by cpwd
Pages: 80, 439

df -h

Check free disk space
Page: 89

dmesg

View current syslog entries
Page: 156

dmesg | grep -i "table overflow"

Search for ARP neighbor overflow messages
Page: 68

dmesg | grep AES

Verify AES-NI support
Page: 259

dmidecode -t cache

View size of CPU fast cache
Page: 220

dmidecode -t processor | grep -i "speed"

View current clock speed of all processors
Page: 36

enabled_blades

Check which Check Point features are currently enabled
Pages: 77, 309

ethtool -a (interface)

Check pause/flow control interface status
Page: 32

ethtool -S (interface)

View extended traffic & error statistics for interface
Pages: 32, 34, 45, 206

ethtool -K (interface) tso off

Disable offload for interface
Page: 201

`fwaccel stats`

Extended SecureXL acceleration statistics
Pages: 260, 341, 387

`fwaccel stats -p`

SecureXL violation statistics
Pages: 332, 336

`fwaccel stats -s`

SecureXL acceleration statistics summary
Pages: 282, 287, 289, 330, 374, 376, 384, 385, 386

`fwaccel templates -s`

SecureXL number of Accept Templates formed
Pages: 376, 379, 383

`fwaffinity_apply`

Apply manual affinity changes made to fwaffinity.conf file
Pages: 452, 453, 455

`fw amw fetch local`

Re-install Threat Prevention policy after disabling with fw amw unload
Page: 294

`fw amw unload`

Disable all Threat Prevention blades except IPS
Page: 294

`fw ctl affinity -l`

Display current kernel, process, and interface affinity
Pages: 200, 202, 203, 221, 448, 449, 450, 452, 455

```
fw ctl affinity -l -a -v
```

Display current kernel, process, and interface affinity - verbose
Pages: 405, 446, 450, 454, 456

```
fw ctl affinity -s -f -k
```

Set manual kernel affinity
Page: 453

```
fw ctl affinity -s -f -n
```

Set manual interface affinity (SecureXL disabled)
Page: 453

```
fw ctl arp
```

Display active firewall Proxy ARP addresses
Page: 157

```
fw ctl conntab
```

View firewall connections state table with idle timers
Page: 164

```
fw ctl get int fwlic_num_of_allowed_cores
```

Display number of licensed cores
Page: 238

```
fw ctl multik dynamic_dispatching get_mode
```

Check Dynamic Dispatcher Status (R80.10+)
Page: 243

```
fw ctl multik get_mode
```

Check Dynamic Dispatcher/Priority Queuing status (R77.30 only)
Page: 243

fw ctl multik stat

View connection counters for individual Firewall Worker cores
Pages: 241, 256, 266, 268

fw ctl pstat

View kernel and ClusterXL state sync statistics
Pages: 241, 256, 266, 268

fw ctl set int fwconn_tcp_state_logging X

Enable TCP state logging (R77.30)
Page: 163

fw ctl set int fw_antispoofing_enabled 0

sim feature anti_spoofing off

fwaccel off;fwaccel on

Disable anti-spoofing enforcement on the fly
Page: 118

fw ctl set int fwx_do_nat_cache 0

Disable NAT policy cache
Page: 152

fw ctl set int fwx_nat_dynamic_port_allocation_print_stats

Print dynamic Hide NAT port allocation statistics to syslog
Page: 156

fw ctl set int fw_rst_expired_conn 1

Send TCP RST when connections are expired by firewall
Page: 162

fw ctl set int fw_reject_non_syn 1

Send TCP RST for connections already expired
Page: 162

`fw ctl set int https_inspection_show_decrypted_data_in_debug 1`

Show decrypted HTTPS data in kernel debug
Page: 365

`fw ctl set int ssl_inspection_extra_debug 1`

Show decrypted HTTPS data in kernel debug
Page: 365

`fw ctl zdebug -T drop`

Show all firewall drops in real-time with timestamps
Page: 414

`fw debug fwd on|off`

Debug process fwd
Page: 83

`fw debug fwm on|off`

Debug process fwm
Page: 83

`fw monitor`

Capture packets in Firewall Path
Pages: 288, 337

`fw samp add`

Add Rate Limiting quotas
Pages: 415, 417

`fw samp get`

View Rate Limiting quotas
Page: 417

`fw stat -b AMW`

Check enforcement status of Threat Prevention blades
Page: 294

`fw tab -t connections -s`

Total number of connections in the state table and peak value
Page: 93

`fw tab -t f2f_addresses`

View IP addresses excluded from SecureXL acceleration
Page: 277

`fw tab -t fwx_cache -s`

View current number of entries in the NAT cache
Pages: 150, 151

`fw tab -t cphwd_db`

View SecureXL connections table
Page: 338

`fw tab -t urlf_cache_tbl -s`

View entry count in URLF cache table
Page: 359

`fw unloadlocal`

Unload firewall's security policy (causes outage)
Page: 189

`grep -c ^processor /proc/cpuinfo`

View total number of CPUs
Pages: 200, 239

grep cul_load_freeze /var/log/messages*

Search for ClusterXL Cluster Under Load events
Page: 189

healthcheck.sh

Gaia/Firewall health check script provided by Check Point
Page: 74

ifconfig

View interface information
Pages: 14, 24, 26, 184, 251

ip route get

Test Gaia routing
Page: 168

ips off

Disable IPS
Page: 293

ips on

Enable IPS
Page: 294

ksar

Graph sar data (not included with Gaia)
Page: 96

ls -1 /sys/class/net | grep -v ^lo | xargs -i ethtool {}

View information for all firewall interfaces
Page: 391

`nslookup`

Perform manual DNS query
Page: 355

`pathping`

Show network path with performance statistics (Windows OS)
Page: 10

`ping -s 1400 129.82.102.32`

Send large ping packet
Page: 6

`ping -l 1400 129.82.102.32`

Send large ping packet (Windows OS)
Page: 6

`pinj`

Check Point packet injector tool
Page: 168

`pstree`

View Gaia process tree to determine parent process relationships
Pages: 83, 84

`rad_admin stats on (urlf|appi|malware|av)`

Enable rad daemon ThreatCloud interaction statistics
Page: 357

`sar`

System Activity Reporter – view Gaia OS statistics
Pages: 98, 428, 429, 431, 436

sar -A

View all sar statistics
Page: 429, 436

sar -f /var/log/sa/sa19 -s 13:30:00 -P ALL

View historical sar data
Page: 431

sar -n EDEV

View extended network interface statistics including errors/drops/overruns
Pages: 95, 205

sar -P ALL

View individual core utilization
Page: 96

sar -u

Show summarized CPU utilization
Pages: 18

save config

Save current active Gaia OS configuration to startup configuration (clish)
Page: 88

set edition 64-bit

Set Gaia for 64-bit operation (clish)
Page: 88

set interface eth0 rx-ringsize X

Set interface RX ring size (clish)
Pages: 230, 232

`sim dbg`

SecureXL debug to determine reason for path selection
Pages: 338, 339

`sim_dos`

Set DoS protections
Page: 415

`sim_dos ctl -m 1`

Set Rate Limiting DoS protections to monitor-only mode
Page: 419

`sim_dos ctl -m 0`

Set Rate Limiting DoS protections to active mode
Page: 419

`sim_dos ctl -x 0`

Apply Rate Limiting DoS protections to all interfaces
Page: 418

`sim dropcfg`

Set SecureXL drop templates
Page: 411

`sim dropcfg -l`

List active SecureXL drop templates
Page: 414

`sim erdos`

Set SecureXL "Penalty Box" protection mechanism
Page: 414

sim feature pbrroute on

Enable support of Policy Based Routing with SecureXL (R77.30)
Page: 278

sim hlqos

Heavy load QoS protections (deprecated)
Page: 410

sim tmplquota

Heavy load QoS protections (deprecated)
Page: 410

sim vpn on|off

Enable/Disable SecureXL acceleration of IPSec VPN traffic only
Pages: 261, 278

strace

Trace process system call execution (not included with Gaia OS)
Page: 84

taskset_us_all

Set global firewall process CPU affinity to Firewall Worker cores only
Page: 225

tcptraceroute

Send TCP-based traceroute for testing routing and policies in lieu of pinj
Pages: 168, 169

top

Monitor Gaia processes, memory, and CPU utilization in real-time
Pages: 79, 83, 84, 87, 98, 99, 197, 217, 293, 327, 329, 393, 397, 447

`top -b -d 5 -n 720 > outputfile`

Run top command in batch mode
Page: 99

`uptime`

Check Gaia system uptime
Pages: 14, 81, 206

`vpn debug on|off`

Debug vpnd process
Page: 83

`vpn tu mstats`

Monitor tunnel statistics for multicore IPSec VPN (R80.10+)
Page: 256

`vpn tu tlist`

Monitor tunnel statistics for multicore IPSec VPN (R80.10+)
Page: 256

`watch -d -n1 fwaccel stats -p`

Monitor SecureXL violations into PXL and F2F
Page: 340

Useful Tcpdump Filters

`tcpdump -vn -s 1500 -i (interface) 'ether[20:2] == 0x200'`

Capture Cisco Discovery Protocol (CDP) packets with decode
Page: 12

`tcpdump -eni any '((ip[6:2] > 0) and (not ip[6] = 64))'`

Capture IP fragments only
Page: 333

`tcpdump -c100 -eni (iface) not ether proto 0x0800 and not ether proto 0x0806`

Capture non-IPv4 packets only
Page: 249

`tcpdump -c 100 -eni (iface) not vlan`

Capture untagged/native traffic only
Page: 252

`tcpdump -vvv -ni (interface) stp`

Capture switch BPDU frames
Page: 42

`tcpdump -c100 -eni (iface) vlan`

Capture only 802.1q-tagged traffic
Page: 251

`tcpdump -c 100 -eni (iface) vlan and not "(ether[14:2]&0x0fff = 4 \`
`or ether[14:2]&0x0fff = 8 or ether[14:2]&0x0fff = 96)"`

Capture traffic not tagged with known VLANs 4, 8, or 96
Page: 251

Network Discovery Commands – Cisco IOS

`set spantree portfast`

Set switchport for portfast operation (Cisco)
Page: 44

`show buffers`

Show buffering statistics including misses (Cisco)
Pages: 14, 205

`show cdp neighbors`

Show adjacent Cisco devices via Cisco Discovery Protocol
Page: 13

`show interface`

Show interface counters (Cisco)
Page: 14

`show proc cpu`

Show Cisco CPU utilization (Cisco)
Page: 14

`show proc mem`

Show Cisco memory utilization
Page: 14

`show run interface (interfacename)`

Show interface information including portfast state (Cisco)
Page: 44

`show spanning-tree detail`

Show STP state – detailed (Cisco)
Page: 42

Made in the USA
Columbia, SC
31 March 2018